FOUNDATIONS OF LAW FOR PARALEGALS: CASES, COMMENTARY, AND ETHICS

TITLES IN THE DELMAR PARALEGAL SERIES

Jonathan Lynton, Donna Masinter, Terri Mick Lyndall,
Law Office Management for Paralegals, 1992.

Peggy N. Kerley, Paul A. Sukys, Joanne Banker Hames, *Civil Litigation
for the Paralegal*, 1992.

Daniel Hall, *Criminal Law and Procedure*, 1992.

Ransford C. Pyle, *Foundations of Law for Paralegals:
Cases, Commentary, and Ethics*, 1992.

FOUNDATIONS OF LAW FOR PARALEGALS: CASES, COMMENTARY, AND ETHICS

Ransford C. Pyle

LAWYERS COOPERATIVE
PUBLISHING

DELMAR
PUBLISHERS INC.

NOTICE TO THE READER

Cover photo courtesy Collection of the Supreme Court of the United States.
Cover design by The Drawing Board.

Delmar Staff:

Administrative Editor: Jay Whitney
Editing Supervisor: Marlene McHugh Pratt
Production Supervisor: Larry Main
Design Coordinator: Karen Kunz Kemp

For information, address

Delmar Publishers Inc.
2 Computer Drive West, Box 15-015
Albany, New York 12212

Printed in the United States of America

10 9 8 7 6 5 4 3 2

Library of Congress Cataloging-in-Publication Data

Pyle, Ransford Comstock, 1936–
    Foundations of law for paralegals: cases, commentary, and ethics
/Ransford C. Pyle
      p. cm.—(Delmar paralegal series)
    Includes bibliographical references and index.
    ISBN 0-8273-4572-0 (textbook)
      1. Legal assistants—United States—Handbooks, manuals, etc.
    2. Law—United States. I. Title. II. Series.
KF320.L4P95 1991
349.73—dc20
[347.3]   91-21466
                                                                CIP

CONTENTS

DELMAR PUBLISHERS INC.

 AND

LAWYERS COOPERATIVE PUBLISHING

ARE PLEASED TO ANNOUNCE THEIR PARTNERSHIP
TO CO-PUBLISH COLLEGE TEXTBOOKS FOR
PARALEGAL EDUCATION.

DELMAR, WITH OFFICES AT ALBANY, NEW YORK, IS A PROFESSIONAL EDUCATION PUBLISHER. DELMAR PUBLISHES QUALITY EDUCATIONAL TEXT-BOOKS TO PREPARE AND SUPPORT INDIVIDUALS FOR LIFE SKILLS AND SPECIFIC OCCUPATIONS.

LAWYERS COOPERATIVE PUBLISHING (LCP), WITH OFFICES AT ROCHESTER, NEW YORK, HAS BEEN THE LEADING PUBLISHER OF ANALYTICAL LEGAL INFORMATION FOR OVER 100 YEARS. IT IS THE PUBLISHER OF SUCH RE-KNOWNED LEGAL ENCYCLOPEDIAS AS **AMERICAN LAW REPORTS, AMERICAN JURISPRUDENCE, UNITED STATES CODE SERVICE, LAWYERS EDITION** AS WELL AS OTHER MATERIAL, AND FEDERAL- AND STATE-SPECIFIC PUBLICATIONS. THESE PUBLICATIONS HAVE BEEN DE-SIGNED TO WORK TOGETHER IN THE DAY-TO-DAY PRACTICE OF LAW AS AN INTEGRATED SYSTEM IN WHAT IS CALLED THE "TOTAL CLIENT-SERVICE LI-BRARY®" (TCSL®). EACH LCP PUBLICATION IS COMPLETE WITHIN ITSELF AS TO SUBJECT COVERAGE, YET ALL HAVE COMMON FEATURES AND EXTEN-SIVE CROSS-REFERENCING TO PROVIDE LINKAGE FOR HIGHLY EFFICIENT LEGAL RESEARCH INTO VIRTUALLY ANY MATTER AN ATTORNEY MIGHT BE CALLED UPON TO HANDLE.

INFORMATION IN ALL PUBLICATIONS IS CAREFULLY AND CONSTANTLY MON-ITORED TO KEEP PACE WITH AND REFLECT EVENTS IN THE LAW AND IN SOCIETY. UPDATING AND SUPPLEMENTAL INFORMATION IS TIMELY AND PROVIDED CONVENIENTLY.

FOR FURTHER REFERENCE, SEE GENERALLY:

AMERICAN JURISPRUDENCE 2D: AN ENCYCLOPEDIC TEXT COVERAGE OF THE COMPLETE BODY OF STATE AND FEDERAL LAW.

AM JUR LEGAL FORMS 2D: A COMPILATION OF BUSINESS AND LEGAL FORMS DEALING WITH A VARIETY OF SUBJECT MATTERS.

AM JUR PLEADING AND PRACTICE FORMS, REV.: MODEL PRACTICE FORMS FOR EVERY STAGE OF A LEGAL PROCEEDING.

AM JUR PROOF OF FACTS: A SERIES OF ARTICLES THAT GUIDE THE READER IN DETERMINING WHICH FACTS ARE ESSENTIAL TO A CASE AND HOW TO PROVE THEM.

AM JUR TRIALS: A SERIES OF ARTICLES DISCUSSING EVERY ASPECT OF PARTICULAR SETTLEMENTS AND TRIALS WRITTEN BY 180 CONSULTING SPECIALISTS.

UNITED STATES CODE SERVICE: A COMPLETE AND AUTHORITATIVE ANNOTATED FEDERAL CODE THAT FOLLOWS THE EXACT LANGUAGE OF THE STATUTES AT LARGE AND DIRECTS YOU TO THE COURT AND AGENCY DECISIONS CONSTRUING EACH PROVISION.

ALR AND ALR FEDERAL: SERIES OF ANNOTATIONS PROVIDING IN-DEPTH ANALYSES OF ALL THE CASE LAW ON PARTICULAR LEGAL ISSUES.

U.S. SUPREME COURT REPORTS, L ED 2D: EVERY REPORTED U.S. SUPREME COURT DECISION PLUS IN-DEPTH DISCUSSIONS OF LEADING ISSUES.

FEDERAL PROCEDURE, L ED: A COMPREHENSIVE, A—Z TREATISE ON FEDERAL PROCEDURE—CIVIL, CRIMINAL, AND ADMINISTRATIVE.

FEDERAL PROCEDURAL FORMS, L ED: STEP-BY-STEP GUIDANCE FOR DRAFTING FORMS FOR FEDERAL COURT OR FEDERAL AGENCY PROCEEDINGS.

BANKRUPTCY SERVICE, L ED: A COMPLETE SERVICE FOR PRACTICE UNDER THE CURRENT BANKRUPTCY REFORM ACT.

IMMIGRATION LAW SERVICE: A PRACTICE-ORIENTED, ANALYTIC TEXT TREATMENT OF SUBSTANTIVE AND PROCEDURAL IMMIGRATION LAW, PLUS UNIQUE "HOW TO" CHAPTERS ON REPRESENTING PARTICULAR CLIENTS.

AMERICAN LAW OF PRODUCTS LIABILITY 3D: A COMPREHENSIVE PRACTICE SET, WHICH INCLUDES ANALYSIS OF GOVERNING PRINCIPLES AND ALL STATE AND FEDERAL STATUTES, RELEVANT CASELAW, FORMS, AND CHECKLISTS.

SOCIAL SECURITY LAW AND PRACTICE: ANALYSIS, FORMS, AND SOURCE MATERIAL RELATING TO THE FIELD OF SOCIAL SECURITY.

TABLE OF CASES

FOREWORD

When I initially offered the Legal Assistant Program at Santa Fe Community College in September, 1973, it was the first such program in the State of Florida. There were no textbooks or any other material at that time designed specifically for teaching legal assistant courses. The concept of *legal assistants* was less than ten years old, and most of those early programs were teaching from law school casebooks. In effect, they were "mini-law schools," teaching the "why" of the law, which was the attorney's prerogative, rather than the "how" to do things in the law office, which was the legal assistant's function.

By the late 1970s and early 1980s, there was a proliferation of legal assistant textbooks as publishers and authors tried to fill a vacuum in what was obviously a dynamic and growing profession. Some of those early textbooks were good, others not so good. The problem with most of the texts was that the legal assistant profession was so dynamic and expanding so rapidly that the books were out of date almost before they were published. This book, *Foundations of Law for Paralegals,* incorporates the most current material necessary for a comprehensive introductory textbook for legal assistant students.

I first met Dr. Ransford Pyle at a legal assistant conference sponsored by the University of Central Florida in Orlando, Florida, in the late 1970s. I was impressed by both his professional credentials and his personality. He was obviously very much interested in promoting the profession of legal assisting. Therefore, when an opening for an adjunct professor became available in my program at Santa Fe Community College, I contacted Dr. Pyle.

He has been teaching the Introduction to Legal Assisting course at Santa Fe Community College for several years, in addition to his full-time appointment at the University of Central Florida. He is eminently qualified to author this text, and his many years in law and teaching have resulted in a text that is readable as well as instructive. I commend it to educators in the legal assistant field.

J. Pope Cheney
Gainesville, Florida
1991

PREFACE

This book is based on fifteen years' experience teaching full time in a four-year university paralegal program and several years teaching as a part-time instructor at a community college. The choice of subject matter was also guided by personal experience recalled from the first weeks and months in law school without prior legal training. The book is designed to provide the student with the knowledge necessary to proceed to more advanced courses, integrating them into a coherent whole.

While the book may be considered a general overview of American law and the American legal system, it is not intended merely to provide concepts that will be repeated in subsequent courses. Quite generally, law and paralegal curricula are divided into substantive courses (e.g., property and contracts), procedural courses, and skills (or technical) courses. The need for an introductory course does not rest simply on the acquisition of a few terms of art, the jargon of the legal profession, although that is certainly a useful purpose. It is necessary to introduce the student to a wide variety of concepts that are commonly neglected in more specifically oriented courses. Far too often, instructors and texts in specialized courses assume that the student has already acquired an understanding of how the judicial system works, the principle of precedent, statutory interpretation, and appellate procedure. Basic concepts such as these that drive the legal system and the practice of law are taken for granted and seen as relatively simple to the experienced practitioner but are quite mysterious to the novice. It is assumed here that the paralegal is distinguished from other law office staff in having an understanding and knowledge of the law as a whole and an understanding of how the legal system operates in addition to whatever legal skills are called upon. The acquisition of skills and knowledge in specialized courses in legal training programs must be grounded on a basic understanding of the whole. Learning law has some analogy to putting together a jigsaw puzzle. The more the puzzle approaches completeness, the more clear the meaning of each piece becomes.

The book is divided into text and cases. The purpose of the textual materials is to explain with as much clarity as possible the basic concepts of our law and legal system. The decision to include cases was made for a number of reasons. Most of the cases are excerpts from appellate decisions that are written to decide disputes between parties ordinarily on narrowly focused legal issues drawn from results of trial decisions. At some point, every paralegal must be able to read and analyze cases. While the text is explanatory, the cases provide judges' reasoning, adding detail to the concepts raised in the text. Cases, of course, are law in action, dealing with real disputes and real parties. They often provide judges with difficult choices. If time permitted, it would be very instructive to follow each important legal concept with a case dealing with that concept. Unfortunately, such an approach would inevitably result in a law-school length casebook, where an inordinate amount of time is spent dissecting cases while learning relatively few principles.

Since most of the cases included in this text are severely edited from the actual decision, the opportunity for analytical reading is quite limited. The cases are intended more to expose the student to legal writing, reasoning, and style in preparation for the sort of analysis that will be necessary in legal research and writing classes. For those students who wish to have a greater exposure to the analytical process, involving the principle of precedent, using cases, and interpreting statutes and constitution, Appendix B has three cases presented in their entirety, except for numerous footnotes, which have been omitted. The cases in Appendix B describe the ultimate demise of the doctrine of sovereign immunity in the Commonwealth of Pennsylvania. They show how a once-favored principle became slowly discredited and how the courts and the legislature agonized over how to do away with it. In the process, it shows how courts deal with state constitution, legislation, and prior decisions. For those instructors who decide to run their students through this exercise in legal analysis, the appropriate assignment of Appendix B should follow the chapters on legal sources, Chapter 4 (cases) and Chapter 5 (legislation), and may be assigned prior to the chapters on substantive law, beginning with Chapter 8, since sovereign immunity is marginal to the specialized concepts of these substantive fields.

Appendix A should be assigned prior to Appendix B. Appendix A, "How to Read a Case," is designed to familiarize students with reported decisions, their form, and the reasoning that goes into them. Appendix A is an important section of the book, but because students in paralegal programs demonstrate a variety of backgrounds (some even employed as paralegals prior to the paralegal training programs), the discussion may be rather elementary to those experienced in reading judicial decisions. If Appendix A is assigned, it would logically fall early in the course, preferably prior to Chapter 4. Cases included in later chapters assume the acquisition of skills and understanding concerning the legal system, appellate review, and process. Many of the cases are followed by case questions designed to direct the students to key features of the case as well as to raise peripheral but important issues suggested by the case and provide an opportunity for discussion.

Most chapters end with questions and exercises. The purpose of the chapter questions is to review the key concepts raised in the chapter. They may or may not be used by the instructor for the purpose of discussion. The chapter exercises provide some relatively simple tasks for the students to perform. Since the book is aimed at a national readership, many of the exercises are designed so the student can discover the particular features of the law of his or her state. Since legal materials differ from state to state, as does the accessibility of legal materials for any particular student body, the instructor must tailor the exercises to the context of the training program.

Legal terms introduced in the text using bold-faced type may be found in the glossaries located in the margins of the text, as well as in a full glossary at the end of the book. Students should be aware, however, that many concepts are explained adequately in the text and therefore are not bold-faced and included in the glossaries.

As far as form is concerned, cases referred to by name or party are italicized, in part to draw attention to the fact that they are cases and to distinguish between *Anderson,* the case, and Anderson, the person. They're also italicized to familiarize the student with the manner in which cases are customarily referenced in textual materials. Brackets are used to indicate comments by the author. The brackets used in the cases are comments of the author of the judicial decision. The difference should be clear from the context. In order to shorten the cases, most citations in the cases have been omitted; their presence is indicated by [C.] for a single citation and [Cc.] for multiple citations.

When dealing with fifty different state jurisdictions, not to mention the federal jurisdiction, countless generalizations are made. Effort has been made to qualify those generalizations known by the author to lack uniformity among the states, and exceptions have been noted where important differences known to the author exist. Nevertheless, some of the statements are undoubtedly inappropriate to specific jurisdictions, and the instructor should exercise some caution in noting to the students when a pertinent state provides an exception to the rule.

From the outset, ethics has been considered an integral part of this book. Chapter 3 is dedicated to ethics in areas with which the paralegal should be familiar. In addition, Appendix C includes materials pertinent to specific chapters of the book. The goal here is to deal with ethics in relation to other subjects in order to show its relevance to the practice of law rather than follow the common practice of discussing ethics as a tedious afterthought.

Chapters 1 and 2 discuss the lawyer–paralegal team, emphasizing the nature of its work and responsibilities. Chapters 4 and 5 discuss the major sources of American law, viz., judicial opinions and legislation. (Constitutions as a source of law are treated as pertinent to specific subjects in the text.) Chapters 6 and 7 cover the organization of the court system, the functions of trial and appellate courts, and the differences between federal and state jurisdictions. Chapters 8 and 9 give an overview of civil and criminal procedure. Chapters 10 through 14 provide foundations in major areas of substantive law (torts, contracts, property, and criminal law) and basic principles of administrative law. Chapter 15 discusses the future of the paralegal profession and the law office, emphasizing expected developments in law office technology, licensing, and specialization.

ACKNOWLEDGMENTS

More than any other sort of book, an introductory text expresses the sum of the author's view of a vast terrain. While the personality and imagination belong to the author, most of the ideas belong to others. Many insights about law were assimilated so long ago that their attribution is no longer possible. Nevertheless, numerous debts have accrued, which may in some small way be paid here.

I was quite fortunate in having an editor, Jay Whitney, who was supportive of both my goals and my modus operandi. I was given a freedom not usually afforded authors of texts, and Jay's contributions invariably enhanced the text. From the beginning, we envisioned a book aimed at the paralegal embarking on a new field of study both mysterious and complex. The goal, which we hope we have realized, was to provide a guide through the labyrinth of law and legal system that could be readily learned and readily taught.

Fortunately for the teacher, learning is a collaborative effort. In fifteen years of teaching law to students at the University of Central Florida, I have formed very definite thoughts concerning what students can learn from an introductory course and what they need to know as they proceed to more advanced studies. My students have been both critical and supportive of my efforts to convey a picture of American law in the classroom. The subject matter and approach of this book owe much to their comments.

As luck would have it, I enjoyed a special windfall as I began this text in having two extremely able students whose help with the book was invaluable. Jolee Farinacci and Thomas diLustro tirelessly performed endless research. No aspect of the text was tackled without first consulting these two gifted individuals.

Early drafts and the final manuscript were read by the following reviewers:

Richard S. Fisher
Greenville Tech
Greenville, SC

Joyce W. Birdoff
Nassau Community College
Garden City, NY

Jan Halverson
Pierce College
Tacoma, WA

Cathy J. Okrent
Schenectady County Community College
Schenectady, NY

Kathleen M. Reed
University of Toledo Community & Technical College
Toledo, OH

A.Y. McCoin
Cleveland State Community College
Cleveland, TN

Bernard G. Helldorfer
St. John's University
Jamaica, NY

Joseph J. Mallini, Jr.
Midlands Technical College
Columbia, SC

Each provided a wealth of detailed comment that rectified inaccuracies, misstatements, and questionable generalizations. Alas, they cannot be held responsible for what faults still remain.

It is customary to thank one's marital partner in the author's acknowledgments, but my wife Laura deserves far more than the usual credit. Not only did she furnish the necessary encouragement and patience that are essential to the completion of a lengthy and exhausting project, but she helped with tedious tasks of typing and proofreading as well as with questions of style and content. Most important, however, Laura created an environment in which productive work was possible.

Finally, I would like to thank my children for accepting that their father was often unavailable to meet their daily needs, take them to the beach, the springs, or go tubing down the Ichitucknee. I must now spoil them for a spell.

Ransford C. Pyle
Gainesville, Florida
1991

FOUNDATIONS OF LAW FOR PARALEGALS: CASES, COMMENTARY, AND ETHICS

PROFESSIONAL PROFILE

Excerpted with permission from James Publishing Inc., Legal Assistant Today (September/October 1990).

A paralegal for fourteen years, Jolene Miller earned a B.S. in business at Emporia State College (Kansas), then moved to Topeka and was a legal secretary for a sole practitioner. "Within a year, I worked into a dual-capacity role, with lots of substantive legal work. He was busy, and glad to have me take on more responsibility." She became a legal technician in the U.S. Attorney's office in Topeka for nearly five years, working in civil litigation and collections. The Attorney General's office had a bigger civil than criminal practice: bankruptcies, foreclosures, other real estate transactions.

When Miller's boss took an appointment to the U.S. Court of Appeals, she called a paralegal she knew at the Atchison Topeka & Santa Fe Railroad. An opening happened to be coming up; Miller got the job. Starting out in 1984 in the law department, she worked primarily in personal injury litigation. Gradually, she shifted into the collection area, which she liked better. In 1988 she moved fully into collections, out of litigation, and now works in the accounting department, due to restructuring.

Jolene Miller
Corporate Paralegal/Supervisor

"I dial for dollars," Miller quips; much of her job involves talking to the railroad's shipping clients in debt. "Calling people we continue to have a business relationship with, I have to balance sensitivity to the customer with resolving disputes. Customers dispute rates, for example. I may have to work through a maze of facts to resolve things." Miller sometimes makes a decision about whether a lawsuit is worth it, evaluating what might happen in court. She also goes outside the office, when appropriate, to negotiate with a customer. The railroad employs outside legal help in collections, and Miller coordinates documents and drafts pleadings, utilizing her litigation experience.

Miller has been promoted several times within the paralegal classification, and now supervises nine people. "I find working in a law office much more challenging than anything else I could do—every case is new and different." Miller, who turned down the opportunity to go to law school, jokes that she likes being a paralegal "because I can have all the fun and none of the responsibility." More seriously, she observes, "It's not MY name on the dotted line. I have less pressure and fewer demands on me than the attorneys do." Currently president of the National Federation of Paralegal Associations (NFPA), Miller has completed a part-time A.A. degree in paralegal studies at Washburn University (not ABA-approved, but in compliance).

NFPA President Miller states, "Being involved in your state or local association, especially the national, definitely develops your leadership skills. It requires the support of your employer—which I've been lucky to have. You develop a network of contacts that can be useful to your employer and yourself."

"For Topeka, I have very good fringe benefits: health and dental," says Miller. "It's a trade-off. I would not have them at a private firm in Topeka. Smaller firms in smaller cities can't afford to be lavish with benefits."

Miller reports the Atchison Topeka Railroad offers $18,000-20,000 for entry-level paralegals. "The railroad has been shortsighted in terms of seeing the economic benefits they could derive from more effective use of paralegals," she believes. "When the proposed Southern Pacific merger failed, the railroad began downsizing and restructuring. In this kind of environment, employment of paralegals is the right approach."

CHAPTER 1
Paralegals

Simply put, paralegals are nonlawyers who perform legal tasks that were once done only by lawyers.

— *Barbara Bernardo,*
Paralegal (1990)

A legal assistant is a person, qualified through education, training, or work experience who is employed or retained by a lawyer, law office, governmental agency, or other entity in a capacity or function which involves the performance, under the intimate direction and supervision of an attorney, of specifically–delegated substantive legal work, which work, for the most part, requires a sufficient knowledge of legal

1

concepts that absent such assistant, the attorney would perform the task.

— *Standing Committee on Legal Assistants,*
American Bar Association (1986)

While lawyers must be licensed, those who assist lawyers in their legal work do not as yet need to be licensed. The position of legal assistant or paralegal has in recent years become fairly well defined, but since its definition is unofficial, anyone may use this designation in most states. Nevertheless, the advent of numerous respected paralegal training programs and the growing employment of paralegals in law firms have contributed to defining a paralegal. Although the American Bar Association (ABA) definition quoted above comes from a lawyers' group and reflects lawyers' concerns, it demonstrates that paralegals have come to occupy a recognized place of importance in the legal profession. Like lawyers, paralegals perform a broad range of tasks, only some of which will be performed by any one paralegal. This makes the field exciting; there is a place for anyone willing to work and learn. Since the law touches every aspect of human life, the opportunities are limitless.

This chapter attempts to define paralegals and describe some of the tasks they perform.

ORIGINS

The terms *paralegal* and *legal assistant* today are used interchangeably, though only a few years ago there was some debate over which term was more descriptive. Whichever term is used, the paralegal/legal assistant career has become clearly defined in the last twenty years.

In general, paralegals do not perform any tasks that were not performed in law offices prior to the rise in importance of their field. In fact, paralegals do not perform any tasks that lawyers did not perform in the past. Paralegals assist lawyers in providing legal services to clients, but there are a number of things they cannot do because they are not licensed to practice law, a matter that will be discussed later in this chapter. Since paralegals are employees of lawyers and law firms, the nature of their work depends largely on how their work is defined by their employers, but the types of tasks they perform have become increasingly standardized, in part because of the uniformity of the formal training they are receiving in educational institutions.

Although the paralegal profession is relatively recent in origin, lawyers have been using legal assistants in some form since the founding of our republic. Before bar associations, bar examinations, and law schools, it was the custom in the legal profession to learn law by apprenticeship in a law office, often called "reading the law." Except for those affluent enough to study law at the **Inns of Court** in London, early nineteenth-century lawyers learned law by assisting lawyers for a period of time, taking what opportunities they could to read cases and treatises about the law. This often took on an aspect of exploitation at low wages, but eventually the novice was sponsored by his employer to be accepted into practice by the courts of his jurisdiction. This form of legal education qualified bar applicants in most states well into the twentieth century, and contemporary law school students continue to serve much the same function when they work as law clerks in law offices during summer vacations from law school. It would be appropriate to refer to these students as paralegals, though many of them might not be comfortable with such a designation. In communities with large law schools, law students and paralegals often compete for employment.

Before the rise of paralegalism, many lawyers trained their legal secretaries to perform legal tasks beyond the usual scope of secretarial work, and some attorneys still prefer this approach to hiring formally trained assistants. Many present-day paralegals were trained in this way. As the attorney's practice increased, the secretary was gradually converted into a full-time paralegal, and a new secretary was hired to do the secretarial work. The advantage of such an arrangement was that the lawyer was able to take an employee with whom a good working relationship had been established and train that person to do the specific auxiliary tasks the lawyer needed. The disadvantage was that both the lawyer and the secretary took time away from their work for the training.

The paralegal position would never have been invented if it had not proven economically advantageous to law firms. The prime movers in paralegalism have been the largest law firms in the largest American cities. In large law firms, attorneys tend to be highly specialized, which tends to produce attorneys very knowledgeable and competent within their field of practice. They charge premium fees because they can provide quick delivery of high-quality legal services to large corporate and affluent private clients. But this can be accomplished effectively only if the firm is a well-managed business. The lawyers are free to concentrate on important tasks by the assistance of a competent staff, consisting primarily of law office managers, paralegals, and secretaries. The more support staff a lawyer has, the more time the lawyer can devote to delivering legal services and the more money can be

Inns of Court
For centuries, English lawyers were trained in the Inns of Court, where students learned the law in association with legal scholars, lawyers, and judges. (The reputation of these institutions has had its ups and downs, at times appearing more like young gentleman's clubs than legal institutions.) English lawyers are divided into two groups: *barristers*, roughly equivalent to our trial lawyers, and the more numerous *solicitors*, who handle legal matters other than trial work. The Inns of Court provided the traditional training ground for barristers.

brought into the firm. In many instances, this benefits the clients, who can be billed, for paralegal research for example, at a significantly lower rate than the attorney's hourly rate. In short, paralegals came to occupy defined positions in large law firms simply because they were part of a rational allocation of work that improved the quality of legal services at the same time that it increased profit for the firm.

Paralegal Training

Since paralegals are as yet unlicensed, no formal training is required. As mentioned above, many paralegals have been trained at work by their supervising attorney; some have even trained themselves. While we may call some persons paralegals by virtue of the completion of formal training, others are best defined by the nature of the work they do. In addition, many individuals working in law firms perform secretarial work as well as legal work that goes beyond what would normally be expected of a legal secretary. Whether we call such individuals legal secretaries or paralegals is presently a matter of choice.

In their book *Paralegals,* Johnstone and Wenglinsky provide an insightful sketch of the plight of paralegal schools in attempting to develop quality curricula and graduate employable paralegals. They compiled questionnaires and conducted interviews with hundreds of paralegals in New York City. *Paralegals* is not only an excellent source of data on paralegals but also a very thoughtful analysis of the field. Although published in 1985 and focused on New York City, the book provides data that can be generalized with some caution to the nation in 1990. Johnstone and Wenglinsky found that a minority (36%) of their subjects working as paralegals had formal paralegal training, but the proliferation of paralegal courses in recent years is likely to have an upward impact on this figure as more trained paralegals enter the market. The lowest percentage figures for formal training were encountered in governmental law offices (14%) and large firms (18%), while the largest was in medium-sized firms (64%). The low percentages come from large, bureaucratic offices, which are best able to organize training programs and are most likely to require specialized expertise that is still difficult to obtain in a paralegal school. The federal government has also been under budgetary restraints for a number of years and has tended to recruit paralegals from within rather than add new personnel.

Johnstone and Wenglinsky defined large law firms as those with more than fifty attorneys, which would exclude all but a handful of firms nationwide and eliminate entirely firms in most of our smaller cities. Thus, their figures would seem to be low when viewed from a national perspective, and the proliferation of paralegal training programs in recent years furnishes a resource not available in the past.

The number of paralegals with formal training will vary considerably locally since many cities do not have or have only recently developed paralegal schools, while others are producing more trained paralegals than can be utilized locally. An apt comparison can be made between Jacksonville and Gainesville, Florida, only seventy miles apart. Santa Fe Community College in Gainesville, with the oldest paralegal program in Florida, has for many years warned its incoming students that they may not be able to find employment in Gainesville, which has the disadvantage (for paralegals) of being a small city with a large state law school with many law students willing to work for meager wages as law clerks in the local firms. On the other hand, Jacksonville, a much larger city, had for many years been without a paralegal training school, so Jacksonville law firms were recruiting paralegals from Atlanta and beyond. Thus, people contemplating a paralegal career who cannot move from their present locale should do some preliminary market analysis. A word of caution should be added, however, that gossip and rumor abound in the employment field so that it is easy to get a distorted picture from only one or two sources.

All it takes to obtain a job as a paralegal is to convince an employer to hire you. The only qualifications needed are those the particular law firm requires. Nevertheless, we live in a society that cherishes credentials in the workplace. It seems inevitable that the paralegal field, like the legal profession before it, will gravitate toward formal training, certificates, and degrees. Paralegal schools will be ranked by reputation, and the graduates of a "good" school will have an edge over others.

Paralegal Schools

Paralegal training is not currently monopolized by any one type of institution. This is unusual since training in most fields is clearly either vocational or academic. Paralegals should be viewed as professionals since they must possess not only technical skills but also a firm grounding in the subject matter of their field, which is law. A *professional* is a person who applies a body of knowledge to aid people in solving their problems.

Perhaps an analogy with the English legal profession will be helpful. In England, the legal profession is divided into barristers and solicitors. Solicitors perform the day-to-day tasks of handling commercial transactions and advising clients with legal problems. Barristers are similar to what we in America call *trial lawyers*; they take from solicitors cases that cannot be resolved by negotiation and must be decided by trial in court. Although English solicitors have broader authority than American paralegals, the two are similar in the sense that their authority stops short of representation in court. Solicitors are not merely technicians but must have an intimate knowledge of the law in order to adequately represent the interests of their clients.

In 1990, California and New York began to consider licensing independent paralegals for limited legal representation. Parallels with the English system are obvious, and recognition of paralegals as a profession in its own right is imminent. In practical terms this means that, like other professionals, paralegals must possess more than technical skills; they must also acquire a broad body of knowledge to help them exercise wise and effective judgments. When viewed in this light, paralegal training takes on a serious mission.

Who can claim a legitimate role in training paralegals? Should traditional academic programs in colleges and universities enjoy a monopoly, or should technical and vocational schools do the training? Both have legitimate claims because of the need for both technical and academic training appropriate to the field. Fortunately, both kinds of programs usually employ practitioners who have an understanding of the needs of the profession and endeavor to impart the skills and knowledge necessary.

Academic institutions conform to the traditions of academic training and the requirements of regional accrediting agencies, which monitor the activities of the institutions that seek continuing approval. The ABA has added its own approval process, which entails a detailed initial approval application and periodic scrutiny to maintain approval. Any program that has obtained ABA approval has received careful attention to ensure it meets stringent requirements. At this writing, the ABA is the only body that sets standards for paralegal programs and gives or refuses its stamp of approval. The American Association for Paralegal Education (AAfPE) has grown significantly in recent years and will no doubt play a significant role in setting future standards, probably in cooperation with the ABA.

Regional accreditation subjects an educational institution as a whole to intense scrutiny, but will not necessarily subject its paralegal program to the same scrutiny, which is largely up to the institution itself. An institution like a community college or university that has both regional accreditation and ABA approval has undergone scrutiny through two processes. While neither of these guarantees high quality, they demonstrate that a program has met important minimal standards. A less formal, but nonetheless important, measure of any program is its reputation among local attorneys. Good programs that graduate good paralegals will ultimately be recognized through the legal grapevine since attorneys have a serious interest in hiring competent paralegals.

Paralegal training programs can also be divided into degree programs and certificate programs. Degree programs are more typical of traditional academic programs, like those found in community college, college, and university settings, where a degree such as Associate of Science, Associate of Arts, or Bachelor of Arts is awarded. In these programs, the institution usually requires that the academic training meet a general standard that may require courses in addition to paralegal courses. In certificate programs, a certificate of satisfactory completion is conferred, and the programs usually limit themselves to the particular field of study. *Certificate programs* should not be confused with *certification* by the National Association of Legal Assistants (NALA), which conducts an optional examination of qualified paralegals leading to the designation *Certified Legal Assistant*. While this designation has no official legal status, NALA was an early entry into the paralegal field, assigning itself the mission of establishing standards for practicing paralegals; certification, like passing a bar exam, is evidence of professional knowledge and competence.

There are literally hundreds of paralegal schools, and the number has been growing consistently in recent years in response to predictions of continually rising paralegal employment through the end of the century. Two-year programs are the most numerous, but four-year colleges and universities sometimes offer paralegal training. There are a number of proprietary schools unaffiliated with colleges that offer only paralegal training.

The quality of training is difficult to measure for a number of reasons. First, it is not clear exactly what should be taught. A primary issue is whether training should be general or specific. Although law firms frequently want specialists for whom they do not need to provide extensive training, few schools can afford to offer many specialized courses. Training a student in bankruptcy or government contracts has minimal usefulness if that student is hired by a personal injury firm. Unless the locality has a clearly defined specialized need or the students have already obtained employment, highly specialized courses are simply not economical for the school. As paralegal employment expands and competition increases, it is likely that individual schools will develop one or two specialties they have determined to be marketable.

A second factor making curriculum planning difficult is the diverse nature of paralegal students. Some are young, seeking their first career employment; many are older, seeking a career

substantive law and procedural law
Our legal system makes a critical distinction between substance and procedure. Substantive law describes rights and duties, while procedural law outlines the procedures that are available or must be followed to enforce or remedy legal rights and duties. The property rights one enjoys are a matter of substantive law; the means by which a deed to property may become part of official records is a matter of procedural law.

torts
is a major area of substantive law concerning causes of action to redress injuries that arise out of non-contractual incidents such as auto accidents and medical and other professional malpractice.

domestic relations
is the traditional name for an area of law also referred to as family law, which is concerned with marriage, divorce, child custody, and guardianship.

corporations, partnerships, and sole proprietorships
are three forms of business organizations, each with its own legal aspects.

change or returning to the workforce after a period of child-rearing. Many paralegal students are legal secretaries or office-trained paralegals who are attempting to upgrade their skills and their employment. Many have college degrees or some college training, while others have none. Some schools have resolved the problem of diversity by requiring prior college training, but the typical community college program cannot logically limit admittance on this basis.

In 1988, a group of attorneys, paralegals, and educators called The Conclave made recommendations for paralegal education that may spell a trend toward more extensive education. The group recommended that programs include a minimum of thirty hours of general education courses, including math and accounting, computers, history, and government.

A third problem is faculty. The typical paralegal instructor is a full-time practicing attorney teaching in a paralegal school on a part-time basis. The advantage of this arrangement is that the schools can recruit attorneys who specialize in the field that they teach and are up-to-date on the law and practices of their field. The disadvantage is that part-time academic salaries are low, especially when compared with the compensation received by a successful specialist practitioner. Part-time instructors are rarely available to students outside of class and have a limited commitment to the institution, which in turn may often find it difficult to assess the quality of the instruction.

It is particularly difficult for the paralegal student who has no prior experience in a law office to assess the quality of the school and the quality of individual courses. The competent paralegal must have practical skills as well as a general knowledge of the law but must rely on the instructors to decide how much of either is desirable in any given course. Paralegal students commonly experience a high level of anxiety about what they are learning and whether they will be competent to perform the tasks they will be assigned once they obtain employment. Understanding a few simple facts can reduce this anxiety:

No one knows all the law or even a major part of it—not paralegals, not lawyers, not even the Chief Justice of the United States Supreme Court.

With a general understanding of the law and the legal system, skills and specifics can always be learned. It is up to the individual to ask, study, and learn. Nothing contributes more to success in law than thoroughness and perseverance.

Every case has something unique about it; something that the lawyer or paralegal must think about for the first time; something they could not have been prepared for.

Legal study often seems overwhelming, but the student should learn to enjoy the challenge of the law. There is always more to be learned, but it is never enough.

Curriculum

Paralegal schools vary significantly in their curricula, though a number of courses are offered nearly universally. Curricula are planned by program administrators to fulfill their perceptions of the needs of the local market, student needs, and the basic core of American law. In some respects the curricula appear to be versions of law school curricula with a different emphasis. This is partly because lawyers typically are designing the programs and partly because law school curricula reflect market needs and essential subject areas of law. ABA-approved paralegal schools must have an advisory board composed of lawyers and paralegals who provide input into the perceived needs of the local bar. Curricula can be separated into the areas of **substantive law, procedure**, research and writing, office skills, and miscellaneous courses.

Substantive law curricula frequently begin with an overview course on American law and the American legal system. This course introduces students to substantive law and the court system and provides a basic introduction to fundamental legal concepts and the vocabulary that expresses them.

More specific subject areas are always included in the substantive law curriculum under a variety of names. Two subject areas are almost universally included, property law and contract law, though the former is commonly called "Real Estate Transactions" and the latter "Business Law." The difference in terminology reflects a philosophical difference between paralegal training, which is directed primarily to law office tasks, and law school training, which is geared to analytical reasoning and general knowledge of the law. Other subject areas commonly offered are **torts**, often referred to as personal injury law, **domestic relations** (family law), and criminal law. The field of business law often includes a course on business organizations, likely to be called "**Corporations**" or "Corporate Law," which usually also covers **partnerships** and **sole proprietorships**. Advanced courses in property law typically include a course in **estates and trusts** and sometimes a course in **estate planning**. Property and business law courses tend to dominate the substantive law curriculum because these are the fields that offer a great deal of paralegal work.

Procedural law is traditionally divided into **civil procedure** and **criminal procedure**, though a course in the latter is rarely

estates and trusts deals principally with the distribution of the property of a deceased person, commonly referred to as *decedents' estates*. Trusts involve formal agreements that establish management of property by a trustee on behalf of someone else, called a *beneficiary*. Trusts are frequently associated with wills but may also be set up without reference to a will.

estate planning An attorney and/or an accountant helps someone plan for the management of his or her property with particular concern for distribution at death. Much of estate planning is concerned with taxation, since large estates may be subject to heavy taxes at death.

civil procedure courses address the complex rules governing the steps appropriate to noncriminal cases as they progress from the initial filing of a lawsuit through trial and even post–trial stages.

criminal procedure ordinarily is taught as a separate course from civil procedure because many of its rules are different, such as laws governing searches and seizure of evidence and the right not to testify against oneself (privilege against self-incrimination).

required since it may be included in a criminal law course. Criminal law constitutes a small portion of legal practice and has not kept pace with civil law in terms of paralegal employment. Civil procedure is sometimes called *litigation* and is likely to overlap with other areas of the curriculum by requiring extensive drafting of litigation forms and management of case materials. Legal research is an essential paralegal course since it familiarizes the student with the law library and teaches how to look up laws. Legal writing may be included in the research course or may form a separate course; it instructs the student in legal writing format and style. While paralegals are usually not hired primarily for research and writing, they will be expected to have skills in these areas.

Law office skills courses may be organized in many different combinations but include law office management and computer usage. Programs at four-year colleges and programs requiring college degrees may expect students to have already acquired basic keyboarding skills or to learn them outside the curriculum.

Among miscellaneous courses, legal ethics is commonly offered, in part because it has been mandated by the American Bar Association for ABA approval. Interviewing and counseling courses are sometimes offered. Many schools provide credit for internships in law offices. Specialty courses are offered where the local market provides special opportunities for employment.

WHAT PARALEGALS MAY NOT DO

Before we discuss what paralegals actually do, it may be helpful to clarify what they may *not* do. This summary will not include all the areas in which paralegals may run into difficulties, such as fee-splitting with attorneys, soliciting business for attorneys, and other ethical problems covered in Chapter Three; for now we will confine the discussion to work tasks.

Problem areas are found under what is called *unauthorized practice of law*. Some things may be done legally only by licensed attorneys, and most states have a statute that restricts the practice of law to attorneys. Limited exceptions may be made for realtors and accountants, for example, within their respective fields, and paralegals may enjoy limited privileges if the state has specifically authorized them. Those few states that have addressed this issue by statute have been largely concerned with what paralegals cannot do rather than with what they can do. It is incumbent upon paralegals to become familiar with restrictions and privileges in effect in their state.

Despite variations among the states, it is possible to arrive at general principles since there is a consensus on what an attorney's license permits. Lawyers are privileged to provide legal advice and legal representation to clients. Legal advice means advising a client about legal rights and duties and especially about the proper course of action as it relates to the law. While a paralegal may properly advise someone, "I think you ought to see a lawyer," it would not be proper to say, "I think you ought to file a motion to dismiss." This extends even to matters of law clearly within the paralegal's knowledge and competence. *The temptation to advise must be resisted.* This proscription extends beyond actual clients since whenever a paralegal gives legal advice she may be engaged in the unauthorized practice of law. The line is not always easy to draw. Consider the example of a friend laboring under the misconception that the **statute of limitations** is four years when the paralegal knows it to be only two. Should she quietly sit by and let her friend lose a suit? Without advising the friend on a course of legal action, the paralegal can certainly question the friend's knowledge and suggest a visit to an attorney or provide a copy of pertinent state statutes without interpretation.

Legal representation includes a number of important activities, including representation before a court, which is the privileged domain of attorneys. This monopoly of the bar is necessary to exercise control over attorneys who act improperly and to enable clients who are improperly represented to sue their attorneys for malpractice. Nonlawyers may not represent others in court, may not sign documents submitted to the court in any proceeding, nor sign any documents that call for attorneys' signatures. The paralegal is not an agent of a client and must avoid any appearance of being one. There may be limited exceptions to this rule, but paralegals act at their peril in such matters and must be very clear on state law when interviewing clients or engaging in negotiations.

Observing two cardinal rules can avoid the dangers of legal representation by the paralegal. First, the client must always be aware that the paralegal is not an attorney. In any consultations with a client in which the paralegal may participate, especially in initial contacts, the status of paralegal should be clear to the client. Letters written on law firm stationery (some states do not allow paralegals' names on the letterhead), should make clear that the letter is not from an attorney, e.g., "As Mr. Clinton's paralegal, I have been asked to write concerning . . . [signed] Erin Summer, Paralegal." Even this might not be sufficient if legal advice is offered. Many clients do not know that paralegals are not lawyers.

The second rule concerns attorney supervision. As long as the paralegal is under the control and supervision of an attorney and the attorney exercises supervision properly, nearly all

statute of limitations
Nearly all civil and criminal actions have time limits within which suits must be filed. These are spelled out in state and federal statutes and vary from one action to another and from state to state. An attorney who neglects to file an action within the time period has committed a serious mistake that may be grounds for a malpractice suit.

potential problems are avoided. Many legal documents, including **pleadings,** are prepared by paralegals and signed by lawyers. The attorney is responsible for ascertaining the paralegal's competence to prepare the documents and must review and amend the documents before signing them. Responsibility rests with the supervising attorney, who may be sanctioned by the court or the bar association for problems created by a failure to supervise properly, but the paralegal must be aware of the dangers of such situations.

Legal Technicians

The terms *paralegal* and *legal assistant* both imply attorney supervision. There are also a number of persons now calling themselves *legal technicians,* who provide legal services without attorney supervision. A movement toward licensing appears to have started in California, where a significant number of independent paralegals risked legal sanctions in providing services to the public. Although the California Bar Association disapproved the proposed licensing of paralegals in November 1990, the issue survives. Several states have formalized licensing bills in the state legislatures, including Illinois, Minnesota, Washington, and Oregon. The issue of the 1990s is likely to shift from *whether* to license paralegals to who will be responsible for regulating them.

pleadings
These are formal documents filed with the court that establish the nature of a lawsuit and its defenses. The initial pleading is usually called a *complaint* or a *petition.*

CASE NO. 1-1   Rosemary Furman Fights the Florida Bar Association

On April 26, 1984, the Florida Supreme Court in *The Florida Bar v. Furman,* 451 So. 2d 808 (Fla. 1984), sentenced Rosemary Furman to thirty days in jail for **contempt of court**. The contempt charge was based on her violation of a 1979 order from the same court **enjoining** her from engaging in the unauthorized practice of law. In her long-standing fight with the Florida Bar, Furman had become a folk hero to many. Governor Bob Graham excused her from serving the jail sentence.

Rosemary Furman is outspoken in her criticisms of the legal profession. Her primary complaint concerns the excessive fees many lawyers charge people of modest means for providing routine legal services. Prior to her difficulties with the Florida Bar, she had served for more than twenty years as a court stenographer. In 1972, she assisted in creating a house for battered wives. The women who came to this house were typically without financial resources, and Ms. Furman began to help them obtain divorces. Eventually she opened her own office, offering services primarily for obtaining divorces. For her services the charges generally ranged from fifty to one hundred dollars.

Ms. Furman was not a member of the bar, not licensed to practice law. While she maintained that she was simply helping people to fill out forms for routine legal matters, the Florida Bar thought otherwise, contending that she was giving legal advice constituting unauthorized practice of law. Subsequent to the 1979 order of the Florida Supreme Court, Furman continued in her business and was again pursued by the Florida Bar. The matter was referred by the Florida Supreme Court to a referee, who concluded from the evidence presented by the Bar that Furman was practicing law in violation of the court order and recommended a four-month prison term. The court accepted the referee's findings but reduced the term to thirty days on condition that she comply with the original court order for two years. Under Florida law, Furman was not entitled to and did not receive a jury trial.

In finding her in contempt of court, the Florida Supreme Court cited evidence of several instances in which Furman had advised clients to distort what they put in their petitions for divorce and how to proceed. Evidence cited by the referee included occasions on which Furman advised clients to submit inaccurate information. In holding against Ms. Furman, the Florida Supreme Court emphasized its responsibility under the law to ensure that competent legal services be provided to the public.

In **commuting** Ms. Furman's sentence, with assurances that she would not continue her business, Governor Graham emphasized the continuing need for inexpensive public access to the courts.

CASE GLOSSARY

contempt of court American courts have authority to punish those who behave improperly in court proceedings or who defy court orders by holding them in contempt of court. Judges may assess fines or order incarceration. Criminal contempt usually applies to offensive behavior in the courtroom, while civil contempt usually applies when someone defies a court order to do something or to refrain from doing something, for example, when a father fails to pay court-ordered child support. Rosemary Furman was held in *indirect criminal contempt of court* since she did not misbehave in the courtroom (direct criminal contempt) but nevertheless defied a court order designed to assure the orderly administration of justice.

enjoin On occasion lawsuits seek a remedy called *injunction,* which asks the court to order the opposing party to refrain from doing something. If the court agrees, the opposing party will be *enjoined* from such activity. In the Furman case, the Florida bar sought to enjoin Rosemary Furman from continuing activities characterized as the unauthorized practice of law.

commute Governors and the President have the authority to cancel the punishments awarded to convicted criminals in the form of a pardon. Distinguish this from *commutation of sentence,* wherein the same officials have the authority to substitute a lesser sentence for a greater one, most notably from the death penalty to life imprisonment.

WHAT PARALEGALS DO

Once impermissible tasks are eliminated, paralegals may do anything from typing and filing to preparing **appellate briefs**. An efficiently run law office will clarify the boundaries between paralegal work and the work of the rest of the office staff. Routine typing and filing should be assigned to the secretarial staff simply because such tasks do not effectively utilize the knowledge and skills of the paralegal. Appellate briefs probably should be written by attorneys, though paralegals can provide valuable assistance.

Rather than catalog the myriad tasks that a paralegal can do, it is more instructive to consider what a paralegal might do in a case. In a complex case that may result in litigation, a paralegal may be assigned extensive duties of management and coordination. A supervising attorney can delegate tasks to a trusted and experienced paralegal to free the attorney from the routine activities that can be so time-consuming. In our hypothetical case, the attorney is working on a **contingency fee** basis so that the final fee will be the same regardless of who performs the work. In such a situation, the use of paralegals, who presumably earn considerably less than the supervising attorney, is very cost-efficient. Keep in mind that consultations with the attorney should be frequent, and the attorney should directly supervise the paralegal's work. Depending on the complexity of the case, a paralegal may actually supervise other paralegals.

Hypothetical case: The parents of a five-year-old boy who has been struck by a rare form of cancer consult a personal injury firm concerning a possible lawsuit against a business adjacent to their residence that has been investigated for and charged with dumping toxic waste in back of the business premises. It has been determined by a public investigating agency that some of the effluent has caused contamination of the well water serving the surrounding neighborhood. The parents have received information that the particular chemicals disposed of have been linked elsewhere with their son's form of cancer. After a preliminary investigation, the law firm decides that the business wrongfully dumped toxic waste that caused contamination of the water supply, that a strong case can be made for a causal connection between the contamination and the child's cancer, and that the injuries sustained were sufficient to pursue the case on a contingency fee basis. What are some of the tasks that might be assigned to the paralegal working on the case?

There are numerous tasks that could be performed by a paralegal assigned as case manager. A paralegal may be put in charge of many tasks and report directly to a supervising attorney.

appellate briefs
are written arguments submitted to an appellate (appeals) court. The party initiating the appeal (the appellant) files an appellant's brief, after which the other party (the appellee) is given a period to reply with appellee's brief.

contingency fee contracts
are agreements between an attorney and a client in which the attorney will receive compensation in the form of a percentage of money recovered in a lawsuit, whether the amount is negotiated without a trial or awarded at the end of trial. This is the usual form of compensation in personal injury cases but is unethical in most other sorts of cases. The contingency fee has come under attack through the years and is likely to be subject to statutory limitations in coming years.

Some tasks may be delegated to a secretary or another assisting paralegal. Without a paralegal, some tasks, such as telephone calls to collect information and arrange meetings, would be performed by a legal secretary, while others would be performed by an attorney.

An attorney may prefer to have the paralegal present from the outset in any consultations with a client. In fact, the client may see the paralegal first in an interview to determine the nature of the case. All this depends on the practices of the firm and the relationship between attorney and paralegal. An advantage of having a paralegal present is that the client can be introduced in a setting in which the client perceives the paralegal as a trusted assistant to the attorney. In addition, the paralegal can take notes, thus freeing the attorney from talking and taking notes at the same time. If the paralegal is not present, the attorney must later take time to explain the case to the paralegal.

The paralegal will engage in some investigative activities. The facts as represented by a client are necessarily incomplete. Facts must thus be collected from other sources to get a complete picture and also to minimize any distortions the client may have conveyed. A report of the agency investigating the dumping of wastes will be sought. Any action taken against the business will be researched and its status followed through any final decision. The paralegal may make a visit to the site to take pictures of the client's property and its relation to the property on which the chemicals were dumped. The paralegal may question neighbors named by the client who have suffered illness they believe to be caused by the dumping of waste. In short, a full picture of the background in which these events took place should be established, both through informal investigation and questioning and through public and private records.

Pretrial preparation also involves formal devices for collecting information from the opposing party called **discovery**. The paralegal can be instrumental in the pretrial process. He can arrange for depositions to be taken of the employees of the business and any other witnesses for the opposition. During the case, the attorney will develop what is often loosely called the "theory" of the case, i.e., the most probable legal basis for winning the case, tying it into the facts of the case. It is called *theory* for two reasons: First, no one can be certain that the judge will agree until the final decision. Second, the approach and even the basis for the lawsuit may change as the factual basis becomes clearer.

In a good working relationship, attorney and paralegal share the story of a case and develop a strategy to deal with it. If a paralegal enjoys the confidence of the attorney, the paralegal can formulate questions for depositions, draft **interrogatories** to the opposing counsel to obtain basic information, and participate in and sometimes direct other discovery processes such as

discovery
refers to devices used to request information from the opposing side of a lawsuit prior to trial. The court is not ordinarily involved in this process unless one side refuses to comply with requests from the other.

interrogatories
are a discovery device in which one party sends written questions to the other party. These are particularly useful in obtaining factual information that cannot easily be denied, such as previous marriages, employment, addresses, etc. but would be troublesome to obtain through investigation.

requesting documents from the other side. The fact that the attorney is responsible for reviewing and approving or signing appropriate documents does not prevent the paralegal from doing most of the work. Oral depositions must be arranged at times convenient to attorneys for both sides as well as the person to be deposed. It is more economical for a paralegal or secretary to make such arrangements than an attorney. The case manager can track the process on the attorney's calendar to see that these tasks are completed. Obviously secretaries can perform such tasks, but it is more efficient to have someone in charge of the loose ends of a particular case to ensure that everything has been done.

Whether or not the paralegal is directly involved in the deposition itself, in a complicated case it is essential that the deposition be summarized and indexed. The court reporter typically reduces the deposition to a verbatim written **transcript**, which can often run to several hundred pages. Long transcripts are unmanageable without summaries and references to the pages of important topics discussed. Summarizing and indexing should be done by someone familiar with the case and its theory. This is a time-consuming job that can be accomplished by a paralegal, allowing better time management by the attorney.

Extensive legal research will be necessary in the case. As much as possible, the client's legal position must be bolstered by persuasive legal authority. This is not only important to persuade the trial judge but is also instrumental in negotiations with the opposing counsel. If a defendant's attorney is convinced that under the law his client has a losing case, focus will change to saving the client money by a favorable negotiation. A strong case built on solid research is an essential part of the negotiation process. While some attorneys insist on doing most or all of the legal research, many paralegals are accomplished researchers. The most important ingredients in good research are thoroughness and perseverance.

Management of a complex case requires an orderly filing system. The many documents that accumulate in the course of the case must be readily available for review and preparation for trial. In our computer age, file management has been made much easier. Many software packages are available for litigation files, and a program can be tailored for specific styles of organization. Material can be stored by computers in ways that make retrieval fast and efficient. Nevertheless, a human being is still necessary to record and file the material with the computer, and paralegal case managers are often selected to perform or delegate these responsibilities.

Writing can also form an important activity for the paralegal. In complex litigation, a paralegal case manager may at many points in the case have a greater mastery of the legal and factual details of the case than the attorney, who as the decision-maker has an overview of the case. The attorney may ask the paralegal to write memoranda about the case and especially the legal issues of the case in such a way that the major issues are summarized in an analytical form that makes a quick review of the case status possible. While analysis and writing require more skill than does research, experience is a great teacher. The fortunate paralegal works for an attorney who will take time to help build these skills.

Paralegals can also be instrumental in maintaining good client relations. One of the most frequent client complaints is the difficulty in reaching their attorneys by phone and in receiving return calls. Paralegals often have direct contact with clients and may have a better feel for clients' concerns. Clients may be reluctant to discuss all their concerns with the attorney, especially if they think of that two-dollar-a-minute clock ticking. The paralegal is often a more sympathetic and patient listener and can reassure the client that the case is proceeding in a timely fashion as well as relay the client's concerns to the attorney. Clients often feel that nothing is happening in their case if their attorney has not corresponded with them for some time. It is helpful for a client to know that more than one person is concerned about the case. The paralegal can call, receive calls, make sure that copies of letters and legal documents are sent to the client, and in other ways make the client appreciate that the case is receiving attention. The paralegal can also alert the attorney to angry clients and help head off an unpleasant confrontation.

The tasks performed by paralegals are too numerous to catalog completely, but the following lists give some indication of paralegal duties. They borrow heavily from lists prepared by the Subcommittee on Legal Assistance of the New York State Bar Association:

Real Estate Transactions

1. Review the contract for sale of real property.
2. Request and obtain title searches.
3. Request and obtain survey of the property.
4. Prepare deeds.
5. Review title opinion and/or title insurance documents.
6. Prepare and review closing statements.
7. Forward, receive, and track documents for closing.
8. Monitor closing file for completeness and accuracy.
9. Track deadlines.

Wills and Trusts

1. Maintain files and indexes.
2. Initial interview with fiduciary.

transcript
refers to a written verbatim statement. In law, transcripts are used most frequently in reference to depositions and trials.

3. Prepare and file probate documents.
4. Arrange for publication and service of citation.
5. Prepare application for tax identification number.
6. Value assets.
7. Transfer property to trust.
8. Prepare decedent's final income tax return.
9. Prepare estate tax return.
10. Prepare applications for life insurance benefits.
11. Inventory investments, bank accounts, etc.
12. Pay decedent's debts and costs of administration.
13. Cancel credit cards.
14. Prepare final accounting.
15. Prepare final probate petition.

Similar lists could be compiled for corporate paralegals, tax paralegals, bankruptcy paralegals, or virtually any other specialty using paralegals. The lists indicate the variety of formal document preparation and management required for activities involving property transfers. A great deal of work is generated in order to ensure that these events are accurate, complete, and timely.

CASE NO. 1–2   Limits on Legal Representation

The following case is the written decision of Justice Aldrich of the Supreme Court of Dutchess County, New York. Note that New York uses the designation "Supreme Court" for a lower or trial court rather than for the highest court, the customary usage in most states and in the federal court system.

The *Maldonado* case represents an intransigent attitude toward legal representation by nonlawyers. As long as the Bench and Bar view the world as divided into those who are legally competent (lawyers) and those who are not (laypersons), large portions of our society may be deprived of legal services. At the time of this decision, the paralegal profession was in its infancy. It is interesting to speculate whether the case would be decided differently if the prisoner were represented by a paralegal twenty years from now.

**In the Matter of the Application of Miguel
MALDONADO, Petitioner, for a Judgment
Pursuant to Article 78 of the Civil
Practice Law and Rules**
v.
NEW YORK STATE BOARD OF PAROLE, Respondent.

Supreme Court, Dutchess County
108 Misc. 2d 880, 424 N.Y.S.2d 589 (1969)

RAYMOND E. ALDRICH, Jr., Justice.

The motion of petitioner captioned as a **CPLR**, Article 78 proceeding seeks to proceed **pro se** and that Robert Dana, an inmate law clerk, be appointed as his spokesman or advocate with respect to this proceeding in the place of his designated attorney-at-law duly admitted to practice law under our judicial system, is denied as the Court is unaware of any authority which permits a lay person to appear on another person's behalf and to act as his attorney in a court of law unless admitted to so practice. Under the statutes of this state, only those persons permitted by law to practice before the courts of this state may act as a legal representative of another person in a courtroom proceeding or fulfill the capacity of a practicing attorney.

The Court further observes that the motion to relieve the court appointed attorney has not been served upon him, although even if petitioner or Robert Dana had done so, the relief would be denied.

If petitioner wishes to proceed pro se he may do so, and he will not be denied that right, but he cannot have Robert Dana act as his attorney or in any capacity other than as a witness or an advisor out of court for no person may practice law without being first admitted to the Bar.

Pursuant to the provisions of the Judiciary Law 478 and 484, only persons admitted to practice before the courts of this state (with certain enumerated exceptions not applicable herein) may do so, the Legislature acknowledging that those who receive legal assistance must obtain same from those who have had adequate training and experience to fully inform them of the intricacies of the legal circumstances confronting them. Violation of that proscription is punishable as a misdemeanor (Judiciary Law 485).

Were this a criminal proceeding, the Court also notes that while petitioner may have a constitutional right to defend himself pro se should he elect to do the same [C.], said right to pro se representation in a criminal proceeding does not carry with it the right to request the designation as a representative in court of a person not admitted to practice before the courts of the jurisdiction under which the proceeding had been commenced [Cc.].

While the Court is not fully aware of the qualifications of Mr. Dana, there is no indication or representation made to the Court that he is an attorney duly admitted to practice before the courts. Given the nature of his job title within the institution, it appears that his capacity is one that is comparable to a librarian whose responsibility is to assist individuals in their own research while utilizing facilities in the prison law library.

For the foregoing reasons, the motion is denied.

The Court further recommends that the Board of Parole and the Superintendents of the State correctional institutions inform each Inmate Law Clerk under their jurisdiction to advise any inmate seeking his assistance that he cannot appear in a legal proceeding as his spokesman or advocate for he would thus be practicing law without admission to the Bar by the Appellate Division.

CASE GLOSSARY

CPLR is an abbreviation of Civil Practice Law and Rules of New York State.

pro se is Latin for "in one's own behalf," "for oneself." In law it usually refers to representing oneself without an attorney.

CASE QUESTIONS

1. How does the court justify its denial of Maldonado's request to be represented by a nonattorney?
2. Assuming from Miguel Maldonado's name that he is Hispanic-American, would this decision seem fair if his first language were Spanish and he was not at ease with English, especially in legal proceedings, and he did not like his appointed attorney?
3. If we have a constitutional right to represent ourselves and a constitutional right to be represented by an attorney, why do we not have a right to be represented by a layperson?
4. Does this decision disadvantage prisoners more than those who are free to go about preparing their defense?
5. Would this case be decided similarly today?

CASE NO. 1–3 To Practice or Not to Practice

The *Winder* case that follows draws a fine line between what is the practice of law and what is not. In drawing its conclusions it cites a case involving a well-known book titled *How to Avoid Probate!*, which caused considerable consternation among state bar associations. Probate is the court procedure whereby the estate of a deceased person is administered and distributed. When poorly planned by the decedent, the estate may be subject to significant costs during the probate process, which in some jurisdictions has been abused by lawyers and judges. In writing his book, Dacey appealed to the fears of those who had heard horror stories of probate. There are a number of legal devices for passing on property without going through probate. Members of the legal profession, nevertheless, were properly concerned that a general book about probate failed to take into account the peculiarities of various state laws and the individualized needs of those who sought a proper division of their property.

The STATE of New York, Respondent,

v.

James A. WINDER, Individually and dba Divorce Yourself,
Do It Yourself Divorce Kits and Divorce Aid
Service Enterprises, Appellant.

Supreme Court, Appellate Division, Fourth Dept.
348 N.Y.S.2d 270 (1973)

Before DEL VECCHIO, J.P., and MARSH, MOULE, CARDAMONE AND SIMONS, JJ.

MEMORANDUM:

The Divorce Yourself Kit offered for sale by defendant, a layman, purports to offer forms and instructions in law and procedure in certain areas of matrimonial law and the judicial process. **In Matter of New York Co. Lawyers' Ass'n v. Dacey**, 28 A.D.2d 161 . . . , the court dealt with the publishing of a book "How to Avoid Probate!" consisting of 55 pages of text and 310 pages of forms. In the dissenting opinion adopted by the Court of Appeals, Justice Stevens, analyzing the pertinent rules of law, stated . . . : "It cannot be claimed that the publication of a legal text which purports to say what the law is amounts to legal practice. And the mere fact that the principles or rules stated in the text may be accepted by a particular reader as a solution to his problem does not affect this. . . . Apparently it is urged that the conjoining of these two, that is, the text and the forms, with advice as to how the forms should be filled out, constitutes the unlawful practice of law. But that is the situation with many approved and accepted texts. Dacey's book is sold to the public at large. There is no personal contact or relationship with a particular individual. Nor does there exist that relation of confidence and trust so necessary to the status of attorney and client. This is the essential of legal practice—the representation and the advising of a particular person in a particular situation. . . . At most the book assumes to offer general advice on common problems, and does not purport to give personal advice on a specific problem peculiar to a designated or readily identified person." Similarly the defendant's publication does not purport "to give personal advice on a specific problem peculiar to a designated or readily identified person," and because

of the absence of the essential element of "legal practice—the representation and the advising of a particular person in a particular situation" in the publication and sale of the kits, such publication and sale did not constitute the unlawful practice of law in violation of Sec. 478 of the Judiciary Law and was improperly enjoined by paragraph I of the judgment appealed from. There being no legal impediment under the statute to the sale of the kit, there was no proper basis for the injunction in paragraph G against defendant maintaining an office for the purpose of selling to persons seeking a divorce, separation, annulment or separation agreement any printed material or writings relating to matrimonial law or the prohibition in the memorandum of modification of the judgment against defendant having an interest in any publishing house publishing his manuscript on divorce and against his having any personal contact with any prospective purchaser. The record does fully support, however, the finding of the court that for the charge of $75 or $100 for the kit, the defendant gave legal advice in the course of personal contacts concerning particular problems which might arise in the reparation and presentation of the purchaser's asserted matrimonial cause of action or pursuit of other legal remedies and assistance in the preparation of necessary documents. The ordering paragraphs of the injunction A through F, H and J all enjoin conduct constituting the practice of law, particularly with reference to the giving of advice and counsel by the defendant relating to specific problems of particular individuals in connection with a divorce, separation, annulment of [sic] sought and should be affirmed.

Judgment unanimously modified on the law and facts in accordance with Memorandum and as modified affirmed without costs.

CASE QUESTIONS

1. What does the court describe as the essential ingredient of legal practice?
2. Why may a nonlawyer give advice in a book but not in person?
3. Is the legal profession protecting its fees or protecting the public from charlatans?

SUMMARY

Paralegals perform a variety of tasks in law offices that depend largely on the needs of the firm. It is easier to say what paralegals cannot do than what they can do. Since legal advice and legal representation are restricted to licensed members of the Bar, paralegals must be careful not to cross the line into these areas, but they may do virtually anything else that lawyers have traditionally done. Where paralegal work is supervised by an attorney, most potential problems of unauthorized practice of law and malpractice suits against the attorney are minimized.

Paralegal training is available at a variety of schools, and many paralegals are trained by their firms or attorneys. Paralegals are distinguished from other law office staff by specialized legal knowledge and skills and the manner in which they apply these.

EXERCISES

1. Check the want ads in the local newspaper for paralegals. What qualifications are mentioned? If you have access to a newsletter of a local city or county bar association, check to see if it has advertisements for paralegals. Also see if it mentions local paralegal associations.
2. Find out if your state has a state paralegal association and if your city or county (or region) has a paralegal association. See what information you can obtain from these groups. The National Association of Legal Assistants also has representatives in most metropolitan areas.

SUGGESTED READING

Paralegal by Barbara Bernardo (Peterson's Guides, Princeton, N.J., 1990) is a clearly written and informative paperback guide to the profession, highly recommended for those seeking a career as a paralegal.

PROFESSIONAL PROFILE

Ransford Pyle says, "Although I have taught many different subjects, I have found the teaching of law extremely demanding." One of the most satisfying aspects of teaching law is the fact that students will apply the knowledge gained in training to real situations, adding something useful and productive to our society. He sees the profession of law as a productive one. To those who would say that there are too many lawyers or that our society is too litigious, Pyle answers that Americans are devoted to the rule of law—believing that each of us has fundamental rights that can be vindicated, if necessary, in a court of law, and believing that change can be brought about through a lawful, democratic process. The hope that faith in the rule of law inspires in Americans contrasts starkly with the fatalistic submission to authority and the revolutionary terrorism to be found among citizens of many other countries.

"The practice of law presents endless challenge," Pyle says. It is intellectually demanding, personally rewarding, and politically exciting. As a group, lawyers are well-informed, and socially and politically active. Their contributions to society in and out of the practice of law is unsurpassed by any other profession. No other profession confronts the variety of human problems nor maintains the optimism for solving them as does the legal profession.

Pyle believes that the most exciting aspect of the practice of law lies in solving clients' problems. Every lawyer has a wealth of stories about unusual clients, bizarre problems, and strange judicial behavior. The lawyer is constantly thrown into novel situations that call for quick thinking, clever talking, and a good sense of humor. It is a field that is at the same time exhausting and energizing.

Pyle does not recall a case that did not have something interesting about it or one from which nothing could be learned. The endless process of learning required by the law is very appealing. "Admittedly, there are areas that simply do not interest me," Pyle says, "yet I can still understand why others find them interesting." Fortunately, the practice of law offers a niche for every personality and every intellectual orientation.

A BRIEF CURRICULUM VITAE

Education:

Ph.D. (Anthropology), University of Florida, 1974
Juris Doctor, University of Florida College of Law, 1967
A.B., Harvard University, Major in Fine Arts (Art History), 1958

Teaching:

Paralegal Program, Santa Fe Community College, 1985-present
Coordinator, Legal Studies Program, University of Central Florida, 1976-present
West Georgia College, 1973-1976
Also taught at Emory University, Atlanta; Rollins College, Winter Park, Florida; and the University of Costa Rica

Bar Memberships:

Member, Florida Bar
Former Member, Georgia Bar

Practiced law in Georgia and Florida

Japanese linguist, Military Intelligence, U.S. Army, 1958-1962

Ransford C. Pyle
Attorney, College Educator, and Author

CHAPTER 2
Lawyers

> **The first thing we do, let's kill all the lawyers.**
>
> — *Shakespeare, Henry VI, Pt. II*

> **There is no group . . . which has become more socially conscientious and more understanding of their obligation than the members of the bar.**
>
> — *Lyndon B. Johnson,*
> *36th President of the United States*

Characters in Shakespeare's plays are not alone in their distaste for lawyers. One generation after the founding of the Virginia and Massachusetts Bay colonies, private lawyers were

jurisprudence
is commonly defined as the science or philosophy of law. It is generally concerned with the nature of law and legal systems and their rules rather than with ethics and morality, though these latter topics can rarely be excluded.

plea bargaining
One accused of a crime can "bargain" through his or her attorney with the prosecutor. The trade usually involves an agreement by the accused to plead guilty rather than not guilty, in return for which the prosecutor agrees to charge the accused with a lesser crime, e.g., voluntary manslaughter in lieu of murder, or to recommend a lesser sentence. The court may enter a written agreement to this effect, though the rules vary by state.

docket
as used here, refers to the court calendar with listings of court proceedings to be heard during a certain time period or term of court.

prosecutor
In criminal cases, suits are brought in behalf of a state or the United States. The attorney charged with prosecuting such cases is a public official, commonly called state attorney, district attorney, or United States attorney.

forbidden to practice before their courts. As the legal historian Lawrence M. Friedman remarks, the American lawyer "has played a useful role, sometimes admired, but rarely loved." Suspicion, distrust, and outright hostility toward lawyers is still much a part of American folklore. The truth is, however, that few outside the legal profession understand exactly what lawyers do or why they do what they do. In this chapter we will discuss lawyers and the legal profession to arrive at a basic understanding of their place in our legal system and our society.

THE LAW AND THE LAWYER

The legal profession is named after its subject matter, the law. Unfortunately, this field is not as easily described as, say, electrical engineering. The problem of defining law may be left to legal philosophers and scholars of **jurisprudence**. We are concerned with law in operation or "in practice." Lawyers are called professionals but are also referred to as *practitioners* since the practice of law includes a great variety of services furnished by lawyers to their clients.

Law may be defined as a process, a system, or a set of rules governing society. As a process, law can be viewed as the means by which rights and duties are created and implemented. As a system, law interconnects rules governing society with a hierarchy of courts served by the legal profession and the police. As a set of rules, law is a complex code of conduct and values formally established and published, backed by the threat of enforcement. This last view of law as rules is what law students regularly study and what the public generally views as the law.

Failure to understand law as system and process, however, leads to a distorted view of law and lawyers. For example, nonlawyers often regard **plea bargaining** as an unethical device used by criminal defense lawyers to circumvent justice. Plea bargaining only makes sense in the context of the pressures and problems inherent in the process and system behind the administration of criminal justice. It has become an indispensable aid, some might say a necessary evil, in resolving criminal cases in the context of overcrowded jails, overburdened court **dockets**, and overworked **prosecutors**.

One must never forget that law continually undergoes change. Not only do the rules change, but the legal system also changes. As society changes, so must law. Law has a particularly important place in American society, which is extremely diverse and complex in comparison with other societies. The various parts of American society express differing and often conflicting values, so a major task of law is to convert values into functioning rules. In the last thirty years, America has encountered major value confrontations over racial integration, civil disobedience in the Vietnam era, and abortion. While these are social, political, and even spiritual issues, Americans have looked to law and the legal system for their resolution.

The law we will discuss in the following chapters is American law, the law of the American legal system as practiced by the legal profession. It is more properly labeled Anglo-American law, since we have the very special distinction of having more than nine hundred years of unbroken legal tradition inherited from England. The severing of political bonds with England in 1776 did not bring a corresponding break with the English legal tradition. In fact, it has been argued convincingly that the American colonials were fighting for the rights normally accorded Englishmen in England but denied to Americans by colonial governments.

Law is concerned with rights, duties, obligations, and privileges and their enforcement. Under the U.S. constitutional model, political authority is divided among the executive, legislative, and judicial branches of government. The study of law generally focuses on the judiciary since the courts in our system are entrusted with interpreting the law, and it is in the courts that disputes between opposing sides are resolved.

Disputes form the heart of our legal system, which has evolved as an **adversarial** system in which legal battle is waged by conflicting parties employing legal counsel to take their sides before an impartial judge and, if necessary, an impartial jury. The practice of law commonly involves advancing and protecting the interests of a client in a dispute, but equally important is preventing disputes. No ethical lawyer would write a **will** or **contract** or close a real estate transaction hoping that **litigation** would result. The test of a well-written will is whether its provisions are carried out uncontested; the test of a good contract is whether it has resolved all reasonable potential conflicts in advance and allows the contracting parties to perform their obligations to their mutual satisfaction. Perhaps it is in this area of preventive law, in which lawyers foresee and prevent future problems, that they do their best work and provide their most valuable services. The public rarely recognizes that lawyers routinely perform this function. The **uncontested will**, the contract that is not **breached**, and the transaction that runs smoothly do not make headlines. For most lawyers, however, an appreciative and satisfied client is one of the frequent personal rewards of the practice of law.

adversarial
In an adversarial legal system like ours, litigants, typically represented by attorneys, argue their respective sides in a dispute before an impartial judge and jury. Ideally, parties to a suit are at liberty to present their cases and challenge their opponents. The adversarial system is often contrasted with an inquisitorial one in which an accused is questioned by officials without rights of defense in a relentless search for the truth. An inquisitorial process provides no protection against abuse by the officials.

will or contract
A document through which a person directs how his or her property will be distributed at death. The formal requisites of a valid will are established by state law. A person who dies without a valid will is called an *intestate*, and the decedent's property passes by state law governing *intestate succession*. *See also* **Uncontested will.**

litigation
Bringing a dispute to court; derived from the Latin *lis*, which means lawsuit. We Americans are said to be *litigious*, meaning that we are prone to resolve our disputes through lawsuits rather

than by other means. In a curriculum, may serve as the title for a course called "Civil Procedure" at other schools.

uncontested will
Wills are sometimes challenged by those who would benefit if the will were declared invalid. If there is no challenge, the will is said to be uncontested.

breached
commonly means breaking a law or obligation. In contract law, a breaching party is one who fails to perform part or all of his obligations under the contracts.

disbarment
is the most severe professional disciplinary sanction in which an attorney's license to practice law is canceled. In addition to professional discipline, an attorney may be subject to civil and criminal actions.

associate
is the title usually given to a full-time member of a law firm who has not yet been elevated to partner. The associate is salaried, whereas the partners share in the profits of the firm.

law review
Most accredited law schools publish a law review on a quarterly basis with scholarly articles and comments on legal issues. Law reviews are edited

BECOMING A LAWYER

In order to represent a client before a court, a person must become a member of the Bar. In a general sense of the term, the Bar refers to the licensed members of the legal profession, the community of American lawyers, just as the Bench refers to all judges collectively. Requirements for membership, however, differ from state to state, and membership in one state bar does not confer membership in another state. In most states, licensing is regulated by a state bar association to which members pay annual dues. The state bar associations have responsibility for maintaining standards of conduct within the profession and for determining misconduct or assisting the court in disciplining members for misconduct with a variety of sanctions, the most severe of which is **disbarment**. Bar disciplinary boards are particularly concerned with misconduct in relations with clients, such as misuse of client's funds or the failure to provide promised services. Bar associations also engage in review and reform of laws and provide a sounding board and even lobbying activities for the legal profession. If a state attempts to place new restrictions or taxes on lawyers, they will be quick to respond through their respective bar associations. The authority and activities of the different associations can vary considerably from state to state.

Admission to the Bar requires passing a bar examination and submission to scrutiny by the bar association. Traditionally, bar membership has required that each candidate be approved on the basis of moral character as determined by the licensing association.

Approval of an application to take the bar examination generally requires completion of law school and the receipt of a law degree, usually called a J.D. (Juris Doctor) or LL.B. (Bachelor of Laws). Admission to law school is usually predicated on the completion of a four-year undergraduate degree.

Law School

In order to understand how lawyers think, some appreciation of the law school experience is helpful. Law school provides a rigorous training that formally and informally molds a certain sort of thinking.

Admission to law school is highly competitive. Prestige and reputation are important in the legal profession and equally so to the law student because placement and salary upon graduation from law school depend upon the prestige of the law school and performance in law school. Entry to law school is based principally on undergraduate grade point average and scores obtained on the Law School Admissions Test (LSAT). The more prestigious the law school, the higher grades and scores must be to obtain admission. Intense competition is characteristic of law students and happily encouraged by their professors, most of whom were once law school achievers.

Among law schools, the most elite are considered "national law schools" because their orientation as well as their reputations are national. Yale Law School in New Haven, Connecticut, for example, is not a training ground for Connecticut lawyers but an entree to large New York law firms, the so-called "Wall Street firms," which represent national business interests. The archetype of the perfect new **associate** just hired by a law firm went to Harvard Law School, became editor of the **Harvard Law Review**, and served a year or two as a **law clerk** for a United States Supreme Court **Justice**. Such credentials would guarantee a handsome salary at a top law firm.

Law school training continues to follow a model established in the 1890s by Dean Christopher Columbus Langdell of the Harvard Law School. He invented the *case method* in which students read judicial opinions, or cases, rather than treatises about law. His reasoning was that the practice of law in the United States was based on discovering the law through these decisions since it was in the courts that law was interpreted and explained. A natural corollary to the case method is the *Socratic dialogue* between professor and student. Instead of lecturing, the law professor asks questions of the students about cases they have been assigned to read in order to determine the issues and reasoning in the opinions. For the freshman law student, this is a grueling and often humiliating experience and has been called a "game that only one (the professor) can play." It is a rite of passage in which students are forced to shed their former ways of thinking and reacting to issues and problems and begin to "think like a lawyer." This method of teaching has been seriously criticized as promoting a tunnel-vision, but it succeeds in its goal of fostering analytical thinking and objective argument. Because of this criticism, however, many law schools have in recent years shown a greater sensitivity to the needs of students, offering counseling and tutoring by staff and peers.

The product of an American law school has read hundreds of judicial opinions and spent countless hours finding his or her way about an extensive law library learning the law but may never have been in a courtroom and may not know the difference between a **bailiff** and a **court reporter**. In recent years law schools have initiated or expanded the number of clinical programs in which students practice law under the supervision of an instructor. In

by outstanding students, who gain considerable prestige by serving on law review. Law reviews tend to reflect the prestige of their schools, the Harvard Law Review occupying center stage for most of this century.

law clerk
Top law students often seek clerkships with judges after graduating from law school. It is a very great honor to serve as a clerk for a United States Supreme Court Justice. Law clerks frequently make major contributions to drafting written decisions. Law clerk also refers to law school students who work summers or part time for private attorneys. They do much the same work as paralegals.

justice
The judges on the United States Supreme Court and the highest state courts are called Justices, though the term may be used for other judges, depending on the custom of the jurisdiction.

bailiff
An officer of the court charged with keeping order in the courtroom, having custody over prisoners and the jury.

court reporters
make verbatim recordings of court proceedings and, when necessary, reduce them to typewritten

addition, many law students gain experience by serving as law clerks for law firms during the summers between academic years. Despite this occasional practical education, the law school focuses on developing an attitude of mind that seeks the relevant legal issue in each human transaction and applies a technical analytical approach to solving problems.

Obtaining a License to Practice Law

In order to represent a client in legal matters, an attorney must be licensed in the jurisdiction in which he or she practices. Each state has its own requirements for admission to practice, and the federal courts have their own requirements. Many states relax their requirements for long-term members of the bar of other states, but the process by which the newly graduated law student becomes an attorney follows a similar pattern in most states.

Application for licensing generally requires graduation from a law school approved by the American Bar Association (in some states nonapproved law schools are allowed). The applicant must also show good moral character, but the extent to which this is scrutinized depends on the state. Moral fitness is difficult to define and must be determined on a case-by-case basis; but bar examiners are especially concerned about defects in character that suggest a potential for betraying a client's trust or deceiving a court. For example, an individual previously convicted of **perjury** would be a poor candidate for the practice of law, having demonstrated a disregard for the integrity of the justice system. Finally, admission is usually predicated on a passing score on the bar examination.

Bar Examination

Upon completion of law school or just before graduation, aspiring candidates face the dreaded ordeal of the bar examination. This generally consists of two or three days of a written examination, which in most states consists of two parts. One part is the Multistate Bar Examination, a standardized national test that contains two hundred multiple choice questions based on general legal topics such as property, contracts, and constitutional law. Each question is based on a hypothetical fact situation, and the examination requires a thorough knowledge of **black letter law**. This mentally exhausting part of the examination lasts six hours.

While the Multistate is based on general principles of law, most states require a second part that addresses the law specific to the state administering the examination. This part of the

transcripts. They are also employed to make transcripts of out-of-court sworn statements such as depositions.

perjury
A person who makes a false statement under oath in a judicial proceeding, knowing the statement to be false, has committed perjury. The false statement must concern a material issue or fact in the proceeding.

black letter law
is lawyer's slang for the basic, well-established rules of law. It is a common custom in annotated statutes and legal treatises to bold-face (hence "black letter") the rules and statutes while leaving comments and annotations in normal type.

examination often requires written essay questions based on hypothetical legal disputes and resembles the sorts of examinations typically given as final examinations in law school. Applicants must then wait several weeks, even months, to receive the final results. Each state licensing board is free to establish its own standards, so a passing grade on the Multistate in one state may be a failing grade in another. In most states between sixty-five and ninety percent of examinees pass. A failing candidate can usually retake the examination, though some states limit the number of times the examination can be taken.

The bar examination not only establishes a minimum standard of competence for lawyers, it also represents a psychological ordeal shared by attorneys; most recall vividly the events of the examination. The Multistate in particular calls for an approach for which law students have not been prepared, namely, to command a broad knowledge of the law and apply it all at once to a series of multiple choice questions. For this reason, most applicants take a bar review course lasting several weeks prior to the examination itself. While law students have been accustomed to limiting their study to a particular subject over the course of an academic term, the bar examination requires the applicant to recall the sum of three years of legal study.

Attorney Employment

The vast majority of new bar members join private law firms, but significant numbers obtain employment as government attorneys or as **house counsel** for private corporations. A few brave souls decide to "hang out their shingles" and begin practicing law as sole practitioners or jointly with one or more law school colleagues. Despite three years of intensive training, few law school graduates are prepared for the demands of practice. They are unfamiliar with law office routine and management, the peculiarities of court systems, interviewing clients, negotiating settlements, and collecting for services. Successful practice requires interpersonal skills that are sorely neglected in law school. In addition, since law school focuses on major legal issues, a law school graduate before preparing for the bar exam is likely to be totally ignorant of many areas of state law. A new lawyer is unlikely to know how to do a **bankruptcy**, a tenant eviction, get a **zoning variance** from a city, or even conduct a **real estate closing**. Because of unfamiliarity with so many features of day-to-day practice, the new lawyer is most comfortable in the company of more experienced practitioners and their legal staff.

house counsel
Many corporations and other businesses employ full-time attorneys, called house counsel, as part of their administrative staff. When attorneys from private firms are retained to represent corporate interests, they are usually called *outside counsel.*

bankruptcy
While there are different forms of bankruptcy, the term generally refers to the situation in which a person, business, or government cannot or will not pay its debts, so its property is entrusted to a trustee in bankruptcy who distributes the property to creditors.

zoning variance
It is customary in the United States for local governments to create zones within city and county boundaries with restrictions primarily on the form of use, e.g., agricultural or residential zones. Permission by local government to depart from the restrictions is called a variance.

real estate closing (settlement)
Real estate transactions are completed by a closing at which numerous documents are signed and

The competitive spirit of law school also directs many new lawyers to large firms. Already oriented toward achievement and success, graduating law students often measure themselves by starting salaries and the prestige of the law firms they join. Big city law firms compete with each other for top law school graduates, and the largest Wall Street firms offer starting salaries more than twice the average.

Fortunately for our society, many law graduates are not seduced by the drive to enrich themselves. It is very common for a graduate to return to his or her home town to assume a respected position among friends and associates. Lawyers who choose this path inevitably find that the rewards of service to the community outweigh monetary compensation. The practice of law, like most other professions, offers an opportunity for personal satisfaction difficult to find in other kinds of employment.

Some law school graduates have specific goals for their training, such as preserving the environment, providing legal services to the poor, prosecuting criminals, or serving as elected legislators. The legal profession provides a unique foundation for contributing to change or improvement of one's society.

Obtaining prestigious employment, however, does not guarantee a successful career. New attorneys in a firm are called *associates*, a position from which they may never graduate. The traditional course of a legal career in a private firm entails working for a few years as an associate until invited to become a partner in the firm, which means moving from a salary to sharing in the profits of the firm. In the largest firms, only a small number of associates are ever asked to become partners. Associates who do not make partner commonly move to other firms or set up their own practice. This is a brutally competitive system that has been improved somewhat by many firms by establishing intermediate positions like senior associate or junior partner. This allows firms to reward attorneys without forcing a partnership decision.

The pressures on attorneys to perform do not consist simply of providing good services to clients. A law firm is also a business, and attorneys who do not add significant profits to the business by way of new clients and many hours of work billable to clients are unlikely to become partners in a firm. For some, the advantage of employment with government or a private corporation is that an attorney is more often measured by the quality of work rather than the quantity of business generated.

Paralegals must understand the stresses involved in the work of attorneys in order to work better with their employers. One of the advantages of paralegal work over that of an attorney is that paralegals do not bear ultimate responsibility for the outcome of clients' problems. The difference in stress can be great. Paralegals

exchanged, payment is made, and property deeds are transferred. Paralegals are frequently employed in the preparation and organization of documents, but states differ on the extent to which paralegals can actively participate in closings. Exceeding the limits set by the state may subject a paralegal to the charge of "unauthorized practice of law."

occupy a position similar to corporate lawyers in that performance is measured by the quality of their work.

WHAT LAWYERS DO

The United States has more than a half a million lawyers. They are assisted by over one hundred thousand paralegals, whose numbers are projected to double by the year 2000. Obviously, a great deal of legal work exists to support this workforce. What is it exactly that lawyers do?

Acquisition of knowledge in law school is merely the first step in becoming a competent attorney; this knowledge must be put into practice. Just as the LSAT is an imprecise predictor of performance in law school, law school grades are an imperfect predictor of success in the practice of law. Even the bar examination fails to measure many of those qualities essential to future success. An attorney is not simply a repository of legal knowledge and technical skills. An attorney is a problem solver who must rely on imagination, creativity, common sense, and psychology as well as the analytical skills learned in school. The rules that make up the body of the law are abstractions that only take on their meaning in the course of human events. Attorneys are frequently addressed as "counselor," and this perhaps comes closer than any other word to the nature of their work. Attorneys act as providers of legal services, advisors, counselors, negotiators, and agents for their clients.

The Lawyer as a Provider of Legal Services

It is as a furnisher of services in legal problem solving that the lawyer is generally pictured. Although this may be the primary function of an attorney, we will see in the following sections that attorneys also play many other roles.

The dramatic popular image of the lawyer focuses on the trial lawyer, when in actuality very few attorneys spend a significant portion of their time in court. Many lawyers never try cases, and most trial lawyers spend most of their time preparing for trial. Lawyers are basically problem solvers. Sometimes the problems are actual disputes that may lead to lawsuits and eventually to trial. Most disputes never reach the trial stage but are settled with the lawyer acting principally as negotiator or conciliator, which will be discussed below.

Much of the work that lawyers do has nothing to do with disputes. Many client problems do not involve an adversary, varying from things as simple as changing one's legal name to something as complicated as obtaining approval for a major airport. Potential adversaries may be lurking on the sidelines, but most problems require legal help largely because they have legal consequences. Incorporating a business must be accomplished in accordance with state law; writing a will must be done with formalities dictated by state law. While these may be done without an attorney, it is wiser and safer to employ professional services.

Most lawyers are specialists whether they realize it or not. Some, for instance, handle only tax matters, while others, who may call themselves general practitioners, may refuse to handle criminal cases or divorce cases. The body of the law is immense and constantly growing. No lawyer can adequately keep up with the changes in all areas of the law. If a lawyer accepts a case in an area in which she is not expert, it is her duty to educate herself before proceeding.

Because of specialization, the distribution of legal work for any particular lawyer varies considerably, but we may make some generalizations about how lawyers spend their time. They talk with clients, first to understand the problem, then to explain its legal ramifications to the client. They write many letters, to clients, to other attorneys, to request information from a variety of sources. They are constantly reading. They read contracts their clients furnish them; they read wills and deeds and many other legal documents in order to assess their clients' duties, rights, and risks. They read a lot of "law," which may be focused on research for a problem or a dispute or may be designed to remain current on the areas of law of particular concern to them. Lawyers must be well informed about matters affecting their clients. It has been said that some lawyers specializing in **medical malpractice** cases know more about many fields of medicine than the average physician. In short, the attorney must know enough to provide competent legal representation to a client, an ethical duty imposed by the ABA **Canons of Ethics** and every state bar association.

In short, lawyers must rely on their communication skills; they talk, they write, and they read. Those who view lawyers as merely clever manipulators of words fail to recognize that a primary function of law in our society is to reduce rules of conduct to precise language that can be applied to real situations. Lawyers exercise their verbal skills with a knowledge of the law and supported by analytical training. In a legal context, words simply may not be used in the manner of casual speech. The attorney must use not only legal terms in a precise way but ordinary words as well. When dealing with the written word, attorneys read with a verbal microscope, analyzing each word and phrase for its legal implications. They are adept at what we might call "legal semantics," and it is for this that their services are needed. Anyone can memorize rules or fill out forms; but training, experience, and intelligence are required to use the special language of the law.

Lawyers are also organizers. There are many transactions that require detail and coordination. The merger of two corporations, for example, is a complex transaction that should be performed without leaving loose ends. Lawyers serve in such transactions to ensure that no legal problems will arise that could have been foreseen and avoided during the negotiations. They establish an orderly process to facilitate a smooth transition. Similarly, preparation for trial requires a step-by-step process in which all necessary information is collected and organized in a way that builds a logical and convincing presentation of the client's side of the lawsuit. As the case is built, it must be constantly reevaluated; lack of proper organization will produce poor results.

The Lawyer as Advisor

Clients consult lawyers when they feel they need legal advice. Many transactions and events take place in our society that have legal significance, and common sense dictates that they be entrusted at least in part to someone knowledgeable in their legal ramifications. Probably most of these involve property transactions in some way, but those who are accused of a crime or are seeking compensation for injury can best protect their interests by employing an attorney.

A person making a will or buying a residence is involved in serious property planning. For most, purchasing a home constitutes the largest investment of a lifetime, and the consequences of such a transaction should not be left to chance and ignorance. This transaction involves two principal areas of law—the law of real property and the law of contracts. Property law has evolved over many centuries and contains many relics of the past that present hidden traps for the unwary. The buyer may be presented with a standard contract for sale that provides reasonable protections for buyer and seller or may be presented with a contract that was designed primarily for the benefit of the seller. In either case, it is unlikely that the buyer understands the full import of the many clauses contained in the document. An attorney well-versed in property law can explain the contract and advise the client about its possible dangers and how to prepare for them.

As an advisor in these circumstances, the attorney does not give only legal advice. The attorney is likely to have a wealth of practical knowledge that has nothing to do with law, strictly speaking, such as the current state of local real estate prices, the

medical malpractice
Malpractice generally refers to professional negligence. If a person is injured due to negligent performance of professional services, he or she may sue for malpractice. A major difference between professional malpractice and ordinary negligence is that the professional is held to a higher standard of care when providing professional services.

Canons of Ethics
Refers to a set of basic principles established by the ABA to govern professional conduct. Their meaning has been elaborated by additional rules and interpretations in the various states.

most favorable mortgage rates, and planned or proposed development in the area. The attorney may know that the airport is about to change its flight paths in such a way that flights will pass directly over the home in question. Such information may be more valuable to a client than the explanation of rights and duties or the legal consequences of the contract itself.

Attorneys may be successful for many reasons, including politics and even luck, but most attorneys succeed because they provide valuable services. They are in a position to acquire a great deal of practical knowledge because they deal on a daily basis with countless problems that arise in the course of practice. An attorney who specializes in wills and **trusts**, for example, has seen countless examples of what can happen when someone dies if relatives and in-laws fight over the deceased's **estate**. Writing a will for a client may appear to be a technical legal matter, yet an attorney's knowledge of human nature will influence the legal advice that is given.

This role of the lawyer as personal, practical advisor is also important with business clients. Many businesses require legal help on a frequent basis. Not only are they concerned with making contracts and buying and selling, but they must be concerned with employee relations, government regulation, and taxation, not to mention the type of business organization that is appropriate to the enterprise. It is common for a close relation to develop between an attorney and a business client. The attorney comes to understand the business and its needs, and the client will often turn to the attorney for advice of a business and personal nature. The client also enjoys the **attorney–client privilege,** which allows the client to treat the attorney as a confidante who may be told matters that would not be disclosed to anyone else.

The Lawyer as Counselor

The role of counselor includes the role of advisor and more. The term is commonly used to refer to legal counsel, but in fact attorneys are often called upon to do much more. Certain areas of the practice of law entail personal counseling skills beyond legal skills, most notably divorce law. Lawyers must be prepared for the fact that clients deliver problems to them, that the clients are not competent to handle themselves. When dealing with a client seeking divorce or one accused of a crime, the lawyer must be aware that inevitably the client is dealing with intensely emotional personal problems as well as immediate legal problems. Law school training rarely prepares the new attorney for this kind of conflict.

While the function of the lawyer is to resolve a client's legal difficulties, the close personal and confidential relationship that often develops between lawyer and client can put the attorney in a role similar to that of a mental health counselor. Some lawyers avoid this role by taking a distant, strictly professional attitude toward their clients, but many recognize that this can seem callous and insensitive to a client who may be very much in need of caring and understanding. To a person who may be full of guilt and pain and have low self-esteem, personal rejection by the person they are looking to for solving their problems can make them feel very alone.

On the surface, the lawyer's responsibility would seem to end with the furnishing of legal services, but the nature of the relationship between attorney and client affects the quality of the services rendered. A divorcing spouse or an incarcerated person may well be in an emotional state that weakens his or her ability to achieve a reasonable legal solution. Persons suing for compensation for personal injury often face loss of work, medical expenses, and other financial difficulties that render them vulnerable to unfair negotiations with an insurance company or corporation that views the dispute objectively as a business transaction. An attorney insensitive to these personal problems may do a client a disservice.

Attorneys must also learn that a fine line must be drawn between caring and understanding and emotional involvement with a client's problems. It is one thing to have a personal relationship with a client and quite another to have a social or even romantic relationship. Taking a cue from mental health counselors, the lawyer should maintain a professional attitude without losing sight of the fact that clients are human beings deserving respect and understanding.

The Lawyer as Negotiator

The attorney must give a client the best representation possible. In the adversarial legal system, a lawyer often appears to be the "hired gun," using all the tricks of the trade to destroy the opposing party. This picture misrepresents the role of the lawyer, who is more often a negotiator, mediator, and conciliator. In a personal injury case, for example, the attorney must weigh a number of factors besides winning. If a person injured in an auto accident is suing an insurance company, both sides will have made an estimate of reasonable compensation. Their estimates are based on past experience, both in negotiations and with awards made by juries and judges. If the initial estimates, which are kept secret,

trust
A device whereby title to property is transferred to one person, the trustee, for the benefit of another, the beneficiary. An example might be the creation of a trust for a minor child, who might receive payments as directed by the trust until reaching a certain age, at which time the remainder of the trust would be transferred.

estate
Estate has several legal meanings but when used in reference to a decedent means the property rights distributed by someone appointed by the court (called the personal representative, administrator, or executor) to those entitled by law to receive the decedent's property.

attorney–client privilege
Confidential statements made by a client to an attorney may not be disclosed to others by the attorney without the client's permission, including court proceedings. Staffs of law firms, including paralegals, enjoy this privilege and must scrupulously avoid breaking client confidentiality. The privilege is for the benefit and protection of the client.

are close, it is likely that the two sides can come to an early agreement. If this happens, a number of advantages accrue to the client. First, the client will not experience the considerable unpleasantness of a trial. Second, the client will not endure prolonged negotiations. Third, the expenses, including attorneys' fees, will be minimized.

The client in this case is best served by an attorney who is a persuasive negotiator and can convince the other side that it is in their best interests to present reasonable offers of compensation. The attorney not only negotiates with the insurance company's attorney but must also apprise the client of the risks and strategies on both sides so that the client has reasonable expectations. Although the client must make the final decision to accept or reject an offer of settlement, the attorney commonly acts as a mediator between the two sides, ultimately persuading the client that an offer should be accepted. It should be noted, however, that some insurance companies adopt a strategy of nonnegotiation, in which case the plaintiff's attorney must assume an aggressive and threatening posture.

The adversarial role is especially problematic in divorce cases. The legal process of divorce tends to aggravate an already painful and sometimes hostile relationship between husband and wife. The best interests of clients go beyond maximizing economic benefits and parental rights. If minor children are involved, the divorcing couple need to establish at least a minimal basis of cooperation for the children's sake. A court battle is likely to leave everyone severely scarred emotionally. Nowhere are ethical and professional duties more perplexing than in divorce law. Divorce does not make unhappy people happy. Perhaps no area of the practice of law produces so many dissatisfied clients. Interpersonal skills in negotiation, mediation, and conciliation are just as essential as legal skills in this field.

Negotiating skills are essential in commercial law as well. In business and real estate transactions, in contracts, and in structuring business organizations, the objective is usually to establish an agreement of all concerned within the requirements of the law. While different parties have different self-interests, business transactions are normally entered into because everyone benefits. The attorney acts as a facilitator and negotiator, at the same time protecting the client's interests. In some long-standing business relationships based on personal trust, legal counsel may actually be intrusive. If agreements have been customarily cemented with a handshake, the sudden appearance of a contract written by an attorney may be insulting and could damage the relationship. Again, the lawyer's legal skills must be tempered with sensitivity.

SUMMARY

In this chapter we have seen that law school training and admission to the Bar are merely the first steps in becoming a competent attorney. While law school imparts a basic knowledge of important fields of the law, its emphasis on developing analytical skills does not provide either training for the daily tasks of the practice of law or the communication skills necessary for providing valuable legal services.

Attorneys are paid for their verbal skills. Most of their time is spent talking, writing, and reading, but law is a specialized language that must be used with care and precision. Words have legal implications often only fully appreciated by lawyers. Clients' goals are facilitated by lawyers who rephrase their wishes in language that establishes legal rights and duties, whether it be a business contract, a will, or a divorce settlement.

Lawyers are problem solvers; they help remove the legal hurdles in the way of a client's path. Sometimes this means fighting a legal battle in court to protect a client's interests, but more often it involves resolving a dispute without going to trial. Perhaps attorneys spend an even greater portion of their time preventing disputes and aiding in personal and business transactions by anticipating potential conflicts and either eliminating them or providing for their amicable resolution if they occur.

The practice of law entails many skills that are not taught in law school and are often absent in the popular image of the lawyer. These are primarily interpersonal communication skills that cast the attorney in the role of advisor, counselor, and negotiator. Lawyers regularly find themselves in difficult and complex situations that call for stamina, intelligence, patience, creativity, and most of all an understanding of human nature.

PROFESSIONAL PROFILE

Excerpted with permission from James Publishing, Inc
Legal Assistant Today (September/October 1990)

Linda Katz loves what she found in her job: "Intellectual stimulation and a balanced lifestyle. I know a lot of unhappy lawyers! I really feel I'm making a contribution, working with some of the brightest people in the country on some fascinating cases. I enjoy the creative aspects of my position now: It's dynamic, never dull, and brings new challenges every year."

"Make sure this is what you want to do," urges Katz. "New legal assistants continue to have lots of surprises: They do not do research all day, and they don't always work for lawyers who know how to manage people. Newcomers can do a lot more homework. Talk to paralegal associations and to the people who do the job. Ask questions. It's worth making a few phone calls."

According to Katz, "Starting salaries are fairly good in Houston—around $20,000 for legal assistants, varying with credentials." At Baker & Botts, a junior position, legal assistant clerk, begins at about $13-14,000. As for hours, Katz, notes, "Legal assistants do work some overtime hours, but it depends on what's happening. They have to have a flexible lifestyle. This is not a forty-hour, five-day per week job in a law firm! Our legal assistants go out of their way to help each other. Some even manage with small children."

With her new B.A. from the University of Bridgeport, Katz went to law school at St. Mary's (San Antonio, Texas) for a year. "I didn't like law school, but I was interested in law," recalls the Washington, D.C. native, who loved Texas and wanted to stay there. She worked briefly as a legal secretary in San Antonio before moving to Houston in search of a better opportunity. Holding out for an opening at her first-choice employer, Katz got the job she wanted in 1977.

Founded just after the Civil War, Baker & Botts is Houston's oldest law firm. Katz calls it "a full-service corporate firm with a strong Southwestern presence. I felt I did a good job and was never convinced I'd be as good a lawyer as I was a legal assistant. I got everything I wanted from the intellectually challenging job and made a lifestyle decision: It was nice having a lot of responsibility, but not ultimate responsibility. I had an opportunity to lead a balanced life."

Katz started on collection cases, then transferred to the labor area. "It sounded boring, but was a great career move. I worked on large employment-discrimination cases and arbitration hearings for refineries or chemical plants. My business trips were to Oil City or Pasadena, Texas—no glamour, but great people," observes Katz, who found labor arbitration fun and challenging. The attorney she reported to had her write briefs and assist lawyers at hearings. As administrator for a settled class action case she had worked on, she notified potential claimants, placed ads to find others, and looked for thousands of class members to get them to file claims. Each claim then had to be evaluated and analyzed. With this large employment-discrimination case around her department for seven years, Katz got involved in negotiations.

In 1984, Baker & Botts' new managing and administrative partners decided to upgrade their legal assistant program, and needed a nonlawyer to run it. They offered Katz the new position. "The firm is segmented into practice areas, with legal assistants dispersed throughout the areas," Katz explains. "They report to supervising attorneys for work assignments each day. I serve as administrative supervisor, assuring consistency in how legal assistants are treated and utilized, and what opportunities they have for benefits and advancement." Katz hires the legal assistants; her assistant hires the clerks who report to legal assistants.

Linda Katz
Managers Association (LAMA)
Vice President/Western Region

CHAPTER 3
Ethics

Men are not rewarded or punished for what they do, but rather for how their acts are defined. This is why men are more interested in better justifying themselves than in better behaving themselves.

— *Thomas Szasz*

The study of ethics is a branch of philosophy. The ethics discussed in this chapter is more appropriately labeled *legal ethics,* which has developed over the last century from a primitive sense of duty and responsibility to an explicit set of rules governing the professional conduct of attorneys, the violation of which may subject attorneys to disciplinary action.

Since paralegals are not members of the Bar, they have no licenses that can be suspended or revoked, but an understanding of ethical principles is nonetheless vitally important for paralegals because unethical conduct may result in serious problems for themselves, the attorneys they work for, and the clients they serve. For example, a paralegal who gives legal advice may be prosecuted by the state for unauthorized practice of law, and the paralegal's supervising attorney may be disciplined for negligent supervision. If the advice is faulty, the client receiving that advice may suffer a detriment, the supervising lawyer and law firm may be sued for malpractice, and the paralegal's career may come to a sudden conclusion.

It must be cautioned at the outset that a strong sense of right and wrong will not guarantee avoidance of the violation of professional ethics, though it certainly minimizes the danger. The practice of law involves duties to clients, to the public, to the courts, and to colleagues. Lawyers have access to sensitive, confidential information about their clients, information that must often necessarily be shared with law office staff. In the representation of clients, attorneys are frequently faced with ethical dilemmas that are not easily solved. Ethical codes are designed to provide answers to most of these dilemmas, but they cannot precisely address every possible situation. Clients can be unpredictable and even unscrupulous, consciously or unconsciously putting attorneys in positions that lead to unfavorable outcomes. It is only by strictly following the ethical codes and acting in utmost good faith that attorneys can avoid the many traps that the practice of law entails.

In the last two decades, the legal profession has expended great effort to define and refine the principles that govern the ethical conduct of attorneys. More than any other profession, the legal profession has embarked on a campaign to identify and police unethical conduct and fulfill its primary duty of serving the public and the legal system.

In the discussion that follows, the subject of legal ethics in general will be covered, but greatest attention will be given to those areas of particular concern to paralegals.

HISTORY OF ETHICAL RULES

Formulating ethical principles has been an ongoing task of the American Bar Association, which established Canons of Ethics as early as 1908. The ABA has no disciplinary authority, but it is the logical forum for discussing ethical principles since it represents the Bar nationwide. The Canons are general statements of principle urging proper conduct. They have been elaborated over the years through the addition and amendment of *Disciplinary Rules* and *Ethical Considerations,* which describe more specifically conduct that is subject to discipline (Disciplinary Rules) and conduct that is improper even though not subject to discipline (Ethical Considerations).

In 1970, these principles crystallized in the ABA's *Model Code of Professional Responsibility* and were quickly adopted by nearly all states. Once these principles were adopted, the Multistate Bar Examination devised a separate ethics test, which most states then made a part of their state bar examination (the Multistate Professional Responsibility Examination). The ABA additionally provided advisory opinions on specific applications of the *Model Code,* and many state bar associations have similarly answered ethical questions posed by their members in formal opinions.

In 1983, after several years of intense study and dialogue, the ABA reformulated legal ethics in the *Model Rules of Professional Conduct.* The *Model Rules* (as distinguished from the earlier *Model Code*) attempted to reflect changes in the legal profession; e.g., former prohibition of certain advertising was found by the U.S. Supreme Court to be an unconstitutional invasion of freedom of speech. The *Model Rules* also addressed conduct more specifically, narrowing the principles to increase clarity and enforceability. The *Model Rules* did away with *Disciplinary Rules* and *Ethical Considerations,* substituting "shall" and "shall not" ("a lawyer shall not seek to influence a judge, juror . . . except as permitted by law or the rules of court") as language warranting disciplinary action and "may" ("a lawyer may refuse to offer evidence that the lawyer reasonably believes is false") as language expressing conduct that is discretionary and not subject to disciplinary action.

The *Model Code* must be discussed with the more recent *Model Rules* for three reasons:

1. The basic principles are quite similar.
2. Since the *Model Code* was the initial set of rules adopted in the states, a host of opinions and judicial decisions serve as precedents for interpretations of the *Rules.*

3. The *Model Rules* have not received the same degree of acceptance from state bar associations as the *Model Code* enjoyed previously.

THE MODEL CODE AND THE MODEL RULES

The Canons of Professional Responsibility of the *Model Code* are listed below with corresponding sections of the *Model Rules*. Although the same issues are addressed, a comparison reveals a distinct difference. The Canons somewhat resemble the Ten Commandments, a moral code to live by, while the *Model Rules* reflect a more sophisticated legislative approach, organized into related subject areas with specific proscriptions that provide better guidance to disciplinary boards and tribunals. The *Model Rules* are eminently more practical, both in terms of enforcement and in terms of the clarity provided to attorneys.

Keep in mind that the Canons were extensively supplemented by *Disciplinary Rules* and *Ethical Considerations* that spelled out specific problems. Displaying the *Model Rules* in this way does not show their higher degree of organization. The *Model Rules* were published with supplementary comments that address problems routinely confronted by attorneys and are a distinct improvement over the *Model Code* as guidelines for attorneys. Nevertheless, because the *Model Rules* are more specific and more clearly enforceable, not all sectors of the Bar have been satisfied with them, and the states have not received the *Model Rules* with the wholehearted approval that generally met the *Model Code*.

CODES FOR LEGAL ASSISTANTS

Legal assistant organizations have also formulated ethical codes designed specifically for paralegals. Deborah Orlik in *Ethics for the Legal Assistant* (Glenview, IL: Scott, Foresman Company, 1986) describes these as "overly broad and moralistic." This is undoubtedly due to their lack of enforceability since they have no official or legal force. Making specific prohibitions that cannot be enforced is problematic. Additionally, the paralegal associations must as yet function reactively to the bar associations, which set the standards for lawyers, including the lawyers' responsibility for supervision of their legal staffs.

The National Association of Legal Assistants (NALA) has followed its earlier *Code of Ethics and Professional Responsibility*

Model Code and Model Rules Compared

Model Code of Professional Responsibility	Model Rules of Professional Conduct
Canons:	Rules:
1. A lawyer should assist in maintaining the integrity and competence of the legal profession.	**8 Maintaining the integrity of the profession.** **8.3 Reporting professional misconduct.** (a) A lawyer having knowledge that another lawyer has committed a violation of the Rules of Professional Conduct . . . shall inform the appropriate professional authority.
2. A lawyer should assist the legal profession in fulfilling its duty to make legal counsel available.	**6 Public service.** **6.1 Pro bono publico service.** A lawyer should render public interest legal service . . . **6.2 Accepting appointments.** A lawyer shall not seek to avoid appointment by a tribunal to represent a person except for good cause . . .
3. A lawyer should assist in preventing the unauthorized practice of law.	**5.5 Unlicensed (or unauthorized?) practice of law.** A lawyer shall not: (a) practice in a jurisdiction where doing so violates the regulation of the legal profession in that jurisdiction; or (b) assist a person who is not a member of the bar in the performance of activity that constitutes the unauthorized practice of law.
4. A lawyer should preserve the confidences and secrets of a client.	**1.6 Confidentiality of information.** (a) A lawyer shall not reveal information relating to representation of a client except as stated in paragraphs (b), (c), and (d) unless the client consents after disclosure to the client.
5. A lawyer should exercise independent professional judgment on behalf of a client.	**5.4 Professional independence of a lawyer.** (a) A lawyer or law firm shall not share legal fees with a nonlawyer, except . . .

(b) A lawyer shall not form a partnership with a nonlawyer if any of the activities of the partnership consist of the practice of law.

(c) A lawyer shall not permit a person who recommends, employs, or pays the lawyer to render legal services for another to direct or regulate the lawyer's professional judgment in rendering such legal services.

6. A lawyer should represent a client competently.

1.1 Competence. A lawyer shall provide competent representation to a client. Competent representation requires the legal knowledge, skill, thoroughness, and preparation reasonably necessary for the representation.

7. A lawyer should represent a client zealously within the bounds of the law.

[Canon 7 is arguably spread among the many subsections of Rules 1 (Client–Lawyer Relationship), 2 (Counselor), and 3 (Advocate).]

8. A lawyer should assist in improving the legal system.

[Canon 8 is primarily exhortatory rather than disciplinary and is implied in many of the Rules and the Preamble.]

9. A lawyer should avoid even the appearance of professional impropriety.

[The vagueness of Canon 9 has been resolved by addressing specific improprieties within the Rules.]

---

with the 1984 *Model Standards and Guidelines for Legal Assistants.* The National Federation of Paralegal Associations (NFPA) has published an *Affirmation of Responsibility.* In general, the substantive sections of both codes are derivative of the ethical principles embodied by the ABA codes. As a practical matter, the paralegal should concentrate on the ABA codes since the paralegal is not simply concerned about ethical conduct but also is concerned about conduct that would put a supervising attorney in an ethical dilemma.

DISCLOSURE

Many ethical problems can be resolved or mitigated by full disclosure to clients. Many conflict of interest situations may be eliminated by disclosure of the conflict to the client and opposing party and consent by both to continued representation. Even if an attorney represents a client in the mistaken belief that the ethical problem has been resolved, evidence of full disclosure indicates a good faith attempt by the attorney to resolve the ethical problem and may mitigate any disciplinary action that might result.

In addition to disclosure to the parties, ethical questions over which some uncertainty exists may be addressed to an appropriate state bar ethics committee for an opinion on the ethical issues if such procedure is available.

DEFINING THE PRACTICE OF LAW

The practice of law may be defined in two ways as it relates to professional ethics. An attorney may or may not be rendering legal services. For example, a lawyer may engage in mediation activities (see Chapter Fifteen), which does not entail providing legal services and is not covered by legal ethics per se, but any linkage of mediation services and the practice of law suggests ethical problems. For example, an attorney might mediate a divorce between husband and wife and then represent one of them in the divorce or refer them to the attorney's firm for representation. Such action would invoke ethical problems of conflict of interest and confidentiality constituting a serious breach of ethics. Thus, an attorney may engage in activities other than the practice of law, but such activities must be consistent with the attorney's professional position.

The practice of law is defined differently in terms of the unauthorized practice of law. In this instance, it is not so much what lawyers do as what may be done only by lawyers that defines the practice of law. For ethical purposes, the practice of law is best defined in the context of unauthorized practice of law, which is subject to criminal and civil sanctions by the court. In applying these sanctions, the courts have been forced to address the definition of the practice of law.

UNAUTHORIZED PRACTICE OF LAW

The following discussion should be supplemented with a review of the comments already made on this subject in Chapter One.

Each state restricts the practice of law to licensed attorneys and provides for a penalty, commonly criminal, to enforce these prohibitions. The problem, concerning which the states show wide variation, lies in defining what constitutes the practice of law. From an ethical standpoint, the restrictions on providing legal services can only be justified by an interest in protecting the public and not in preserving a professional monopoly. There are two issues in protecting the public: (1) the public should be protected against incompetence, and (2) some agency, usually a court, must have the power to protect the public. Licensing protects the public by requiring a level of competence necessary to obtain the license and by establishing authority to revoke the license for misconduct. Those without licenses can be punished for practicing law.

Lawyers are agents of their clients; they can represent clients before the court, sign certain documents on behalf of their clients, and act as direct contact in matters in which they represent their clients. Because of this agency relationship, the lawyer is held to ethical standards in representing clients and can be disciplined for misconduct, even sued by the client for breach of the limits of the relationship. Abuse of the representation can have serious consequences to the client and so justifies this control over attorney misconduct. Unlicensed persons providing legal services are much less subject to the scrutiny of the court and the profession.

The practice of law is much less specific than the practice of other professions, such as medicine and dentistry. For example, lawyers give advice on the conduct of personal and business affairs, but so do many others, such as accountants, real estate brokers, stock brokers, insurance agents, bankers, etc. These persons commonly give advice concerning the legal consequences of their clients' personal and business decisions. In fact, advice that could be considered legal is furnished by just about everyone. Anyone arrested for speeding, anyone buying land, or anyone getting a divorce can find no end of people who will advise on the legal aspects of each of these. When are such people practicing law?

The answer to this question is by no means easy, as a review of court cases on unauthorized practice of law attest. It is not sufficient to define the practice of law, as some early cases did, as what lawyers traditionally do. Lawyers do a great many things that do not require legal expertise. For the purposes of unauthorized practice of law, the issue has come down to identifying what it is that *only* lawyers may do. While the states vary considerably on the specifics of activities restricted to lawyers, three activities are universally identified:

1. Legal representation before a court.
2. Preparation of legal documents.

3. Giving legal advice.

Note that the first two categories relate to the attorney–client agency relationship under control of the court, while the third category is concerned with legal competence.

Legal Representation Before a Court

Because of the technical requirement of procedural law as well as the intricacies of specific kinds of lawsuits, a litigant without a lawyer is severely disadvantaged, especially if the opposing party has legal representation. In our legal system, it is not required that a person have an attorney to bring or defend a suit, but a person may not be represented by someone other than a licensed attorney. The court relies on the competence and accountability of the attorney.

A successful outcome to a trial generally requires legal skills, experience, and knowledge of a high order; the adversarial system does not work fairly when one of the parties lacks legal representation. However, many nontrial court appearances involve routine matters that do not involve legal argument or expertise and could easily be managed by legal staff acting on behalf of an attorney at a great savings to clients without risk. In his *Introduction to Paralegalism*, William Statsky relates that in Allen County, Indiana, paralegals registered with the local bar association may appear in court in a wide variety of matters, such as uncontested divorces, scheduling of pretrial hearings, default judgments, and other routine matters. Most jurisdictions require attorney attendance for these matters, though it is common to send a junior associate of the firm when the senior partner has more important matters to attend to.

The appearance of the attorney in court is certainly necessary when a legal argument may ensue or rights and duties of clients are decided, otherwise the court need only be reassured that an attorney is ultimately responsible for the action taken. The legal system and the practice of law would be more efficient and less costly if paralegals were authorized to perform a number of routine tasks. Nevertheless, no paralegal should ever appear in court to represent a client unless absolutely certain that this is permissible.

Many administrative agencies, like the Social Security Administration, permit representation by any person of the claimant's choosing. Before undertaking such representation, a paralegal should ascertain the extent and scope of such representation under the agency's rules and regulations and make certain the person represented consents (in writing) to such representation with full knowledge that the paralegal is not a member of the Bar.

CASE NO. 3–1 Appearance in Court

The following case is notable for its early date. The law student clerk charged with unauthorized practice of law might today be described as a paralegal. The trial court took a broad view of the practice of law, a protectionist attitude toward the Bar, and was perhaps affronted by the appearance of a nonlawyer in the courtroom. The appellate court, however, showed a progressive attitude toward the allocation of legal services benefiting the Bench, the Bar, and the public.

Note that the individual in question was not prosecuted for unauthorized practice of law but was disciplined by the court for contempt of court, a sanction available to a judge for punishing misconduct in court.

PEOPLE of the State of Illinois, Plaintiff—Appellee,
v.
Walton ALEXANDER, Defendant-Appellant.
Appellate Court of Illinois,
First District, Fourth Division
53 Ill. App. 2d 299, 202 N.E.2d 841
(1964)

DRUCKER, Justice.

This is an appeal from a judgment order adjudging defendant guilty of contempt of court for the unauthorized practice of law. The Supreme Court transferred this case to our court and it is to be considered here as a direct contempt.

Defendant is a clerk employed by a firm of attorneys and is not licensed as a lawyer, although he is studying to be an attorney. On October 19, 1962, defendant was present in court when the case of Ryan v. Monson was called. Thereafter, he prepared an order spreading of record the fact that after a trial of the case of Ryan v. Monson the jury had disagreed and continuing the case until October 22. The trial judge added to that order "a mistrial declared."

Before entering the contempt order, the court issued a rule to show cause and a hearing was held at which only defendant testified. He was examined by his attorney, cross-examined and also interrogated by the judge. A summary of part of this testimony is incorporated in the trial judge's opinion.

In his testimony defendant stated that after the case was called on October 19, he and plaintiff's attorney in the Ryan v. Monson case stepped up; that the judge inquired whether they knew of the disagreement by the jury; that the court requested that an order be prepared spreading the mistrial of record; that both defendant and plaintiff's lawyer sat down at a counsel's table and defendant wrote the order which they then presented to the judge in chambers.

An order of court reciting the verdict of a jury or setting out its failure to agree on a verdict is the responsibility of the court and the court clerk is usually ordered by the court to enter an order showing the result of a jury's deliberations. This is reflected in Freeport Motor Casualty Co. v. Tharp, 406 Ill. 295, at 299, 94 N.E.2d 139, at 141 . . .

The preparation of an order, in the instant case, with the collaboration of opposing counsel was a ministerial act for the benefit of the court and a mere recordation of what had transpired. We cannot hold that this conduct of defendant constituted the unauthorized practice of law.

The opinion of the trial court also states as a basis for contempt that on October 22 the judge inquired of defendant whether the case of Ryan v. Monson was settled and that defendant answered in the negative. It appears that on that date the court held the case for trial. Defendant testified that he advised the court that the trial attorney was actually engaged in a trial in the Federal Court. The court held that the appearance of defendant constituted the unauthorized practice of law.

Plaintiff contends that any appearance by a non-lawyer before a court for the purpose of apprising the court of an engagement of counsel or transmitting to the court information supplied by the attorney in the case regarding the availability of counsel or the status of the case is the unauthorized practice of law.

. . . In the case of People ex rel. Illinois State Bar Ass'n v. People's Stock Yards State Bank, 344 Ill. 462, at page 476, 176 N.E. 901, at page 907, wherein a bank was prosecuted for the unauthorized practice of law, the following quotation is relied upon:

"According to the generally understood definition of the practice of law in this country, it embraces the preparation of pleadings, and other papers incident to actions and special proceedings, and the management of such actions and proceedings on behalf of clients before judges and courts * * *."

Since this statement relates to the appearance and management of proceedings in court on behalf of a client, we do not believe it can be applied to a situation where a clerk hired by a law firm presents information to the court on behalf of his employer.

We agree with the trial judge that clerks should not be permitted to make motions or participate in other proceedings which can be considered as "managing" the litigation. However, if apprising the court of an employer's engagement or inability to be present constitutes the making of a motion, we must hold that clerks may make such motions for continuances without being guilty of the unauthorized practice of law. Certainly with the large volume of cases appearing on the trial calls these days, it is imperative that this practice be followed.

CASE QUESTIONS

1. The court distinguishes between appearance in court "in behalf of a client" and appearance "in behalf of the attorney-employer." Is this a relevant distinction?
2. Is there an implied distinction between "management of proceedings" and routine clerical activities?

Preparation of Legal Documents

This category refers to "preparation of legal instruments and contracts by which legal rights are secured." A major function of paralegals is the preparation of such documents; real estate agents ordinarily prepare contracts for sale that allocate legal rights and duties in great detail; and accountants prepare tax forms. So the word "preparation" may be a poor choice since it is not the preparation per se that is at issue but the final product at the time it takes legal effect and the person who takes ultimate responsibility for the document.

In many instances, paralegals prepare documents that are signed by attorneys. There is no ethical problem with this as long as the supervising attorney reads and approves the document prior to signing. Many documents require little skill in draftsmanship, sometimes only requiring that names, dates, and the like be inserted into a standard form. Nevertheless, the attorney is responsible for the legal sufficiency of documents prepared for clients. There is a danger that an attorney with a large workload assisted by a long-term, competent paralegal may place too much reliance on the paralegal and begin signing documents without reading them even when the documents are not standard forms. The concern here is not the competence of the paralegal but a proper allocation of responsibility.

In reality, a paralegal may be more knowledgeable about a particular legal matter than an attorney, but in theory the paralegal is a trained technician while the attorney is a legal analyst. This is an excellent combination of skills to serve clients; paralegal and attorney working as a team provide legal services of high quality. If the attorney, however, relies on the paralegal entirely, the equation fails; the client has not received the services contracted.

As an employee of an attorney, a paralegal is understandably reluctant to criticize the boss; but it is important to ensure that the attorney reads a document before signing. The paralegal can tactfully express doubts about a document and thereby urge the attorney to read with care. In fact, if the paralegal has any doubts about the form of the document, its legal consequences, or the propriety of the language used, these doubts should be brought to the attention of the attorney, who may then take special care in reading relevant parts of the document. Even though the paralegal is not legally accountable for a document signed by a supervising attorney, the paralegal's ethical duty does not end with the exercise of technical skills. Service to client and service to attorney require attention to these details.

Despite their best urging and protestations, many paralegals work for attorneys who do not read many of the documents prepared by the paralegals. Despite confidence in the quality of the documents, the paralegal may nonetheless have the uncomfortable feeling that the process is not as it should be. The paralegal faces an ethical dilemma because of the attorney's lack of diligence. It may be that no one is harmed in that the legal documents are sound. But a fraud has been perpetrated on the client, who has contracted and dearly paid for the legal expertise of a licensed member of the Bar. On such occasions a paralegal should seek counsel from an appropriate source such as a trusted member of the firm.

It is anticipated that in the 1990s legal technicians will come to enjoy limited authority to help individuals fill out legal forms, much as H & R Block helps individuals fill out tax forms. If the Bar makes good on its commitment to ensure that legal services are provided to the public, such a development should be one of the consequences since numerous legal documents require little or no advice necessitating an attorney and can be completed by legal technicians (independent paralegals) at minimal cost to the client.

Giving Legal Advice

Paralegals must be careful not only to refrain from giving legal advice but also to avoid even giving that impression. It is important that each client clearly understand that the paralegal is not a lawyer and not licensed to practice law. Clients will often seek advice from paralegals, especially when the attorney is temporarily unavailable. Paralegals possess a competence and knowledge of the law that tends to encourage clients and friends to ask for legal advice.

Defining *legal advice* is not an easy task because there is a fine line between providing information and giving advice. For example, it is neither unethical nor an unauthorized practice of law to sell standard legal forms (office supply stores regularly sell legal forms). Nor is the provision of typing services improper. A logical conclusion might be that assisting a person in typing in the blanks on a standard legal form is not improper or illegal (this may be unauthorized practice of law in New York). In the course of filling out a form, however, a client may ask a question concerning the legal consequences of an item in the form. Rosemary Furman (see Case No. 1–1) was accused of telling her clients to include or exclude information on the divorce forms. The most serious charges against her concerned encouraging her clients to lie on the forms. The Furman case presents some legitimate concerns of the Bar—it is not the giving of legal advice per se that is wrong but the giving of incompetent or inaccurate advice. Since the Bar and the Court have little control over nonlawyers, the public has little protection against incompetents and charlatans.

As a practical matter, the paralegal should be alert to making statements to a client. Statements that may induce the client to do or refrain from doing something that may have legal consequences may be construed as legal advice. There is a big difference between saying "Don't do that" and "You ought to talk to the attorney before doing that." When pressed for advice, the paralegal must always refer the questions to the attorney. Although often a conduit or messenger between attorney and client, the paralegal must exercise care in conveying information or advice. Even when instructions are unambiguous, such as "Tell the client to go ahead and sign the contract," a paralegal should ascertain the exact instructions to be conveyed and indicate to the client that the instructions are those of the attorney. Of course, it is far better for the attorney to speak personally with the client.

Ironically, a paralegal is more constrained in giving legal advice than is the man-in-the-street. The justification for this is that the paralegal is knowledgeable in the law, so paralegal advice is likely to be construed as accurate and thus acted upon. Presumably, individuals understand that legal advice from the man-in-the-street has no authority behind it. Paralegals must be aware of their special vulnerability in this regard. In coming years the boundaries of paralegal responsibilities will undoubtedly undergo significant clarification. It should be noted that at present the states differ significantly in where they draw these boundaries.

CONFIDENTIALITY

Perhaps the most important aspect of legal ethics is confidentiality. In the course of legal consultation, a client typically reveals information that is personal, private, and often secret. Competent legal advice is predicated on the assurance that none of these private facts will be disclosed to third parties beyond the attorney and the attorney's staff. In order to deal effectively with client affairs, the attorney must be fully informed about all matters relating to the client's need for legal service and advice. For this reason, statements made in confidence to an attorney by a client are privileged and may only be disclosed with the consent of the client or when special circumstances provide clear exceptions to the rule.

The privilege extends to law firm employees who necessarily have access to confidential material in order to provide legal services, including especially legal secretaries, clerks, and paralegals. Although paralegals are not subject to disciplinary actions for improper disclosures, a supervising attorney can be held responsible both by attorney disciplinary rules and by a possible suit by the client.

The paralegal must be scrupulous in protecting clients' confidences. It is a great temptation for attorneys and paralegals alike to relate the facts of an interesting case to friends and associates outside the law firm, but any disclosure incurs the risk that the listener may identify a client and thereby learn facts that are privileged. If third parties not covered by the privilege learn confidential communications, the disclosures may lose their confidential status. Extreme caution must be exercised in discussing specific matters involving specific clients. Attorneys and law firms routinely warn staff about confidentiality, but paralegals must also constantly remind themselves of their responsibilities toward the clients.

Confidentiality can lead to bizarre predicaments, as illustrated by the following real-life situation. A woman was working as an intake paralegal for a Legal Aid office that provided legal services in civil cases for indigents. As such, she interviewed prospective clients for the office. A woman seeking divorce came to the office and was accepted as a client. The attorney in charge of the case was encountering difficulties finding the woman's husband to serve notice of the pending divorce action. It so happened that the husband later came to the office for legal representation. In the course of collecting intake information, the paralegal recognized that the man was the husband of a client of the office. While the office could not represent both husband and wife, it was now in possession of the husband's address and telephone number, which was now considered privileged information since the husband had furnished it in confidence in attempting to establish a lawyer-client relationship.

Although the attorney for the wife was informed that the husband had furnished this information, she and the paralegal concluded that it might be improper to give it to the wife's attorney, so the husband's file was locked away where the attorney did not have access to it. The attorney took the appropriate action of asking the Bar's Ethics Committee for an opinion on whether the address and telephone were privileged. An opinion had not yet been issued as of this writing. The lesson, however, is that the paralegal and the attorney were appropriately sensitive to the confidentiality question.

A client's actions may render disclosures nonconfidential. Statements made before third parties who are not covered by confidentiality are disclosable. If, for instance, the client brings a friend along to a meeting with the attorney and the friend has no relation to the case, statements made are not confidential. Attorneys and paralegals are careful to exclude third parties from discussions, especially when confidential statements are expected. The problem with nonconfidential statements is that their content is subject to discovery by the opposing side, and in criminal cases, the third parties may be required to disclose the statements on the witness stand.

Whether or not the confidential attorney–client relationship applies depends on the circumstances. Even though an attorney may have represented a client in the past, statements made with regard to an unrelated current problem may not be confidential if the client has not expressed an intention to retain the attorney in the current matter.

On the other hand, the attorney–client relationship may be understood to be ongoing. A client who employs an attorney on all business matters may implicitly intend all business statements to be confidential. A client may also pay an attorney a general retainer with the understanding that the attorney and client have a continuing relationship. Once confidentiality is established, the confidentiality does not end with the termination of client representation, though it may not extend to subsequent nonconfidential information.

CASE NO. 3–2 The Limits of Confidentiality

The PEOPLE of the State of New
York, Respondent,
v.
John C. MITCHELL, Appellant.
Court of Appeals of New York
58 N.Y.2d 368, 448 N.E.2d 121 (1983)
OPINION OF THE COURT

SIMONS, Judge.

. . . .

Defendant was a resident of Waterloo, New York, and, at the time these events occurred, he was under indictment for causing the stabbing death of his girlfriend, Audrey Miller, in February, 1976. He was represented on that charge by Rochester attorney Felix Lapine. In January, 1977, defendant went to Rochester to take care of some personal matters and registered at the Cadillac Hotel. On the evening of January 5 while sitting at the hotel bar, he met O'Hare McMillon. They had two or three highballs and then were seen to leave the bar about 11:00 p.m. and take the

elevator to the floor on which Mitchell's room was located. No one saw either of them leave defendant's room that night or the next morning, but in the afternoon of January 6, on a tip from attorney Lapine, the police went to defendant's hotel room and found the partially clad dead body of O'Hare McMillon on the bed. She had been stabbed 11–12 times in the face, chest and back. At least four of the wounds were sufficient to cause her death by exsanguination.

After leaving the hotel room that morning, defendant went to attorney Lapine's office. Lapine was not in but defendant met and spoke to a legal secretary, Molly Altman, in the reception area. She testified that he seemed nervous and as if he was looking for someone. Apparently he could not find whomever it was he was looking for so he left only to return a minute later and start telling her about what happened the night before. She testified that he said: "he wanted to go out and have a last fling * * * he had been out drinking and met a girl and then he woke up in the morning and she was dead. He had stayed there all night and then he walked out again".

While he was talking to Ms. Altman, Judith Peacock, another legal secretary, entered the reception area. She testified that defendant was kind of rambling on but he said that: "he had laid next to someone all night and they didn't move, and he [was] in a bar and *** in a hotel *** this person who he had laid next to was black and he was worried because when the black people find out about it, they protect their own and he would be in danger". She also testified that he muttered something about a knife.

Ms. Pope-Johnson entered the room. She asked defendant what was wrong and he told her: "that there was a dead body and he felt that he had done it and that the person was dead, that she was dead because of being stabbed."

Shortly thereafter, Lapine entered the office and talked privately with defendant. After defendant left Lapine called the police and had them check defendant's hotel room. The body was discovered, defendant's identification learned from the hotel registration and defendant found and arrested at a bar near the courthouse.

. . . .

On this state of the record, we conclude that defendant has not met his burden of establishing that when he spoke to these unknown women in a common reception area, his statements were intended to be confidential and made to an employee of his attorney for the purpose of obtaining legal advice. The only evidence identifying the women came from Lapine who responded to a question whether he had "any female employees" by saying "Yes, Robin Pope-Johnson". She, it turns out, was the last woman in the office to hear defendant's inculpatory statements and even if statements made to her at the time could have been privileged, the privilege was lost because of the prior publication to nonemployees and the utterance of the statements to Pope-Johnson in front of the non-employees [Cc.] Taking this view we need not consider whether the statements could be privileged because of an on-going retainer between defendant and Lapine or if they could be privileged if made to the attorney's employee before a formal retainer was agreed upon.

Exceptions to Confidentiality

Rule 1.6 Confidentiality of information.

(a) A lawyer shall not reveal information relating to representation of a client except as stated in paragraphs (b), (c), and (d) unless the client consents after disclosure to the client.

(b) A lawyer shall reveal such information to the extent the lawyer believes necessary:

(1) To prevent a client from committing a crime; or

(2) To prevent a death or substantial bodily harm to another.

    (c) A lawyer may reveal such information to the extent the lawyer believes necessary:

       (1) To serve the client's interest unless it is information the client specifically requires not to be disclosed;

       (2) To establish a claim or defense on behalf of the lawyer in a controversy between the lawyer and client;

       (3) To establish a defense to a criminal charge or civil claim against the lawyer based upon conduct in which the client was involved;

       (4) To respond to allegations in any proceeding concerning the lawyer's representation of the client; or

       (5) To comply with the *Rules of Professional Conduct.*

    (d) When required by a tribunal to reveal such information, a lawyer may first exhaust all appellate remedies.

The exceptions to confidentiality privilege are primarily aimed at protecting the public [(b)(1) and (b)(2)] and protecting the attorney in a conflict with the client [(c)]. Although confidential statements about past crimes and misconduct are privileged, a client's intention to commit a crime in the future is not. An attorney has an ethical duty to attempt to dissuade a client from committing a crime and a duty to inform appropriate authorities if unable to dissuade the client. The most difficult case arises when a client plans to commit perjury at trial and, despite the attorney's admonitions, proceeds to lie on the witness stand. Attempted withdrawal by the attorney at that stage of the process will ordinarily be refused by the court, but the attorney also is not free to disclose the confidences that would reveal the perjury. The complexities of this situation are illustrated by the following:

ABA Project on Standards for Criminal Justice; Proposed Defense Function Standard 4-7.7 (2d ed. 1980).

(a) If the defendant has admitted to defense counsel facts which establish guilt and counsel's independent investigation established that the admissions are true but the defendant insists on the right to trial, counsel must strongly discourage the defendant against taking the witness stand to testify perjuriously.

(b) If, in advance of trial, the defendant insists that he or she will take the stand to testify perjuriously, the lawyer may withdraw from the case, if that is feasible, seeking leave of the court if necessary, but the court should not be advised of the lawyer's reason for seeking to do so.

(c)   If withdrawal from the case is not feasible or is not permitted by the court, or if the situation arises immediately preceding trial or during the trial and the defendant insists upon testifying perjuriously in his or her own behalf, it is unprofessional conduct for the lawyer to lend aid to the perjury or use the perjured testimony. Before the defendant takes the stand in these circumstances, the lawyer should make a record of the fact that the defendant is taking the stand against the advice of counsel in some appropriate manner without revealing to the court the client's intent to perjure himself. The lawyer may identify the witness as the defendant and may ask appropriate questions of the defendant when it is believed that the defendant's answers will not be perjurious. As to matters for which it is believed the defendant will offer perjurious testimony, the lawyer should seek to avoid direct examination of the defendant in the conventional manner; instead, the lawyer should ask the defendant if he or she wishes to make any additional statement concerning the case to the trier or triers of the facts. A lawyer may not later argue the defendant's known false version of facts to the jury as worthy of belief, and may not recite or rely upon the false testimony in his or her closing argument.

CONFLICTS OF INTEREST

A common conflict of interest problem arises when an attorney leaves one firm for another and the second firm represents a party suing or being sued by a client of the former firm. The risk of disclosure of attorney–client confidences by the attorney to the new employers raises serious ethical concerns. The extremes are not difficult to decide. If the attorney worked on the client's case at his first employment, it would be clearly unethical to work for the opposing party. On the other hand, if an attorney moves from one large law firm to another and had no exposure to the case at either firm, the risk of disclosure is minimal. The risk can be further minimized by erecting a "Chinese wall" between the attorney and those dealing with the case, i.e., preventing access to the case file and warning all concerned not to discuss the case with the firm-switching attorney. If no exception is made, an attorney working for a large firm becomes a "typhoid Mary," virtually unemployable at other large firms for fear the firm may have or may take on a client who may be involved in a dispute against a client of the other firm.

Since paralegals regularly deal with confidential material, an identical problem arises; the entire firm may be disqualified from representing a client if the court concludes that the risk of improper disclosure cannot be purged. In fact, some paralegals will have contact with a greater number of files than any single attorney.

This particular form of conflict of interest poses a practical as well as an ethical problem since the firm representing a client can request that the court disqualify an opposing firm's representation. This action has resulted in numerous reported decisions of the courts that not only clarify the ethical principles but also give them the force of law. In *Silver Chrysler Plymouth, Inc. v. Chrysler Motors Corp.*, 518 F.2d 751 (2d Cir. 1975), the U.S. Court of Appeals articulated the "substantially related" test subsequently adopted by the courts of many jurisdictions. *Silver Chrysler* distinguished between the activities of a lawyer or law clerk at a former law firm that were substantially related to representation in a current case at a second law firm employing the attorney. The court thereby attempted to distinguish situations in which a distinct risk of confidential disclosures exists from those in which the risk is insignificant.

CASE NO. 3–3 "Substantially Related"

In the following case the Second Circuit Court of Appeals reiterated its test in *Silver Chrysler* decided a year earlier. Note that in both cases, the attorney who switched firms was an associate who had limited access to files and limited decision making in the cases under consideration.

GAS—A—TRON OF ARIZONA and Coinoco, Plaintiffs-Appellants,

v.

UNION OIL COMPANY OF CALIFORNIA et al., Defendants-Appellees.

PETROL STOPS NORTHWEST, Plaintiff-Appellant,

v.

CONTINENTAL OIL COMPANY et al., Defendants-Appellees.

United States Court of Appeals, Ninth Circuit
534 F.2d 1322 (1976)

PER CURIAM

. . . .

We recognize that the primary responsibility for controlling the conduct of lawyers practicing before the district court lies with that court, and not with us. We will not disturb the district court's exercise of its discretion in fulfilling that responsibility if the record reveals any sound basis for its discretion disqualifying or refusing to disqualify a lawyer. The record in this case does not support the district court's decision. The district court's disqualification of Mr. Burbidge rested upon its determination that the pending litigation was "substantially related" to the matters in which he had previously represented Shell and Exxon while he was associated with McCutchen. Mr. Burbidge's situation was almost identical to that of the young associates whose claimed disqualification was considered in *Silver Chrysler Plymouth, Inc. v. Chrysler Motors Corp.*, 518 F.2d 751 (2d Cir. 1975), and *Bonus Oil Co. v. American Petrofina Co.*, No. CV—73—L—165 (D.Neb. May 1, 1975). *See also Redd v. Shell Oil Co.*, Civ. No. C—104-71 (D.Utah, Sept. 2, 1974), *rev'd on other grounds* 518 F.2d 311 (10th Cir. 1975) (in another case involving Mr. Burbidge, Berman and McCutchen, district court found motion for disqualification a sham). In each case, the court decided that the associate was not disqualified because no substantial relationship existed between the pending litigation and the matters upon which he had worked for the client during his prior association. We agree with the reasoning in those cases. Here, as in those cases, the associate had not actually obtained any confidential infor-

mation about either Shell or Exxon that would be relevant to the pending litigation, and he had not worked on matters that were "substantially related" to the pending litigation.

We share the district court's concern for the appearance of impropriety. However, we are convinced that any initial inference of impropriety that arose from Mr. Burbidge's potential physical access to the files of Exxon and Shell and from his association with lawyers who did know confidential information about them was dispelled by evidence that he saw none of the files other than those relating to the cases assigned to him heretofore described and that he heard no confidences about Exxon and Shell from the lawyers with whom he was earlier associated.

Berman's disqualification was based solely on Mr. Burbidge's disqualification, and that disqualification vanishes with Mr. Burbidge's nondisqualification.

Reversed.

The ABA *Model Rules* adopted the "substantially related" test in 1980:

Rule 1.9 A lawyer who has formerly represented a client in a matter shall not thereafter:

(a) represent another person in the same or a substantially related matter to which that person's interests are materially adverse to the interests of the former client unless the former client consents after consultation; or

(b) use information relating to the representation to the disadvantage of the former client except as Rule 1.6 would permit with respect to a client or when the information has become generally known.

CASE NO. 3–4 Conflict of Interests

The *Cheng* case below demonstrates the fine line between relationships that constitute a conflict of interests and those that do not. The Court of Appeals might well have decided the case differently, as did the trial court. The strictness of the decision reflects the importance the court places on protecting client confidences.

**James K. J. CHENG,
Plaintiff—Appellant,
v.
GAF CORPORATION,
Defendant—Appellee.**

United States Court of Appeals,
Second Circuit
631 F.2d 1052 (1980)

MESKILL, Circuit Judge:

. . . .

Determination of a violation of Canon 4 sufficient to disqualify an attorney traditionally has been based on a finding of concurrent or successive representation in the same or substantially related matters.

[T]he former client need show no more than that the matters embraced within the pending suit wherein his former attorney appears on behalf of his adversary are substantially related to the matters or cause of action wherein the attorney previously represented him, the former client. The Court will assume that during the course of the former representation confidences were disclosed to the attorney bearing on the subject matter of the representation.

T. C. Theatre Corp. v. Warner Bros. Pictures, 113 F. Supp. 265, 268 (S.D.N.Y. 1953). It is well established that a court may not inquire into the nature of the confidences alleged to have been revealed

to the tainted attorney. To require proof of access to privileged information would "put the former client to the Hobson's choice of either having to disclose his privileged information in order to disqualify his former attorney or having to refrain from the disqualification motion altogether." [Cc.] (Kaufman, *J.*) ("complainant need only show *access* to such *substantially related* material and the inference that defendant received these confidences will follow.") (emphasis in original). In the instant case, there is no dispute that the matters involved in Gassel's former association with Cheng are substantially related to his present association; the suit and the parties have remained the same throughout the proceedings. The only changing factor has been Gassel, who has moved from the plaintiff's firm to the defendant's firm, thus becoming subject to a disqualification challenge.

In *Silver Chrysler Plymouth, Inc. v. Chrysler Motors Corp.,* 518 F.2d 751 (2d Cir. 1975) . . . we recognized that although there may be an inference that an attorney has knowledge of the confidences and secrets of his firm's clients, that inference is rebuttable. We also noted an earlier caution that the standard of proof to rebut this presumption should not become "unattainably high. . . . "

. . . .

II. *The "Chinese Wall" Defense*

Anticipating difficulties caused by a strict application of Disciplinary Rule 5—105(D), law firms have employed various methods of screening a possibly tainted attorney from the rest of the firm's involvement in a particular case. The

Epstein firm in the instant case cites the division of duties within its firm to demonstrate the height and thickness of the "Chinese Wall" they have constructed between Gassel and the *Cheng* case. They note in their affidavits that Gassel has been assigned to the health law division of their firm while GAF's defense is being handled by its labor division. The affidavits also aver that Gassel has not worked on the *Cheng* case, disclosed Cheng's confidences nor discussed the merits of the case while at the Epstein firm, and that the firm will not permit him to have any substantive involvement in the *Cheng* defense. Judge Owen accepted the Epstein firm's position, finding that the "risk of disclosure of confidential information is negligible." We take a different view of the potential for disclosure, keeping in mind that, as Judge Owen noted, one of the purposes of disqualification is "to guard against the danger of inadvertent use of confidential information" [Cc.].

Although Gassel may not be personally involved in the *Cheng* defense, he is a member of a relatively small firm. The matter involved in his prior exposure to Cheng while at LSEP is still being actively pursued by attorneys for GAF at the Epstein firm. Despite the Epstein firm's protestations, it is unclear to us how disclosures, admittedly inadvertent, can be prevented throughout the course of this representation. Unlike many disqualification motions that appear before this Court, here there exists a continuing danger that Gassel may unintentionally transmit information he gained through his prior association with Cheng during his day-to-day contact with defense counsel. [Cc.] If after considering all of the precautions taken by the Epstein firm this Court still harbors doubts as to the sufficiency of these preventive measures, then we can hardly expect Cheng or members of the public to consider the attempted quarantine to be impenetrable. . . .

The order of the district court is reversed and the case is remanded for entry of an order of disqualification.

SOLICITATION

For many years, the legal profession banned advertising legal services, and many disciplinary cases considered such issues as listings in the yellow pages, the sending of Christmas cards, the size of law office signs, etc. In 1977, the U.S. Supreme Court in *Bates v. State Bar of Arizona*, 433 U.S. 350, held that the ban on advertising violated First Amendment freedom of speech. Since that time, ethical concerns have aimed at distinguishing advertising from solicitation. The Bar continues to attempt to thwart "ambulance chasing," the practice of hunting down injured parties and twisting their arms to hire the attorney. While *Bates* made it clear that attorneys were free to announce their services to the public in general, the aggressive solicitation of individual clients is still condemned.

Model Rules of Professional Conduct:

Rule 7.3 Direct contact with prospective clients.

A lawyer may not solicit professional employment from a prospective client with whom the lawyer has no family or prior professional relationship, in person or otherwise, when a significant motive for the lawyer's doing so is the lawyer's pecuniary gain. The term "solicit" includes contact in person, by telephone or telegraph, by letter or other writing, or by other communication directed to a specific recipient. . . .

An attorney also may not solicit through another person, including a paralegal. Paralegals must be careful in generating business for the attorneys for whom they work. It is very tempting when hearing a story of a personal injury or some other promising legal case to encourage a visit to the law office, but paralegals must be cautious in their treatment of such situations. Certainly it is unethical to loiter at the hospital handing out business cards to accident victims, but it is not necessary to keep one's employment a secret or, when asked, to recommend an attorney. Suggesting that a person seek legal help is ethical if the paralegal has not sought out clients. The paralegal should not disparage other attorneys nor encourage a person to switch from one attorney to another nor criticize an attorney's handling of a client. When learning of possible misconduct by an attorney, the paralegal should discuss the matter with an attorney associate, who has an ethical duty to address attorney misconduct.

FEES

The *Model Rules* treat fee arrangements with considerably more specificity than did the *Model Code*. Fees are based on contracts between the attorney and the client and should be specifically discussed by the attorney with the client. Whenever fees have not been adequately explained to a client a potential conflict emerges. If at all possible, a contract signed by the client should clearly explain the basis on which the fees are established. When the *Model Rules* were debated, the framers wanted to require that all fee arrangements be in writing, but sole practitioners and rural lawyers argued that this would hurt their relationships with many of their clients, so the writing was not made mandatory.

A recurring issue regarding fees concerns contingency fees, whereby the attorney is paid a percentage of the award or recovery in favor of the client. There is a strong national movement favoring limitations on contingency fees. Personal injury cases are typically based on contingency fees, which are unethical in criminal cases and divorce proceedings. It is essential that the client understand that the percentage does not include costs other than the attorney's services. In cases using expert witnesses, the costs can be quite large; the client must be aware of this and the fact that the client must pay the costs regardless of who wins the case.

Work performed by a paralegal is commonly billed to a client. Ordinarily the paralegal's work is charged at a rate significantly less than that for an attorney, though not necessarily proportional to the compensation paid the paralegal. Clients should not be charged for attorney's work if paralegals actually did the work, nor should they be billed for more time than was actually spent. The latter is not only unethical but illegal as well. Even though paralegals may not be responsible for the billing, they should not participate, actively or passively, in a fraud on the client.

REPORTING MISCONDUCT

Model Rules of Professional Conduct:

Rule 8.3 Reporting professional misconduct.

(a) A lawyer having knowledge that another lawyer has committed a violation of the *Rules of Professional Conduct* . . . shall inform the appropriate professional authority.

Although lawyers are understandably reluctant to inform on each other, the above rule is clear, and failure to report misconduct is an ethical violation. The object is not simply to punish the wrongdoer but to protect the public and the legal system. Choice of the authority to which the misconduct should be reported depends on whether the misconduct is a professional matter or matter before the Court.

The duty of paralegals to report misconduct is more problematic. If the misconduct is also criminal, a legal duty to report a crime falls upon the paralegal. If the misconduct is of a professional, noncriminal nature, the duty is less clear. There is an ethical duty in an abstract sense, but not one that subjects the paralegal to discipline, the paralegal not being a member of the Bar. If misconduct results in an injury to a client, the paralegal who overlooks the misconduct may be viewed as contributing to the injury. In any event, such matters must be treated with great delicacy. Accusations of misconduct can have serious ramifications for an attorney. The paralegal is quite vulnerable as well, having a subordinate position in the legal hierarchy. Hopefully in such a situation, the paralegal will know a lawyer who can give counsel. If the misconduct can be corrected, approaching the wrongdoer rather than informing may be the best policy. In any event, diplomacy and caution should be exercised.

TRUST ACCOUNTS

One of the most common reasons for attorney discipline involves the misuse of client funds. This is considered by disciplinary committees to be one of the most serious transgressions. Clients deposit funds with attorneys for a number of reasons besides paying fees. Money held for a client must never be commingled (mixed) with an attorney's personal accounts nor should separate trust accounts be commingled in any way. Accurate record keeping is essential in order to properly account for monies received and disbursed.

Misuse of client funds may constitute the crime of embezzlement. A paralegal must not participate or contribute to improper use of client funds.

SUMMARY

The legal profession is governed by a code of professional ethics that is enforced by the courts and the profession. Each state has an ethical code for lawyers. The ABA has been the leader in developing ethical codes, adopting the *Model Code of Professional Responsibility* in 1970 and the *Model Rules of Professional Conduct* in 1983. Most states have adopted these codes nearly verbatim so that there is considerable uniformity in principle, at least.

The interpretation of the codes in the courts shows some disparities, especially in defining the unauthorized practice of law, which especially concerns paralegals since they risk unauthorized practice of law if they engage in activities only permitted to licensed attorneys, namely:

1. Legal representation before a court;
2. Preparation of legal documents;
3. Giving legal advice.

The unauthorized practice of law may be prosecuted under criminal statutes or by the court as contempt of court.

Confidentiality of client statements is protected by the attorney–client privilege, which extends to law office personnel. Paralegals must take great pains not to disclose confidential information on clients to persons not covered by the privilege. The attorney–client privilege belongs to the client and not the attorney. Major exceptions to the privilege occur when a client proposes to commit a crime or when the client sues the attorney.

Confidentiality gives rise to problems of conflict of interest when an attorney or a paralegal changes employment from one firm to another. If the new firm represents a party adverse to a party represented by the firm from which the new employee came, the risk that confidential information may be disclosed to the disadvantage of a former client is great. The entire firm may be disqualified. However, in this age of large law firms, a lawyer or paralegal frequently has no contact with a client of the firm in which employed. As a result, the courts and the *Model Rules* have adopted the "substantially related" test: The adverse representation must be substantially related to matters with which the attorney dealt in prior employment. Law firms must additionally take pains to isolate the attorney from the case, the so-called "Chinese wall" approach.

CHAPTER QUESTIONS

Hypothetical 1:

You have been working as a paralegal for five years for an attorney specializing in divorce and family law. A close friend comes to you for help. He says that his wife has filed for divorce and has presented him with a **marital settlement agreement** drawn up by her attorney, and he wants you to read it and tell him what you think of it. You have prepared many of these agreements yourself and know that in your jurisdiction the judges routinely approve such agreements when signed by both parties unless they appear grossly unfair to one party. Your friend says that the agreement appears to him to reflect his oral agreements with his wife before she consulted an attorney. He has consulted several attorneys, and all want at least $1500 to represent him. He says he cannot afford this additional expense and will not hire an attorney unless absolutely necessary. If you do not read the agreement, he says, he will simply take his chances by signing it. He knows you are a paralegal and not licensed to practice law.

What are the ethical considerations?

1. Does it matter whether or not your friend pays you for this service?

marital settlement agreement
refers to a contract drawn up for a divorcing couple to distribute marital property and set the terms for child custody, child support payments, and alimony.

2. Must you advise your friend to consult an attorney?
3. Must you refuse to read the agreement?
4. If you read the agreement and are convinced that it is fair and legally sound, can you so inform your friend?
5. If you read the agreement and have doubts about some of its clauses, what can you tell your friend?
6. Can you advise your friend with a disclaimer to the effect that you are not an attorney, that your advice may be incorrect, and that he should consult an attorney?

Hypothetical 2:

You are assisting an attorney in the defense of a man accused of murder. Two days before the trial the client declares that he will perjure himself in order to present a more plausible argument for self-defense.

7. May the attorney withdraw from the case?
8. Must the attorney disclose the perjury?
9. What are the risks to the attorney?

EXERCISES

1. Find out whether your state has adopted either the *Model Code* or the *Model Rules* or has its own ethical code.
2. Does your state have a statute covering unauthorized practice of law? What does it say?
3. How are attorney grievances processed in your state?
4. Can you find out from a local paralegal association or other source what paralegals are permitted and prohibited from doing in your state?

PROFESSIONAL PROFILE

Excerpted with permission from James Publishing, Inc., Legal Assistant Today (September/October 1990).

Barbara Gerletti's first job—clerk/matron in a small police department while an evening student at the University of Southern California—got her interested in law. With a B.A. in English, she became probation department clerical supervisor for four years, in charge of producing reports for juvenile court. Transferring to the county clerk's office, her involvement with probate law soon helped her to get appointed courtroom clerk to a probate judge. "I was promoted to probate file examiner, a rare opportunity, like a reserach assistant or law clerk job requiring a lot of research in the law library. I also had to look at pleas, for information and procedures. My five years there convinced me to return to school for a paralegal certificate," Gerletti remembers.

As a member of the file examiner's office, Gerletti began presenting seminars at informal brown-bag luncheons her department held for attorneys and paralegals to inform them of the proper way to submit pleadings. "I also did seminars for Continuing Education of the Bar, and really enjoyed the public speaking. It was a very good experience," she feels.

In 1983, Gerletti moved to Sacramento, where a year as probate paralegal in a large law firm convinced her she preferred government work. "My father was a public servant. I'm very comfortable in a bureaucracy. I like to feel I can change things from inside and make it easier for people to deal with the system." Her next goal: a job in the Attorney General's office. "I pestered them, wrote letters, asked for meetings—and got to see them on two different occasions. Finally they had an opening, in 1984, for a job with little client contact." Her new employer saw it as a glorified administrative assistant post, but Gerletti had other plans.

"My boss, Steve White, head of the criminal law division, gave me a lot of support and latitude. Whenever I went in with an idea, he encouraged me. He had to go the state comptroller to convince them to create my current position. We got a new clerk line. He let me develop a paralegal internship program, which I supervise in our four offices throughout the state," Gerletti recounts.

To help government employees compete with people from outside, Gerletti told her boss she'd like to set up a training committee. She couldn't get any money, but convinced other directors to assign committee members, and set up on-site college courses for any school requesting them, as well as in-house training on substantive or procedural areas of law. "The program is not certified training—just knowledge," explains Gerletti, who is committed to making her field more professional. "It made a great difference in the quality of paralegals we have in our office." Gerletti now sits on the panel for promotions, and finds attorney general staff competing effectively with other candidates.

Gerletti teaches two courses in the paralegal program at University of California, Davis. "I love teaching! I learn so much from students," she exclaims. Very interested in politics in relation to paralegals, Gerletti admits she'd love to get into the governor's office and make changes in the rules governing her field. President of the Sacramento Association of Legal Assistants, she hopes for greater statewide impact.

Gerletti identifies four major areas of professional growth: "Teaching—we need quality paralegal instructors; writing books—by and for paralegals; managers of paralegals in law offices; and litigation support by computer—document control and trial support. These specialists will be able to take their personal computers to the courtroom and call up details for the attorney."

Barbara Gerletti
Paralegal Coordinator

CHAPTER 4

Sources of the Law: Cases

There is no jewel in the world comparable to learning: no learning so excellent both for Prince and subject, as knowledge of laws; and no knowledge of any laws (I speak of human) so necessary for all estates and for all causes, concerning goods, lands or life, as the common laws of England.

— *Sir Edward Coke (1552–1634),*
Chief Justice of the King's Bench

During the Renaissance, European legal scholarship was dazzled by the power and beauty of the rediscovered Roman law. One country, however, managed to resist the so-called "reception," that is, the acceptance of Roman law. England alone was not seduced. It held fast to its native traditions. . . . This tenacious local system was the so-called common law. . . .

71

The basic principles of law were not found primarily in acts of Parliament, but in the case law—the body of opinions written by judges, and developed by judges in the course of deciding particular cases. The doctrine of "precedent"—the maxim that a judge is bound in some way by what has already been decided—is strictly a common-law doctrine.

—Lawrence M. Friedman,
American Law, p. 16 (1984)

LAW AND THE COURTS

The law in practice revolves around disputes and problems. The primary forum for dispute resolution is the Court. Even though most disputes brought to lawyers do not result in trials, the courts, through their spokespersons, the judges, are the final arbiters of what the law is. Since courts are the last legitimate resort of disputants, judges must decide. No matter how difficult or complex a case, the judge may not plead ignorance, frustration, or indecision. In deciding a case, the judge must provide reasons and rules, the final product of the process of adjudication. Without reasons and rules, decision making is purely political. This is particularly true in our constitutional system in which the lines between the judicial function and the administrative and legislative functions are relatively distinct.

Where does a judge find the rules? The judicial imagination is not sufficient authority even though some judicial decisions seem to suggest otherwise. There are several sources for the law, the primary ones being the Constitution, legislation, and prior judicial decisions, this last forming the subject matter of this chapter.

Judicial Restraint

In the American judiciary, a principle has evolved called *judicial restraint*. The United States Constitution set the stage by separating executive, legislative, and judicial functions into the three basic branches of government. Taking their cues from European Enlightenment thinkers of the eighteenth century, the framers of the Constitution established a political charter designed to break completely from the archaic remnants of feudalism in which power and status were based on the accident of birth and society was ruled by an aristocracy with ultimate power residing in the monarch. The Constitution, by contrast, attempted to create a "government of laws and not of men" and allocated authority to the three branches of government in such a way that each could serve as a check on the other.

From the beginning, the President and the members of Congress were elected officials and ipso facto involved in politics and the political process. The political nature of the courts was not clearly defined in the Constitution, and it can fairly be said that Chief Justice John Marshall, who dominated the United States Supreme Court during the early nineteenth century, singlehandedly defined the role of the federal judiciary. Among the important doctrines Marshall established, two stand out as fundamental principles that have guided American law ever since:

1. Marshall argued that the U.S. Constitution was the "law of the land," meaning that no law or official act that violated the Constitution was lawful; the Constitution stood as the guiding light superior to every other law. Since the U.S. Supreme Court is the final interpreter of the meaning of the Constitution, this doctrine of constitutional supremacy provided the Supreme Court with great political power. This phrase in the Constitution is referred to as the **supremacy clause**. The power of the court to examine legislative and executive acts is called *judicial review.*

2. This power was severely limited by another principle established by Marshall, which was dubbed *judicial restraint.* Since ultimate authority resides in the Court, which is made up of judges who are appointed for life subject only to removal by impeachment, it is necessary that judges restrain themselves from actively entering the political arena. This can be effectively accomplished by judges devoting themselves to deciding cases according to existing law. In simple terms, this means that judges interpret the law rather than make it, the latter function being reserved to the legislature. Ideally, judicial decisions are based on the authority of legal principles already in existence and not on the moral, political, or social preferences of the judges.

The Common Law

The American legal system is said to follow the common law tradition inherited from England. We are perhaps unique, along with England, Canada, Australia, and New Zealand, in enjoying nine hundred years of virtually uninterrupted legal evolution since the Norman Conquest of England in 1066. Since that time England has not been invaded by foreign powers imposing their own legal institutions, nor have political or legal revolutions

supremacy clause
Article VI of the U.S. Constitution provides: "This Constitution and the laws of the United States which shall be made in pursuance thereof; and all treaties made, or which shall be made, under the authority of the United States, shall be supreme law of the land, and the Judges in every State shall be bound thereby, any thing in the Constitution or laws of any State to the contrary notwithstanding."

seriously disrupted the steady development of English law. When the British came to America, they brought their law with them. The American Revolution made a political break with the mother country and established a more democratic political organization, but it did not change the fundamental process of the law. When our judges sought legal authority for their decisions, they logically turned to the basic principles of English law, which they knew and trusted even if they did not trust George III.

When the Normans organized England into a unified kingdom, they eliminated the pockets of local authority and jurisdiction characteristic of continental European countries. Although local legal process continued for a time for purely local matters, England gradually became a nation in the true sense of the word and gave birth to the "common law of England," under which developed a body of law common to all citizens of the nation. This undoubtedly led eventually to the reverence for the rule of law in the minds of the British people.

The common law has come to mean something more than simply English law. In American jurisprudence, the common law refers to judge-made law, which is distinguished from continental European legal systems, which are civil law systems. From the seventeenth century onward, with the rise of European nationhood, centralized governments were formed that required corresponding legal institutions. Rather than building on existing custom and institutions, these governments compiled sets of laws into codes, borrowing heavily from the **Corpus Juris** of the Roman Emperor Justinian, the first European to attempt to collect and organize legal principles into comprehensive written form. This movement had significantly less impact on England, which had long enjoyed a central government and a national court system.

While the sources of English law included edicts of the monarch and acts of Parliament, the daily life of the law was conducted in the courts, where pronouncements of the law were made on matters great and small. Today we are accustomed to view the legislature as the source of new law and expect judges to exercise judicial restraint and merely interpret and enforce the laws, but this was not always so. Until well into the nineteenth century, the English Parliament, the U.S. Congress, and the various state legislatures were by modern standards virtually inactive. The law was declared by judges in the process of resolving disputes, relying on traditional principles. In modern times society and polity have grown more complex at an accelerating rate, and it is no longer possible to deal with modern problems by relying on slowly evolving legal principles. As a result, modern legislatures have assumed the major burdens of lawmaking, and the courts have assumed a sharply reduced role.

Corpus Juris
Corpus Juris Civilis, literally, "the body of the civil law," was the name later given to a compilation of Roman civil law ordered by the Emperor Justinian in the first half of the sixth century. In the late Renaissance under the desire to establish national codes of law, the Corpus Juris was revived and studied and served as a model for all European nations except England, which stubbornly kept the common law. A major American encyclopedia of the common law, the Corpus Juris Secundum ("the Second Body of the Laws"), borrowed from the name without borrowing from the early code.

Judges Make Law

It is currently part of the American democratic folklore that judges merely interpret but do not "make" law. The fallacy of this notion lies in the fact that the power to interpret the law inevitably leads to making the law. Every time a judge is called upon to interpret the law, lawmaking occurs. Since judges ordinarily rely on the authority of existing law, judicial interpretation of the law invokes changes that are nearly imperceptible, but when faced with novel or difficult cases, judges occasionally formulate statements of the law that form important new principles.

It may be helpful to give an example of judicial lawmaking. In the landmark case of *MacPherson v. Buick Motor Co.*, 217 N.Y. 382, 111 N.E. 1050 (1916), Justice Cardozo of the New York Court of Appeals wrote an opinion that ushered in a new era in liability of manufacturers for injuries caused by their products, leading many years later to the field of **products liability.** Mr. MacPherson sued for injuries caused by the collapse of a defective wooden spoke wheel on the Buick he had purchased. The company defended against the suit on the grounds that it had sold the car to a dealer, which in turn sold the car to MacPherson. Since Buick did not have a contractual relation with MacPherson, it was not liable, stated attorneys for the company. In a carefully reasoned opinion, Cardozo explained why the company could not be protected by the traditional principle of **privity of contract** and held the company liable. The appearance of the automobile on the American scene put in the hands of the American public a potentially dangerous machine. Cardozo held that the manufacturer was responsible for inspection of the vehicles it sold and refused to allow the manufacturer to pass liability on to the dealer under the guise of privity of contract. In handing down his decision, Cardozo charted a course for compensation law in the United States.

Stare Decisis

Today the importance of the common law tradition lies largely in the principle of *precedent,* or *stare decisis,* by which judicial lawmaking is rendered orderly, predictable, and legitimate. The principle of *stare decisis* dictates that in making decisions judges should follow prior precedents. In practice this means that disputes involving similar fact situations should be decided by similar rules. Former decisions are thus called precedents and are examined for guidance in making present decisions. When the Court is faced with a novel fact situation ("case of first impression") and

products liability
is a branch of tort law that assigns liability to a manufacturer when injury occurs due to a "dangerously defective product." A major feature of products liability is that it dispenses with the traditional concept of fault that has been an essential element of intentional torts (e.g., battery, slander) and negligence.

privity of contract
The relationship between two parties to a contract. Originally this was a bar to a suit brought by a consumer against a manufacturer who did not have a direct contractual relationship, but this requirement has been abandoned in products liability cases.

formulates a rule to decide the case, the Court "sets a precedent" that should be followed should a similar case arise.

As an example, let us suppose that a state court is faced with the following unusual situation: a man and woman who have been living together for several years without benefit of marriage separate; the woman sues the man for breach of contract, claiming that when they entered into a cohabitation arrangement, the man promised to share his earnings equally with her if she refrained from employment and provided him with homemaking services and companionship, to which she agreed. The man defends on the basis of an established principle of contract law that a contract to perform illegal acts is unenforceable. Since sexual cohabitation is illegal in the state and that was the purpose of any promises that might have been exchanged, claimed the man, the contract cannot be enforced.

Assuming the court has never been faced with this precise situation before, it must apply the rules of contract law and set a precedent for cohabitation agreements. Judging from similar cases already decided in several states, the court will probably rule that a cohabitation agreement is enforceable like any other contract unless its purpose is compensation for sexual services. Once this precedent has been set, the next dispute over a cohabitation agreement should be decided by the application of the same rule. In this way, the first case is precedent for the second. If the rule is applied in many similar cases over a period of time, the court is likely to refer to it as a "well-established principle of law."

The force of a precedent depends upon the court that hands it down. A precedent is considered binding on the court that sets it and all lower courts within its jurisdiction. In a typical state court system decisions can be rendered at three levels: trial court (lowest), court of appeals (intermediate appellate), and state supreme court (highest). Decisions of the highest state court are binding on all state courts. Decisions of courts of appeals are binding on that court and on lower courts within its jurisdiction. There is frequently more than one court of appeals, each with specific regional jurisdiction within the state. The hierarchy of federal courts follows this pattern, also.

It sometimes happens that different courts of appeals within the same system (i.e., a state or the federal system) will formulate different rules for the same fact situation, creating considerable confusion. Trial courts in the First Circuit may feel bound by a different rule than those in the Fifth Circuit, and courts in the Third Circuit, whose court of appeals may not have decided an equivalent case, may be in a quandary about whether to follow the First Circuit rule or the Fifth Circuit rule. The logical solution is to obtain a ruling from the highest court, which is at liberty to adopt either rule or even a different rule, which would then be binding on all the courts within its jurisdiction.

The quagmire of American jurisdiction can be clarified by certain important principles. First, not only are federal and state court systems separate, but state and federal laws are separate as well. Where federal law is concerned, federal courts set the precedents, and the U.S. Supreme Court has final authority in declaring what the law is. In matters of state law, state courts have authority, and the highest court of a state has final authority to declare what the law is. Many Americans labor under the misconception that the U.S. Supreme Court is the final authority for interpreting state law. On the contrary, the highest court of each state is the ultimate authority for the law of that state. One of the reasons for the confusion arises from the supremacy clause of the U.S. Constitution, under which the U.S. Supreme Court may declare state law, whether judicial precedent or state statute, invalid if it is deemed to be in violation of the U.S. Constitution. This power of the U.S. Supreme Court is not derived from any authority to define state law but from authority to interpret the meaning of the U.S. Constitution, which is the "supreme law of the land."

CASE NO. 4–1　Overruling Prior Precedent

The following case is an example of a court overruling a well-established precedent and thus substituting a new rule. The issue facing the Supreme Court of California was whether to abolish the doctrine of contributory negligence and replace it with the doctrine of comparative negligence. Negligence will be discussed in some detail in the chapter on torts, but in layman's terms, negligence occurs when one person injures another by failing to exercise care, for example, if someone carelessly causes an auto accident. Since negligence is grounded in fault, the courts in the nineteenth century developed the doctrine of *contributory negligence,* which held that a negligent defendant would not be liable if it could be shown that the plaintiff's negligence also contributed to the injury. It soon became apparent that the doctrine was inequitable in cases in which the defendant's negligence was great, while plaintiff's negligence was minimal. Gradually the states began to replace contributory negligence with the doctrine of *comparative negligence,* which apportioned fault between plaintiff and defendant so that the plaintiff, even if also negligent, could recover a diminished compensation if the jury found the plaintiff less responsible for the cause of the injury (e.g., plaintiff 20 percent at fault and defendant 80 percent at fault).

In *Li v. Yellow Cab Co.* below, the plaintiff made an improper turn through an intersection and was struck by defendant who was racing to pass through the intersection while the stoplight was yellow. The case was heard without a jury, and the judge found both plaintiff and defendant negligent and entered a judgment in favor of the defendant based on California law. Plaintiff then appealed in the hope that she could persuade the Supreme Court of California to overrule prior precedent, in which effort she was successful.

A careful reading of the case reveals that four of the six justices ruling on the case wanted to change the law. Their decision was complicated by the fact that although contributory negligence originally arose through judicial decision, the California legislature had enacted a statute in 1872 establishing the doctrine of contributory negligence. In a lengthy discussion of the statute and its history that has been omitted from the case below, the court concluded that the statute had not been intended to permanently establish contributory negligence as the law of the state.

LI
v.
YELLOW CAB COMPANY OF CALIFORNIA et al., Defendants and Respondents

13 Cal. 3d 804, 532 P.2d 1226, 119 Cal. Rptr. 858 (1975)

SULLIVAN, J., delivered the opinion of the court.

In this case we address the grave and recurrent question whether we should judicially declare no longer applicable in California courts the doctrine of contributory negligence, which bars all recovery when the plaintiff's negligent conduct has contributed as a legal cause in any degree to the harm suffered by him, and hold that it must give way to a system of comparative negligence, which assesses liability in direct proportion to fault. . . .

It is unnecessary for us to catalogue the enormous amount of critical comment that has been directed over the years against the "all-or-nothing" approach of the doctrine of contributory negligence. The essence of that criticism has been constant and clear: the doctrine is inequitable in its operation because it fails to distribute responsibility in proportion to fault.

. . . .

It is in view of these theoretical and practical considerations that to this date 25 states have abrogated the "all or nothing" rule of contributory negligence and have enacted in its place general apportionment statutes calculated in one manner or another to assess liability in proportion to fault. In 1973 these states were joined by Florida, which effected the same result by judicial decision. (*Hoffman v. Jones* (Fla. 1973) 280 So.2d 431.) We are likewise persuaded that logic, practical experience, and fundamental justice counsel against the retention of the doctrine rendering contributory negligence a complete bar to recovery—and that it should be replaced in this state by a system under which liability for damage will be borne by those whose negligence caused it in direct proportion to their respective fault. . . .

It is urged that any change in the law of contributory negligence must be made by the Legislature, not by this court. Although the doctrine of contributory negligence is of judicial origin . . . subsequent cases of this court, it is pointed out, have unanimously affirmed that . . . the "all-or-nothing" rule is the law of this state and shall remain so until the Legislature directs otherwise. . . .

[There follows a discussion of why the court may nevertheless abolish the doctrine of contributory negligence followed by a discussion of the different forms of comparative negligence adopted in the other states.]

For all of the foregoing reasons we conclude that the "all-or-nothing" rule of contributory negligence as it presently exists in this state should be and is herewith superseded by a system of "pure" comparative negligence, the fundamental purpose of which shall be to assign responsibility and liability for damage in direct proportion to the amount of negligence of each of the parties.

. . . .

The judgment is reversed.

. . . .

CLARK, J., dissenting. . . . [T]he Legislature is the branch best able to effect transition from contributory to comparative or some other doctrine of negligence. Numerous and differing negligence systems have been urged over the years, yet there remains widespread disagreement among both the commentators and the states as to which one is best. . . . This court is not an investigatory body, and we lack the means of fairly appraising the merits of these competing systems. Constrained by settled rules of judicial review, we must consider only matters within the record or susceptible to judicial notice. That this court is inadequate to the task of carefully selecting the best replacement system is reflected in the majority's summary manner of eliminating from consideration all but two of the many competing proposals— including models adopted by some of our sister states.

By abolishing this century old doctrine today, the majority seriously erodes our constitutional function. We are again guilty of judicial chauvinism.

CASE QUESTIONS

1. Is abolishing contributory negligence a question more properly addressed by the legislature than the court? (Consider this question when reading the section below comparing adjudication and legislation.)
2. If the court sets a "bad" precedent, must it wait for the legislature to rectify the mistake?
3. What if the California legislature, after the decision in *Li*, passed a law unequivocally declaring that contributory negligence and not comparative negligence were the law of California? Does a legislature have authority to do this? Must the court follow the statute?

Legislation versus Adjudication

Although judges may be said to "make law," they do so in a way quite different from legislators. Judges resolve disputes between parties; *adjudication* refers to the process of making these decisions. In the American system, a person (which can also be a business, a corporation, or a city) files a lawsuit against another to redress an injury or to establish rights and duties. When a case reaches trial, the judge is faced with past events that have been framed by attorneys for both sides for submission to the judge for resolution. Ordinarily only the facts of the events relating to the dispute are relevant to its resolution. Evidence presented at trial will reveal those facts in great detail in order to determine which rule of law is applicable. The judge will decide which laws are relevant to the facts as determined by the evidence presented in court. Thus, the process of adjudication focuses on past events specific to one dispute, and only the law the judge deems appropriate to that case will be applied.

In short, the judge looks through a magnifying glass at one case and declares what law is applicable. If law is made in the process, it is a byproduct of the case. The function of the judge is to settle the dispute, not to determine how the law applies to other cases in the future. The judge will look to the authority of the past to make the decision.

Legislation is a very different process with a different orientation. The characteristics of legislation are universal application and future effect. Legislators do not resolve individual cases, though they are often motivated by dissatisfaction with the outcomes of cases decided in the courts. For example, the "Baby M" case in New Jersey (*In re Baby M*, 109 N.J. 396, 537 A.2d 1227 [1988]) in which a surrogate mother fought unsuccessfully to gain custody from the couple who had arranged for the baby's adoption, resulted in many legislatures, including New Jersey, enacting laws regulating surrogate mother contracts. But the New Jersey legislature did not decide the Baby M case nor change the ruling of the court; its enactment provided for the contracts between surrogate mothers and adoptive parents in future cases.

The legislative process typically operates by first recognizing a problem and then through investigation and deliberation attempting to solve the problem by enacting a law. When the legislative process is complete, the law is a matter of public record, and everyone must comply or risk legal consequences. Only rarely can legislation apply retroactively. The surrogate mother case brought to public attention the moral issues in the commercialization of pregnancy and adoption. Some people felt that such contracts should be illegal or unenforceable, some felt that the natural mother should have the option to revoke the contract, and others felt that ordinary contract law provided sufficient protection. State legislatures deliberated these questions and arrived at laws designed to deal with the question. These laws, however, did not change adoptions that had already taken place but instead served as the legal standards that would govern surrogate mother contracts subsequent to the enactment of the law.

While adjudication can be said to be particularized in the sense that cases focus on particular events and particular parties, legislation is generalized in that it is designed to make rules that apply to everyone.

CASE NO. 4–2 Adjudication versus Legislation

The following two cases illustrate the difference between legislation and adjudication and illuminate the judicial attitude exemplified in the doctrine of **stare decisis**.

American courts in the nineteenth century created or expanded immunity to suit for several categories of parties, including charitable institutions, which are the subject of the two cases that follow. Immunity from suit leaves an injured party without a remedy, and in the twentieth century the courts and legislatures of our country began to question the wisdom and legality of immunity to suit. The rise of the insurance industry made such immunities obsolete. The Supreme Judicial Court of Massachusetts was presented with an archaic principle of charitable immunity that it had created a century before. By the time these cases were decided, nearly every other state had abolished charitable immunity by statute or by the highest state court overruling its own prior decisions.

Even though the court was inclined to abolish charitable immunity, it found itself in a dilemma. Since the precedents were clear, i.e., charitable institutions were immune from suit according to a well-established line of precedents, the Supreme Judicial Court was reluctant to suddenly change the rule, but at the same time the doctrine of charitable immunity was just as clearly discredited as a principle of American law. Charitable institutions should be able to rely on the law as stated by the courts. Why should a nonprofit hospital buy insurance if it cannot be sued?

Edwin A. COLBY, Administrator

v.

CARNEY HOSPITAL

356 Mass. 527, 254 N.E.2d 407 (1969)

WILKINS, Chief Justice.

The plaintiff **administrator** brings this action of tort and contract for the death and conscious suffering of his **intestate**. The defendant hospital set up, among other things, the defence of charitable immunity. The plaintiff **demurred** to this part of the answer, stating that it "does not set forth a valid or legal defense, in that said defense as alleged violates and abrogates certain rights, privileges and immunities granted to, and preserved for the citizens of the Commonwealth" under arts. 1, 10, 11, 12, 20, and 30 of our Declaration of Rights and also under the Fifth and Fourteenth Amendments to the Constitution of the United States. A judge in the Superior Court overruled the demurrer, and the plaintiff appealed.

The demurrer was rightly overruled. Nothing has been brought to our attention suggesting that the doctrine of charitable immunity is repugnant to any provision of the Constitutions of the United States and the Commonwealth.

In the past on many occasions we have declined to renounce the defence of charitable immunity set forth in *McDonald v. Massachusetts Gen. Hosp.*, 120 Mass. 432, and *Roosen v. Peter Bent Brigham Hosp.*, 235 Mass. 66, 126 N.E. 392, 14 A.L.R. 563. [citations omitted] We took this position because we were of opinion that any renunciation preferably should be accomplished prospectively and that this should be best done by legislative action. Now it appears that only three or four States still adhere to the doctrine. . . . It seems likely that no legislative action in this Commonwealth is probable in the near future. Accordingly, we take this occasion to give adequate warning that the next time we are squarely confronted by a legal question respecting the charitable immunity doctrine it is our intention to abolish it.

Order overruling demurrer affirmed.

John HIGGINS

v.

EMERSON HOSPITAL

328 N.E.2d 488 (1975)

HENNESSEY, Justice.

This appeal brings before us the issue whether, by reason of the language in *Colby v. Carney Hosp.*, 356 Mass. 527, 528, 254 N.E.2d 407 (1969), we should hold that the defense of charitable immunity is not available to the defendant hospital. . . .

The plaintiff brought an action in tort and contract for injuries allegedly sustained by him on June 17, 1970, while he was an inpatient at the defendant hospital. The case was tried on June 20, 1974, before a Superior Court judge and a jury. The plaintiff's attorney made an opening statement that asserted the facts of the plaintiff's accident and injury, including a stipulation that the defendant hospital . . . was operated exclusively for charitable purposes. The judge thereupon **directed verdicts** for the defendant as to both counts of the plaintiff's declaration.

. . . The parties and the judge have clearly considered that the single issue is whether, by reason of the *Colby* case, or any other consideration, we should hold that charitable immunity is not applicable in this case. We hold that the doctrine is applicable and the judge properly directed verdicts for the defendant as to both counts.

The injury here occurred after the date of the decision of the *Colby* case (December 23, 1969), but before the effective date, September 16, 1971, of [the statute] which abolished the doctrine of charitable immunity. We have since held that the statute is not retrospective in effect (*Ricker v. Northeastern Univ.*, ___ Mass. ___, 279 N.E.2d 671 [1972]), and it is thus clear that the plaintiff here takes no benefit from the statute.

The plaintiff contends that, because of the intimation in the *Colby* case as to the possible future abolishment of charitable immunity, that doctrine is not applicable in this case. He argues that from the date of the decision the various charitable institutions, as well as the insurance industry and members of the public, were clearly given notice of and could conform their conduct in reliance on the fact that claims of charitable immunity raised with respect to incidents occurring after the date of the decision, December 23, 1969, would be rejected.

He further contends that had the Legislature not acted on the subject matter in 1971 there would be no question that this court would rule the charitable immunity doctrine abolished as to the instant case.

We reject the arguments. In *Colby v. Carney Hosp.*, 356 Mass. 527, 528,

254 N.E.2d 407, 408 (1969), we said that any renunciation of the doctrine of charitable immunity "should be accomplished *prospectively* and that this should be best done by legislative action" (emphasis supplied). At no time has this court abolished the doctrine. In *Ricker v. Northeastern Univ., supra,* ___ at ___, 279 N.E.2d at 672, we said, speaking of the *Colby* case, "This language does not by itself abolish the doctrine of charitable immunity as of December 23, 1969 . . . [the language] makes it clear that no change of the doctrine was then being made." The Legislature chose to act subsequent to the *Colby*

decision. We recognize the factual distinction between the instant case and the *Ricker* case, to wit, that the injury to Ricker occurred prior to December 23, 1969, the date of our decision in the *Colby* case, while the injury underlying this action occurred subsequent to that decision. Nevertheless, we see no persuasive reason now to rule, as in practical effect the plaintiff urges here, that the doctrine of charitable immunity does not apply to an injury which occurred after December 23, 1969, but before the effective date of [the statute].

. . . .

Judgment affirmed.

CASE GLOSSARY

stare decisis   is a Latin phrase meaning "to stand by decided cases," that is, by judicial precedents. Much of this chapter is devoted to explaining the operation of this doctrine.

administrator   A person appointed by the court to manage and distribute the estate of a person who dies without a will (intestate) is called an administrator or occasionally administratrix if a woman.

intestate   A person who dies without a valid will.

demurrer   This old Law French term is more precisely stated by the long-winded "motion to dismiss for failure to state a claim upon which relief can be granted." It is a pretrial motion usually made by the defendant in response to the complaint by the plaintiff and argues that the complaint is legally insufficient to make a lawsuit.

directed verdict   In a jury trial, the judge may grant a motion for a directed verdict when it is clear as a matter of law that the party making the motion must win and there are no material facts in dispute that must be decided by the jury. Granting the motion terminates the case in favor of the moving party.

CASE QUESTIONS

1. If the court was so clearly opposed to charitable immunity, why did it not simply abolish it in *Colby*?
2. Since the doctrine of charitable immunity was a judicial creation in the first place, why did the court look to the legislature to abolish it?
3. How do these cases express the judicial attitude toward precedent in Massachusetts?
4. If you had been Higgins' attorney in *Higgins v. Emerson Hospital*, would you have predicted a win or a loss in the Supreme Judicial Court?

Obiter Dictum

Not everything that is expressed in an opinion is precedent. The author of an opinion is free to make comments that go beyond the immediate issues that must be decided. The remarks, opinions, and comments in a decision that exceed the scope of the issues and the rules that decide them are called *dictum*, plural *dicta*, from the older Latin phrase **obiter dictum**, and are not binding on future cases. As we have already seen, the process of adjudication commonly results in making new rules or interpreting existing rules. This is an unavoidable result of the necessity of resolving disputes. However, when a judge attempts to expand an argument to issues or facts not before the court in the dispute, adjudication ends and legislation begins. While these statements are worthy of consideration in subsequent cases, they are not considered binding precedent and need not be followed; they are *dicta* rather than rule.

Analytically, the way to distinguish *dictum* from the rule of law is to determine the legal and factual issues presented by a dispute and analyze the reasoning that leads to their resolution. Anything outside this reasoning and the rule behind it is *dictum*.

This can be applied to the *Colby* and *Higgins* cases above. In *Colby*, the court faced the issue of whether charitable immunity was still the rule in Massachusetts. Although the court expressed its disapproval of the rule, it nevertheless followed prior precedent and held that charitable immunity was still in effect, suggesting that it would be better for the legislature to abolish the doctrine. The court added that it intended to abolish the doctrine the next time it was faced with the same issue. This assertion of the court's future intentions was *dictum*. When the trial court in *Higgins* was faced with the same issue five years later, it upheld charitable immunity and directed verdicts in favor of defendant. The trial court was legally correct since the Supreme Judicial Court in *Colby* had not abolished the doctrine but merely expressed its intention to do so. The Supreme Judicial Court agreed with the lower court that the doctrine had not been abolished by the court and indicated that its expression of future intentions had no legally binding force on Massachusetts courts. As a practical matter, the fact that the legislature had subsequently abolished charitable immunity meant that the Supreme Judicial Court need not take it upon itself to abolish the doctrine, which only affected those unfortunate few who were injured prior to the legislative act.

The principle of *obiter dictum* thus tells us that not everything written in a judicial opinion is the law. This requires a careful reading of cases before citing them as authority.

Nonbinding Authority

In practical terms, the law consists of state and federal constitutions, statutes, and judicial opinions. If a trial court in Rhode Island is faced with a difficult legal issue, it will attempt to determine the applicable law by resorting to Rhode Island statutes and case law that conforms to mandates of the Rhode Island and federal constitutions. It is bound by these authorities alone. Nevertheless, the court may confront an issue that clearly demands judicial resolution and for which the usual binding sources of the law provide little or no guidance. Typically this arises in a case of first impression in which the factual situation giving rise to the dispute has never been decided by a court of the state nor been addressed by the state legislature.

Reasoning from authority

In order to arrive at a reasonable solution, the court will use the best authority it can find. It may reason from existing state law using logic and analogy to infer a rule. For instance, until recently state courts universally rejected the notion that a professional license was property that could be used to establish property settlements upon divorce. This was particularly problematic in cases in which spouses, usually wives, had worked to support their husbands through professional school only to be divorced soon after when their professional husbands had not yet practiced long enough to acquire much property to be divided between husband and wife. In attempting to classify professional licenses, the courts, while admitting the license clearly had value for its holders, noted that the licenses did not have the usual attributes of property, namely, that they could not be transferred, sold, leased, or given away, and noted that they could be revoked by the licensing authority. While many courts obviously felt that this traditional definition of property resulted in an injustice to many wives, they felt compelled to follow the law. Finally, in *O'Brien v. O'Brien*, 489 N.E.2d 712 (NY 1985), the New York court defined professional licenses as "marital property," justifying its departure from prior law on the basis of recent divorce legislation that provided a broad definition of marital property in divorce.

obiter dictum
Dictum is a Latin word meaning "said" or "stated." *Obiter* means "by the way" or "incidentally." *Obiter dictum*, then, means something stated incidentally and not necessary to the discussion.

Law from sister states

When binding authority is absent, the court often looks to nonbinding authority from other states. A case unique in one state may very well have been decided in another. It seems reasonable to examine such decisions to see whether the rules handed down and the reasoning behind them are applicable to the law of the state faced with a case of first impression. Often the pioneering state will give its name to the principle; for example, one of the comparative negligence rules mentioned in *Li* (in Case No. 4–1) as the "50 percent" rule might also be referred to as the "Wisconsin rule," as opposed to the "Florida rule," which is normally referred to as "pure" comparative negligence.

Decisions of other state courts are commonly referred to as *persuasive authority;* they command respect since they represent the law of another American jurisdiction even though they are not binding outside of that jurisdiction. The persuasiveness of such authority is greatest in areas of common law, especially torts, and weakest in decisions based on statutory interpretation. For example, in the area of family law, there is considerable variation among the states concerning divorce law so that the reasoning of the court of one state may be considered inappropriate in another by virtue of differences between their respective statutes. For example, California is a **community property** state, while New York is an **equitable distribution** state, making California decisions regarding the distribution of property upon divorce often inapplicable to New York cases. On the other hand, since the **Uniform Commercial Code** (UCC) has been adopted in every state except Louisiana, decisions interpreting the UCC are often used as persuasive authority.

Secondary sources

In addition to cases from other states, a vast array of legal materials used in arguments by lawyers and opinions by judges that are not officially the law anywhere are called *secondary authority.* Principal among these are law review articles, **treatises**, and the **Restatements**. Law review articles written by legal scholars commonly address contemporary problems in the law and suggest carefully reasoned solutions. For example, the surrogate motherhood question that arose in New Jersey in the "Baby M" case gave rise to numerous articles critiquing the court's decision and discussing appropriate solutions to the issues raised in that case. Treatises by eminent scholars are often cited in cases, and the Restatements are especially respected since they attempt to provide a general statement of American law rather than focus on any particular state.

In addition to cases of first impression, courts, usually the highest state courts, are sometimes presented with cases that urge the overruling of precedent. In rationalizing the departure from what would otherwise appear to be binding precedent, the court

---

community property
Eight states borrowing from French (Louisiana) or Spanish (Texas west to California) law incorporated the concept of community property into marital law. The most important feature of this concept is that earnings of husband and wife during the marriage are considered to be owned equally by both. Husband and wife form an inseparable *marital community.* Consequences of this law are important upon divorce or death of one of the spouses.

equitable distribution
Many of the states that are not community property states have by legislation or judicial decision established principles of equitable distribution for the purpose of dividing property at divorce. Among other features, this law incorporates the modern trend in family law that values homemaking on a par with earnings. The result often resembles what is achieved under community property principles.

will muster all the available persuasive authority and secondary authority it can.

Since cases raise serious legal issues and judges are entrusted with the administration of justice, decisions are not mechanical products of legal scholarship. Much attention is given in written opinions to fairness to the parties and the consequences to society of the rules that are constructed or enforced. The search for authority on which to base a rule helps to ensure that judges are not acting merely on their own personal value systems but instead reflect a consensus of the wisdom of their peers. This is the legacy of the common law, a system of judicial decision making that has endured many centuries of political and social change and has perhaps greatly assisted in making those changes.

SUMMARY

The Anglo-American legal tradition has a rich history of judge-made law known as the common law. It is governed by the principle of *stare decisis,* which urges that the courts abide by past precedents unless there is a compelling reason for departure from prior cases. The process of adjudication focuses on disputes, in contrast to the legislative process, which enacts general laws for future application.

In determining and interpreting the law, courts base decisions on authority, principally statutes and prior case law. When these do not provide a clear answer to the case at hand, secondary authority may be the source of reasoning and rules.

The statements of the law made in higher courts must be followed by the lower courts, but the force of precedent applies only to that part of the decision pertinent to the facts of the dispute before the court and not to incidental statements of the author of a judicial opinion.

CHAPTER QUESTIONS

1. Why is the American system called a common law system?
2. What does judicial restraint restrain?
3. Why is *dictum* not binding?
4. What is the difference in process between legislation and adjudication?
5. When may a court overrule a prior precedent?

Uniform Commercial Code
   The Uniform Commercial Code, commonly referred to simply as the UCC, is a set of comprehensive statutes governing most commercial transactions and has been adopted in every state except Louisiana.

treatises
   in the legal context are scholarly books about the law, usually covering one of the basic fields of law, such as torts or contracts, or a significant subfield of the law, such as worker's compensation or products liability. The persuasiveness of the treatise rests largely on the prestige of the author.

Restatements
   The American Law Institute, which was founded in 1923, sponsored the compilation of major fields of common law and published a number of works, beginning with the *Restatement of Contracts* in 1932. These works state basic legal principles and provide comments on them. While courts are free to accept or reject these principles, they frequently quote them in cases.

EXERCISES

1. Find out what regional reporter publishes your state's appellate decisions. How is the reporter abbreviated in citations?
2. Does your state have a reporter that reports decisions of the trial courts?
3. At the beginning or end of reporter series in law libraries are sets of bound and paperback indexes called "Shepard's Citations," which list cases citing other cases; thus, you can look up a case and find what subsequent cases have cited it. See if you can find out if a case has been overruled.

PROFESSIONAL PROFILE

Cheryl Perillo graduated from the State University at Albany with a B.A. in psychology in December 1982. Raised in a small town, Medina, New York, Perillo was anxious to move to New York City and find work. "I was thinking about going to law school, so I wanted to work in the legal field first and learn more about it," Perillo remembers. She says, "The most interesting positions I had were as a legal assistant handling trusts and estates for a two-attorney firm in New York and as a title and survey reader for a law firm in Albany, which represented a major mortgage-lending institution. I learned to be a paralegal through on-the-job training with direct attorney supervision and instruction." The attorneys worked very closely with the paralegals, making them feel a part of the firm.

Perillo recalls, "I responded to an advertisement in the *New York Times* for my first job as a legal assistant. They wanted someone without experience who could be trained in their own office procedures. The firm offered tuition-reimbursement, which made this position appear particularly attractive. While the responsibilities and deadlines were similar to those for attorneys, I was excited to accept the offer."

Initially the job as legal assistant in trusts and estates was very secretarial. "My duties included typing, filing, and photocopying, as well as grocery shopping and making coffee! But my employer was very supportive and anxious to educate his employees in the field of trusts and estates," Perillo says. He encouraged research, on-the-job training, and participation in planning conferences. "Many times I made the commute to and from Manhattan while listening to cassettes on the fine points of revocable trusts or reading articles on the merits of taking a marital deduction. While working in this office, I developed what I believe is the necessary quality for a paralegal: attention to detail. I learned to be exacting, proofread, keep diaries, and make checklists. This skill has served me well in all my subsequent work. When I finally left this office, my job responsibilities had grown to drafting clauses in and drawing outlines for wills, preparing documents, marshalling assets, assisting in the preparation of tax returns, and billing," Perillo says.

As a title and survey reader at a large law firm, Perillo oversaw all aspects of the home-equity lending department. She reported directly to the managing partner and supervised two paralegals. Typically the office would handle an average of sixty real estate closings per week. Perillo says, "My duties included ordering title searches, reviewing titles, plotting deed descriptions, and working with the bank and attorneys to cure defects in titles. I also set up a system to computerize the loan documents, which streamlined loan preparation and reduced turn-around time. I also established a catalog system for closed files, handled the billings to the bank, produced weekly status reports, and charted the volume of files flowing in and out of the office. I basically dealt exclusively with bank personnel and title companies."

The most rewarding aspects of her work were helping people by solving their problems, working independently, and completing a job well. Perillo, who now devotes her time to raising two small children, advises prospective paralegals with the following:

"Be exacting and careful, and pay a lot of attention to detail."

Cheryl Perillo

CHAPTER 5
Legislation

> One of the greatest delusions in the world is the hope that the evils of this world can be cured by legislation.
>
> — *Thomas B. Reed (1839–1902)*

> No man, woman, or child is safe while the legislature is in session.
>
> — *source unknown*

Historically judicial decisions have played the major role in the evolution of Anglo-American law, but the courts as the source of law have been eclipsed in modern times by the ascendancy of legislatures as primary lawmaking bodies.

EVOLUTION OF LEGISLATION

During most of the development of Anglo-American law, the pronouncement of law was accomplished by courts deciding cases in which customs, practices, and informal principles of conduct were formalized in written decisions. Although our law largely escaped the **codification** movements that revolutionized continental European law, the nineteenth century brought a new attitude in America with regard to legislation. The English Parliament enacted numerous statutes over the centuries that clarified or changed the common law but its legislative output was minor in comparison to the courts as a source of law.

The American situation was different. The United States had approved a written federal constitution that allocated political authority among the three branches of government, providing specific important spheres of authority for *Congress*.* The legal profession and the courts were viewed by some with suspicion because of the elitist tradition of these institutions in England and colonial America. Congress, on the other hand, was elected by the people and thus viewed as representative of the people. It was natural that antiaristocratic sentiment in the new republic would turn to Congress and the state legislatures for lawmaking, which is their constitutional and customary function.

The last half of the nineteenth century saw a major movement toward codification in the United States. In addition to the reasons

---

* The United States Constitution provides as follows:
  Article I, Section 1. All legislative powers herein granted shall be vested in a Congress of the United States, which shall consist of a Senate and House of Representatives.
  Section 8. The Congress shall have the power
   1. To lay and collect taxes . . . ;
   3. To regulate commerce with foreign nations . . . ;
   5. To coin money . . . ;
   7. To establish post offices and post roads;
   8. To promote the progress of science and useful arts, by securing for limited times to authors and inventors the exclusive right to their respective writings and discoveries; [patent and copyright law]
   9. To constitute tribunals inferior to the Supreme Court;
   11. To declare war . . . ;
   12. To raise and support armies . . . ;
   18. To make all laws which shall be necessary and proper for carrying into execution the foregoing powers, and all other powers vested by this Constitution in the government of the United States, or any department or officer thereof.

given above for favoring legislation, two others provided impetus. First, Americans had learned through revolution and the establishment of the Constitution that the people could guide their own destiny by making law through their representatives, a democratic and rational process. Second, the country was undergoing rapid change and development, and Americans were disinclined to preserve ancient customs simply because they were ancient. Americans were ambitious and ready for change. To wait for the evolution of legal principles through the cumbersome and conservative judicial process was probably never truly part of the American character.

The most renowned spokesman for codification was David Dudley Field, a New York lawyer who was appointed to a law revision commission that authored the *Code of Civil Procedure* enacted in 1848 and often called simply the "Field Code." While Field advocated and authored several other codes, their reception in New York and other eastern states was poor. Western states, on the contrary, wholeheartedly jumped at the chance for ready-made law, perhaps because their brief history and lack of tradition made them impatient for a system of laws from which they could set new horizons.

The complex problems of the twentieth century have encouraged timely responses from legislative bodies, which have become politically very powerful, often seeming to eclipse the common law tradition. Although the states differ in the extent to which they have codified state law, every state has enacted a complex body of statutes that serves as a principal source of law. The rise of the power of legislatures is reflected in the courts, which now defer to the statutes. Nevertheless, since disputes over the law must ultimately be resolved in the courts, the meaning of legislation is decided by the courts and applied to specific cases.

THE NATURE OF LEGISLATION

In Chapter Four, legislation was distinguished from judge-made law by its characteristics of "general application and future effect." The line drawn between the characteristics of legislation and adjudication has not always been clear. In the past legislatures have often passed special bills to define narrow rights of individuals or local entities, but this practice has always been viewed with suspicion (see the 1851 case of *Ponder v. Graham*, below). When a legislative body narrows its focus to resolve a particularized dispute, it may be challenged in court as violating

codification
The term *codify* may refer to the simple process of turning a custom or common law rule into legislation, but usually it refers to making *codes*, i.e., comprehensive legislation covering a particular area, such as civil procedure. Codification movements have been inspired by efforts of lawyers, judges, and legislators to organize a body of law into a coherent and consistent statutory form.

the principle of separation of judicial and legislative powers embodied in federal and state constitutions.

Legislation strives to reduce principles of law to a coherent written form in which the intent of the law can be determined from the words alone—statutes are pure rules, often without policy statements or statements of intent. In this respect they differ in nature from the common law, which, while relying on past precedent when available, may be characterized as customary law since it is based on unwritten principles of justice and proper conduct rooted in the values of society and is elaborated in often lengthy critical comments in the decisions. The rules in judicial decisions are formulated to apply to the case before the court and are tailored to the dispute. They express an underlying principle rather than an exact rule, as is the case with legislation. The reasoning is as much a part of the rule as the precise statement of the rule in the decision.

The common law treats law as an evolving process. Ultimately it is what a case comes to stand for rather than what it actually states. For example, the landmark school case *Goss v. Lopez*, 419 U.S. 565 (1975), which defined the rights of public school students in certain disciplinary actions, is frequently cited as establishing a constitutional right to a public education. In fact, *Goss v. Lopez* did not hold that there was such a right in the U.S. Constitution but rather that once a state (Ohio) established such a right, it could not take that right away without due process of law. Nonetheless, if the U.S. Supreme Court or state courts dealing with state law declare that *Goss v. Lopez* holds that there is a constitutional right to a public education, then that principle becomes the law, regardless of the actual language of the prior case. Since all states provide public education, the distinction is largely academic, but the point here is that judicial statements of law are not always taken at face value in the way that statutes are.

This distinction may be shown more simply by the difference in attitude of a court in dealing with legislation as opposed to judicial precedent. The court "interprets" statutes, that is, attempts to determine the meaning of the words and phrases in the statute, while the specific rules laid down in cases are examined to determine the underlying principles on which they are based. For example, in *Goss v. Lopez*, the majority concluded with the statement:

> We should also make it clear that we have addressed ourselves solely to the short suspension, not exceeding 10 days. Longer suspensions or expulsions for the remainder of the school term, or permanently, may require more formal procedures.

In so stating, the court made its ruling quite limited, leaving clarification for future cases. Such an imprecise approach would be unacceptable for legislation.

The end result of legislation is the enactment of written laws with an effective date and publication in the statute books. From the lawyer's point of view, the best legislation is clearly written and unambiguous. Since lawyers must be able to predict the outcomes of their clients' disputes, carefully framed statutes are an important aid. But legislators are not clairvoyant; they cannot predict every future scenario and provide for every possibility. Numerous cases arise in which the applicability of a statute to a particular case is unclear. A court may ultimately be asked to define the statute with regard to its application to a real-life dispute. Keep in mind, however, that when statutes are later found to be faulty or unclear, the legislature is free to amend or change the statute to reflect its intent.

CASE NO. 5–1   Limits of Legislative Authority

The following case reflects a fundamental difference between legislative and adjudicative functions in our political system, but it also reveals an interesting facet of the history of family law. In England, prior to American independence, family law matters were handled by ecclesiastical courts. There was no divorce in the modern sense, although a cumbersome procedure involving common law courts and an act of Parliament could result in a legal divorce. It was rare and, practically speaking, only available to men of influence and power. Since the United States did not incorporate ecclesiastical courts into the legal system, family law eventually fell within the courts of equity (see Chapter Seven) rather than the common law courts. In the meantime, several state legislatures borrowed from the English practice of legislative divorce and passed special acts divorcing married couples. In the twentieth century state legislatures have regulated marriage and

divorce through statute, and the courts have assumed the task of granting divorces and determining the rights of divorcing parties. At the time *Ponder v. Graham* was decided, this separation of function was still evolving.

WILLIAM G. PONDER, EXECUTOR OF
ARCHIBALD GRAHAM, APPELLANT
v.
MARY GRAHAM, APPELLEE

4 Fla. 23 (1851)

[Mary Graham was not satisfied with the provisions made for her by her husband, Archibald Graham, in his will, and petitioned to take her **dower** right to one-third interest in his estate in lieu of the will. Ponder was appointed under the will to distribute Archibald's estate and challenged Mary's right on the grounds that she was not lawfully married to Archibald. The jury found for Mary and the court awarded her a one-third interest in Archibald's real estate.]

. . . .

The facts of the case are succinctly these: The respondent, then Mary Buccles, about the year 1820, in South Carolina, intermarried with one Solomon Canady. Some time afterwards, they removed to, and resided in Georgia, but soon, in consequence of domestic dissensions, separated. Mary went to reside with Graham, a bachelor, and continued to live with him, under circumstances from which an adulterous cohabitation might be inferred.

In 1832, and while the said cohabitation continued, a bill was passed by the Legislative Council of the then Territory of Florida, entitled "An act for the relief of Mary Canady."

By this act, the Legislative Council, for the cause expressed in the preamble, assumed to judge and declare that the said Mary Graham was thereby divorced from her said husband, Solomon, and that the bonds of matrimony subsisting between them, were thereby to be entirely and absolutely dissolved, as if the same had never been solemnized. . . . There does not appear to have been any petition, affidavit, or proofs—a reference to a committee to ascertain the facts, or any notice to the absent husband. In 1834, the cohabitation between Mary and the testator still subsisting, the ceremony of marriage is celebrated between them, and from the time up to the period of the testator's death, which occurred in 1848, he lived with her, and acknowledged her as his wife, and in his will he provides for her by that name, and in that relation.

. . . .

SEMMES, *Justice*, delivered the opinion of the court.

. . . .

The main question raised in this case, as to the power of a Legislative body, *as such*, to grant divorces, is not altogether a new one. It has been investigated by some of the American Courts, and grave constitutional questions have been necessarily involved in the discussion; and yet the question still remains an open one—opinions clashing—nothing settled. . . .

. . . .

No one doubts the right of the people by their constitution, to invest the power in the Legislature, or any where else; but the question is, when the constitution is silent on the subject, in what department of government does this authority rest? I believe that much, if not the whole difficulty, has arisen from overlooking some of the great principles which enter into the constitutional government of the States, and from not preserving the obvious distinction between legislative and judicial functions—by confounding the *right* which a legislative body has to pass *general laws* on the subject of divorce, with the *power* of dissolving the marriage *contract*.

. . . .

[The court goes on to dispute the notion that the English Parliament granted divorces, noting that both ecclesiastical courts and common law courts were required to rule on a divorce before it went for approval by the House of Lords, which served as the English supreme court as well as a legislative body.]

In every respect in which I have been able to see this case, I can find no reason to sustain the act of the legislature. It appears by the record, that the parties were domiciled in the State of Georgia, where, it is alleged; the desertion and ill treatment occurred. The wife, living with the testator, Graham, removed to Florida—while the husband returned to Carolina, his former residence. The bill was introduced into the legislature one day, and passed the next. It is very clear that this divorce would not be recognized by the courts of Georgia or Carolina, were any rights asserted under it in those States. . . .

I am, therefore, of opinion that the act of the Legislative Council of February 11th, 1832, was in conflict with the organic law of Florida and the Constitution of the United States, and is, therefore, void.

Per Curiam—Let the judgment of the court below be reversed.

CASE GLOSSARY

dower refers to a widow's right to her deceased husband's estate, traditionally a one-third share in real property of which her husband was seized (see above) at his death. She could claim this share in lieu of whatever might have been left to her by will. Mary Graham apparently was not satisfied with her share under the will and was attempting to receive dower instead. In Florida today, dower has been replaced by *elective share,* which provides that a surviving spouse may elect to take thirty percent of the deceased spouse's estate.

THE LEGISLATIVE PROCESS

While individual states are free to regulate and order the process of lawmaking, we find a common pattern by which principles are enacted into law. The following discussion describes a formal political process. It does not take into account the influence on legislation of informal political activities, the conflicts inherent in the two-party system, lobbying, interest groups, constituencies, etc., because their interaction varies from issue to issue and locality to locality.

The hallmark of the legislative process is discussion and debate. (Note that their absence was criticized implicitly in the legislative divorce that the Supreme Court of Florida invalidated in *Ponder v. Graham.*) Passage of a bill into law ultimately requires open debate within the legislative body, which may be quite extensive with complex or controversial legislation or quite brief with laws over which there is a general consensus or lack of interest.

Among the many problems that arise in our society, some come to the attention of lawmakers as problems that may be helped by the enactment of laws. Typically, legislators serve on legislative committees that deal with a defined area of interest. These committees are assigned to conduct an examination of proposed legislation and frame the law. In studying the problem, the committee collects a wide range of data and information and often conducts hearings on the subject. The purpose is to frame the legislation in the best way to solve the underlying problem, and this is best accomplished if legislators are fully informed about the problem so they can estimate the effectiveness of the solution. Each legislature has its rules by which the proposed legislation reaches the floor of the legislature for open debate and vote. All states except Nebraska have a **bicameral** legislature modeled on the U.S. Senate and House of Representatives; the different views of these two bodies often require compromise for passage of a law.

The process is quite different from adjudication in that the legislators must view the law in its general effect for the future, taking into consideration the effects on all who may be subject to the law. Enactment into law makes a public record and serves as notice to the public of the requirements of the law.

JUDICIAL INVALIDATION OF LEGISLATION

Although the courts are bound to uphold legislation, there are two grounds on which courts have struck down legislation:

1. Defective procedure. The passage of the law may have been procedurally defective as measured by state law. Since our legislatures have been operating for many decades, the legal requisites of statutory enactment are well known and generally orderly, so that procedural challenges are uncommon.
2. Unconstitutionality. The law itself may violate principles of state or federal constitutions. Statutes may also be declared unconstitutional in substance rather than procedure. A statute may be unconstitutional "on its face," meaning that a careful reading of the statute reveals that it violates some constitutional prohibition; or a statute may be unconstitutional in its effects or applications, which is more difficult to establish.

bicameral
legislature has two bodies, such as a House of Representatives and a Senate. Only Nebraska has a single, or *unicameral*, legislature.

JUDICIAL DEFERENCE TO LEGISLATION

Our constitutional system allocates legislative powers to Congress and authority to decide cases and "controversies" to the federal judiciary. This constitutional mandate has been followed by state constitutions so that the principle of separation of legislative and judicial functions is a fundamental part of our legal system.

CASE NO. 5–2   Legislation Violating the Constitution

The following case held a Jacksonville, Florida, vagrancy ordinance unconstitutional both on its face and in its potential for abuse by the police, an abuse made apparent from the facts of the various parties to the case. Note that local legislative bodies, such as a county commission or a city council, enact legislation, commonly called *ordinances,* which have the force of law and are subject to the same constitutional requirements as state and federal statutes. The principal challenge to the ordinance was based on the principle of *void for vagueness,* which applies to a statute that "fails to give a person of ordinary intelligence fair notice that his contemplated conduct is forbidden by the statute." This principle is based on the notion that the statutes serve as public notice of the conduct required by the law. If a law cannot be understood as written, it does not furnish notice. The void-for-vagueness doctrine is derived from the constitutional requirement in the Fourteenth Amendment that no state shall "deprive any person of life, liberty, or property, without due process of law."

The Jacksonville ordinance includes peculiar language that comes from much earlier English poor laws used to control the working class:

> Rogues and vagabonds, or dissolute persons who go about begging, common gamblers, persons who use juggling or unlawful games or plays, common drunkards, common night thieves, pilferers or pickpockets, traders in stolen property, lewd, wanton and lascivious persons, keepers of gambling places, common railers and brawlers, persons wandering or strolling around from place to place without any lawful

purpose or object, habitual loafers, disorderly persons, persons neglecting all lawful business and habitually spending their time by frequenting houses of ill fame, gaming houses, or places where alcoholic beverages are sold or served, persons able to work but habitually living upon the earnings of their wives or minor children shall be deemed vagrants and, upon conviction in the Municipal court shall be punished as provided for Class D offenses. (Jacksonville Ordinance Code §26–57.)

**MARGARET PAPACHRISTOU et al.,
Petitioners,
v.
CITY OF JACKSONVILLE**
405 U.S. 156 (1972)

MR. JUSTICE DOUGLAS delivered the opinion of the Court.

. . . .

The facts are stipulated. Papachristou and Calloway are white females. Melton and Johnson are black males. Papachristou was enrolled in a job-training program sponsored by the State Employment Service at Florida Junior College in Jacksonville. Calloway was a typing and shorthand teacher at a state mental institution located near Jacksonville. She was the owner of the automobile in which the four defendants were arrested. Melton was a Vietnam war veteran who had been released from the Navy after nine months in a veterans' hospital. On the date of his arrest he was a part-time computer helper while attending college as a full-time student in Jacksonville. Johnson was a tow-motor operator in a grocery chain warehouse and was a lifelong resident of Jacksonville.

At the time of their arrest the four of them were riding in Calloway's car on the main thoroughfare in Jacksonville. They had left a restaurant owned by Johnson's uncle where they had eaten and were on their way to a night club. The arresting officers denied that the racial mixture in the car played any part in the decision to make the arrest. The arrest, they said, was made because the defendants had stopped near a used-car lot which had been broken into several times. There was, however, no evidence of any breaking and entering on the night in question.

Of these four charged with "prowling by auto" none had been previously arrested except Papachristou who had once been convicted of a municipal offense.

. . . .

[The court goes on to describe each of the arrests of the several petitioners—including those in companion cases, which were consolidated upon appeal—none of whom were engaged in conduct that would be criminal except for the ordinance.] . . . [Heath and his companion] and the automobile were searched. Although no contraband or incriminating evidence was found, they were both arrested, Heath being charged with being a "common thief" because he was reputed to be a thief. The codefendant was charged with "loitering" because he was standing in the driveway, an act which the officers admitted was done only at their command.

. . . .

This ordinance is void-for-vagueness, both in the sense that it "fails to give a person of ordinary intelligence fair notice that his contemplated conduct is forbidden by the statute," *United States v. Harriss*, 347 U.S. 612, 617, and because

it encourages arbitrary and erratic arrests and convictions. [Cc.]

Living under a rule of law entails various suppositions, one of which is that "[all persons] are entitled to be informed as to what the State commands or forbids." [C.]

. . . .

The Jacksonville ordinance makes criminal activities which by modern standards are normally innocent. "Nightwalking" is one. . . .

"[P]ersons able to work but habitually living upon the earnings of their wives and minor children"—like habitually living "without visible means of support"—might implicate unemployed pillars of the community who have married rich wives.

"[P]ersons able to work but habitually living upon the earnings of their wives or minor children" may also embrace unemployed people out of the labor market, by reason of a recession or disemployed by reason of technological or so-called structural displacements.

. . . .

Another aspect of the ordinance's vagueness appears when we focus, not on the lack of notice given a potential offender, but on the effect of the unfettered discretion it places in the hands of the Jacksonville police. . . .

A direction by a legislature to the police to arrest all "suspicious" persons would not pass constitutional muster. A vagrancy prosecution may be merely the cloak for a conviction which could not be obtained on the real but undisclosed grounds for the arrest. . . .

The Jacksonville ordinance cannot be squared with our constitutional standards and is plainly unconstitutional.

Reversed.

Inherent in this scheme is the notion that legislatures make law and courts interpret and enforce them.

This does not abolish the common law system, which is still held in high esteem. Nevertheless, legislatures have surpassed the courts as the major source of new law. The evolution of a complex society and legal system in America brought these two legal institutions into direct and frequent confrontation. The separation of powers and the self-imposed custom of judicial restraint ultimately resulted in judicial subservience to statutes. If a statute is procedurally correct and constitutional in substance, American courts are bound to enforce it. Individual judges and courts have expressed dislike for particular statutes at the same time that they have upheld them. If the legislature passes a "bad" law, it is the job of the legislature, not the courts, to revise the law. Courts often send strong messages to the legislature by way of their written decisions, but the legislature may or may not heed these messages.

In the evolutionary process of defining legislative and judicial functions, legislative bodies have also been subject to certain constraints. While legislatures enact laws and even provide for the means of enforcement by establishing and funding regulatory, judicial, and law enforcement agencies, the task of enforcement is not a legislative function. The courts are the final arbiters of the disputes that arise under the laws, whether common law or legislation. The power of the legislature to make the rules is counterbalanced by the power of the judiciary to interpret and apply them. It is not uncommon for a court to give lip service to the language of a statute at the same time that its interpretation of the statute makes serious inroads into its intended purpose. Lawmaking and interpretation take place in a political, social, and economic environment that is often more influential than legal technicalities or even the Constitution.

STATUTORY INTERPRETATION

For the legal practitioner, the most important problem with legislation is interpretion. Over the course of many years, a number of principles have been developed to guide the courts in resolving disputes over the meaning of statutes. The principles governing statutory interpretation are commonly called *rules of construction*, referring to the manner in which courts are to *construe* the meaning of statutes. The overriding principle governing statutory interpretation is to determine the intent of the legislature and give force to that intent. Some of the rules and priorities employed in this goal are set forth below.

Legislative Intent

The underlying policy behind statutory construction is the search to determine *legislative intent.*

The Plain Meaning Rule

This rule can actually be used to defy legislative intent. The *plain meaning rule* states simply that if the language of a statute is unambiguous and its meaning clear, the terms of the statute should be construed and applied according to their ordinary meaning. Behind this rule is the assumption that the legislature understood the meaning of the words it used and expressed its intent thereby. This rule operates to restrain the court from substituting its notion of what the legislature *really* meant if the meaning is already clear.

The application of the plain meaning rule may in fact undermine legislative intent. While legislation is usually carefully drafted, language is by its nature susceptible to ambiguity, distortion, or simple lack of clarity. Since legislation is designed to control disputes that have not yet arisen, the "perfect" statute requires a degree of clairvoyance absent in the ordinary human being, including legislators, so that a statute may apply to a situation not foreseen by the legislators, who might have stated otherwise had they imagined such a situation.

The plain meaning rule obviates the need to pursue a lengthy inquiry into intent. Consider the nature of the legislative process. First, legislative intent is difficult to determine. The final product of the legislative process, the statute, would thus seem to be the best evidence of legislative intent. Legislatures are composed of numerous members who intend different things. In many instances, legislators do not even read the laws for which they vote. To believe there is a single legislative intent is to ignore reality. Many statutes are the result of compromise, the politics of which are not a matter of public record and cannot be accurately determined by a court. The precise language of the statute, then, is the best guide to intent. If, in the eyes of the legislature, the court errs in its application of the statute, the legislature may revise the statute for future application.

Limitations on the Plain Meaning Rule

Adherence to the plain meaning rule is neither blind nor simple-minded. A statute that is unambiguous in its language may be found to conflict with other statutes. Statutes are typically enacted in "packages," as part of a legislative effort to regulate a broad area of concern. Thus, alimony is ordinarily defined in several statutes embraced within a package of statutes covering divorce, which in turn may be part of a statutory chapter on domestic relations. The more comprehensive the package, the more likely some of its provisions may prove to be inconsistent. A sentence that seems unambiguous may be ambiguous in relation to a paragraph, a section, or a chapter.

Language must thus be interpreted in its context. In fact, this principle often operates to dispel ambiguity. Comprehensive statutes commonly begin with a preamble or introductory section stating the general purpose of the statutes collected under its heading. This statement of purpose is intended to avoid an overly technical interpretation of the statutes that could achieve results contrary to the general purpose.

The preamble is frequently followed by a section defining terms used in the statutes. This, too, limits the application of the plain meaning rule but in a different way: The definitions pinpoint terms that have technical or legal significance to avoid what might otherwise be a nontechnical, ordinary interpretation.

On occasion, a provision in a statute may turn out to defeat the purpose of the statute in a particular set of circumstances; the Court is then faced with the problem of giving meaning to the purpose of the statute or the language of the clause within the statute. In *Texas & Pac. Ry. v. Abilene Cotton Oil Co.*, 204 U.S. 426 (1907), the U.S. Supreme Court was called upon to interpret the Interstate Commerce Act, which set up the Interstate Commerce Commission (ICC) and made it responsible for setting rates and routes for the railroads. A disgruntled shipper sued the railroad under an old common law action for "unreasonable rates." The Act had a provision, commonly included in legislation, that stated that the Act did not abolish other existing remedies. However, the court reasoned that if persons were able to bring such actions any time they were unhappy with the rates, the rate structures established by the ICC would have little meaning, depending instead upon what a particular jury or judge considered reasonable. The court limited the effect of the clause and argued that the Congress could not have intended for the clause to be used to completely undermine the purpose of the Act, "in other words, the act cannot be held to destroy itself. . . . "

Aids to Statutory Interpretation

Single statutes do not exist in a legal vacuum. They are part of a section, chapter, and the state or federal code as a whole. Historically, statutes developed as an adjunct to the traditional common law system that established law from custom.

Like case law, statutory construction relies heavily on *authority*. Interpretation is a formal reasoning process in the law, which in our legal tradition depends less on the creative imagination than on sources of the law. In the reasoning process, an overriding judicial policy insists that the body of laws be as consistent and harmonious as possible. It was for this reason that the court held in *Abilene Oil, supra,* that the statute "cannot be held to destroy itself."

If a clause seems to conflict with its immediate statutory context, it will be interpreted so as to further the general legislative intent, if such can be ascertained. In a sense, this is simply intelligent reading; words and phrases take their meaning from their contexts. The principle can be extended further, however. Statutes taken from different parts of a state or federal code may be found to conflict. The court will interpret the language to harmonize the inconsistency whenever possible. Legislative intent may become quite obscure in such situations since the presumption that the legislature meant what it said is confronted by the problem that it said something different elsewhere. In reconciling the conflict, the court may use its sense of overall legislative policy and even the general history of the law, including the common law. The obvious solution to these conflicts is action by the legislature to rewrite the statutes to resolve the inconsistencies and provide future courts with a clear statement of intent.

Strict Construction

Words by their nature have different meanings and nuances. Shades of meaning change in the context of other words and phrases. Tradition has determined that certain situations call for broad or liberal constructions, while others call for narrow or strict construction, meaning that the statute in question will not be expanded beyond a very literal reading of its meaning.

"Criminal statutes are strictly construed." This rule of construction has its source in the evolution of our criminal law, in particular, in the many rights we afford those accused of crime. Out of fear of abuse of the criminal justice system, we have provided protection for the accused against kangaroo courts, overzealous prosecutors, and corrupt police. It is an accepted value of our legal system that the innocent must be protected even if it means that the guilty will sometimes go free.

Although many basic crimes, such as murder, burglary, and assault were formulated by the common law in the distant past, today most states do not recognize common law crimes but insist that crimes be specified by statute. We consider it unjust for someone to be charged with a crime if the conduct constituting the crime has not been clearly prohibited by statute. Conversely, if a statute defines certain conduct as criminal, "ignorance of the law excuses no one" (*ignorantia legis neminem excusat*). If public notice of prohibited conduct is an essential ingredient of criminal law, strict construction is its logical conclusion. If conduct is not clearly within the prohibitions of a statute, the court will decline to expand its coverage.

CASE NO. 5–3   Is a Fetus a Human Being?

In the case below, a husband and wife in the process of divorce were involved in an altercation over the wife's pregnancy by another man. The husband shoved his knee in her abdomen, and the fetus was stillborn with a fractured skull. The husband contended that he could not be charged with murder under California law.

Robert Harrison KEELER, Petitioner,

v.

The SUPERIOR COURT OF AMADOR COUNTY, Respondent,

The PEOPLE, Real Party In Interest

Supreme Court of California
2 Cal.3d 619, 470 P.2d 617 (1970)

MOSK, J. In this proceeding for **writ of prohibition** we are called upon to decide whether an unborn but viable fetus is a "human being" within the meaning of the California statute defining murder (Pen. Code, §187). We conclude that the

Legislature did not intend such a meaning, and that for us to construe the statute to the contrary and apply it to this petitioner would exceed our judicial power and deny petitioner due process of law.

. . . .

Penal Code Section 187 provides: "Murder is the unlawful killing of a human being, with **malice aforethought**." The dispositive question is whether the fetus which petitioner is accused of killing was, on February 23, 1969, a "human being" within the meaning of the statute. If it was not, petitioner cannot be charged with its "murder" and prohibition will lie.

Section 187 was enacted as part of the Penal Code of 1872 . . . section 187 was, in turn, taken verbatim from the first California statute defining murder. . . . Penal Code section 5 (also enacted in 1872) declares: "The provisions of this code, so far as they are substantially the same as existing statutes, must be construed as continuations thereof, and not as new enactments." We begin, accordingly, by inquiring into the intent of the Legislature in 1850 when it first defined murder as the unlawful and malicious killing of a "human being."

It will be presumed, of course, that in enacting a statute the Legislature was familiar with the relevant rules of the common law, and, when it couches its enactment in common law language, that its intent was to continue those rules in statutory form. . . .

We conclude that in declaring murder to be the unlawful and malicious killing of a "human being" the Legislature of 1850 intended that term to have the settled common law meaning of a person who had been born alive, and did not intend the act of feticide—as distinguished from abortion—to be an offense under the laws of California.

. . . .

It is the policy of this state to construe a penal statute as favorably to the defendant as its language and the circumstances of its application may reasonably permit; just as in the case of a question of fact, the defendant is entitled to the benefit of every reasonable doubt as to the true interpretation of words or the construction of language used in a statute. . . . We hold that in adopting the definition of murder in Penal Code section 187 the Legislature intended to exclude from its reach the act of killing an unborn fetus. [italics added]

The People urge, however, that the sciences of obstetrics and pediatrics have greatly progressed since 1872, to the point where with proper medical care a normally developed fetus prematurely born at 28 weeks or more has an excellent chance of survival . . . and that one who unlawfully and maliciously terminates such a life should therefore be liable to prosecution for murder under section 187. . . .

. . . .

. . . it is clear the courts cannot go so far as to create an offense by enlarging a statute, by inserting or deleting words, or by giving the terms used false or unusual meanings. . . . *Penal statutes will not be made to reach beyond their plain intent; they include only those offenses coming clearly within the import of their language.* . . . [italics added]

. . . We recognize that the killing of an unborn but viable fetus may be deemed by some to be an offense of similar nature and gravity; but as Chief Justice Marshall warned long ago, "It would be dangerous, indeed, to carry the principle that a case which is within the reason or mischief of a statute is within its provisions, so far as to punish a crime not enumerated in the statute, because it is of equal atrocity, or of kindred character, with those which are enumerated." (United States v. Wiltberger (1820) 18 U.S. (5 Wheat.) 76, 96.) Whether to thus extend liability for murder in California is a determination solely within the province of the Legislature. . . .

CASE GLOSSARY

writ of prohibition   is an order by a higher court to a lower court instructing the lower court not to exercise its jurisdiction over a case. This order is ordinarily sought by a petitioner claiming that the lower court does not have jurisdiction or has exceeded its authority.

malice aforethought   is a special requirement in murder cases; it requires more than the criminal intent necessary for conviction of other crimes. To establish malice aforethought, the prosecution must show that the killing was planned or that the defendant had time to consider what he or she was doing and yet proceeded with the killing. Malice aforethought distinguishes homicides that are the result of instantaneous anger or passion from those in which the killer had time to reflect. Malice aforethought is also called *premeditation* and *malice prepense.*

A second category of statutes that are strictly construed is expressed by the principle that "statutes in derogation of the common law are strictly construed." State legislatures frequently pass laws that alter, modify, or abolish traditional common law rules. The principle that such changes are narrowly construed not only shows respect for the common law but also reflects the difference between legislative and judicial decision making. While judicial decisions explain the reasons for the application of a particular rule, allowing for later interpretations and modifications, statutes are presumed to mean what they say. The intent of the legislature is embodied in the language of the statute itself, which if well drafted can be seen to apply to the situations for which it was intended.

A statute should stand alone, its meaning clear. Unfortunately, this is not always possible. If there is some question of meaning, a statute that appears to conflict with prior principles of the common law can be measured against that body of law. In other words, the Court has recourse to a wealth of time-tested principles and need not strain to guess legislative intent. This is particularly helpful when the statute neglects to cover a situation that has been decided in the past. If the statute is incomplete or ambiguous, the Court will resolve the dispute by following the common law.

Legislative History

If the application of a statute remains unclear in its language and in its written context, the intent of the legislature may be ascertained by researching the statute's legislative history. This includes the records and documents concerning the process whereby the statute became law. The purpose and application of the statute may sometimes become clear with these additional materials. Several committees may have held hearings or discussions on the law during its enactment that have become part of the public record and demonstrate the concerns of legislators and the reasons for enactment. Inferences may be made based on different drafts of the statute and the reasons expressed for the changes. If two houses of the legislature began with different language, the final compromise language may also suggest conclusions. Legislative debates may similarly clarify legislative intent.

Research into legislative history can be a lengthy process involving extensive analytical skills; but an examination of the entire process for a particular enactment will tend to dispel plausible, but incorrect, interpretations of legislative intent. The informal politics of negotiation and compromise, however, are not always reflected in the record, so the reasons for the final decisions on the language of the statute may remain obscure.

A Caveat on Statutory Interpretation

We have touched here on only a few of a multitude of rules of interpretation employed by the courts in resolving issues of statutory meaning. In fact, there are so many rules and exceptions to them that the courts enjoy considerable freedom to select the rules that support the interpretation a given court or judge would favor. For example, any specific rule may be avoided by declaring that it conflicts with the primary intent of the legislature. There is a subjective element to this analysis that provides a court great discretion.

Courts will ordinarily attempt to give force to legislative intent. They are assisted by a great variety of technical rules of construction that have been developed in the precedents of prior judges faced with the problem of statutory meaning. But judges differ in their thinking from legislators. They not only deal with abstract rules, but on a daily basis must also resolve difficult problems with justice and fairness. Very few judges will blindly follow a technical rule if the result would be manifestly unfair. They can justly reason that the legislature never intended an unjust result. When arguing the interpretation of a statute, a lawyer or paralegal must keep in mind the importance of persuading the court that the proposed interpretation is not only correct but also fair and just.

STATUTE AND PRECEDENT

It would be a mistake to think that the existence of a statute suspends the common law principle of precedent. While a statute may supersede a common law rule, the court's interpretation of the statute is law. When researching a case covered by statute, it is not enough to look merely to the statute. One must look at the cases that have remarked on the meaning of the statute as well as on its constitutionality. In many instances, the application of a statute to a client's case is clear; if any doubt exists, judicial decisions must be gathered.

SUMMARY

In modern times, legislation has replaced the common law as the major source of changes in the law. Legislative bodies enact laws to be applied generally to future situations rather than deciding existing disputes, which is the task of the courts. Unless they are procedurally defective or unconstitutional, statutes must be enforced by the courts without changing or distorting their language. For cases in which the application of a statute is unclear, the courts have developed a multitude of rules of construction with the purpose of ascertaining the intent of the legislature. Once a higher court has interpreted the meaning of a statute, that decision becomes precedent for it and lower courts. The legislature always has the option of rewriting the statute for clarification or revision, or if it objects to the interpretation the court has given it.

CHAPTER QUESTIONS

1. What statutes are strictly construed?
2. What is the primary goal of statutory interpretation?
3. What is the effect of a state statute found to violate the U.S. Constitution?
4. Which is more binding on a court, judicial precedent or statute?
5. What is "legislative history"?
6. Why are divorces now granted by courts rather than legislatures?

EXERCISES

1. Does your state recognize charitable immunity? If not, was it abolished and who abolished it?
2. What are the steps legislation must go through in your state legislature to become law?

PROFESSIONAL PROFILE

George Urquiola is reported to have compiled the longest legal memorandum on record, a stack of paper about five feet high regarding the DuPont Plaza hotel fire in Puerto Rico. Urquiola is one of the few paralegals around who manages teams of paralegals in major litigation cases.

Urquiola never intended to be a paralegal. He wanted to be a lawyer but thought he should find out what it would be like to work within a law firm environment. While attending the University of Central Florida, he obtained an administrative assistant position with a local law firm specializing in real estate and general litigation, performing such tasks as general office work, local filings, title searches, and maintaining the law library. As the firm's attorneys gained confidence in his abilities, Urquiola was given a wider range of responsibilities, including client interviews and research assignments.

Urquiola joined the Army, where he received intense training in legal studies. He became a staff member of the Judge Advocate General (JAG) Corps, where he worked both for the prosecution and the defense in over fifty cases.

Upon completion of his military commitment, Urquiola joined a New York firm that contained over 100 attorneys. He served as a coordinator responsible for overseeing the paralegal program, recruiting, hiring, and continuing education. While in New York, he continued his paralegal studies and received a paralegal diploma from New York University's Department of Law & Taxation.

In 1987 Urquiola joined the law firm of Maguire, Voorhis & Wells, where he works for a senior partner who specializes in mass tort and product liability cases. He assists with discovery and investigation, client interviews, drafting preliminary pleadings and the preparation of case status reports.

Urquiola is the litigation support manager in charge of organizing complex litigation cases. Good organization and management skills (along with the ability to juggle various projects in pressured and hectic situations) have afforded him the opportunity to work on high-profile cases, including the notorious DuPont Plaza fire. "I thoroughly enjoy being an important part of a very special litigation team," Urquiola says.

For the prospective paralegal, Urquiola advises that one be sure of the professional choice and commitment. "Most important, be aggressive, do not be intimidated, and believe in yourself," he says. Urquiola is married and has two children.

George Urquiola
Litigation Support Manager

CHAPTER 6
Trial and Appellate Courts

Juries are not qualified to judge questions of law, but they are very capable of judging questions of fact.

— *Thomas Jefferson*

It is no answer to say that the jury's verdict involved speculation and conjecture. Whenever facts are in dispute or the evidence is such that fair-minded men may draw different inferences, a measure of speculation and conjecture is required on the part of those whose duty it is to settle the dispute by choosing what seem to them to be the most reasonable inference. Only when there is a complete absence of probative facts to support the conclusion reached does a reversible error appear. But where, as here, there is an evidentiary basis for the jury's verdict, the jury is free to discard or disbelieve whatever facts are inconsistent with its conclusion. And the appellate court's function is exhausted when that evidentiary basis becomes apparent, it being immaterial that the court might draw a contrary inference or feel that another conclusion is more reasonable.

— Justice Murphy, **Lavender v. Kurn, 327 U.S. 645 (1946)**

THE ADVERSARY PROCESS

The American legal system is based on certain assumptions that are responsible for its organization and structure, its strengths and its weaknesses. The system is a competitive one that reflects the political process and the competitive market economy. In the legal arena, this competitive form is referred to as the *adversary process.* Any legitimate legal system must assert justice as its primary goal. Our system maintains that justice can best be achieved on the basis of rules that provide a fair procedure for those engaged in a dispute. The procedure embodies a search for truth by allowing disputing parties to present their cases through partisan, legally competent agents before an impartial tribunal. The agents are duly licensed attorneys, and the impartial tribunal is composed of a disinterested judge and a disinterested jury.

The adversary process has been likened to a game and a fight, but as a game it has serious consequences and as a fight it is controlled by numerous rules that attempt to make the fight fair and civilized. Whichever metaphor is used, the judge may be viewed as an "umpire," ensuring that the rules are followed and each party is treated with fairness.

Although there may be several parties to a lawsuit, there are only two sides. Each side is provided with equal opportunity to present its evidence and arguments and to challenge the evidence and arguments from the other side. It is to be expected that each side will present a very different picture of the dispute, but the underlying assumption is that objective observers will be able to come close to the truth of the events behind the dispute and that the judge, trained and experienced in the law, will be able to weigh the legal arguments of both sides and come to a correct application of the law in each case.

Critics of the adversary system point to certain inherent weaknesses: the partisanship of the attorneys often operates to cloud the truth rather than reveal it; judges and juries are neither objective nor totally disinterested; the competitive market model reflects a patriarchal, elitist, capitalist bias that prevents litigants from obtaining equality before the law; the system is old-fashioned, awkward, and inefficient. There is some truth to all of these criticisms, yet the Anglo-American legal system has made remarkable achievements that have been out of reach for legal systems based on a different model.

Like any human institution, the legal system has its faults, but it has within it the means to diminish or eliminate its own weaknesses. A major means of correcting mistakes in the system lies in the appellate process, which provides the opportunity to litigants to challenge the propriety of the results of trial.

FACT AND LAW

In order to understand the difference between trial and appellate courts an appreciation of the fact/law distinction is necessary. As the modern court system has developed, the functions of judge and jury have become distinct. The word trial refers to *trial of fact;* the fact-finder at trial is also called the *trier of fact.* In jury cases, the jury is the trier of fact; if there is no jury, for example if the parties have waived a jury trial, the judge, sometimes simply referred to as the court, is the trier of fact. The trier of fact determines, from the evidence presented, the facts of the case in dispute. Once the facts are determined, appropriate law is applied. Decision, declaration, and determination of the law are the sole province of the judge. The jury's fact-finding is called the *verdict,* and upon the verdict the judge makes a *judgment,* which determines the respective rights and obligations of the parties.

Facts in a legal case must be distinguished from what is considered fact in the layperson's sense of the word and from what might be considered scientific fact. While the purpose of trial is to get at facts and truth, neither of these is clear at the outset or there would be no need for a trial; if both parties agree to all the facts relevant to a case, there is nothing left to do but apply the law—no jury is necessary. In a trial, each side presents a different version of the facts. The jury, or the judge in a nonjury trial, must decide what actually happened based on inferences and conclusions drawn from the evidence. The jury (or judge) may believe one side and disbelieve the other, or it may conclude that the truth lies somewhere in between. In many cases, the truth is not readily apparent.

Sometimes the fact determinations are supported by very persuasive evidence, but sometimes they are not. Suppose, for example, two litigants were involved in a head-on collision, and each asserts that the other crossed the median line and caused the collision. Assuming one is telling the truth, how is the jury to determine the facts months after the accident? The jury would be very much aided by disinterested eye-witnesses who confirmed one version rather than the other. Expert witnesses may be called upon to reconstruct the accident by skidmarks, the position of the cars after the accident, and the nature of the injuries. But eyewitnesses and expert witnesses can be as equivocal as the participants. Jurors may rely on other inferences—the experience of the drivers, the evidence that one driver had been drinking, and the demeanor of the parties as witnesses (one may seem honest and sincere, while the other seems furtive and evasive). The absolute truth may never be known, but the jury is obliged to draw conclusions about the facts. If standards of scientific proof of fact were required, cases could not be resolved.

Under the adversary system, then, the facts are assumed to be as concluded by the trier of fact. Even though inferences drawn by the trier of fact may differ from the absolute truth, the assumption of the legal system is that when impartial, reasonable persons deliberate about the facts, their conclusions are as close to the truth as possible and that the process of arriving at the facts is fair to both parties.

Distinguishing fact from law is not a simple matter. Generally facts are concerned with what happened—answers to questions of who, when, what, and how. These are questions or issues of fact. A question of law involves the application or meaning of law. As a rule of thumb, questions of law and fact are distinguished by whether a particular question requires legal training or knowledge. For example, whether or not the defendant in an auto accident/negligence case was drinking prior to the accident is a question requiring no special legal training. A judge is no better qualified to answer that question from the evidence presented than a layperson, thus identifying this as a question of fact. On the other hand, the issue of whether or not particular evidence of the defendant's drinking is admissible in court is a question of law; the judge is trained and experienced in the rules of evidence and must decide which evidence may properly be presented and which is inadmissible.

The fact/law distinction is not only important for the assignment of labor between judge and jury; it can be critical on appeal. Once a trial has reached final judgment, a disappointed party may seek reversal on appeal. The appellate courts treat questions of law and questions of fact quite differently. Questions of law decided by

substitution of judgment
refers to the standard for appellate reversal of trial court action on questions of law. The appellate court is free to substitute its judgment for that of the trial court. Compare this with the clearly erroneous test below of judicial fact-finding. Since the appellate courts are a higher authority for statements of law, they need show no deference for rulings by the lower courts. In fact, their primary purpose is to correct improper statements of the law.

prejudicial
error refers to mistakes made at trial that are sufficiently serious to prejudice the result against one of the parties; in other words, it is sufficiently serious that, if it had not occurred, the case might have reached a different result. It is also called *reversible* or *harmful* error. Error that does not reach this degree of seriousness is called *nonprejudicial* or *harmless* error.

the trial court judge are not treated deferentially by an appellate court that disagrees. For example, if the trial judge gave the jury an instruction that the appellate court concludes was an incorrect statement of the law, the appellate court would **substitute its judgment** for that of the trial court and order a new trial if the improper instructions were **prejudicial**. Fact-finding by judge or jury, however, is treated by the appellate court with great deference and will only be overturned if it is **clearly erroneous** or without **substantial evidence** to support it. This standard makes it extremely difficult to challenge fact-finding on appeal.

Questions of law and questions of fact are not always distinct. For example, the meaning of words may be either a law or fact question. The common meaning of a word is a question of fact; the interpretation of a legal term is a question of law. While judges may not be more competent than laypersons to define "tree," "employee" may be used in either a legal sense or an everyday sense. So if "employee" is used in a statute, its meaning would seem to be a question of law. However, it may not have been used with any particular legal reference and may have been used simply as an ordinary term. Whether or not a person is an "employee" for the purposes of inclusion in the collective bargaining unit under the National Labor Relations Act could be treated as either a question of law or a question of fact. Who decides whether it is a question of law or a question of fact? The judge, of course, or as put by Isaacs: "Whether a particular question is to be treated as a question of law or a question of fact is not in itself a question of fact, but a highly artificial question of law." [22 Col. L. Rev. 1, 11-12 (1922)]

clearly erroneous and **substantial evidence** express the standard by which trial court fact-finding is measured by appellate courts. The appellate court will not reverse fact-finding unless it is clearly erroneous or there is no substantial evidence to support it. Clearly erroneous is more commonly applied; although technically speaking it applies to judicial fact-finding while substantial evidence applies to jury fact-finding, no one has ever been able to show the difference. The quote by Justice Murphy at the beginning of the chapter explains the policy basis for the test.

CASE NO. 6–1   Not Clearly Erroneous

Petitioner Anderson in the case below filed a Title VII case (Title VII of the Civil Rights Act of 1964) against Bessemer City, alleging discrimination in hiring. Ms. Anderson was the only woman applying among eight candidates for the city's Recreation Director. The committee that interviewed the candidates was composed of four men and one woman. The four men voted to offer the position to one of the male applicants; the woman voted for Ms. Anderson.

Ms. Anderson was arguably better qualified on the basis of education and experience. At trial one of the committee members acknowledged he questioned whether a woman could effectively perform the job. Another had solicited applications only from males. The District Court held that Ms. Anderson had been discriminated against on the basis of sex. The Court of Appeals reversed on the basis that the District Court's findings of fact were "clearly erroneous," and the case reached the U.S. Supreme Court on a writ of certiorari. The opinion by Justice White discusses in great detail the clearly erroneous test and the policy and rationale behind it.

The test for fact-finding at the trial level in civil cases is "preponderance of the evidence," which means that the fact-finder must weigh the evidence and find facts according to the evidence that is most persuasive. The test of fact-finding on appeal is very different than that at trial, as shown in Justice White's opinion.

The opinion refers to a common practice of trial court judges whereby they ask the attorney for the prevailing party to submit a written statement of findings of fact. It is to be expected that this submission will present a somewhat biased view of the facts, but the judge may adopt this statement verbatim in the final judicial opinion. Bessemer City argued that the trial judge acted in such a fashion, but review of the decision suggested otherwise.

PHYLLIS A. ANDERSON
v.
CITY OF BESSEMER CITY, NORTH CAROLINA
U.S. Supreme Court
470 U.S. 564 (1985)

Justice **White** delivered the opinion of the Court.

. . . .

According to the court, the vice of the procedure lay in the trial court's solicitation of findings after it had already announced its decision and in the court's adoption of the "substance" of petitioner's proposed findings.

We, too, have criticized courts for their verbatim adoption of findings of fact prepared by prevailing parties, particularly when those findings have taken the form of conclusory statements unsupported by citation to the record. [Cc.] Nonetheless . . . the findings are those of the court and may be reversed only if clearly erroneous. [Cc.]

. . . .

[Because a finding of intentional discrimination is a finding of fact] the question is whether the Court of Appeals erred in holding the District Court's finding of discrimination to be clearly erroneous.

Although the meaning of the phrase "clearly erroneous" is not immediately apparent, certain general principles governing the exercise of the appellate court's power to overturn findings of a district court may be derived from our cases. The foremost of these principles, as the Fourth Circuit itself recognized, is that "[a] finding is 'clearly erroneous' when although there is evidence to support it, the reviewing court on the entire evidence is left with the definite and firm conviction that a mistake has been committed." *United States v. United States Gypsum Co.* 333 US 364, 395, 92 L Ed 746, 68 S Ct 525 (1948). . . . If the district court's account of the evidence is plausible in light of the record viewed in its entirety, the court of appeals may not reverse it even though convinced that had it been sitting as the trier of fact, it would have weighed the evidence differently. Where there are two permissible views of the evidence, the factfinder's choice between them cannot be clearly erroneous. [Cc.]

. . . .

The rationale for deference to the original finder of fact is not limited to the superiority of the trial judge's position to make determinations of credibility. The trial judge's major role is the determination of fact, and with experience in fulfilling that role comes expertise. Duplication of the trial judge's efforts in the court of appeals would very likely contribute only negligibly to the accuracy of fact determination at a huge cost in diversion of judicial resources. In addition, the parties to a case on appeal have already been forced to concentrate their energies and resources on persuading the trial judge that their account of the facts is the correct one; requiring them to persuade three more judges at the appellate level is requiring too much. As the Court has stated in a different context, the trial on the merits should be "the 'main event'. . . rather than a 'tryout on the road.' " *Wainwright v. Sykes*, 433 US 72, 90, 53 L Ed 2d 594, 97 S Ct 2497 (1977). For these reasons, review of factual findings under the clearly-erroneous standard—with its deference to the trier of fact—is the rule, not the exception.

When findings are based on determinations regarding the credibility of witnesses, Rule 52(a) demands even greater deference to the trial court's findings; for only the trial judge can be aware of the variations in demeanor and tone of voice that bear so heavily on the listener's understanding of and belief in what is said. [C.]

. . . .

. . . Our task—and the task of appellate tribunals generally—is more limited still: we must determine whether the trial judge's conclusions are clearly erroneous. On the record before us, we cannot say that they are. Accordingly, the judgment of the Court of Appeals is reversed.

TRIALS AND TRIAL COURTS

A trial is an "on the record" evidentiary hearing. On the record refers to the requirement that the facts be determined exclusively on the basis of evidence presented at trial. Evidence of disputed facts is presented by both sides. The plaintiff attempts to establish facts substantiating claims against the defendant, and the defendant attempts to counter plaintiff's case by questioning and objecting to plaintiff's evidence as well as presenting additional evidence. Evidence takes several forms, including witness **testimony, physical evidence,** and documents. The evidence forms the "record." Naturally the jury will make factual inferences based on common sense and experience gained outside the trial, but it is improper for jurors to use knowledge of events that gave rise to the dispute acquired outside of the record. It would be improper, for instance, for a juror to visit the scene of the crime or ask questions of witnesses or bystanders.

testimony
consists of statements made by witnesses in the course of trial.

physical evidence
consists of physical objects introduced as evidence, such as a gun, a lock, drugs, etc.

CASE NO. 6–2　What Record?

What should the appellate court do when the record from the court below is insufficient? In the following case, the trial court did not provide findings of fact on which the appellate court could determine the adequacy of fact-finding. The trial court treated this case quite casually, apparently because it seemed a relatively routine exercise of the state's power to take private property for a public use ("eminent domain"). The only requirement placed on the state to obtain judicial approval was to show the property was being taken for a "public use and necessity." It is usually a fairly easy task to get this rubber-stamped by the court. Apparently the trial judge gave his reasons for denial orally but did not make them part of the record.

The STATE of Washington, Petitioner,

v.

**W. Kenneth KINGMAN and Julia E. Kingman,
his wife, et al., Respondents.**

Supreme Court of Washington,
Department 1
463 P.2d 638 (1970)

WEAVER, Judge.

By writ of certiorari, the state seeks review of an order denying its petition for an order of public use and necessity.

. . . .

It appears from briefs of counsel (a) that the land to be acquired is a 300 foot strip of waterfront approximately 150 feet wide between the public highway and Lake Chelan; . . . specifically, it is to preserve a beautiful view of Lake Chelan and the foothills beyond. Photographs illustrate the state's position.

Except for the phrase "good cause appearing," the trial court, in its order after trial, gives no reasons for denying the certificate of public use and necessity.

. . . .

Here we run into a void. For some reason, which does not appear in the record, the trial court did not make and enter findings of fact and conclusions of law.

. . . .

A judgment entered in a case tried to the court where findings are required, without findings of fact having been made, is subject to a motion to vacate within the time for the taking of an appeal. After vacation, the judgment shall not be re-entered . . .

The order denying the petition for public use and necessity is set aside; the case is remanded for further proceedings not inconsistent with this opinion.

It is so ordered.

Jury Instructions

The jury is given detailed instructions by the judge about its functions in the lawsuit. Judges vary in their explanations of the proceedings before and during the trial, but the most important instructions are given to the jury at the close of the evidence as the jury prepares to deliberate its verdict. These instructions will provide only as much explanation of the law as is needed for the jury to dispose of factual questions. For example, in a lawsuit for slander, the judge would instruct the jury about the facts it would need to find in order to hold defendant liable for slander, namely: (1) the utterance alleged to be slanderous was communicated to a third party and (2) injured the reputation of the plaintiff. In addition, the judge would instruct the jury that if it found the statement to be true, the defendant would not be liable. The jury would also be instructed on what would constitute compensation for injuries sustained. The specifics of these instructions could vary considerably from case to case.

In short, the court delineates the facts the jury must decide in making its verdict according to the nature of the case, confining the jury to its fact-finding function. When the jury reaches a consensus on the facts and presents the judge with its results, the judge makes conclusions of law and enters a judgment.

Before and during trial, the judge makes a series of decisions on the law, of which the most important concern motions to dismiss the lawsuit in favor of one of the parties, admission of evidence and the propriety of its presentation, and instructions to the jury. In each decision, the judge applies legal principles, which the judge could interpret or apply incorrectly. The correctness of the judge's rulings forms the basis for appeal.

APPELLATE COURTS

The courts above the trial court level to which appeals may be taken are called *appellate courts.* The most common arrangement in the state hierarchy echoes that of the federal court system, with an intermediate appellate court and a court of last resort (e.g., Colorado Court of Appeals, Colorado Supreme Court). Some states have a two-tiered trial court system in which one court handles cases of lesser import, often limited by a dollar amount, and misdemeanor cases, while the other court has jurisdiction over felonies and civil cases above the specified dollar amount. In this arrangement the "higher" court may serve as an appellate court for cases decided in the lower court.

Although the drama of the courtroom receives greatest attention from the media and the public, legal professionals are primarily concerned with appellate court decisions because of *stare decisis.* Trial courts interpret and apply the law, but appellate courts state the law with greater authority. Because they establish precedent for future cases, appellate courts not only settle disputes but also have an impact beyond the case at hand.

The appellate process is quite different from trial. The appellate court does not retry facts, does not call witnesses. It receives a record from the trial court, which includes a written transcript of the testimony at trial, exhibits introduced during trial, copies of the pleadings and motions filed with the court before and during trial, and written briefs submitted by the attorneys for **appellant** and **appellee** arguing the issues raised on appeal.

Attorneys for the parties are given a limited time to make oral arguments before the appellate court, during which the appellate judges may ask questions concerning the case. Deliberation of the case following oral argument is governed by the customs of the particular court, but at some point a vote is taken and usually a single judge will be assigned to write the opinion for the court in consultation with the other judges. Judges disagreeing with the result may write dissenting opinions; judges agreeing with the result may wish to add comments in a concurring opinion. There can be a considerable lapse of time between the oral argument and the issuance of a written opinion, depending largely on the complexities of the legal issues raised and the extent of disagreement among the judges.

Although the appellate court is limited to the record before it with regard to the dispute, its research of the law and its legal arguments may go beyond the cases and arguments made by attorneys for appellant and appellee in their briefs and oral arguments. Since decisions of the appellate courts may establish precedent for future cases, appellate judges are not concerned simply with resolving the dispute at hand but also with the impact of their interpretation of the law on future cases. At trial, the judge is constrained to proceed in a timely fashion, making rulings that will not delay the process and issuing a decision as soon as possible to define the rights of the parties. By contrast, the appellate process may be described as deliberative. The attorneys representing the parties have the opportunity to reflect on their arguments and craft carefully reasoned briefs, and the appellate court will take the time necessary to examine the law to write a reasoned decision. Steadily rising case loads in appellate courts have put pressure on the courts, but it is fair to say that cases of great import receive a corresponding attention by appellate courts.

Appellate courts have two primary functions in deciding appeals: (1) resolve the dispute and (2) state the law. Many cases raise minor issues, dispute well-established rules, or have no particular merit (e.g., many criminal appeals are at government expense so the convicted party has nothing to lose by appealing). When no significant issue of law is decided or if prior law is followed, many jurisdictions do not require that the opinion be published. In some instances the court will write a cursory

memorandum or **per curiam** opinion that disposes of the case without elaborate reasoning. Lengthy reasoning is reserved for cases that raise new or controversial legal issues.

Prejudicial Error

The appellate court examines the record and arguments to determine whether prejudicial, also called reversible or harmful, error occurred at the lower court level. The court does not impose an impossibly perfect standard on the trial court but must determine whether mistaken actions constitute grounds for reversal. For example, the court may conclude that one of the instructions to the jury was not an exact statement of the law but, given the facts and circumstances of the case, a precise statement of the law would not have changed the jury's verdict. This would be considered harmless error that did not prejudice the case and would not be grounds for reversal. In some instances the appellate court may agree with the trial court's result but disagree with its reasoning, in which case the court may substitute its reasoning in an affirming opinion or remand the case for the lower court to rewrite the decision in accord with the appellate court's instructions. A remand for a new decision would also be appropriate where no error was committed in fact-finding, but there was prejudicial error in application of law. For instance, the appellate court might hold that the trial court had no authority to award **punitive damages** so that portion of the decision would be deleted, leaving the award of **compensatory damages** intact.

Reversible error may or may not call for a new trial. The appellate court might find, for example, that the trial court was incorrect in ruling that the statute of limitations had not run, thereby barring further suit. The appellate court may conclude that the trial court was wrong in granting plaintiff's motion for judgment notwithstanding the verdict, the effect of which was to reject the verdict in favor of defendant and enter a judgment in favor of plaintiff; the result of the appellate reversal would be to reinstate the jury's verdict and enter a judgment in favor of defendant. On the other hand, the appellate court might find that instructions to the jury or a ruling on admissibility of evidence so prejudiced the fact-finding process that the error can only be corrected by a new trial.

In short, reversible error refers to the reversal of the *judgment* of the lower court. Since the judgment is based on findings of fact and conclusions of law, either or both could constitute harmful error, and the order of the appellate court would be designed to correct the error in the most expeditious manner.

appellant
is the party bringing the appeal; the **appellee** is the party against whom the appeal is brought.

memorandum and **per curiam**
opinions reflect unanimity of the appellate court without individual authorship. These are usually brief opinions dealing with a settled question of law not requiring lengthy explanation.

punitive damages
are sometimes awarded to punish the defendant, while **compensatory damages** are designed solely to repay the plaintiff for injuries sustained.

CASE NO. 6–3   The Missing Transcript

The defendant-appellant was convicted of second-degree murder, but a significant portion of the stenographic record of the trial was lost. Errors in serious felony cases are scrutinized much more critically than in lesser crimes and in civil cases. Defendant wanted a new trial because of the incomplete record. Defendant also challenged the jury instructions.

STATE of Kansas, Appellee,

v.

Clifton Lorrin STAFFORD, Appellant.

Supreme Court of Kansas
223 Kan. 62, 573 P.2d 970 (1977)

. . . .

The testimony comprising the state's case came from twelve witnesses. Defendant was the only person to testify on his behalf. Thirty pages of defendant's testimony were transcribed, but another fifty pages were lost. On order of the district court an attempt was made to reconstruct the missing transcript through testimony of defendant's trial attorney. The lost transcript formulates defendant's first point on appeal.

. . . .

The inability of the state to provide a full transcript of the trial proceedings does not entitle a defendant to a new trial per se. Before defendant can claim he is entitled to a new trial he must demonstrate that despite a good faith effort it is impossible to reconstruct the missing portion of the record and this precludes effective appellate review of the issues. [C.]

. . . .

The rest of defendant's claims of error relate to instructions given by the trial court. The trial court instructed on first and second degree murder and voluntary and involuntary manslaughter, using PIK (Criminal) 56.04(a)–(d). The court did not define "heat of passion" as set out in PIK (Criminal) 56.04(e). There was an instruction on the effect of voluntary intoxication. The jury was instructed on defendant's presumption of innocence, weight of the testimony of the witnesses, and the duty to reach a verdict in light of all the evidence.

It is to be noted that none of the objections to instructions now raised were presented to the trial court; therefore, our scope of review is limited to a determination of whether the instructions are "clearly erroneous." [Cc.] An instruction is clearly erroneous when the reviewing court reaches a firm conviction that if the trial error had not occurred there was a real possibility the jury would have returned a different verdict.

. . . .

We find no reversible error and the judgment is affirmed.

CASE QUESTIONS

1. Since the correctness of jury instructions is a question of law rather than a question of fact, why did the reviewing court apply the clearly erroneous test rather than substitution of judgment?
2. Was the loss of the transcript prejudicial to the defendant?

IMPACT OF THE APPELLATE SYSTEM

Appellate courts serve as a brake on the arbitrariness of trial judges as well as a forum for establishing uniformity in the interpretation of the law. The right to appeal is a fundamental custom of our legal system. Trial court judges naturally dislike being reversed, so the appellate system encourages them to conform to the law as stated by higher authority. In states having both intermediate courts and courts of last resort, a disappointed litigant has two opportunities for appellate review of the case. Courts of last resort have great discretion in choosing cases for review and decline to hear most cases. Intermediate appellate courts also have significant discretion in the cases they hear and in the attention to be given any specific case.

These factors limit the numbers of appeals, as does the cost of appeal. Not only are significant attorney's fees involved in preparing for appeal, but the cost of reproducing the trial transcript in a lengthy trial is an economic burden as well. Appeals therefore tend to involve cases in which the cost of appeal is borne by the government, as in criminal cases, or which involve substantial amounts of money. Some appeals are subsidized by outside groups that have an interest in setting a precedent or in representing appellants such as in a civil rights action. Because of these factors, appeals are not representative of the cases that go to trial.

Appellate decisions also affect lawyers, who must evaluate their client's chances by predicting the outcome of trial and appeal. Most cases are settled without going to trial or appeal; settlement is encouraged by well-established principles of law that make potential litigant's cases winners or losers. Indirectly, the costs of trial and appeal encourage litigants to realistically gauge their chances of winning and losing.

MISCELLANEOUS JUDICIAL DUTIES

In attempting to learn the law, one tends to concentrate study on appellate decisions, which provide authoritative statements of the law. Most of these are appeals from final judgments from trials, but judges engage in many other duties that consume much time and energy.

Trial Courts

Lower court judges must act on a number of problems that are not truly adversarial in nature but that require orders from a court. The advent of **no-fault divorce**, for example, has converted a formerly adversarial proceeding into one that frequently involves a judge simply approving a marital settlement agreement negotiated by the divorcing parties through their attorneys. A five- or ten-minute hearing disposes of the matter. The major purpose of no-fault divorce laws has been to diminish the adversarial aspect of divorce and give the parties rather than the court control over their destinies. Of course, if the parties cannot agree on the distribution of marital assets, alimony, and child support, the proceedings take on the former adversarial character, forcing the judge to decide these issues.

Some actions, like a legal name change, in which no defendant is involved, are rather perfunctory actions requiring a court order. Others, like **garnishment** of wages, can be adversarial but usually are not. In addition, the court must take action on issues prior to trial and enforce judgments after trial. And, depending on the jurisdiction, judges may spend a good deal of time on purely administrative duties.

Appellate Courts

In general appellate courts are responsible for overseeing the orderly process of the court system. This includes not only hearing appeals, but also ruling on requests for delays in the appellate process, staying decisions of lower courts, applications for bail, etc. Appellate courts may also be involved in matters relating to admission to the Bar and disciplinary actions.

Appellate courts also have responsibility for administrative duties managing their own activities as well as some supervisory functions over the lower courts. Onerous administrative duties are often bestowed on the chief judge of a district or circuit, or the chief justice of a supreme court. The time spent in administrative duties may be directly related to the staff available to a judge.

Unlike trials, which are conducted by a single judge, appellate proceedings involve three or more judges, usually an odd number to prevent evenly divided decisions; assignment of duties also becomes an administrative matter since someone must make the assignments.

no-fault divorce refers to recent statutory changes in the grounds for divorce. Formerly, divorce in every state was an adversarial procedure in which one spouse sued the other for divorce on the basis of fault, asserting grounds like adultery or extreme cruelty. Under no-fault divorce, the basis for the action is "marriage irretrievably broken" or "irreconcilable differences" without alleging fault. No-fault divorce generally precludes defenses by the other spouse since no fault is alleged.

garnishment is an action by which one who is owed a debt may collect payments through a third party. For instance, creditors often garnish wages, i.e., have an employer subtract part of an employee's wages for payment to the creditor.

CASE NO. 6-4 Writ of Prohibition

This case is an example of the regulatory feature of appellate courts. The newspaper in the case was charged with contempt of court for violating a "gag" order of the court in a juvenile case by publishing letters from the parents. The newspaper petitioned for a writ of prohibition, which is a common law remedy asking an appellate court to restrain a lower court from doing something it has no authority to do.

**MINNEAPOLIS STAR AND TRIBUNE COMPANY, La Crosse Tribune Company,
and Northwest Publications, Inc., Petitioners,
v.
Honorable Robert E. LEE, Judge of County Court for Houston County, Respondent.**

Court of Appeals of Minnesota
353 N.W.2d 213 (1984)

POPOVICH, Chief Judge.

FACTS

The petitioners request a writ of prohibition. In June 1984, the trial court issued an order that all parties in what was presumably a juvenile dependency case cease and desist from publishing letters or statements having to do with the proceeding. Subsequently, the minor's parents wrote two letters to the editor of a newspaper in the area. On July 27, 1984, the trial court, believing the letters to be a violation of its order, ordered a contempt hearing. . . .

ISSUE

May a court issue an order forbidding publication of information about a juvenile case obtained from involved parties and at the contempt hearing which was open to the public?

ANALYSIS

. . . .

Prior restraints of speech have long been deemed unconstitutional except in the most drastic of situations. [C.]

. . . .

Such a restraint must be "necessitated by a compelling governmental interest, and * * * narrowly tailored to serve that interest."
[C.]

. . . .

In this case, the governmental interest is not constitutional but statutory: privacy in a juvenile proceeding. It is an important and substantial government interest, but also with limits.

. . . .

In this case, there has been no showing of any illegality; the trial court simply wanted to stop people from reading about the case. [The trial court judge] said he wanted to protect the child and have a better relationship between Houston County Social Services and the parties. Such an interest does not rise to the level required to justify a prior restraint. The order violated a fundamental constitutional right. Although the court's motives were honorable, nonetheless it was a violation of a fundamental right. There is no adequate remedy at law to redress such a violation and, therefore, the writ must issue.

DECISION

The trial court's order was an unconstitutional prior restraint of speech. It is hereby vacated.

The writ of prohibition is granted.

SUMMARY

In the United States, the judicial system has a hierarchy that is divided into trial and appellate courts. The function of the trial court is to resolve disputes between parties in an adversarial process in which an impartial and disinterested judge presides over the presentation of evidence of fact by attorneys for the two sides. When a jury is present at trial, it determines issues of fact, while the judge applies the law in the conduct of the trial and in rendering a judgment on the verdict. In a nonjury trial, the judge serves as the trier of fact and then applies the law.

The distinction between law and fact is important on appeal. The appellate court does not try facts, although it is sometimes called upon to determine whether the trial record indicates that fact-finding at the trial was clearly erroneous, warranting reversal. This is a much higher standard than that the appellate court exercises in reversing application of law by the trial judge. In that case the appellate court is free to substitute its judgment for that of the lower court and need not show any deference to the lower court. As a result, most reversals are based on legal rather than factual arguments.

For an appellant to win a reversal on appeal, the appellate court must be convinced that there was reversible error at the trial level. Reversible error is a mistake in the law or the facts that was so prejudicial to appellant that a different result may have resulted if the mistake had not occurred. Minor mistakes may be deemed to be nonprejudicial or harmless error. In some cases reversible error requires a new trial, while in others the error can be corrected by the appellate court or remanded to the lower court to write a new decision and order.

The appellate process provides a means to make the actions of trial courts consistent with the law, decide new issues of law, and protect litigants from misapplication of the law.

CHAPTER QUESTIONS

1. What is the policy reason for excluding jurors from a criminal trial if they have observed the defendant being arrested on television?
2. Explain the difference between "substitution of judgment" and "clearly erroneous."
3. Why is it necessary for the judge to give jury instructions?
4. Why is there a greater proportion of criminal cases appealed than civil?

5. Why are more cases appealed on questions of law than questions of fact?
6. Does the adversarial system work?
7. Does the truth come out in the course of a trial?

EXERCISES

1. Determine for each of the following whether it is a question of law or a question of fact. One of the questions could be considered a mixed question of law and fact—can you find it?
   a. Whether the defendant was present at the crime scene.
   b. Whether the proposed evidence is irrelevant and inadmissible.
   c. Whether a juror is disqualified.
   d. Whether the defendant in an auto collision was negligent.
   e. The meaning of the premeditation requirement for a conviction of murder.
   f. Whether the defendant killed with premeditation.
   g. The meaning of "guilt beyond a reasonable doubt."
   h. Whether the defendant was "guilty beyond a reasonable doubt."
   i. The value in dollars of plaintiff's injuries.
   j. What can be considered in estimating the value of plaintiff's injuries.
2. How many appellate courts does your state have? What are their names? How many justices are there on the state's highest court?
3. How many levels of trial court does your state have, and what are they called?

PROFESSIONAL PROFILE

On the advice of her parents, Marion Gillerlain applied to the Philadelphia Institute of Paralegal Training. This advice was sound, as her paralegal degree and subsequent experience opened doors to another career.

Gillerlain landed her first paralegal job in the litigation department of a large law firm in her hometown of Kansas City, Missouri. Because of the relative newness of the profession, she had several job interviews before actually receiving an offer. Hired to work on a complex, multi-district products liability case, everything she learned was "baptism by fire." It was a great experience for her, and when she rotated off the case after three-and-one-half years, she was able to work on a variety of different matters. The most gratifying (but also the most testing) experience was when Gillerlain had to assume responsibility for preparing the exhibit and witness lists, trial exhibits, and witness files on a matter that had been pending for four years. She had but one month to prepare over 1,300 exhibits! However, because she became so familiar with those exhibits, the attorneys asked her to sit with them throughout the month-long trial. Gillerlain remained with that firm for five-and-one-half years.

Gillerlain's next firm had a reputation for its innovative paralegal program. Once again, her role was as a jurisdictional manager in yet another complex, litigious matter. She was responsible for about 300 federal and state cases, dealing with both medical and product liability aspects. The firm computerized the entire project due to the number and complexity of the cases. Between the computer usage and trial preparation, she was able to add to her skill base. Gillerlain remained with that firm for two-and-one-half years.

Today Gillerlain is an independent legal assistant. She enjoys the freedom that independent work offers. Gillerlain has the best of both worlds, especially with her other part-time work. She was asked, through a networking connection, to design and write a six hour seminar entitled "How to be a Better Legal Assistant". She is scheduled for a week at a time to do regional tours throughout the country and present the seminar. This opportunity pulls together her paralegal expertise with her public-speaking skills. "I have found throughout my travels that most of the problems that paralegals experience are relatively universal," Gillerlain says. But her message echos a one-time paralegal supervisor who always said, "A good paralegal is worth his or her weight in gold."

Marion Gillerlain
Independent Legal Assistant

CHAPTER 7
State and Federal Courts

> The government of the United States, then, though limited in its powers, is supreme; and its laws, when made in pursuance of the constitution, for the supreme law of the land, "anything in the constitution or laws of any state, to the contrary, notwithstanding."
>
> — *Chief Justice John Marshall*, M'Culloch v. Maryland *(1819)*

The United States has a unique court system. Whereas most developed countries have a hierarchical court system in which all courts are subordinate to a central supreme court, the United States has two separate court systems, federal and state, and each state is independent from every other and is free within constitutional limits to make its own laws and administer its own system of justice. This chapter discusses the interrelationships of this court system and its ramifications.

THE UNITED STATES CONSTITUTION

The U.S. Constitution allocates power between the federal and state governments. The aspects of the Constitution discussed below are far more important and complex than this summary treatment suggests, but acquaintance with certain constitutional provisions is essential for an understanding of state and federal court systems.

When the American colonies united into a federal republic, their representatives framed a charter, the United States Constitution, which allocated governmental authority between state and federal governments. The Constitution reflects a certain distrust of government based on the experience of abuses of traditional legal principles by the British colonial governors under a monarchy. Not only was there a distrust of government in general but also a degree of mutual distrust among the states due to differences in local economies (e.g., plantation economies of Virginia and the Carolinas versus commercial economies of New York, Massachusetts, and Pennsylvania) and differences in size and population (e.g., Rhode Island versus New York). As a result, the Constitution was framed to limit the power of the federal government while preserving governmental autonomy among the states.

The Constitution was viewed as a granting of power by the states to the federal government such that the federal government's powers were limited to those enumerated in the Constitution, while all other governmental authority remained in the states without need to specify that authority in the Constitution itself. This principle is embodied in the Ninth and Tenth Amendments:

AMENDMENT IX. The enumeration in the Constitution of certain rights shall not be construed to deny or disparage others retained by the people.

AMENDMENT X. The powers not delegated to the United States by the Constitution, nor prohibited by it to the States, are reserved to the States respectively, or to the people.

This language reflects that the federal government exercises its authority "by grant," while the states exercise authority "by reservation." Note that this language is the language of property law, such as when a property owner transfers or "grants" property rights to another, "reserving" those rights not granted. Like a property transaction, the grant of power is a contract between the people and the government. This is not merely a philosophical point; constitutional cases may best be conceptualized as enforcing property rights in a contractual relationship in which the federal government is bound by the original bargain.

The scope of federal control over the states can be expanded or restricted by constitutional interpretation. In the twentieth century it has been greatly expanded by a broad interpretation of the *commerce clause*, Article I, § 8, cl. 3, which gives Congress power to regulate interstate commerce. Since most business is in some way involved in interstate commerce, Congress has allowed a pervasive regulation of American business. On the other hand, in recent decades the U.S. Supreme Court has recognized inherent privacy rights into which neither the states nor the federal government may intrude, e.g., abortion rights.

Supreme Law of the Land

Article VI, Section 2, of the Constitution provides that the Constitution "shall be supreme law of the land." It was early established by the U.S. Supreme Court that this clause meant that neither state nor federal legislatures could enact laws in conflict with the Constitution, nor could any official or agency of government act in violation of the Constitution. Since the U.S. Supreme Court is the ultimate authority with regard to the interpretation of the Constitution, it can exercise significant authority over state action.

Due Process

The most important phrase in the Constitution for the operation of the legal system is the *due process clause* of the Fifth and

Fourteenth Amendments. The Fifth Amendment provides that no person "shall be deprived of life, liberty or property, without due process of law." Since this applied only to the federal government, the Fourteenth Amendment was ratified in 1868, including the language: "nor shall any State deprive any person of life, liberty, or property, without due process of law." In this way actions by state officials, legislatures, and courts become federal constitutional issues if denial of due process is alleged.

Due process is an elusive concept at best. It has been defined as requiring "fundamental fairness" in judicial process and prohibiting legislation that is "unreasonable, arbitrary, or capricious." These are subjective concepts—fairness and reasonableness are in the eyes of the beholder. What the court says is fair *is* fair, and what the court says is reasonable *is* reasonable. The principles of *stare decisis* and judicial restraint constrain judges from arbitrarily imposing their views on society, and the appellate process encourages trial court judges to stay within the bounds of established law.

Due process has been divided into *procedural* and *substantive* due process. Procedural due process treats the issues of *notice* and *hearing*. Notice requires that a person threatened with legal action or whose legal rights are being affected be notified in such a way as to be able to prepare to protect those rights. *Hearing* requires that the form and nature of legal proceedings be fundamentally fair, e.g., an impartial tribunal, right to counsel, right of cross-examination, etc. Substantive due process requires that legislation be reasonable, that it have a legitimate purpose, that it use reasonable means to effect a reasonable end, etc.

Since the fairness and reasonableness standards of due process are developed on a case-by-case basis, to understand due process one must become acquainted with the principal cases that have interpreted it. But judges tend to perceive as unfair what most citizens perceive as unfair, so the anger and frustration that a person may feel toward treatment at the hands of the law or the courts will often strike a resonant chord in the minds of judges. Whenever the government acts to the detriment of an individual, a due process argument lurks in the background.

It is not possible to catalog all the possibilities for denial of due process, but consider the following in terms of potential lawsuits against government:

1. A state university has a policy not to release course transcripts if a student has a debt outstanding to the university. George Shylock fails to be admitted to law school because his transcripts were not sent due to a $2.00 library fine he failed to pay. George had not been notified of the fine and now must wait an additional year to enter law school.

2. The Town of Uppercrust, Connecticut, passes a new zoning plan that requires residential building lots to be at least half an acre in area. Mohammed Hussein owns a lot that is four tenths of an acre, sufficient under the old ordinance for a building site, but his application for a variance (an exception to the ordinance) is denied, so he cannot build on his lot.
3. Under state law a person can be convicted of manslaughter if involved in a fatal auto accident while driving intoxicated even if the intoxication did not contribute to the accident.
4. In a rule-making hearing held by the Interstate Commerce Commission, representatives of the railroad and trucking industries are permitted to offer oral testimony of expert witnesses concerning the impact of proposed transportation regulations but are not permitted to cross-examine witnesses.

These hypothetical situations raise additional constitutional issues. The zoning case would be challenged as taking private property without just compensation; the manslaughter case would undoubtedly raise the Eighth Amendment issue of cruel and unusual punishment. Due process questions are commonly raised along with other issues.

Equal Protection

The Fourteenth Amendment also prohibits states from denying "any person within its jurisdiction the equal protection of the laws." This language was designed originally to protect former slaves from discriminatory treatment after the Civil War. Its coverage, however, has been expanded to invalidate all laws and procedures that unreasonably discriminate. It has been called upon when classes of persons have been treated unequally by the law; e.g., alimony statutes in many states provided alimony only for women, thus discriminating against men, or public schools budgeted more for male athletics than female athletic programs, discriminating against women. The discriminatory aspect of the law may be more subtle, such as when cable TV companies objected to regulation of their broadcasting that was not also applied to non-cable broadcasting. All laws by their nature discriminate—drunken-driving statutes discriminate against drinkers—but some forms of discrimination are prohibited by the law, while others are not.

Cases and Controversies

Article III of the Constitution vests judicial power in the "Supreme Court, and in such inferior courts as the Congress may from time to time ordain and establish." Article III, Section 2, refers to judicial power over "cases" and "controversies." These words have been interpreted by the U.S. Supreme Court to restrict access to the federal courts in several ways, the most important of which concerns the question of *standing*. In our legal system, not every person may seek redress for every deprivation of a legal right. Standing is a limitation on who may bring an action. In general, only a person who has a "personal stake in the outcome" of a case may bring suit. This gloss on the Constitution encourages litigants to frame their suits in terms of property rights, but even in the violation of abstract rights, such as freedom of speech, suits are limited to those persons directly affected—a person may not sue the government for the abuse of power if that abuse is unrelated to the person desiring to sue.

Case and controversy have also been interpreted as referring to actual disputes between real parties. Not every slight, rebuke, or annoyance is a legal matter. And the courts have refused to hear cases concerning remote or hypothetical questions. This does not mean that some injury or wrong must necessarily have already occurred, but there must at least be an immediate threat of invasion of a right.

CASE NO. 7–1   Georgia Football

If anyone believes that football is not taken seriously in Georgia, they should read the following case in which a high school referee's call was taken all the way to the Georgia Supreme Court.

**GEORGIA HIGH SCHOOL
ASSOCIATION**

v.

WADDELL et al.

Supreme Court of Georgia
248 Ga. 542, 285 S.E.2d 7 (1981)

. . . .

PER CURIAM.

On October 23, 1981, a football game was played between R.L. Osborne and Lithia Springs High Schools, members of region 5 AAAA established by the Georgia High School Association. The winner of this game would be in the play-offs, beginning with Campbell High School.

The score was 7 to 6 in favor of Osborne. With 7 minutes, 1 second, remaining in the game, Osborne had the ball on its 47 yard line, 4th down and 21 yards to go for a first down. Osborne punted but "roughing the kicker" was called on Lithia Springs. The referee officiating the game with the approval and sanction of the Georgia High School Association assessed the 15 yard penalty, placed the ball on the Lithia Springs 38 yard line, and declared it was 4th down and 6 yards to go.

The rules of the National Federation of State High School Associations provide that the penalty for roughing the kicker shall be 15 yards *and* 1st down. There is a dispute as to whether the Osborne coaches properly protested to the referee, before the ball was put in play, the error in the referee's failing to declare a 1st down.

From Lithia Springs' 38, Osborne punted again. Lithia Springs received the punt and drove down the field to score a field goal. Now 2 points behind, Osborne passed. Lithia Springs intercepted and scored again. The final score was Lithia Springs over Osborne, 16 to 7.

. . . .

On November 12, suit was filed in the Superior Court of Cobb County by parents of Osborne players against the GHSA. Hearing was held on November 13. The court found that it had jurisdiction, found that the referee erred in failing to declare an automatic first down, and found that a protest was lodged with the proper officials of GHSA. The court found that the plaintiffs have a property right in the game of football being played according to the rules and that the referee denied plaintiffs and their sons this property right and equal protection of the laws by failing to correctly apply the rules.

The court then entered its order on November 13 canceling the play-off game between Lithia Springs and Campbell High School scheduled for 8 p.m. that evening and ordered ". . . that Lithia Springs High School and R.L. Osborne High School meet on the football field on November 14, 1981 at an agreed upon time between the parties and resume play at the Lithia Springs thirty eight yard line with the ball being in the possession of R.L. Osborne High School and it be first down and ten yards to go for a first down and that the clock be set at seven minutes one second to play and that the quarter be designated as the fourth quarter."

Asserting that the trial court's order was erroneous under *Smith v. Crim*, 240 Ga. 390, 240 S.E.2d 884 (1977), and would disrupt the play-off games not only between Lithia Springs and Campbell but succeeding play-offs, the GHSA filed a motion for **supersedeas** in this court on November 13, 1981, and the court entered its order suspending the trial court's order, pending further order of this court.

In *Smith v. Crim, supra,* we held that a high school football player has no right to participate in interscholastic sports and has no protectable property interest which would give rise to a due process claim. Pretermitting the question of "state action" which is the threshold of the 14th Amendment, we held that Smith was not denied equal protection by the rule of GHSA there involved. Similarly we find no denial of equal protection by the referee's error here. Were our decision to be otherwise, every error in the trial courts would constitute a denial of equal protection. We now go further and hold that courts of equity in this state are without authority to review decisions of football referees because those decisions do not present judicial controversies. The stay granted by this court on November 13, 1981, is hereby reaffirmed.

All the Justices concur.

CASE GLOSSARY

supersedeas is an order commanding a trial court to delay proceedings or to stop enforcement of a trial court's order.

CASE QUESTIONS

1. Why is "state action" the threshold question for an inquiry into a denial of equal protection of the law under the Fourteenth Amendment?
2. Why did the football players have no right and no property interest to qualify for due process protection?
3. Did the players receive fair procedure?

Full Faith and Credit

Article IV of the Constitution begins: "Full faith and credit shall be given in each State to the public acts, records, and judicial proceedings of every other State." As a practical matter, this means that the courts of each state must recognize the validity of the laws and judicial orders of other states. Divorce provides a useful example. Frequently after divorce, an ex-husband ordered to pay child support or alimony moves to another state and stops making payments. The ex-wife may bring action in the state to which the former husband has moved to collect arrears in payments. In the action, the court must recognize the validity of the divorce and the order to make payments.

Full faith and credit has some limitations. A court may find that the law or court order of another state is repugnant to public policy, a rare occurrence. One state may conclude that the court of another state did not have jurisdiction over the matter in the first place. A court without jurisdiction has no authority and its orders no validity. For example, husband and wife separate and live in different states. One brings a divorce action in one state and the other in another state. Only one state should have jurisdiction—two conflicting divorce decrees make no legal or practical sense. A court may conclude that the court of another state did not have jurisdiction and refuse to enforce its orders.

This may have unanticipated results; consider the following case. A man from North Carolina obtained a "quickie" divorce in Nevada, immediately remarried in Nevada, and returned to North Carolina with his new wife. North Carolina charged and convicted him of bigamy, and the case went to the U.S. Supreme Court twice. This created the anomalous situation in which a man was a "bigamist for living in one state with the only one with whom the other state would permit him lawfully to live" [Justice Douglas, *Williams v. State of North Carolina*, 317 U.S. 287 (1942)]. The Court required North Carolina to respect the Nevada decree (with vigorous dissenting opinions). The advent of no-fault divorce has mitigated the need for divorce havens like Nevada, but jurisdictional problems can still create a tangled web in divorce cases.

SUBJECT MATTER JURISDICTION

Although jurisdiction may properly be treated as part of civil and criminal procedure, federal and state court systems are based on jurisdiction so we consider it here. The power and authority of a court in a particular dispute are based on jurisdiction. Without jurisdiction, a court has no authority; its orders are not valid. *Subject matter jurisdiction* refers to the kinds of disputes a court has the authority to decide. For example, the Constitution provides that the federal government has exclusive control over bankruptcy, **patent**, **trademark**, **copyright** and **admiralty**. A state court has no power to decide a bankruptcy case; if it should do so, its orders would have no validity.

General and Limited Jurisdiction

Courts are classified as having *general* or *limited* subject matter jurisdiction. Courts of general jurisdiction have authority to decide a wide variety of cases and apply the full range of judicial remedy and relief. Major trial courts in each jurisdiction fit into this category. However, most states have also established courts of limited jurisdiction to handle only a restricted class of cases. A probate court, for example, handles matters concerning decedents' estates (many probate courts also have jurisdiction over some areas of law relating to juveniles). Thus, a probate court does not hear cases of tenant evictions. Some states divide their courts into criminal and civil courts; Texas even divides appeals into civil and criminal appeals.

There is a wide variety of lower courts handling minor matters with limited subject matter jurisdiction; one example is small claims court (limited to cases involving a low maximum monetary amount and having limited remedial powers—it cannot grant divorces, issue injunctions, etc.). Municipal courts are common in the United States, typically handling violations of city ordinances and other minor civil and criminal matters. Many of these lesser courts are conducted with less formality than higher trial courts. Small claims courts are designed to provide litigants with an inexpensive means to resolve disputes. Lawyers do not usually participate, court reporters are usually not present (therefore no transcript is made), and court costs are minimal; the judge tends to take a more active role in the process since the litigants are unfamiliar with the technicalities of the law.

patent
 A patent is an exclusive right granted by the government to use one's invention.

trademark
 A distinctive mark in symbols or words used to distinguish the products of manufacturers or merchants.

copyright
 A right in literary property giving an author the sole privilege to copy original literary or artistic works.

admiralty
 is that branch of law pertaining to maritime commerce and navigation.

FEDERAL SUBJECT MATTER JURISDICTION

Federal jurisdiction applies to two categories of cases: (1) federal question cases and (2) diversity of citizenship cases.

Federal Question Cases

The Constitution provides that the federal courts have jurisdiction over cases arising under the Constitution, laws, and treaties of the United States. These are called *federal question* cases. A case may directly raise a constitutional issue, or it may arise under a federal statute enacted by Congress, e.g., federal civil rights violations, environmental protection issues.

Each state (and the District of Columbia) has at least one U.S. District Court, the federal trial court to which federal question cases are brought. Many cases involve both state law and federal questions and can be brought in state courts, which must then decide issues of both state and federal law. For instance, the drunken driving manslaughter case in our hypothetical situations considered earlier would begin as a state prosecution in which the defendant would raise as defense arguments based on due process and cruel and unusual punishment clauses of the U.S. Constitution as well as their counterparts in the state constitution (and factual defenses, of course). If convicted, the defendant could appeal to the state court of appeals and the state supreme court, and then petition the U.S. Supreme Court for a writ of certiorari on the federal constitutional issues.

A case originating in the federal district court will stay in the federal system even if an issue of state law must be decided. A case originating in the state courts will remain in the state court system until decided or denied consideration by the state's highest court, from which appeal is made (by way of certiorari) to the U.S. Supreme Court. A defendant may challenge federal question jurisdiction in a case in a U.S. District Court, which would force the case into state court if the challenge is successful. Similarly, a defendant may petition the U.S. District Court for removal from state court to the federal court and will succeed if the federal court concludes that the case could have been brought originally in the federal court.

Keep in mind that state courts have the final authority to declare state law, and federal courts have final authority to declare federal law. State courts will thus use federal cases to determine federal law, while federal courts will rely on decisions of state courts where state law is concerned. The exceptions to this are: (1) if state and federal laws overlap and conflict (e.g., certain state and federal labor laws may give rise to an inconsistency between them), state law must yield to federal law; and (2) any state statute or court decision that is held to be in conflict with the U.S. Constitution is invalid and without authority as to that part of it that is unconstitutional.

Diversity of Citizenship Cases

Article III of the Constitution placed suits between citizens of different states under federal jurisdiction. This jurisdiction is not exclusive, so that a plaintiff of Maryland suing a defendant from Virginia may elect to sue in a state court (most likely Virginia) or in a U.S. District Court. The differences in state citizenship are referred to as *diversity of citizenship,* and jurisdiction is based on the status of the parties without regard to the subject matter of the case, i.e., no federal law other than the diversity clause of the Constitution is required. Diversity cases have the additional requirement that the amount in controversy exceed $50,000 (recently raised from $10,000).

Diversity jurisdiction requires total diversity—if there are multiple plaintiffs or defendants and any plaintiff is a citizen of the same state as any defendant, diversity jurisdiction will be denied. Like federal question cases, a petition for removal is available to the defendant if the plaintiff elects to bring the suit in the state court. The petition, however, is not available if suit is brought in defendant's state. The rationale for this exception is based on the original purpose of the diversity clause. Apparently when the Constitution was framed, it was feared that parties might face prejudice when suing or being sued in a state other than their own. Federal jurisdiction was made available on the belief that federal courts would be less inclined to partiality. Thus, when a defendant is sued at home, the rationale for federal jurisdiction no longer holds.

Many have argued that the diversity clause no longer makes sense and unnecessarily clogs federal courts, which ought to be deciding cases of federal rather than state law.

The Erie Doctrine

In 1938, the U.S. Supreme Court decided the case of *Erie R.R. v. Tompkins,* 304 U.S. 64, which altered the nature of diversity cases forever. Tompkins was injured by a train while walking along a path beside the railroad tracks when an open door on a refrigerator car hit him. Tompkins brought a diversity case in federal court and was awarded $30,000 in damages. The Second Circuit

CASE NO. 7–2 Two Cases in Two Courts

In the *Fine* case, both sides filed suit on the same day, one in state court and one in federal court. As the case indicates, a corporation may be a "citizen" of more than one state for the purposes of diversity jurisdiction. While a defendant sued in state court may petition for removal to federal court, claiming diversity jurisdiction, a defendant sued in federal court in a diversity case may move to remand back to the state court, claiming a lack of diversity jurisdiction.

William M. FINE, et al., Plaintiffs,
v.
DELALANDE, INC., Defendant.
United States District Court,
S.D. New York
545 F.Supp. 275 (1982)

BRIEANT, District Judge.

This lawsuit began on April 1, 1982, in the New York Supreme Court, New York County, the same day on which the defendant Delalande, Inc. filed an action in this Court against the plaintiffs herein based upon claimed diversity of citizenship. [C.] Delalande removed this action from the state court on April 20, 1982, pursuant to 28 U.S.C. § 1441(c).

By motion docketed May 5, 1982, the *Fine* plaintiffs seek the remand of this action to the state court as improvidently removed, because Delalande, Inc. is a citizen of New York by reason of its principal place of business of this state.

For purposes of 18 U.S.C. § 1441, a corporation is deemed to be a citizen of the state wherein it has its principal place of business, and of the state of its incorporation. 28 U.S.C. § 1332(c).

For reasons discussed more fully in this Court's Memorandum and Order of this date in the companion *Delalande* action, 545 F.Supp. 268, familiarity with which is assumed, this Court finds that Delalande has its principal place of business in New York. Accordingly, there is not complete diversity because at least eleven of the plaintiffs are also citizens of New York.

Plaintiff's motion to remand this action to the state court is granted.

Court of Appeals affirmed the award, but the railroad petitioned and received certiorari from the U.S. Supreme Court.

At issue was the substantive law to be followed in a diversity case. The trial judge instructed the jury that the railroad was liable under general law if the jury found simple negligence. The railroad argued from the beginning that the common law of Pennsylvania, the site of the injury, should apply. Under Pennsylvania law, Tompkins would be considered a trespasser since he was walking on the railroad's right of way, so the railroad would not be liable to a trespasser on the basis of ordinary negligence but only if the jury found gross negligence, i.e., wanton and reckless misconduct.

Section 34 of the Federal Judiciary Act of 1789 had provided for the recognition and application of state common law in appropriate cases, but in *Swift v. Tyson*, 41 U.S. 1 (1842), the court had held that the federal courts were free to disregard specific decisions of state common law in favor of general principles of common law.

The effect of *Swift v. Tyson* was to encourage the creation of a general federal common law that could differ significantly from the law of a particular state. This would encourage litigants for whom diversity jurisdiction was available to select the court, state or federal, in which they would have the greatest likelihood of success, precisely what Tompkins' lawyers did. In *Erie* the Supreme Court overruled *Swift v. Tyson* and declared that, henceforth, the federal courts in diversity cases would follow the common law of the state.

Mr. Tompkins lost his case.

Erie has been applied to substantive law but not procedure—when suing in federal court, federal procedure is followed.

CASE NO. 7–3   The Erie Axe Falls

In the following case, like the *Fine* case above, the principal issue is diversity jurisdiction. Once the court determines it has jurisdiction, the case is summarily dismissed by interpreting state law as *Erie* requires. Plaintiff is suing for wrongful discharge, but she is an "at-will" employee, which means that she does not have an employment contract that guarantees a period of employment, so she can be discharged at any time.

Some states allow suits for wrongful discharge for at-will employees; Missouri does not. Why is the plaintiff trying desperately to get into a Missouri state court? The answer may lie in the *Erie* doctrine itself. While the federal court in a diversity case will be extremely reluctant to upset established Missouri precedent, the plaintiff might be able to persuade a Missouri court to overrule precedent in light of a trend in other states to recognize an action for wrongful discharge of an at-will employee.

Deborah BROWN, Plaintiff,
v.
SOUTHLAND CORPORATION, et al., Defendants.
United States District Court,
E.D. Missouri, E.D.
620 F.Supp. 1495 (1985)

GUNN, District Judge.

. . . .

Plaintiff, a resident of Missouri, brought this action for damages in the Circuit Court of the City of St. Louis against Southland Corporation, a Texas corporation, and Clyde Tinsley, a resident of Missouri.

The action arises out of the circumstances surrounding plaintiff's discharge from defendant Southland Corporation's (Southland) employment. Plaintiff was employed as the store manager of a "7-Eleven" store owned by defendant Southland at the time of her discharge in May 1980. Plaintiff alleges that she was wrongfully discharged pursuant to a corporate policy implemented to cover-up top-level employees' negligence. . . .

Title 28 U.S.C. § 1441(b) gives a defendant who meets certain requirements the right to remove a civil action from a state court to a federal district court on the basis of diversity of citizenship. The requirement of complete diversity between plaintiffs and defendants is fully applicable to § 1441(b). A federal court, however, will not allow removal to be defeated by the collusive or fraudulent joinder of a resident defendant. . . .

In the present action, plaintiff's complaint alleges that Tinsley was the zone manager with ultimate supervisory responsibility over the store where plaintiff worked. In support of his removal petition, defendant Tinsley submitted affidavits and plaintiff's own deposition statements to the effect that at the time of the occurrences alleged in plaintiff's complaint, he was not the zone manager of the district in which plaintiff's store was located and that he had no involvement in the said occurrences. Plaintiff states in her deposition that she never spoke with defendant Tinsley. Plaintiff has not disputed this evidence. The Court concludes that defendants have met their burden of proving that defendant Tinsley was improperly joined and dismisses him pursuant to Rule 21, Fed.R.Civ.P. Accordingly, plaintiff's motion to remand is denied.

The next matter for consideration is defendants' motion to dismiss for failure to state a claim. Plaintiff does not allege any contractual or statutory provision that would bar her termination. In Missouri, it is firmly established that an at-will employee cannot maintain an action for wrongful discharge. . . .

. . . The above rulings dispose of all claims in plaintiff's complaint against each defendant. Judgment for defendants.

Bankruptcy

Bankruptcy comes within the exclusive authority of the federal courts because of the provision in the U.S. Constitution, Article I, Section 8, Clause 4, which grants to Congress the power "to establish . . . uniform rules on the subject of bankruptcies throughout the United States." Bankruptcy is a means by which an individual or business (or even a municipality) may resolve the problem of overindebtedness. When debts accumulate to the point that they exceed the debtor's ability to pay (insolvency), bankruptcy is a way to resolve financial distress. It has particular importance to the paralegal field because so much of the work involves administration, preparation of forms and documents, and organization of the bankruptcy process. Although attorneys must advise concerning the initial choice to file for bankruptcy, once the process starts, most of the work follows an orderly procedure often somewhat mechanical and clerical in nature. There are many paralegals specializing exclusively in bankruptcy, and for that reason it is given special attention here.

The underlying rationale behind bankruptcy is to provide relief for the insolvent debtor and to protect creditors by gathering the debtor's assets and distributing them equitably to the creditors. Although the law strongly favors the full payment of legal debts, individuals and businesses frequently find themselves in a position in which they have no reasonable prospect of becoming solvent and so must default on debts. At that point the debtor or the creditors may decide that the only reasonable method of resolving the problem is to file for bankruptcy, which settles the debts at less than their full value. The old English solution of casting the debtor into prison has been discarded. While imprisonment may satisfy some creditors' desire for punishment, an imprisoned debtor cannot contribute either to paying past debts or to returning to productivity. Nor is insolvency usually the product of bad faith or wrongdoing. Recession, unemployment, and other catastrophes are as much responsible for insolvency as misuse of other people's money.

Current bankruptcy law is based on the Bankruptcy Reform Act of 1978, which forms Title 11 of the United States Code. Individual and commercial bankruptcies fall within Chapters 7, 11, and 13 of Title 11 (the chapters are odd-numbered, Chapter 9 deals with municipalities) and are commonly referred to simply as "Chapter 7," "Chapter 11," etc.

Most bankruptcies are voluntary, i.e., the debtor files the petition. Petitions brought by creditors forcing a debtor into bankruptcy are referred to as *involuntary bankruptcy*. Chapter 7 and Chapter 11 petitions may be either voluntary or involuntary, but Chapter 13 proceedings may only be voluntary.

Chapter 7 is titled "Liquidation," which refers to the process of collecting the debtor's assets and distributing them (or the proceeds from their sale) to creditors. A trustee in bankruptcy is appointed to assume control of and distribute the debtor's assets. The trustee has the duty of establishing which claims are valid and payable and of distributing assets according to priorities established by law. Many forms of property interests are exempted from inclusion in the assets, such as $1200 equity in one motor vehicle and child support payments. Some debts may not be discharged in bankruptcy, such as certain taxes, alimony, and child support. Once the trustee has collected nonexempt property and paid nondischargeable debts, the remainder of the assets, if any, are distributed to creditors and the debts are discharged—a bankrupt individual is no longer legally indebted for discharged debts. Discharge is subject to a number of conditions, one of which is that the bankrupt has not been granted a discharge in bankruptcy within the prior six years.

Chapter 11, titled "Reorganization," is designed principally to save failing business organizations such as corporations and partnerships. Many businesses become financially distressed but are nevertheless worth saving. Liquidation of the business could do much more damage to owners, creditors, and employees than attempting to reorganize the business. Chapter 11 requires that the debtor propose a plan of reorganization, which is subject to acceptance by classes of creditors and classes of interests (e.g., stockholders). Ultimately, the Court must decide whether the plan is satisfactory, whether it meets the requirements of the law, and whether acceptance by classes of claims and classes of interests is sufficient. Confirmation of the plan entitles the debtor to a new start, subject to the specific requirements imposed by the decree of the Court. Not all Chapter 11 plans are approved, and not all reorganizations result in successful operations.

Chapter 13, titled "Adjustment of Debts of an Individual with Regular Income," is a voluntary petition designed to defer payments on debts in order to pay them in full under a plan proposed by the debtor and confirmed by the Court. As its title suggests, Chapter 13 applies to individuals and one-owner businesses (sole proprietorships) who are not presently able to pay debts but who have a source of income indicating a future ability to pay. The plan must meet certain statutory requirements, and creditors have the opportunity to accept or reject the plan, though the Court has the authority to confirm or reject the plan. Under Chapter 13, creditors should receive more than they would under a Chapter 7 liquidation and may ultimately receive payment in full.

The effect of both voluntary and involuntary petitions is to prevent creditors from bringing or continuing suits to enforce debt. Because of this feature, bankruptcy has occasionally been used as a strategy to stave off enforcement of debts. For example, when Texaco lost a ten-billion-dollar judgment to Pennzoil, Texaco filed for bankruptcy, eventually settling for four billion dollars; a few years later Texaco was more profitable than ever. It is doubtful that Texaco was ever seriously in danger of going out of business. Frank Lorenzo used bankruptcy to fend off attempts by the unions at Eastern Airlines to take over the company. Eastern, however, was in far more severe financial straits than Texaco had been, and its fortunes proceeded steadily downward.

CONFLICT OF LAWS

Separate state jurisdictions within one nation have also presented a special problem called *conflict of laws* or *choice of law*.

Suppose two Connecticut residents are involved in an auto accident in Massachusetts. With a Connecticut plaintiff and a Connecticut defendant, suit is logically brought in Connecticut, although it could be brought in Massachusetts where the accident occurred. Should Connecticut or Massachusetts law apply? This is a conflict of laws problem. Whatever state is chosen for the suit, the *forum* state, its procedural laws will be followed; but there may arise a question of which forum's substantive law should apply. In some respects this parallels the issue in *Erie*: the result of the lawsuit should not depend on the choice of the forum. Because of differences in state law, a defendant may be liable in one state but not in another so that the residence of the defendant becomes the determining factor in the result.

Conflict of laws rules resolve this problem to some extent. Each state has its own rules to decide the choice of law. If the Connecticut plaintiff sues in Connecticut, Connecticut choice of law must apply. Assuming that Connecticut is in no way involved with the accident (i.e., the accident and its causes occurred wholly within Massachusetts), the substantive law of Massachusetts would apply, just as it would if the case were brought in Massachusetts. Connecticut law would require that the substantive law of Massachusetts govern the outcome of the case.

There is logic to this result. Whether conduct is wrongful should be determined by the law of the place where it occurs. The Connecticut driver in Massachusetts must obey Massachusetts law. To illustrate, many states allow a driver to turn right at a red light after stopping and determining it is safe to turn. Suppose a resident of such a state follows this custom in a state that does not allow turning on red. It would certainly be no defense, either civil or criminal, that the driver's home state has a different rule. Suppose that the turn on red caused an accident and suppose that an injured party sued the nonresident in his home state. Should defendant's conduct be judged differently because it is legal in his home state, the state where the suit was brought? No, wrongful conduct should not be magically transformed into proper conduct by the choice of the forum.

Unfortunately, conflict of laws is not always this simple. Suppose, for example, that the two drivers were crossing the Connecticut–Massachusetts border as the accident occurred. The wrongful act of one driver may have occurred in Connecticut but the injuries inflicted in Massachusetts. Choice of law will depend on the conflict of laws principles of the forum state. In tort cases like an auto accident, two rules are generally applied. The ancient rule, *lex loci delicti*, or "the law of the place of the wrong," holds that choice of law will fall on the site of the last act necessary to make the actor liable, i.e., where the tortious act is complete. In recent times another test, called the *significant relationship test,* has been adopted in many states. Under this test, all the circumstances of the tort are considered in deciding which state has the greatest connection with the wrong.

Contract cases present far more problems for conflict of laws. As a somewhat absurd, but not impossible, example, consider the following:

> Two corporations with nationwide activities negotiate a complex contract. One corporation is incorporated in California, the other in New York. The contract is negotiated and signed in Illinois. The contract is to be performed primarily in Texas but is breached in Louisiana. The contract specifically provides, "in case of breach, this contract will be construed under the law of Michigan." The California corporation sues the New York corporation in New Jersey, its principal place of business.

Theoretically, the law of one of several states might be chosen. If suit is brought in New Jersey and the New Jersey court agrees that it has jurisdiction, the choice of law would depend on New Jersey rules on conflict of laws. New Jersey conflict of laws may be very different from those of Texas or Illinois. Most states give great weight to the agreement of the parties to specify the law that governs, here that of Michigan. But many contracts are silent in this regard, and there may be policy reasons for not enforcing that part of the contract.

There are several conflict of laws principles with regard to contracts, and frequently different rules apply to different circumstances. Like torts, there has been a strong trend toward the significant relationship test, which aims at choosing the state having the greatest connection with the contract. Except for those rare experts on conflict of laws, anyone with a problem in this area can anticipate doing considerable research. To achieve the best results, one should consider which state's law might apply; which would be most favorable; and which of the possible forum states has conflict rules that would invoke the favorable state's law.

LAW AND EQUITY

History has left the American legal system with an arbitrary division of remedies into *legal* and *equitable. Legal* remedies refer to relief granted by common law courts, and equitable remedies to those afforded by courts of equity, also called chancery. Although this subject is usually treated under the heading of remedies, it is

CASE NO. 7–4 The Lost Manuscript

In the following case, a conflict of laws problem becomes a pivotal issue since the plaintiff might well lose in New York and win in Illinois. Note that the case was filed in a federal court in New York, which under *Erie* followed New York law, specifically New York conflict of laws, to determine whether New York or Illinois law should apply. This case was decided in the days before xerography and word processing. Today the court might hold the plaintiff contributorily negligent for not making a copy of the valuable lost manuscript.

Although the court does not discuss these in detail, it uses two of the traditional bases for choice of law in contract cases: (1) the place where the contract was made, and (2) the place where the contract was performed.

NEWMAN
v.
CLAYTON F. SUMMY CO.
Circuit Court of Appeals, Second Circuit
133 F.2d 465 (1943)

FRANK, Circuit Judge.

Appellee, a composer, sent a manuscript, insured for $500, by Railway Express from Florida to appellant, a music publisher, in Chicago. Appellant later procured appellee's permission to send the manuscript to appellant's New York office. But, unknown to appellee, appellant, in shipping the script to New York, also by Railway Express, described the package as containing merely "sheet music." The script was lost in transit. Appellee, having retained no copy, spent considerable time in reproducing the script and later contracted with another publisher who published it under a royalty agreement.

. . . .

The manuscript had no market value and was unique, so that it was proper to measure its value by the reasonable worth of the time and effort spent by appellee in reproducing it. On the basis of evidence, the verdict was not excessive. And appellee's failure to keep a copy of her script did not bar recovery. . . .

. . . .

Appellant asserts that the trial judge erred in instructing the jury as follows: "What is the duty which the bailee, the Summy Company, owed to the bailor, Miss Newman? Being a bailee, the Summy Company owed the plaintiff the duty of exercising reasonable care in handling her manuscripts and in dealing with her manuscripts * * * Negligence is usually defined in these words: Negligence is the failure to exercise a care commensurate to the hazard. That is, the amount and kind of care that would be exercised by an ordinarily prudent person in the same or similar circumstances, or that degree of diligence which the manner and the nature of the employment make it reasonable to expect. The question, therefore, that you must decide is whether the defendant failed in its duty to observe that degree of care in looking after the manuscript which had been entrusted to it." Appellant maintains that the judge should have instructed the jury that it was not liable unless it was grossly negligent because, appellant claims under Erie R.R. v. Tompkins, 304 U.S. 64, 58 S.Ct. 817, 82 L.Ed. 1188, 114 A.L.R. 1487, New York law governs. By the law of New York where the trial was held, appellant was a gratuitous bailee, and a gratuitous bailee is not liable except for gross negligence. There is, however, no need for us to consider what would be the law of New York applicable to such a transaction occurring in New York, for here we must apply the New York doctrine of conflict of laws and that doctrine is to the effect that the applicable legal rules are those of Illinois. There can be no doubt that the arrangements for the bailment were made in Illinois, and that "performance," i.e., the shipment of the manuscripts, occurred in that state. In such circumstances, the New York courts hold that the Illinois law as to bailments should be applied. [Cc.]

Turning then to the Illinois decisions, it appears that the rule is that, regardless of whether or not there was a gratuitous bailment or one for "mutual benefit," the bailee must use the same care as he would with respect to his own property; there is no discussion of "gross negligence". . . .

The instruction given by the trial court in the instant case was not literally in accord with the language used in those cases. Perhaps the differences are not substantial. But even if they are, that is of no import, since, in the trial court, appellant did not except to the instruction on the ground of any such differences but only because of the failure to give instructions as to gross negligence. Accordingly there was no reversible error.

The judgment of the trial court is affirmed.

related to jurisdiction since many states restrict equitable jurisdiction to their highest trial courts.

The existence of legal and equitable remedies can be adequately understood only in historical context. Anglo-American law began with the administrative organization of England in the aftermath of the Norman Conquest. Although the Normans left local tribunals in operation, often applying principles of former English law, the organization of a centralized kingdom included the establishment of laws common to the entire kingdom, hence the name common law. Courts were established that had jurisdiction over the common law. In these courts, actions were initiated by *writs*, a word that does not have an exact counterpart in modern law. A writ stated a cause of action, so it is similar to a modern pleading called a *complaint*. But writs had specific names, such as the writ of trespass *quare clausum fregit*, which corresponds to our modern cause of action for trespass to land, or the writ *de ejectione firmæ*, corresponding to modern ejectment or eviction. The writs were essentially formulas applied to recognized legal wrongs, almost like a catalog of actions in which a party would fill in the blanks. Each action was required to fit precisely into a specific writ. In the first years of the common law courts, new writs were constantly created as different disputes arose that varied from already established actions. Gradually, however, the system crystallized, and the common law court became formal and rigid, resisting the establishment of new writs so that novel cases that did not fall within established writs were rejected by the courts.

This development did not leave litigants without a remedy, however, since from the beginning subjects of the kingdom enjoyed the right of petitioning the king for justice. As more and more cases arose that were not recognized by the common law courts, parties sought relief from the king, who then presented these cases to the chancellor, originally an ecclesiastical office staffed by priests—not to be confused with ecclesiastical courts under the authority of the Church that applied the principles of canon law. Because of a gradually mounting case load, Chancery developed its own courts independent of the common law courts and referred to as courts of equity. Courts of law and equity existed side by side until recent years when the states merged law and equity into a single court having authority to order both legal and equitable remedies. Despite the merger, features of the historical differences between the two courts remain of importance in modern legal practice.

Courts of equity treated the cases before them somewhat differently than the common law courts. Since petitions in equity sought special justice and presented novel situations, equity courts enjoyed greater flexibility and discretion than common law courts. The object of equity was to provide relief appropriate to merits of the case, so courts of equity were described as *courts of conscience*, governed by the moral issues of the case rather than *stare decisis*. Theoretically this is still true today, a judge sitting in equity is not bound by precedent. As a practical matter, modern judges rule in equity on the basis of precedent and expect attorneys to provide precedental authority in their arguments. Nonetheless, since judges sitting in equity have great discretion and are not strictly bound by precedent, appeal from a case in equity is frequently premised on the charge of "abuse of discretion" by the lower court judge. If a judge departs from well-established principles of equity as revealed by prior cases, an appellant may use this effectively to persuade an appellate court that the lower court judge abused discretion.

Jury Trials

Since courts of equity exercised moral authority and originally were cloaked with the spiritual authority of the clergy, juries were deemed unnecessary and inappropriate. This custom remains today; there is no right to a jury trial in a case seeking equitable relief alone. The merger of law and equity compounds the jury question since both legal and equitable remedies may be sought in the same suit, and legal as well as equitable issues may be raised in a suit for equitable relief.

CASE NO. 7–5 Right to a Jury

The following case discusses in some detail the right to a jury trial and the test for determining whether it holds in the context of the modern merger of law and equity.

DEBORAH LESLIE, LTD., Plaintiff,

v.

RONA, INC. and Erwin Rona,
Defendants.

United States District Court,
D. Rhode Island
630 F.Supp. 1250 (1986)
MEMORANDUM AND ORDER

SELYA, District Judge.

. . . .

The seventh amendment to the federal Constitution is the touchstone of any reasoned analysis anent the availability of civil jury trials in the federal courts. The seventh amendment intones:

> In suits at common law, where the value in controversy shall exceed twenty dollars, the right of trial by jury shall be preserved, and no fact tried by a jury, shall be otherwise reexamined in any Court of the United States, than according to the rules of the common law.

As is clear from the text, the Framers preserved the right to jury trial in all suits at common law. Their basic purpose was to maintain the right to a jury trial as it existed when they adopted the amendment in 1791. [Cc.] Because the seventh amendment speaks in terms of preserva-

tion, an historical test has been employed to determine its application. Suits in which traditionally legal rights were to be heard and determined have been jury-eligible; those wherein predominantly equitable remedies were to be administered were thought triable to the court. [C.]

The proposition, however, is more easily stated than applied. The dividing line does not depend on the character of the overall action, but instead is determined by "the nature of the issue to be tried." [C.] An issue is considered "legal" when its resolution involves the ascertainment and determination of legal rights or when it justifies a remedy traditionally granted by common law courts. [Cc.] An "equitable" issue is one where, whether because of the inadequacy of conventional legal remedies or the need to defeat special kinds of unfairness, courts of chancery have historically intervened. [Cc.] . . . Howsoever the standard is phrased, the balance is tilted in favor of trial by jury. [C.] . . .

[The opinion then addresses the difficult issue of the availability of a jury in a case founded on a cause of action based on a federal statute where Congress has been silent concerning the right to a jury. The court rules in favor of Defendant's demand for a jury trial, applying a test set out by the U.S. Supreme Court in *Ross v. Bernard*, 396 U.S. 531 (1970).]

The Supreme Court has provided direction in these precincts by way of a tripartite test. *Ross*, 396 U.S. at 538 n. 10, 90 S.Ct. at 738 n. 10. In the absence of explicit congressional guidance, a court should consider the following factors to determine if a given case or issue implicates seventh amendment concerns: (i) customs prevailing before the merger of law and equity, (ii) the nature of the remedy sought, and (iii) the practical abilities and limitations of juries. *Id.* The burden of *Ross* is, in effect, to make a "what if?" analysis: had the issue arisen before the historic distinction between law and equity became blurred, which "side" of the tribunal would have entertained it? [C.] And, in so doing, the court must factor into the calculus such practical restrictions upon the perceived abilities of jurors as it may deem relevant.

Adequacy of Remedy at Law

Equitable jurisdiction was always discretionary. Since equity courts were originally established to provide remedies when the common law was unavailing, the equity courts refused to hear cases if there was an adequate remedy at law. This became the threshold question in every equity action. The usual common law remedy is *damages*, specifically, monetary compensation for an injury or wrong. There are a number of specific common law remedies such as **replevin** and **ejectment**; various extraordinary remedies titled *writs* (e.g., **writ of mandamus**, writ of prohibition) are common law remedies.

In order to invoke the equitable jurisdiction of the court the claim must be based on some special feature that monetary compensation will not redress. The most common request for equitable relief is for an *injunction*, most commonly a prohibitory injunction, which asks the court to order someone *not* to do something. Injunctions are based on an alleged threat of imminent irreparable injury, asking equity to prevent the injury rather than waiting for the injury to occur and then suing for damages. Affirmative injunctions requiring a party to act, e.g., requiring a school to desegregate, are less common because of enforcement problems.

Inadequacy of legal remedy is often asserted when the subject matter of a contract is unique or irreplaceable. For example, if someone has made a contract to purchase and the seller refuses to deliver the goods, the remedy of specific performance may be sought on the grounds that the goods have some unique quality, such as a family heirloom or a one-of-a-kind classic car. Real property, i.e., land and its improvements, has long been regarded as unique, making available the remedy of specific performance for contracts for the sale of real property.

replevin
is a common law cause of action to recover personal property wrongfully possessed by another person.

ejectment
is a common law cause of action to recover possession of real property.

writ of mandamus
is an order requiring a public officer to perform a duty.

CASE NO. 7–6 In the Days Before Food Coloring

Campbell Soup Co. had a practice of making output contracts with farmers, providing seed and agreeing to purchase the entire crop at prices fixed in advance. The Wentz brothers were Pennsylvania farmers who grew Chantenay carrots for Campbell. During the 1947 season, because of the scarcity of these carrots, the price per ton rose to $90. Since the contract price was $30, the Wentz brothers were not eager to honor the contract and sold 62 of their 100 tons of carrots to Lojeski, who sold half of them to Campbell. Ordinarily, Campbell could pursue a legal remedy by purchasing the carrots elsewhere at the market price and suing for the difference between the market and contract price and so receive the benefit of its bargain. Unfortunately, the carrots were unavailable on the market. Campbell was also undoubtedly concerned about the possibility of other farmers under contract acting similarly in the future and so brought a suit for specific performance, an equitable remedy asking the court to order performance of the contract.

CAMPBELL SOUP CO.
v.
WENTZ et al.

CAMPBELL SOUP CO.
v.
LOJESKI
United States Court of Appeals,
Third Circuit
172 F.2d 80 (1948)

GOODRICH, Circuit Judge.

. . . .

On January 9, 1948, Campbell, suspecting that defendant was selling its "contract carrots," refused to purchase any more, and instituted these suits against the Wentz brothers to enjoin further sale of the contract carrots to others, and to compel specific performance of the contract. . . .

We think that on the question of adequacy of the legal remedy, the case is one appropriate for specific performance. It was expressly found that at the time of the trial it was "virtually impossible to obtain Chantenay carrots in the open market." This Chantenay carrot is one which the plaintiff uses in large quantities, furnishing the seed to the growers with whom it makes contracts. It was not claimed that in nutritive value it is any better than other types of carrots. Its blunt shape makes it easier to handle in processing, and its color and texture differ from other varieties. The color is brighter than other carrots. It appears that the plaintiff uses carrots in 15 of its 21 soups. It also appeared that it uses these Chantenay carrots diced in some of them and that the appearance is uniform. . . .

The trial court concluded that the plaintiff had failed to establish that the carrots, "judged by objective standards," are unique goods . . . that the test for specific performance is not necessarily "objective" is shown by the many cases in which equity has given it to enforce contracts for articles—family heirlooms and the like—the value of which was personal to the plaintiff.

. . . Here the goods of the special type contracted for were unavailable on the open market, the plaintiff had contracted for them long ahead in anticipation of his needs, and had built up general reputation for its products as part of which reputation uniform appearance was important. We think if this were all that was involved in the case, specific performance should have been granted.

The reason that we shall affirm instead of reversing with an order for specific performance is found in the contract itself. We think it is too hard a bargain and too one-sided an agreement to entitle the plaintiff to relief in a court of conscience. . . . This form has quite obviously been drawn by skillful draftsmen with the buyer's interests in mind.

[The Court then discusses the contract paragraph by paragraph, demonstrating that it gives Campbell numerous powers and protections while affording no protection to the farmers and concludes the contract is "unconscionable."]

. . . That equity does not enforce unconscionable bargains is too well established to require elaborate citation.

. . . As already said, we do not suggest that this contract is illegal. All we say is that the sum total of its provisions drives too hard a bargain for a court of conscience to assist.

The judgments will be affirmed.

Clean Hands Principle

Although equity is not bound by *stare decisis,* a number of principles of equity have developed over the years expressed in the form of equitable maxims. One has already been discussed: equity will not intervene if there is an adequate remedy at law. Other maxims reflect the moral basis for equitable relief, one of the important maxims being the *clean hands doctrine.* Since equity is a court of conscience based on moral principles and dispenses special justice, an equity court may refuse to give relief if the petitioner has not acted in good faith or is otherwise undeserving of special consideration.

CASE NO. 7–7 Family Feud

The *Dixon* case below represents an application of the clean hands doctrine. Mother (Dixon) conveyed twelve acres of land to Chapman, who used the property as collateral for a loan to start a restaurant. Mother and Son (Murphy) assumed Chapman's loan and paid it, at which time Chapman conveyed the property to Son. Meanwhile, Mother declared bankruptcy without indicating any interest in the land. After her assets had been distributed in the bankruptcy proceeding to her creditors, Mother asked Son to reconvey the property, or part of it, to her. Son refused and Mother sued and was awarded two of the acres with a home on it. Mother appeals; Son cross-appeals.

DIXON et al.

v.

MURPHY,

MURPHY

v.

DIXON

Supreme Court of Georgia
259 Ga. 643, 385 S.E.2d 408 (1989)

WELTNER, Justice.

. . . .

2. Murphy's defense includes his contention that his mother is barred by the doctrine of unclean hands from seeking equitable relief. We agree.

    The evidence is undisputed that Dixon has completed a fraud upon her creditors, by:

    (a) swearing in the bankruptcy court that she owned *no* interest in the property;

    (b) failing to amend her bankruptcy petition to disclose the interest that she now claims; and

    (c) obtaining the discharge of all of her scheduled debts—notwithstanding that, according to her, she owned twelve acres of land during the pendency of the bankruptcy proceeding.

3. (a) What is presented here is more than a case of silence and inaction evidencing intent to defraud; it is a case of success in defrauding. By extending to her the relief that equity reserves for those whose hands are clean, we can only serve to encourage others to make (or to *say* that they have made) hidden trusts, and then deny their existence in bankruptcy.

    (b) The justice system cannot permit itself to become an implement of fraud. The judgment in Case No. S89A0231 is affirmed insofar as it vests title to any of the property in Murphy.

4. As to Murphy's cross-appeal (Case No. S89X0249), we are aware of no authority that vests in a trial court the power to make equitable distribution in a case of unclean hands. Accordingly, that portion of the judgment awarding the smaller parcel of property to Dixon is reversed.

[The dissenting opinion by Justice Gregory questions the fact-finding by the majority and points out the absurdity of the final result:]

. . . Murphy, who paid nothing for the property, now has it all. Dixon, who acquired it twice, paying close to $21,000 the second time, now has nothing. Dixon's fight is not with her creditors, but with Murphy. The creditors, whom the majority thinks were defrauded, also now have nothing, and Murphy, who failed to keep his promise to his mother, gets it all.

Statutes of Limitation and Laches

Another difference between legal and equitable remedies arises in the context of delay in bringing suit. Common law actions may be barred by statutes of limitation. Each state has legislated that suits must be brought within a certain period of time, usually measured in years. Some statutes creating causes of action fix the period within which suit can be brought. Unless the state legislature has otherwise specified a time period, equity follows the maxim expressed by the word *laches*. Rather than fixing precise periods of time, laches may be used as a defense to an action in equity if the action is unreasonably delayed to the prejudice of a party who has changed position during the delay. Circumstances might dictate that a party bring an action very promptly or, conversely, that since no one was harmed by a long delay, no injustice would occur by allowing the action.

Domestic Relations

Prior to the establishment of the American republic, family law matters fell within the jurisdiction of ecclesiastical courts and were governed by canon law. With the American separation of church and state, the law of domestic relations, having no common law precedent, fell within equity jurisdiction. This has had a profound effect on the law since equity entails great discretion. This is generally appropriate since, in the case of divorce and custody questions, problems tend to be particularized and each case must be examined on its own merits. No-fault divorce, however, has discouraged divorce contests and encouraged parties to negotiate the conditions of custody and the division of property. State legislatures have been active in recent years in setting the standards for child support and providing the means to collect it.

Language

It is important to note that the historical separation of law and equity has given rise to different terms. Since equity actions are brought by petition, the parties to an action in equity are called *petitioner* and *respondent* rather than their common law equivalents, *plaintiff* and *defendant*. Judges sitting in equity are in some jurisdictions referred to as *chancellor* or *master in equity*.

SUMMARY

The American legal system is complicated by the existence of separate state and federal jurisdictions. Not only do these have different spheres of authority, but the states themselves are independent jurisdictions. The division of judicial power is expressed in the U.S. Constitution, which grants specific power to the federal government and reserves the remaining judicial authority to the states. The Constitution is the supreme law of the land and no official act, law, or judicial order may violate it. The federal judiciary exercises significant authority over state law under the due process and equal protection clauses of the Fourteenth Amendment. The Constitution also requires that the states honor the acts, laws, and judicial orders of other states under the full faith and credit clause.

The Constitution also dictates subject matter jurisdiction of the federal courts, which have jurisdiction over federal question cases, those arising under the Constitution, laws, and treaties of the federal government, and diversity of citizenship cases, those given federal jurisdiction because of the grant of authority over citizens of different states. In diversity cases, by virtue of the decision in *Erie R.R. v. Tompkins*, the federal courts apply state law rather than developing a general federal common law.

In cases in which there is some question as to which state's substantive law should apply, each state has its own rules, called conflict of laws, to determine whether it should apply its own law or that of a state more closely involved with the facts giving rise to the lawsuit.

A further complication in the American legal system is the historical existence of common law courts and courts of equity. Equity court first arose several centuries ago in England to provide remedies for disputes the common law courts would not hear. Equity developed special remedies differing from the usual common law remedy of monetary compensation (damages) and developed its own principles based on moral principles. As a result, equitable remedies are more flexible and bound less by precedent than legal remedies. One important feature that distinguishes law from equity is the traditional absence of the right to a jury in equity.

Today law and equity have merged, so that American judges provide both equitable and legal relief, and legal and equitable remedies may be requested in the same suit. Nevertheless, many of the traditional differences have been maintained.

CHAPTER QUESTIONS

1. What is the basis for state power?
2. What establishes the authority of the U.S. Supreme Court?
3. How were U.S. District Courts established?
4. Why does one state enforce decrees of courts of other states?

5. Why do federal courts follow state law in diversity cases?
6. How would a defendant in a diversity case attempt to have the case heard in a state rather than a federal court?
7. What kind of federal jurisdiction requires a minimum amount in controversy to bring a lawsuit?
8. Why did courts of equity first come into existence?
9. What is the threshold question for equity jurisdiction?
10. What is the usual remedy sought in an action at common law?
11. What determines the conflict of laws rules to be followed in a case that requires a choice of law?
12. On what basis does delay in bringing suit bar the suit in law and in equity?

EXERCISES

1. Of the four hypothetical situations described at the end of the section discussing due process, which would you argue on the basis of substantive due process and which on the basis of procedural due process? Explain.
2. Look up the conflict of laws rules in your state to determine which law would apply if the *Newman* (Case 7–4) case were brought in your state.
3. Determine which courts in your state are courts of limited jurisdiction and which are courts of general jurisdiction.

PROFESSIONAL PROFILE

A native of West Monroe, Louisiana, Peggy Kerley recalls, "I worked as a legal secretary for two decades before the formal definition of 'paralegal' was publicized. Much of the training in those twenty years was individual instruction from attorneys, one of whom became a district judge. This personalized training was a wonderful foundation for the subsequent educational instruction in my new career."

Kerley's first paralegal position was with a corporation. She was a legal secretary in the oil and gas division of the corporation, working closely with the corporate legal department. In the fall of 1974, a corporate officer asked her to interview for a "paralegal" position. He proceeded to give his understanding of this newly created position. At the time, Kerley had no college degree. The corporation allowed her to select a course of

Peggy N. Kerley
Freelance Paralegal, Instructor, and Author

paralegal education at a time (the mid-1970s) when there was not a wide choice. One national institute required a college degree for enrollment. However, the University of Oklahoma had a unique program, Bachelor of Liberal Studies. She enrolled, as one of the initial students, in the paralegal studies program at the University of Oklahoma. Kerley completed the first three years of her degree and her paralegal certificate program before moving to Dallas, Texas. Kerley immediately enrolled at the University of Texas at Dallas, where she completed her degree in political economy.

Presently Kerley is an instructor at Southeastern Paralegal Institute and an adjunct professor in the legal assistant program at Southern Methodist University, both ABA-approved programs. Kerley is also the proprietor of a computerized deposition summary service and a freelance paralegal. She is co-author of a new textbook, *Civil Litigation for the Paralegal*, with Paul A. Sukys and Joanne Banker Hames.

"My career path has curved slightly in the past three years. I consider my career a testimonial that a paralegal does not have to burn out after thirty years in the profession. My typical day consists of teaching in either one or two paralegal programs, sitting at the computer in my home and summarizing depositions, or possibly leaving the classroom to rush to a freelance assignment and then returning to my office at home to work on the paralegal textbook. But the most rewarding aspect of my career is encouraging and helping to train new paralegals," says Kerley.

"I was fortunate to work in the litigation section of a major law firm in Dallas for ten years," Kerley remembers. During that time, Kerley, a senior attorney, and a secretary worked as a team to meet incredible deadlines. The highlight of that teamwork included traveling to the United States Supreme Court with the attorney for his oral argument (which he won).

Kerley's advice for those embarking on a legal career: "Secure the maximum amount of education, obtain a paralegal certificate, and NEVER STOP LEARNING."

CHAPTER 8
Procedure in Civil Cases

DISMISSAL MOTIONS
   The Demurrer
   Summary Judgment
   Motion for a Directed Verdict
   Motion for Judgment Notwithstanding the Verdict
RES JUDICATA AND *COLLATERAL ESTOPPEL*
SUMMARY

Procedural law is the oil that greases the legal machine. No area of law has more theoretical or practical importance. From a theoretical perspective, procedural law informs us about the basic premises of the legal system itself. The adversarial premise of the American legal system maintains that our system is based on competition and that individuals act in their own self-interest and cannot be trusted without equalizing their power positions before a disinterested and perhaps indifferent tribunal. The fact that we preserve the jury system tells us that we do not even trust the presumed neutrality of the judges. The rules of evidentiary exclusion suggest that we do not trust the capacity of juries to sift good evidence from bad.

The theoretical premise at the heart of our procedure is: If the means by which conflict in society is resolved are fair and equal, justice will, on the whole, be achieved. Acceptance of this premise is a virtual catechism of lawyers. When criminal defense attorneys are asked, "Would you defend a guilty man? Would you help a guilty man be acquitted and go free?", the answer is usually the same: "Every person is entitled to a competent legal representation; it is not for the attorney to judge, and it is the job of the prosecution to prove guilt beyond a reasonable doubt." This response can only be understood in the context of a system that places procedure on a pedestal.

The practical importance of procedure is equal to its philosophical importance. Rights have no meaning without a means to enforce them. Without a procedure for enforcement, the establishment of a right is merely symbolic.

Each state and the federal system have compiled their own set of rules of civil procedure, which will henceforth be referred to as "the rules." These treat some procedural questions with great specificity, allowing little room for interpretation, but other questions may be adequately understood only by researching rules of court, judicial interpretations, or even local procedural customs. The competent practitioner must have a thorough understanding of the rules of the jurisdictions in which practice is to be conducted, but that is beyond the scope of the treatment of civil procedure here, which is merely a model and an overview.

Procedure is arbitrary and technical, yet it is always subject to attack for its fairness under the due process clause of the Fourteenth Amendment. Cases concerning procedural due process tend to be exceedingly complex and difficult. One of the reasons may be that the social values underlying the rules are obscure at best. In comparison, substantive areas of law, such as tort and contract, may rely on accepted values: In contract law, it is a premise of our society that a person should fulfill lawful promises; in tort law, it is a premise that a person who wrongfully injures another should compensate the injured party. On the other hand, is there any fundamental reason that a jury may not be exposed to hearsay evidence, or that a hearing be adversarial rather than mediatory in nature, or that a complaint must state a cause of action?

PROCEDURAL FRAMEWORK OF LEGAL DISPUTES

There is a basic model of the legal processing of a dispute that underlies American procedural law. In its minute details, it differs from jurisdiction to jurisdiction, but the basic model is the same. This chapter will follow its basic outline as follows:

1. One who proposes to seek relief through the legal system must formally state to a court the basis for a grievance, and the grounds asserted must amount to a grievance that the law recognizes as enforceable.
2. The opponent in a legal action must be notified of the suit and given the opportunity to prepare for a defense.
3. Parties to a lawsuit will have every reasonable means prior to a trial to become fully informed of the factual and legal arguments of the other side.
4. If a dispute proceeds to trial, it will be conducted as an adversarial proceeding in which each side has every opportunity to challenge the arguments of the other side.
5. In an adversarial trial, decisions of the court must be based on the evidence and arguments presented in court before an adversarial party.
6. Any departure from procedural rules will provide a basis for challenging the fairness of the process.
7. Procedural error takes precedence over substantive goals. The corollary to this is that if the procedure was fair, the results cannot be questioned except by extraordinary circumstances.

DETERMINING THE PROPER COURT FOR THE SUIT

In addition to problems of subject matter jurisdiction discussed in the previous chapter, there are a number of obstacles that may arise concerning the exercise of the court's authority in a particular case.

Service of Process

The notification of the defendant in a lawsuit is accomplished by *service of process*. This refers to the presentation to the defendant of a copy of the complaint along with a summons, which informs the defendant that an answer to the complaint must be served on the plaintiff's attorney within a specified number of days, commonly twenty. Service refers to presentation of the documents; service of the complaint and summons is *original service*. (After original service, documents may be served on the attorneys for the parties by mail.) Process refers to the document commanding a party to do or not do something. At common law, original process was formerly called an original writ or writ of process. In equity, it was called a subpoena. Today original process is usually simply called a summons.

Service of process is effected by filing the complaint and summons with the court, followed by presentation to the defendant of the complaint and summons by one authorized to do so, typically a sheriff or deputy or a U.S. Marshall for federal cases. Private process-servers may also be authorized by the law and are typically used if the defendant may be purposely avoiding service or may be difficult to locate. Deputies and marshalls have many duties and cannot be expected to go to great efforts in serving process in civil cases. Attorneys commonly offer assistance in locating defendants, e.g., informing the sheriff of defendant's place of work or the hours defendant is likely to be at home. The place, time, and manner of service of process must be in accord with the rules or other statutes of the jurisdiction in which process is served.

Presenting the summons and complaint personally to the defendant is called *personal service* and is the ideal form of service, especially in jurisdictions in which the defendant signs a paper, thus assuring the court that the defendant was properly notified of the suit and making it difficult for the defendant to later challenge the service. The rules or statutes also provide for *substituted service* whereby process can be served to someone other than the defendant, such as a relative living at defendant's abode. Substituted service that does not strictly comply with the law is invalid. Service may also be made by publication in a newspaper of general circulation if a diligent search for the defendant fails to reveal the defendant's whereabouts. *Publication* refers to the publication of a legal notice in an authorized periodical, such as a newspaper of general circulation. Again, the manner of service by publication must strictly follow the law.

The rules provide for service in special situations. Business entities, for example, call for different service—a corporation may be served by service upon an authorized agent of the corporation; partnerships may be served by service upon a partner. Minors, prisoners, military personnel on active duty, legal incompetents, etc., may call for special treatment.

Service of nonresidents is accomplished under the authority of **long-arm statutes** with the cooperation of the officers of the state of residence of the defendant. If the nonresident is present in the state in which the suit is filed, personal service is effective within the state.

Service other than personal service will be scrutinized carefully by the judge if the defendant does not answer and does not appear for a judicial proceeding. Judges are understandably reluctant to determine rights of an absent defendant.

long-arm statutes provide a state with jurisdiction over persons or entities ordinarily beyond its territory and usual jurisdiction.

CASE NO. 8–1   Service of Process

This case presents several interesting procedural features, some of which are difficult to reconstruct because of the age of the case. In 1937, personal service of process was even more preferred than today. At that time, the causes of action for seduction and breach of promise to marry were recognized in most states as in Florida, which later abolished them, but they were in disrepute, particularly in New York, which may explain why the complaint was filed in Florida rather than New York. Since the defendant did not answer the Florida complaint, the Florida court entered a default judgment, which the plaintiff then attempted to enforce in New York.

WYMAN

v.

NEWHOUSE

Circuit Court of Appeals, Second Circuit
93 F.2d 313 (2d Cir. 1937)

MANTON, J.

This appeal is from a judgment entered dismissing the complaint on motion before trial. The action is on a judgment entered by default in a Florida state court, a jury having assessed the damages. The recovery there was for money loaned, money advanced for appellee, and for seduction under promise of marriage.

. . . .

Appellant and appellee were both married, but before this suit appellant's husband died. They had known each other for some years and had engaged in meretricious relations.

The affidavits submitted by the appellee deemed to be true for the purpose of testing the alleged error of dismissing the complaint established that he was a resident of New York and never lived in Florida. On October 25, 1935, while appellee was in Salt Lake City, Utah, he received a telegram from the appellant, which read: "Account illness home planning leaving. Please come on way back. Must see you." Upon appellee's return to New York he received a letter from appellant stating that her mother was dying in Ireland; that she was leaving the United States for good to go to her mother; that she could not go without seeing the appellee once more; and that she wanted to discuss her affairs with him before she left. Shortly after the receipt of this letter, they spoke to each other on the telephone, whereupon the appellant repeated, in a hysterical and distressed voice, the substance of her letter. Appellee promised to go to Florida in a week or ten days and agreed to notify her when he would arrive. This he did, but before leaving New York by plane he received a letter couched in endearing terms and expressing love and affection for him, as well as her delight at his coming. Before leaving New York, appellee telegraphed appellant, suggesting arrangements for their accommodations together while in Miami, Fla. She telegraphed him at a hotel in Washington D.C., where he was to stop en route, advising him that the arrangements requested had been made. Appellee arrived at 6 o'clock in the morning at the Miami Airport and saw the appellant standing with her sister some 75 feet distant. He was met by a deputy sheriff who, upon identifying appellee, served him with process in a suit for $500,000. A photographer was present who attempted to take his picture. Thereupon a stranger introduced himself and offered to take appellee to his home, stating that he knew a lawyer who was acquainted with the appellant's attorney. The attorney whom appellee was advised to consult came to the stranger's home and seemed to know about the case. The attorney invited appellee to his office, and upon his arrival he found one of the lawyers for the appellant there. Appellee did not retain the Florida attorney to represent him. He returned to New York by plane that evening and consulted his New York counsel, who advised him to ignore the summons served in Florida. He did so, and judgment was entered by default. Within a few days after the service of process, the appellant came to New York and sought an interview with the appellee. It resulted in their meeting at the home of the appellee's attorney. She was accompanied by her Florida counsel.

These facts and reasonable deductions therefrom convincingly establish that fraud perpetrated upon him by the appellant in falsely representing her mother's illness, her intention to leave the United States, and her love and affection for him, when her sole purpose and apparent thought was to induce him to come within the Florida jurisdiction so as to serve him in an action for damages. Appellant does not deny making these representations. All her statements of great and undying love were disproved entirely by her appearance at the airport and participation in the happening there. She never went to Ireland to see her mother, if indeed the latter was sick at all.

In asking for judgment based on these Florida proceedings, appellant relies upon article 4, section 1, of the United States Constitution, providing that "Full Faith and Credit shall be given in each State to the public Acts, Records, and Judicial Proceedings of every other State." . . .

This judgment is attacked for fraud perpetrated upon the appellee which goes to the jurisdiction of the Florida court over his person. A judgment procured fraudulently, as here, lacks jurisdiction and is null and void. A fraud affecting the jurisdiction is equivalent to a lack of jurisdiction. The appellee was not required to proceed against the judgment in Florida. . . .

Judgment affirmed.

CASE QUESTIONS

1. Did the Florida trial court have any reason to believe that the service of process was accomplished by fraud?
2. Does the court's opinion suggest a union of a conniving plaintiff and an unscrupulous attorney?

In Personam Jurisdiction

In personam, or "personal," jurisdiction refers to the authority of the Court to determine the rights of the defendant in a lawsuit. Where service of process is deficient or not in accordance with law, the Court does not have personal jurisdiction over the defendant. The defendant may simply be beyond the reach of the Court. If a resident of Oregon is involved in an accident in Oregon with a resident of California, the Oregon resident can object to personal jurisdiction in California—California would only have personal jurisdiction under its long-arm statute if the accident occurred in California.

Appearance by defendant in court confers personal jurisdiction despite deficient service of process. In many jurisdictions, the defendant may enter a special appearance solely for the purpose of contesting personal jurisdiction, and the appearance will not be construed as conferring personal jurisdiction. Challenges to personal jurisdiction must follow the rules to avoid a waiver of defenses to personal jurisdiction. Of course, a nonresident may remain silent and later challenge jurisdiction of the original court if the plaintiff attempts to enforce a judgment under full faith and credit in defendant's home state, but a significant risk is involved because the defendant's state might reject the defenses and enforce the judgment, leaving defendant without an opportunity to defend the case on its merits.

In Rem Jurisdiction

Under certain circumstances, the purpose of a suit may be to determine the status of property rather than to determine personal rights, and an *in rem* action may be brought. *Rem* is from the Latin word *res,* roughly translated as "thing." Courts generally have jurisdiction over real and personal property located within their jurisdiction. *In rem* proceedings are often brought to prevent the removal of property from the jurisdiction, typically in **attachment** proceedings to secure control of the Court over property subject to a debt. Some actions involve property but operate only between parties to the suit and are called *quasi in rem.* Conceptually it is difficult to distinguish *quasi in rem* from *in personam* actions. *In rem* actions are fairly rare since the primary purpose of most lawsuits is to determine the respective rights of persons.

Certain real property actions in equity are *in rem* or *quasi in rem* actions, such as suits to quiet title or to remove a cloud on title. These suits are usually brought in connection with a real estate transaction when an attorney (or title company) discovers some potential defect in the title that should be cleared up prior to completing the transaction. For example, a person can acquire title by adverse possession, i.e., someone without rightful possession of real property who nevertheless enters on the land and occupies it for a certain number of years (twenty at common law, less under most state statutes) may acquire title. The presence at some past time of adverse possession may raise doubts about title that can be settled in the suit. Essentially, then, the suit is against the property rather than against specific persons. Whenever the parties are known, caution suggests they should be included as defendants.

Another example of an *in rem* action is suit for divorce. In theory, the *res* in a divorce action is the marriage—divorce has the effect of changing the status from married to unmarried. In practice, courts are extremely reluctant to treat divorce actions as *in rem* proceedings since ordinarily divorce actions involve the adjudication of personal rights. Alimony and child support, for example, are considered *in personam* questions.

The aforementioned examples demonstrate that *in rem* proceedings must be restricted to special circumstances; frequently, as in attachment, they are ancillary to a larger *in personam* suit. Whenever a known person's rights are involved, personal jurisdiction should be established to prevent a later attack on the judicial order.

In Personam, in Rem, and Quasi in Rem Compared

In personam, in rem, and *quasi in rem* are difficult to distinguish in the abstract. The cases, the history, and the difference between jurisdictional definitions have left the distinctions quite

attachment
 is a procedure whereby property is seized and a lien placed on it to satisfy a debt or judgment or to secure property in anticipation of a judgment.

confused. With this confusion in mind, the following is designed as a rule-of-thumb guide:

> *In personam* jurisdiction has a party, a person, as a defendant.
> *Example:* Johnson sues Jackson for breach of contract.
> *In rem* jurisdiction has property as a defendant.
> *Example:* State seizure of drugs.
> *Quasi in rem* jurisdiction brings suit against property to satisfy a personal claim.
> *Example:* Plaintiff sues for attachment and sale of property to satisfy a debt owed by another party who has property located within the forum state but is beyond the reach of the personal jurisdiction of the court.

Quasi in rem is used when personal jurisdiction would have been obtained if the defendant could have been served personally. The court has *in rem* jurisdiction over property within the state but does not have *in personam* jurisdiction over out-of-state residents who have no other contact with the state than their ownership of property located within the state.

The distinctions are often obscure, and an inherent due process issue always lurks when rights may be affected without opportunity to be heard. This problem of definition underscores the difficult problems of civil procedure, namely, measuring very technical rules and concepts against the broad, flexible concept of due process.

Venue

Venue refers to the place where jurisdiction is exercised. Venue is easily confused with jurisdiction, but the two must be clearly distinguished. For example, the issue of whether a case should be heard in a state or federal court is a matter of subject matter jurisdiction, as discussed in the last chapter. Venue concerns the question of which court within a system should be the *place* where jurisdiction is exercised. An example from divorce law in Florida may clarify this problem.

Florida circuit courts have jurisdiction over divorce cases (now called "dissolution of marriage"). The jurisdictional requirement for bringing a divorce action is that the petitioner must have resided in the state for six months prior to bringing the action. The action may be brought in any circuit in the state; in fact, some actions are brought in a venue far from the residences of either party to the action in order to avoid local public scrutiny. However, if the respondent objects to the place where the suit is filed, venue may be challenged, and the court will transfer the case to the circuit in which the defendant resides. It is not that the original court does not have jurisdiction but, rather, that another court with similar jurisdiction is determined to be the more appropriate site of the lawsuit.

The divorce example is based on the allegation of *inconvenient venue*, commonly referred to by the Latin phrase *forum non conveniens*. Another venue challenge is based on the allegation that a party cannot obtain a fair trial where the action has been brought, e.g., the plaintiff may have unusual influence over the local population so that the defendant fears that a fair trial is difficult or impossible.

PLEADINGS

Many technical problems may arise concerning proper and necessary parties to a lawsuit, i.e., who may or must be included in the lawsuit. Problems of multiple plaintiffs or defendants, **class action suits,** and other special problems must be left to a more detailed study of litigation and procedure. Discussion here will be limited to the basic documents that frame the issues for trial.

Modern pleading borrows heavily from both law and equity. The basic documents of pleading, the *complaint* and the *answer,* echo the procedure of equity, which required the suitor to file a petition or bill in equity. The petition initiated the suit much like a complaint does today, except that the petition was a lengthy recitation of the facts of the case, much restricted today. After the bill was filed, a subpoena was issued requiring the respondent to appear, and respondent provided an answer, which presented respondent's defenses, thereby closing the pleadings and requiring the plaintiff to go forward to prove his allegations.

Equity also provided for *joinder,* which consolidated related claims and related parties, thus avoiding the necessity of hearing numerous cases. If a defendant had a claim against the plaintiff, this could be brought through a *cross-bill,* analogous to the modern **counterclaim.**

Equity also provided for plaintiff's (and later defendant's) discovery of information possessed by the defendant in order to prepare for hearing.

All these features of equity procedure were incorporated with changes into modern pleading. Common law procedure, on the other hand, was complex and formal. Common law pleading had

class action suits are a modern form of suit in which a group of persons is represented by some members of the class in pursuing a lawsuit. It was designed to enable a class with numerous members to bring a suit in the name of all. In order to bring a class action, federal and state rules require that several criteria be met.

counterclaim is a cause of action brought by a defendant against the plaintiff in a single case.

two principal objects. First, it was necessary for the plaintiff to fit the case into a *form of action* that would support the Court's issuing a corresponding writ or order to the sheriff to compel the defendant to satisfy plaintiff's claim or appear in court to show cause why he need not do so. The form of action corresponds to the *cause of action,* still required in modern pleading; the specific facts required by the formula for each form of action correspond to the *elements* presently required to state a cause of action.

Second, common law pleading was designed to focus the lawsuit on a single issue, and it did this by a series of responsive pleadings back and forth between plaintiff and defendant until the issue was clearly framed. This was a highly technical process with numerous pitfalls. The parties were not allowed to present multiple actions or defenses and attempt to do so would result in a holding for the other side.

The advantage of common law pleading was its precision; the disadvantages were its inflexibility and technicality. The advantages of equity procedure were its flexibility and attention to substance over technicality; its disadvantage was the time-consuming process of setting the case for hearing—the relative simplicity and flexibility of equity procedure failed to focus the case and restrain the parties.

Modern code pleading attempts to borrow the advantages of both processes while minimizing their disadvantages. Equity pleadings are simplified to the allegation of **ultimate** rather than the more detailed **evidentiary** facts. Rather than focusing on a single issue, the pleadings are designed to establish a cause of action and present defenses. Issues are narrowed largely by the pretrial process, including discovery, a concept borrowed from equity. Liberalized pleading allows complaints to be amended, shifting emphasis toward substantive rather than purely technical issues. It must be noted, however, that civil procedure is by its nature technical, and inattention to the rules can be costly.

The Complaint

The complaint is designed to inform the Court and the defendant that a lawsuit has been filed, invoking the attendant legal process. The complaint itself, that is, the document filed with the court and served on the defendant, may be divided into several parts:

1. The *caption* is the heading of the complaint and names the court in which the complaint is filed, the names of the parties to the suit, and the case number of the suit (assigned by the

ultimate facts
In pleading, a distinction is made between ultimate facts and **evidentiary** facts. Evidentiary facts are the specific facts presented at trial; ultimate facts are the general statements of fact that support a cause of action. The complaint should avoid a lengthy detailing of the events of the case and simply allege general facts that support a cause of action and notify the defendant of the basis for the suit. Nor is it sufficient to merely state *conclusions of law,* such as "The defendant was negligent." The boundaries between these three are not very clear.

clerk). The caption begins each document filed with the court. Below the case number (on the right underneath the name of the court) or below the caption itself is the label of the document, e.g., "COMPLAINT," "ANSWER," "MOTION FOR SUMMARY JUDGMENT."

2. The first paragraph of the complaint contains the jurisdictional allegation, which states the grounds for subject matter jurisdiction of the court wherein the complaint has been filed.

3. The remaining numbered paragraphs of the complaint present a brief allegation of general facts designed to state a cause of action and provide notice to the defendant of the basis for the suit.

4. The complaint ends with a *prayer for relief,* sometimes called the *wherefore clause* since it traditionally begins with something like "WHEREFORE, the Plaintiff prays for judgment . . . "

The Answer

To defend the suit, the defendant must file an answer, although other procedural devices to attack the complaint are available at this time. The answer is responsive to the complaint and admits allegations in the complaint that defendant does not wish to contest. It contains denials of allegations in the complaint that the defendant disputes, which allegations then become questions for proof and argument. The answer may also contain *affirmative defenses,* which contain matter not included in the complaint that defendant alleges will prevent the plaintiff from obtaining relief. For example, the defendant may contend that the statute of limitations has run, barring plaintiff's suit. If the plaintiff cannot overcome this defense, the suit must be dismissed. The answer may also present a counterclaim, which is a claim by the defendant against the plaintiff that must contain sufficient allegations to state a cause of action on its own.

The Reply

Although filing an answer usually ends the pleadings, the plaintiff must file a reply if the defendant has made a counterclaim in order to present denials and defenses to the counterclaim. Affirmative defenses do not necessarily require the filing of a reply, but the cautious attorney may do so to avoid certain technical problems later on.

DISCOVERY

Discovery refers to pretrial devices for obtaining information relevant to the suit. It is a modern adoption of procedures in equity and has come to play a major role in civil cases. Long delays in bringing suit to trial are most often related to the discovery process, which has been severely criticized for its contribution to delays and the resulting costs that give a significant advantage to wealthy parties. While it is unethical to delay as a strategy for wearing down an opponent or as leverage to induce settlement, and is subject to sanctions in some states, it is difficult to prove that attorneys have used procedural devices solely for the purpose of delay. Defense attorneys in damage suits have little incentive to effect prompt resolution of a case—their clients are not eager to pay sooner than necessary, and the attorneys continue to receive compensation as the process is prolonged. This is not purely self-serving on the attorneys' part. In the end, the client may save a great deal of money in the settlement, despite increased attorneys' fees. And any eagerness to settle tends to be regarded as a weakness by the other side. This is one of the prices we pay for having an adversarial system.

The discovery process involves a great deal of work that is currently accomplished by paralegals.

Depositions

A primary tool of discovery is the deposition. It consists of an oral questioning of a witness or the parties themselves; present are attorneys for both sides and a court reporter recording verbatim the questions and answers for later transcription. The ostensible purpose of the deposition is to gather information, but it serves also to gauge the credibility of the witness and to make a record of statements under oath to preserve testimony for trial, usually effectively preventing a witness from later changing testimony.

Attorneys arrange for a deposition, often through their paralegals; it is often difficult to schedule because the attorneys and the witness must all be available at the same time. Although several depositions may be taken in sequence on the same day, attorneys frequently arrange one deposition at a time, prolonging the pretrial period for several months or even years. Depositions may last for several hours, and all the attorneys present (except those on contingency fee arrangements) are likely to be paid at an hourly rate. While there is no effective substitute for thoroughness in preparation for trial, thoroughness is profitable for the attorney and costly for the client.

Paralegals frequently draft questions for depositions and may even sit beside an attorney and pass notes concerning objections and follow-up questions to responses made by the deponent.

Interrogatories and Requests for Admissions

Attorneys submit written questions, called *interrogatories*, to the opposing party asking for specific information, usually information not easily denied, such as vital statistics, employment, historical facts of the case. Time of reply is often unduly protracted, although undue delay may be countered by motions to the court to compel compliance. Requests for admissions ask the opposing party to admit specific facts, which once admitted may no longer be put in dispute, thereby narrowing the issues for trial.

Requests for Documents and Mental and Physical Examinations

A party may demand the production of documents and records relevant to the case, e.g., business records, receipts, etc., as well as mental and physical examinations of a party if cause can be shown that an examination is relevant to the case (this is especially common in personal injury actions).

Scope of Discovery

Discovery inquiry is measured by very broad standards and is not limited by the more restrictive standards of admissibility of evidence at trial. Discovery is normally conducted through the attorneys without the intervention of the judge, who may have little knowledge of what is happening. The court becomes involved only when the process breaks down and a party seeks an order from the court requiring the other party to comply with the discovery process.

In theory, discovery is based on the rationale that justice is served by both sides being fully informed and prepared for trial. It is a counterpoise to the "gunslinger" approach to trial in which trial is a battle of wits between great performers, a view favored by popular dramatists. In practice, the trial is a performance that has been carefully rehearsed—both sides are aware of the facts and arguments of the other, the only uncertainty being the unpredictability of the jury.

On the surface, discovery appears to be a reasonable feature of the search for truth and the equalization of the positions of the parties. In fact, it is as much subject to subterfuge as any other part of a lawsuit. Deponents are prepared for depositions as are witnesses for trial and are warned by attorneys not to expand on their answers, to answer merely "Yes" or "No" to questions that can be answered simply by yes or no responses. Answers to interrogatories are drafted by attorneys, rather than the parties, to provide as little information as possible. In short, discovery has become a negotiating tool used as much for strategic purposes as for investigation. It is a part of a lengthy pretrial process devoid of judicial scrutiny, encouraging a continual reevaluation of a case for negotiating settlements. It is responsible for pretrial settlements more than any other feature of civil procedure. The question remains whether this mechanism is fairer, more efficient, or more just than procedure without it.

Discovery and the Paralegal

Discovery affords a great deal of work for paralegals, since most of the work of discovery can be accomplished by paralegals. Building a theory of a case, determining the information necessary to support that theory, analyzing and indexing transcripts from depositions, drafting interrogatories, and organizing the products of discovery are essential tasks that are efficiently handled by the paralegal–attorney team.

PRETRIAL HEARING

In a great many cases a pretrial conference or hearing is held at an advanced stage of the pretrial process. It is frequently held in the judge's chambers rather than in open court and is attended by the judge and attorneys for the parties. A general discussion is held on the issues of the case and the merits of the claim. Ostensibly the pretrial hearing helps the judge assess the progress of the pretrial process and plan for trial time. Depending on the judge and the jurisdiction, pretrial is often used to encourage settlement. The judge may urge the attorneys to focus on real issues and suggest areas for compromise. Attorneys may show a willingness to settle in the pretrial hearing that they were reluctant to show previously. The judge may show some impatience with frivolous claims and issues and ask the attorneys to submit written arguments on questions of law.

Depending on the judge, the attorneys may come away from the conference with a clear idea of where the judge stands on the law and even the judicial attitude toward the merits, weaknesses, and defenses with regard to the claim. It is not that the judge pre-judges the lawsuit, but a frank discussion of the case takes place in which the judge can act as a mediator to resolve the dispute and obviate the necessity for going to trial. It is often in the interests of all present to forego the time and expense of trial. At the pretrial conference, the adversaries finally come face to face with the one person whose job it is to resolve the dispute.

PROCEDURE AT TRIAL

Trial is conducted as an orderly sequence of steps. The model presented here is followed quite generally in federal and state courts.

Jury Selection

The means and manner of selecting a jury vary considerably between jurisdictions and even between judges, largely in the extent to which they wish to control the process. The jury pool is typically selected from the list of registered voters within the jurisdiction, a number of whom are called for jury duty when the court is in session. From a number larger than the number of jurors required in a case, the jury will be selected by an examination called *voir dire*, during which the attorneys and/or the judge will ask the prospective jurors questions with regard to their qualifications to serve in the case. In addition to statutory disqualifications, jurors who are prejudiced with regard to the parties or subject matter of the case or cannot reasonably be expected to judge the facts impartially may be excluded from the jury. An attorney who wishes to so exclude a juror makes a *challenge for cause*. These are unlimited in number since no party should be tried by a biased jury. Cases that receive widespread publicity prior to trial may involve a lengthy *voir dire* to find impartial jurors, though the problem is usually limited to sensational criminal trials.

In addition to challenges for cause, each party is allowed a specific number of *peremptory challenges* which allow the parties to exclude jurors they suspect are unsympathetic to their side of the case but who are not otherwise disqualified. Attorneys do not give reasons for exercising peremptory challenges.

Jury selection is extremely important. Cases commonly go to trial because there are two believable versions of the facts or simply because the facts could be viewed favorably for either side. A case may be won or lost on the basis of the jury or, more often, the amount of damages can vary greatly depending on the jury since, for example, the value of "emotional distress" or an award of punitive damages requires an arbitrary assessment by a jury.

Conduct of the Trial

With the jury selected, the trial begins with *opening statements* by each side, plaintiff first and then defendant, who may reserve opening remarks until later. Opening statements are designed to inform the jury of the nature of the case and the facts each side proposes to show or dispute. In a bench trial, i.e., a nonjury trial, opening statements are usually waived since the judge ordinarily does not need to be prepared in this way.

Plaintiff then presents the evidence that forms the *case-in-chief*. The plaintiff has the burden of proof, meaning that there must be sufficient proof of the allegations of the complaint to sustain a verdict in favor of plaintiff if the evidence is believed. This is called making a *prima facie* case.

Questioning of witnesses proceeds with the party calling the witness conducting a *direct examination,* followed by *cross-examination* by the other side, which attempts to show flaws in the witness's testimony or to discredit the witness. The initial party then has the opportunity to *redirect* questions concerning issues raised "on cross." This is followed by *recross.*

When the plaintiff finishes the case-in-chief, the defendant produces witnesses favorable to the defense, who are questioned in similar fashion with the defense conducting the direct examination. Plaintiff then has the opportunity to present evidence rebutting the defendant's presentation, followed by rebuttal by defendant.

Finally, each side makes a *summation,* or *closing argument,* before the jury, with the defendant usually going first (in opposite order of opening statements). The function of the closing argument is to summarize the evidence and show that an interpretation of the facts consistent with the evidence favors the party making the argument. Considerable latitude is given the attorneys in their closing arguments, provided they stay within the evidence presented and conduct themselves properly.

The Verdict and Judgment

Before the jury retires to deliberate the facts, the judge *charges* them, i.e., gives them instructions. Paralegals assist in the research and preparation of jury instructions. The jury returns when it reaches consensus and reads the verdict before the court. The judge will then ask each juror if he or she concurs in the verdict. After dismissing the jury, the judge may enter judgment on the verdict immediately or wait for a period during which the parties may make posttrial motions.

In a nonjury trial, the judge is the trier-of-fact so no verdict is entered, though the judgment should include findings of fact beyond what would be appropriate in a jury trial. Final judgment is in written form, dated and signed by the judge and filed with the court records.

CASE NO. 8–2 Jury Fact-Finding

The following case presents a peculiarity of Ohio law that existed at the time of decision. The plaintiff's injuries followed a rather unexpected course, and an issue of foreseeability under applicable federal law caused the trial judge to ask twenty-five special interrogatories of the jury. Under Ohio law, no general verdict would then be entered, but the judge would apply the law to the jury's answers. As the dissent points out, a more usual method is for the jury to provide specific answers and then enter a general verdict (for or against the plaintiff). The judge may then be faced with reconciling inconsistencies between the two.

JAMES GALLICK, Petitioner
v.
BALTIMORE & OHIO RAILROAD COMPANY
U.S. Supreme Court
372 U.S. 108 (1963)

Mr. Justice WHITE delivered the opinion of the Court.

Upon a special verdict of the jury, the Common Pleas Court of Cuyahoga County, Ohio, entered judgment awarding damages to petitioner in this Federal Employers' Liability Act suit. The Court of Appeals reversed and the Ohio Supreme Court refused further appellate review, making the decision of the intermediate appellate court the final judgment rendered by the state courts. This Court granted certiorari to consider the question whether the decision below improperly invaded the jury's function. We have concluded that the decision below is erroneous and must be reversed.

Petitioner was a spotting crew foreman working on or about August 10, 1954, along the respondent railroad's right of way in the Cuyahoga River "flats" section of Cleveland, Ohio. At the particular stretch of roadbed where petitioner was working on that afternoon, there had been for many years a pool of stagnant water, in and about which were dead and decayed rats and pigeons, or portions thereof. Insects had been seen on, over, and about this stagnant pool, and the evidence showed, as the Court of Appeals stated, that respondent had long been aware of the fetid condition of this pool.

While he was temporarily working near the pool, petitioner experienced a bite on his left leg just above the knee. He grasped the spot with his hand and felt an object under his trousers which seemed to be a large insect and which, when he crushed it, dropped out of his trouser leg. The wound subsequently became infected. The infection failed to respond to medical treatment, and worsened progressively until it spread throughout petitioner's body, creating pusforming lesions and eventually necessitating the amputation of both his legs. None of the doctors who treated and studied petitioner's case could explain the etiology of his present condition, although some of them diagnosed or characterized it as "pyodermagangrenosa, secondary to insect bite". . . .

After a lengthy trial, the court, pursuant to the State's special verdict statute, under which no general verdict is rendered by the jury, submitted some two dozen interrogatories to the jury and charged them as to what it deemed the applicable law of negligence. The special verdict of the jury, to the extent that it is relevant here, follows (answers italicized):

10. On approximately August 10, 1954, was plaintiff bitten by an insect? *Yes* . . . .

13. Did the defendant B & O provide the plaintiff Mr. Gallick a reasonably safe place to work under the facts and circumstances existing at the time? *Jury can't decide on this question.*

14. [D]id the defendant B & O know that by permitting the accumulation of said pool of stagnant water, dead pigeons, dead rats, bugs, and vermin would be attracted to said area? *Yes.*

15. If the answer to 14 is yes, did the defendant B & O know that its employees would have to work in this area? *Yes.*

16. Was the defendant negligent in one or more of the particulars alleged in the petition? *Yes.*

17. If the answer to Question 16 is yes, indicate in the words of the petition the acts or omissions which constitute defendant's negligence. *There existed a pool of stagnant water on the premises in the possession of and under the control of defendant into which was accumulated dead pigeons, rats, and various forms of bugs and vermin.*

18. Was the illness or diseases from which Mr. Gallick now suffers caused in whole or in part by an insect bite sustained by him on defendant B & O's premises? *Yes.*

19. Were the injuries to the plaintiff proximately caused . . . by . . . the acts or omissions of the defendant? *Yes.*

20. [W]as there any reason for the defendant B & O to anticipate that such [maintaining stagnant, infested pool] would or might probably result in a mishap or an injury? *No.*

21. Is there a proximate causal relationship to the stagnant water, the dead rats, the dead pigeons, the insect bite, and the present physical condition of the plaintiff? *Yes.*

22. If the answer to Question 21 is yes, was it within the realm of reasonable probability or foreseeability of the defendant B & O to appreciate this proximate causal relationship between the stagnant water, the dead rats, the dead pigeons, the insect bite and the present physical condition of the plaintiff? *No.*

. . . It is said that interrogatories Nos. 20 and 22 are findings of no foreseeability, and that there is therefore a fatal inconsistency among the jury's findings and that they cancel one another out, necessitating a judgment for the defendant, or at least a new trial. But it is the duty of the courts to attempt to harmonize the answers, if it is possible under a fair reading of them: "Where there is a view of the case that makes the jury's answers to special interrogatories consistent, they must be resolved that way." Atlantic & Gulf Stevedores, Inc., v. Ellerman Lines, Ltd., 369 U.S. 355, 364. We therefore must attempt to reconcile the jury's findings, by exegesis if necessary, . . . before we are free to disregard the jury's special verdict and remand the case for a new trial.

[The opinion then discusses the jury's answers and concludes that the law does not require foreseeing the specific consequences of wrongful acts and defendant was liable for unexpectedly severe consequences, satisfying the foreseeability requirement of the Federal Employers' Liability Act under which plaintiff sued.]

. . . The Court of Appeals erred in depriving petitioner of the judgment entered upon the special verdict of the jury. The judgment of the Ohio Court of Appeals is reversed and the case is remanded for further proceedings not inconsistent with this opinion.

Reversed.

Mr. Justice HARLAN, dissenting.

Heartrending as the petitioner's accident has turned out to be, I think this case should not have been brought here. It involves no unsettled question of federal law calling for decision by this Court. . . .

Mr. Justice STEWART and Mr. Justice GOLDBERG, dissenting.

. . . .

The duty of courts to attempt to reconcile inconsistent jury findings has emerged from cases in which the jury answered special interrogatories *and also* returned a general verdict.

The inconsistencies which the courts have dealt with in these cases were inconsistencies between a general verdict for one of the parties and seemingly conflicting special findings in answer to added interrogatories. The purpose of such an effort has been to preserve, if possible, the integrity of the jury's general verdict. . . .

Although the Court several times mentions a "special verdict" of the jury, this refers to no more than the answers given to the interrogatories. The fact is that the jury returned no general verdict for either party. . . .

For these reasons we would set aside the judgment and remand this case for a new trial.

CASE QUESTIONS

1. Was the Court applying common law principles? If so, was it justified in doing so because the case was a question of federal law?
2. Since the case involved peculiarities of Ohio procedural law, should the U.S. Supreme Court have deferred to the Ohio Court of Appeals in interpreting the Ohio special verdict law?
3. Was Justice Harlan correct in his dissent when he stated that the case "affords a peculiarly dramatic example of the inadequacy of ordinary negligence law to meet the social obligations of modern industrial society. The cure for that, however, lies with the legislature and not with the courts."?

THE RULES OF EVIDENCE

Evidentiary rules form an independent subject for study that cannot be treated in satisfactory fashion here. In general, the rules of evidence are designed to exclude evidence that is irrelevant, repetitious, or unreliable. They help to prevent filibustering (delaying tactic) by attorneys representing losing causes. But the rules also reveal a distrust of the jury. Much that is excluded could be helpful in learning the truth but is not admissible because of questions of reliability, thus questioning the jury's ability to weigh the import of unreliable evidence. Since the jury may find facts based only on the evidence that it hears and sees, it often receives a limited picture of the circumstances of the case.

The ancient forerunner of the modern jury was composed of members of the community who knew the defendant and could judge the veracity of the plaintiff's claim. Today the jurors are strangers to the parties and the facts and are limited by the rules of evidence in what they can know of the case.

Two examples of evidentiary rules may suffice to illustrate this problem. First, one of the rules of evidence is that a nonexpert witness, or layperson, may not give opinion testimony, while a person qualifying as an expert, let us say a psychiatrist, may express an opinion on the facts of the case. As a result, an eye-witness friend of the defendant may not declare that the defendant was "insane," while a psychiatrist who entered the case long after the events took place may talk at length about how Oedipal conflicts caused the defendant to act as he did.

Second, the *hearsay rule* excludes from testimony out-of-court statements made by a person not present in court ("My friend told me that Joe had been drinking"). There are more than a dozen major exceptions to the hearsay rule, but it excludes what might otherwise be extremely relevant evidence on the grounds of unreliability and the lack of opportunity to cross-examine the person who made the statement.

MOTIONS

Parties to a case have at their disposal numerous motions that ask the court to take particular action by granting or denying the motion. Since the ruling on each motion requires the exercise of legal judgment, denial may be the basis for appeal by the movant (person making the motion), and granting the motion may provide a basis for appeal by the nonmoving party on the grounds of prejudicial error, which must be demonstrated to the satisfaction of an appellate court. The discussion here will be confined to a handful of motions that are designed to terminate the case favorably to the moving party if granted. They have several names but much in common; their differences depend largely on their timing, and so they are often classified as pretrial, trial, and posttrial motions.

Fact/Law Distinction

The purpose of trial must be kept in mind in order to understand the function of these motions. Trial refers to trying facts. Assuming a typical jury trial of a damage suit, the plaintiff must prove the elements of a cause of action and the amount of the damages. The jury must find facts supporting each element and fix the dollar amount of damages in order for plaintiff to recover. The only issues before the jury are those of disputed fact. If no facts are in dispute, the jury has no function. The parties may stipulate the truth of certain facts, thus taking those fact questions out of dispute. For example, in a suit for damages, the defendant might acknowledge liability for compensation to the plaintiff, not disputing the amount claimed by the plaintiff, but arguing that punitive damages are not allowed under the circumstances of the case. Whether punitive damages are allowable is a legal question. If the judge agrees with defendant's argument, there would be no task for the jury; if the judge disagrees, the jury must determine whether the facts of the case warrant punitive damages according to the instructions given the jury by the judge. If the jury finds punitive damages are appropriate, the amount must be fixed by the jury.

The simple model of dispute resolution describes a two-step process in which facts are determined from the evidence presented and law is applied to the facts to establish the prevailing party and the form of relief, if any, to be awarded. This assumes, first, that facts will be found—this is almost always the case, but rarely the jury finds it impossible to reach a consensus, resulting in a mistrial. The model also assumes that the law is there to be found and applied. This is somewhat problematic since the judge will always make conclusions of law, but the peculiarities of a given case may present novel legal issues not easily answered from statutes and cases.

If no material facts are in dispute, the only task before the court is to apply the law. Whether there are or are not facts in dispute is a question of law for the judge. The judge may take the case out of the hands of the jury or take a fact question away from jury determination by converting it into a question of law. This sleight of hand is justified with language such as, "reasonable persons could not disagree that . . . ". The rationale here is that the jury is needed only if some doubt exists with regard to the facts. If the judge concludes no doubt exists, even though the parties dispute the facts, the question can be decided "as a matter of law" ("reasonable persons could not disagree"). Disputed facts should normally go to the jury; a judge who oversteps the authority to decide facts will be reversed on appeal.

In its simplest form, the conversion of a fact question into a question of law is seen in the taking of *judicial notice.* The court may relieve a party of the burden of proving a fact by taking judicial notice of that fact. Ordinarily notice is taken on the basis of common knowledge of a fact (it is dark in Omaha at midnight; Mario Cuomo was governor of New York in 1989). Of course, self-evident facts are rarely disputed so the court does not need to bother with such questions, but sometimes there are facts that seem clear but are nevertheless disputed, as when a party attempted to argue that wine is not intoxicating and the judge took judicial notice of the fact that wine is an intoxicating beverage.

CASE NO. 8–3 The Wages of Sin

In the 1940s, the great silent film actor Charlie Chaplin was sued by Joan Berry over paternity of her daughter, Carol Ann Berry. Chaplin agreed to pay support for the child if blood tests indicated he could be the father. To the contrary, the blood tests indicated he could not have been the father. Carol Ann had blood type B, while Joan had A and Charlie had O. Since Carol Ann must have inherited B from a parent who had a B or AB type blood, Charlie could not have been the father. Joan won a suit that was characterized by histrionics, including putting Charlie and Carol Ann side by side to show a family resemblance. The court refused to take judicial notice of the blood tests as conclusive and sent the case to the jury, which concluded that Charlie was the father. Although judicial notice is usually reserved for matters of common knowledge, the question arises as to whether the court should take fact-finding away from the jury when scientific certainty compels a factual conclusion. Compare *State v. Gray*, below.

Note that bastardy, usually called paternity, proceedings are "quasicriminal" proceedings that are used to establish paternity for related civil suits. The court uses preponderance of the evidence rather than guilt beyond a reasonable doubt as the standard of proof.

STATE of Ohio ex rel. Hope A. STEIGER, Complainant,

v.

Bruce GRAY, Defendant.

Juvenile Court of Ohio, Cuyahoga County

145 N.E.2d 162 (1957)

WOLDMAN, Judge.

Complainant, an unmarried woman, filed a complaint in bastardy alleging that the defendant is the father of her child born to her December 1, 1956.

Defendant himself did not testify on his own behalf. He called but one defense witness—Dr. Roger W. Marsters, a clinical pathologist, who had been appointed by the court to conduct the blood grouping tests of the child, the complainant and the defendant, as requested by the defendant. . . .

Dr. Marsters' qualifications as an expert serologist were not questioned by the complainant. He testified that he carefully tested the blood specimens of the complainant, the defendant and the child "for the International OAB, M and N, and C, D, E, and **c** blood factors by using known blood controls along with the unknowns" . . . .

"The data on the International OAB blood group factors are inconclusive because the mating of a type A individual with a type O individual may produce offspring of either type A or type O.

"The data on the M–N factors are inconclusive, ...

"The data on the Rh blood factor D are inconclusive, ...

"The data on the Rh blood factor E are inconclusive, ...

"The data on the [Rh] factor **c** are inconclusive, ...

"The data on the Rh factor C however indicate that an exclusion of paternity is established on this basis. Both Hope Steiger and Bruce Gray are negative for the C factor and therefore lack this particular blood antigen. On the other hand Baby Norma June Steiger is C-positive and therefore possesses this particular blood antigen. Since these blood factors can only be inherited from the parents and since both of these adults lack the C, then some other man than Bruce Gray must be the father of this child.

"In conclusion, an exclusion of paternity is established by the demonstration of the C factor in this child, Norma Steiger, without the presence of this particular blood factor in the blood of either of these two adults, Hope Steiger or Bruce Gray.

"Respectfully submitted,
Roger W. Marsters, Ph.D.
Clinical Pathologist."

Dr. Marsters stated that he and his associates made five separate blood tests and that all proper safeguards were taken to protect the integrity and accuracy of the blood grouping tests. The accuracy of his conclusion of the exclusion of defendant as the father of the child was not rebutted by any counter medical evidence submitted by complainant. . . .

. . . This court further believes that the near unanimity of medical and legal authorities on the question of the reliability of blood grouping tests as an indicator of the truth in questioned paternity cases justifies the taking of judicial notice of the general recognition of the accuracy and value of the tests when properly performed by persons skilled in conducting them. The law does not hesitate to adopt scientific aids to the discovery of the truth which have achieved such recognition. Cortese v. Cortese, 1950, 10 N.J.Super. 152, 72 A.2d 117. . . .

I hold, further, that because this great weight must be accorded to the blood grouping test results as testified to by Dr. Marsters, complainant has failed to prove the guilt of the defendant by a preponderance of the evidence.

Accordingly, I find the defendant not guilty as charged in the complaint.

DISMISSAL MOTIONS

On motion a judge may end a case because one side has no legal basis for its claims or because no material fact is in dispute and it is time to enter judgment. Since the granting of such motions cuts short further discussion or presentation of facts and denies a person's "day in court," the court uses a strict test. Although it is phrased somewhat differently according to the motions, generally it states that the court will test the motion by looking at the case "in the light most favorable to the nonmoving party." This test must be examined by considering the motions.

The Demurrer

The first dismissal motion that can arise in a case is one made by the defendant attacking the complaint by a "motion to dismiss for failure to state a claim upon which relief can be granted." Since this is quite a mouthful, it is abbreviated to "motion to dismiss for failure to state a claim," "motion to dismiss for failure to state a cause of action," or, borrowing from equity, a "demurrer." Granting of this motion stops the action dead in its tracks. With a demurrer, the defendant argues that the complaint is legally insufficient, it does not state a cause of action, or the law has no remedy for the grievance asserted by the plaintiff.

The test used by the court for a demurrer is as follows: If all the allegations of the complaint were true, the complaint would still not allow plaintiff any relief. In a sense the demurrer says "So what?" Some essential ingredient is missing. The *Georgia High School Association* case in the previous chapter is a case that *should* have been dismissed if the trial court judge had taken the position the appellate court did, namely, plaintiffs had no property rights that were infringed by the referee's bad call; the law does not allow relief for such a case—no cause of action exists.

The assumption of the truth of plaintiff's allegations is made only for the purpose of testing the demurrer. By making the demurrer, the defendant does not admit the allegations are true for any other purpose. If the demurrer is denied (the usual outcome) the defendant may proceed to dispute the facts alleged.

Summary Judgment

A motion for summary judgment can be both a trial and pretrial motion. As a pretrial motion, it is made at some point before trial when it appears that one side must win. For example, although the complaint may appear to state a cause of action, after all pleadings have been filed and discovery has taken place, plaintiff's case may reveal some fatal weakness so defendant moves for summary judgment. In such a case, the test to be applied is whether, viewing the case in the light most favorable to the plaintiff, the nonmoving party, the plaintiff could not win. Again, if there are material facts in dispute, the motion will be denied.

Motion for a Directed Verdict

At trial, after the plaintiff has presented his case-in-chief, the defendant may make a motion for a directed verdict. Construing all the evidence in the light most favorable to the plaintiff, the motion will be granted if it appears that plaintiff has not provided sufficient proof to prevail. If granted, judgment is entered for the defendant, and the case is over. Usually there are sufficient facts that a jury might find in plaintiff's favor, so the case will continue. The motion for directed verdict is made routinely, and almost as routinely denied, so that defendant preserves the right to appeal on the basis of its denial. Even if plaintiff's case is weak, the judge may be reluctant to take the fact-finding away from the jury.

At the close of all the evidence, both sides commonly make motions for a directed verdict. At first glance it might seem that one would be granted, but since each is measured in terms most favorable to the nonmoving party, if there is a reasonable dispute over the facts, the evidence could be interpreted to support either side, so that task is left to the jury.

In a nonjury trial, the judge is the fact-finder so the appropriate motions are called motions for summary judgment since the judge may immediately enter judgment. Formerly judges directed the juries to enter verdicts, which explains the "directed verdict" label of the motion, but this is no longer followed. A motion for a directed verdict is also called a motion for nonsuit in some jurisdictions.

Motion for Judgment Notwithstanding the Verdict

After the jury has returned a verdict, either party may make a motion for judgment notwithstanding the verdict, usually referred to as a motion n.o.v. from the Latin *non obstante veredicto* ("notwithstanding the verdict"). This will be granted if the judge finds as a matter of law that the verdict is against the manifest weight of the evidence. On occasion a jury will return a verdict that appears absurd on the basis of the record, or the jury's fact-finding may be legally inconsistent; for example, the jury may find that the plaintiff was negligent as well as the defendant, giving the defendant an absolute defense to the suit (in a state that recognizes contributory negligence), and yet award compensation to the plaintiff. In such a case, the judge would enter a judgment in favor of defendant on a motion for judgment n.o.v.

The aforementioned motions terminate the proceedings if granted. Usually they are denied; in most instances a case should not proceed to trial if one side's case is fatally flawed—the case should have been settled short of trial. Nevertheless, the expense of trial is a threat that is used for bargaining, and sometimes both sides are so stubborn in the negotiating process that trial is held regardless of the merits of the case. When the dispute is based on novel or controversial interpretations of the law, the trial may be primarily a prelude to appeal. Negotiations may continue during trial and prior to appeal. In addition, there are posttrial motions designed to set aside the judgment or to ask for a new trial. These and other pretrial procedures will be left to further study. Specific devices of civil procedure vary considerably from one jurisdiction to another, and it is best to learn the peculiarities of the jurisdiction in which one intends to practice.

RES JUDICATA AND COLLATERAL ESTOPPEL

While it is possible to obtain a new trial if an appellate court has determined that prejudicial error in the first trial justifies relitigating the case, the losing plaintiff does not have the right to a retrial simply by filing the cause of action again. This is represented by the principle of *res judicata*, Latin for "the thing has been decided." A party may not bring a suit over and over again until a favorable result is achieved. *Res judicata* is an affirmative defense that bars further suit. It is also called *merger and bar*, referring to the principle that the claim of the winning plaintiff is "merged" in the judgment of the court and enforceable by the judgment, but the claim is "barred" from further suit when the plaintiff loses.

Although this seems straightforward, a number of problems complicate the principle. Overlapping state and federal jurisdictions allow a claim in either or both courts. State and federal law may cover similar subjects in different ways. Then problem then becomes whether a suit brought in one court is really the same case as that later brought in another. And since the law provides different causes of action that can arise from the same events, e.g., threatening someone with physical harm might be grounds for "assault" or "intentional infliction of mental distress," the question can arise whether one suit bars the later suit.

There are important conflicting policies in claim preclusion (*res judicata*). On the one hand, fairness would prevent a defendant from being forced to defend the same case more than once. On the other hand, plaintiff should have full access to the courts. The court will not invoke *res judicata* if there is a difference in the parties to the claim or if the case involves different issues than those brought in the first case. This discussion seriously oversimplifies *res judicata*, which can become very complex with multiple parties and multiple claims.

Collateral estoppel is directly related to *res judicata*; it is a bar to the relitigation of specific issues that have been previously adjudicated, even though the suits may not satisfy the requirements of *res judicata* (if all the issues in a new suit are identical to those in the prior suit, collateral estoppel and *res judicata* may both be said to apply). Occasionally a new suit raises issues from a former case as well as additional issues not barred by the prior suit. Nevertheless, those issues raised in the former suit and decided in it may not again be raised because of collateral estoppel.

Res judicata and collateral estoppel are simple in principle but often difficult in application.

SUMMARY

Civil procedure has both theoretical and practical importance. Theoretically, examination of our system of civil procedure reveals an adversarial system in which the fairness of the procedural rules takes on special significance. Reliance is placed on procedure to achieve justice. Practically, the legal practitioner must understand the procedure of the jurisdiction, both to enforce the rights of clients and to protect them from the maneuvers of the opposing side.

Lawsuits are initiated by the filing of a complaint and service of process on the defendant. In order to determine the rights of the parties, the Court must have personal jurisdiction over them. In restricted cases a suit may be filed against a thing (*in rem* jurisdiction). When there is a choice of courts having jurisdiction over a case, proper venue is determined by the rules and the circumstances of the parties.

Most American jurisdictions follow code pleading, which is a statutory refinement of common law, and equity pleading, which requires that a complaint state a cause of action, to which the defendant files a responsive pleading called an answer.

In some cases the plaintiff will then file a pleading responding to the answer.

An important feature of pretrial procedure is the discovery process in which the parties enjoy great latitude in learning about the case for the other side through deposition, interrogatories, requests for documents, etc.

Key features of the jury trial are jury selection and presentation of evidence. Each side has ample opportunity to present evidence and challenge the evidence for the other side. The plaintiff carries the burden of proving the elements of the cause of action.

Each side has at its disposal several motions at the pretrial, trial, and posttrial stages. The most important of these are motions that test the validity of the case for the other side, such as a motion for summary judgment. When granted, these motions terminate the litigation at that point.

CHAPTER QUESTIONS

1. Why is it necessary to be thoroughly familiar with the rules of civil procedure in one's jurisdiction?
2. Why is *voir dire* so important?
3. How does a defendant attack a complaint for legal insufficiency?
4. Why are depositions important?
5. What causes the most delay in reaching trial?
6. How does the pretrial hearing encourage settlement?
7. How does the paralegal play a part in discovery?
8. What is the difference between *res judicata* and collateral estoppel?
9. How does venue differ from subject matter jurisdiction?
10. On what basis can the judge keep a case from going to the jury?

EXERCISES

Discovery

Suppose you are a paralegal working for the attorneys representing the Baltimore & Ohio Railroad in the *Gallick* case. You are assigned the following tasks during the discovery process:

1. Frame ten questions that should be asked during oral deposition of Gallick aimed at determining the foreseeability of his injuries and the amount of damages for his injuries.
2. Frame five written interrogatories to obtain written responses that might be helpful in preparing the defense.
3. What documents would you request from Gallick?
4. Write a Request for Admissions aimed at facts that might be helpful to your case and would be difficult for Gallick to deny.

Voir dire

5. Frame five questions you would ask the potential jurors in the *Gallick* case if you were representing Baltimore & Ohio Railroad.
6. Frame five questions you would ask the potential jurors in the *Gallick* case if you were representing Gallick.

Opening Statement

7. Prepare a one-page outline of the opening statement by the attorney for Baltimore & Ohio Railroad.

PROFESSIONAL PROFILE

"The sky is the limit," declares Susan Hock. She believes that a flexible and positive attitude is the most important element of success. "Once the paralegal has been able to establish basic skills, there are many nontraditional jobs available outside of the law firm setting," she says. Hock helped establish Paralegals Plus, Inc., a freelance agency.

Hock graduated from the University of Central Florida in 1981, following her internship at the state's attorney's office in Orange County, Florida. Initially Hock's days were spent assisting the attorneys in court, drafting documents, and analyzing records as a family law paralegal.

Upon relocating to Dallas, Texas, Hock applied to Burleson, Pate & Gibson, where she was hired by Phil Burleson, former president of the Dallas Bar Association. One week before Hock applied for the position, Burleson had addressed the Dallas Association of Legal Assistants (DALA). Following an embarrassing question-and-answer session, Mr. Burleson promised to learn more about paralegals and about what they do; he hired Hock. "In entering the profession," according to Hock, "it is important to become involved with local and national organizations." These groups assist entry level paralegals by providing a "placement network."

Currently Hock consults with law firms and corporate legal departments regarding the management of paralegals. Hock says, "Once my client's needs are analyzed, I match paralegals and their skills with the positions available." Paralegals assist employers by making the legal process more cost-effective and efficient. "And the most rewarding aspect for the paralegals is the ability to help clients solve their problems," Hock says.

Working with attorneys is a team effort. For the legal team to work efficiently together, the attorney and paralegal must establish a relationship based on trust and adherence to legal ethics. As a professional, the paralegal must assist the attorney in defining the parameters of responsibility delegated. Paralegals should also demonstrate professionalism in order to gain attorneys' confidence and receive more substantive assignments, advises Hock.

Susan Mooney Hock
Vice President, Paralegals Plus, Inc.

CHAPTER 9
The Law of
Criminal Procedure

The quality of a nation's civilization can be largely measured by the methods it uses in the enforcement of its criminal law.

— *Schaefer, Federalism and State Criminal Procedure,*
70 Harv L Rev 1, 26 (1956)

> It is better that ten guilty persons escape than one innocent suffer.
>
> — *William Blackstone*

THE CONSTITUTIONAL BASIS OF CRIMINAL PROCEDURE

Criminal procedure follows many of the patterns of civil procedure, but major differences are largely due to the special provisions of the U.S. Constitution, which are usually echoed in state constitutions. The Constitution, and especially the first ten amendments (the Bill of Rights), expresses a basic code of criminal procedure by enumerating rights of the citizens against government intrusion and rights of those accused of crimes. The provisions of the Constitution have been subject to intense scrutiny by state and federal courts, particularly since the 1950s. Criminal procedure cannot be understood without reference to these rights. The following excerpts from the Constitution highlight these rights with brief annotations or explanations of the terms emphasized in **boldface**.

Excerpts from the Constitution of the United States

ARTICLE I

Section 9:

(2) The privilege of the **Writ of Habeas Corpus** shall not be suspended, unless when in Cases of Rebellion or Invasion the public Safety may require it.

(3) No **Bill of Attainder** or **ex post facto Law** shall be passed.

ARTICLE III

Section 2:

(3) The trial of all Crimes, except in Cases of Impeachment, shall be by **Jury**; and such Trial shall be held in the State where the said Crimes shall have been committed; but when not committed within any State, the Trial shall be at such Place or Places as the Congress may by Law have directed.

AMENDMENT IV

The right of the people to be secure in their persons, houses, papers, and effects, against **unreasonable searches and seizures**, shall not be violated, and **no warrants shall issue, but upon probable cause, supported** by oath or affirmation, and particularly describing the place to be searched, and the persons or things to be seized.

AMENDMENT V

No person shall be held to answer for a capital, or otherwise infamous crime, unless on a presentment or **indictment of a grand jury**, except in cases arising in the land or naval forces, or in the militia, when in actual service in time of war or public danger; nor shall any person be subject for the same offense to be **twice put in jeopardy** of life or limb; nor shall be compelled in any criminal case to be a **witness against himself, nor be deprived of life, liberty, or property, without due process of law**; nor shall private property be taken for public use, without just compensation.

AMENDMENT VI

In all criminal prosecutions, the accused shall enjoy the **right to a speedy and public trial**, by an **impartial jury** of the State and district wherein the crime shall have been committed, which district shall have been previously ascertained by law, and to be informed of the **nature and cause of the accusation**; to be **confronted with the witnesses against him**; to have **compulsory process** for obtaining witnesses in his favor, and to have the **assistance of counsel for his defense**.

AMENDMENT VIII

Excessive bail shall not be required, nor excessive fines imposed, nor **cruel and unusual punishments** inflicted.

AMENDMENT XIV

. . . No State shall make or enforce any law which shall abridge the privileges or immunities of citizens of the United States; nor shall any State deprive any person of life, liberty, or property, without **due process** of law; nor deny to any person within its jurisdiction the **equal protection** of the laws. . . .

Annotations

A **Writ of Habeas Corpus** is brought by a petition, the purpose of which is to challenge the lawfulness of a detention by the government. This includes institutions other than prisons, but most habeas corpus actions are brought by imprisoned criminals. It is often used as a form of federal review after state appeals have failed.

A **Bill of Attainder** is a law that singles out a person or a very small group of persons for penal sanctions. An example of such a law would be one that made it a crime to be the Grand Wizard of the Ku Klux Klan.

An **ex post facto Law** is a penal law that operates retroactively. For example, under such a law a person could be charged with a crime for an action that was not a crime at the time it took place, or a person's sentence for a crime could be increased to a greater sentence than was permissible at the time the crime occurred.

The right to a **Jury** trial applies to all criminal prosecutions. Disciplinary actions in prisons do not fall into this category.

The right to be free from **unreasonable searches and seizures** is designed primarily to protect citizens from excessive intrusions by government and police into their homes and persons, but interpretation of search and seizure has extended to places of business as well. The reasonableness of a search must necessarily remain a subjective judgment.

" . . . **no warrants shall issue, but upon probable cause, supported by oath or affirmation, and particularly describing the place to be searched, and the persons or things to be seized.**" Warrants are carefully scrutinized by criminal defense attorneys to determine whether they conform to this constitutional requirement. If the warrant or the search exceeds constitutional limits, the evidence seized may be excluded from trial, which frequently destroys the case for the prosecution. For example, drugs illegally seized may not be used as evidence, so the prosecution then has no case.

A **grand jury indictment** requires a hearing before a special body of citizens gathered to review the prosecutor's evidence in support of taking the accused to trial. If the grand jury concludes that there is probable cause to believe the accused committed the crime, it issues an indictment, which is a written accusation by the grand jury charging the accused with a criminal act. It is also referred to as a *true bill,* but when the grand jury does not indict, it is called a *no bill.* The grand jury proceeding is controlled by the prosecutor to such an extent that a chief judge of the New York Court of Appeals remarked that a grand jury would indict a ham sandwich if the prosecutor recommended it.

A grand jury, although composed of citizens, is different from the petit jury which serves at trial. The grand jury has been used as an investigatory tool of the prosecutor's office on many occasions, as where the federal prosecutor investigated activities of the Black Panther Party, whose leaders had indicated an intent to kill President Nixon and had advocated sabotage by Black soldiers in Vietnam. Since witnesses before the grand jury are not represented in the hearings by their attorneys and since the grand jury cannot convict, the prosecutor enjoys a freedom from the usual limitations imposed at trial, [so] the grand jury can be used oppressively.

In 1734, William Cosby, the English governor of New York, sought to have the publisher of a radical newspaper with extremely limited circulation indicted for criminal libel. The grand jury twice refused to indict. Thereafter, the publisher, Peter Zenger, was charged with libel, and one of the most celebrated trials in American history followed. It was with this and similar precedents fresh in their memories that our founding fathers incorporated into the Fifth Amendment the requirement that no person shall be held to answer for an infamous crime except upon the presentment or indictment of a grand jury.

Today, courts across this country are faced with an increasing flow of cases arising out of grand jury proceedings concerned with the possible punishment of political dissidents. It would be a cruel twist of history to allow the institution of the grand jury that was designed at least partially to protect political dissent to become an instrument of political suppression. *Bursey v. United States*, 466 F.2d 1059 (9th Cir. 1972)

[After a dramatic trial characterized by hostility between an arrogant judge appointed specially by Governor Cosby and a brave and unrelenting defense attorney, Mr. Zenger was found by the jury to be *not guilty*, an historic victory for the people and the cause of freedom of speech and of the press.]

Double jeopardy prevents a person from being tried twice for the same crime. Jeopardy attaches once the accused has been put on trial before judge or jury; until that time, the case may be postponed without violating this provision. Double jeopardy applies to bringing the same charges in the same jurisdiction even if the courts are different, e.g., a lower criminal court versus a higher criminal court. This does not apply to state and federal jurisdictions. In the famous case of the three civil rights workers who were killed in Mississippi, an acquittal of homicide in the state court was followed by prosecution and conviction in federal court for depriving the victims of their civil rights.

A person cannot be held to be a **witness against himself**. This is usually referred to as the *privilege against self-incrimination*, generally restricted to a testimonial privilege; i.e., a person may not be required to testify to matters that would tend to incriminate him. Blood tests, fingerprints, and most documents that might incriminate are not considered "testimony" and not covered by this privilege. This provision of the Fifth Amendment is the basis for the *Miranda* rights, particularly the right to remain silent during a police interrogation.

" . . . **nor be deprived of life, liberty or property, without due process of law"** is an important feature of criminal law because of the inclusion of the words *life* and *liberty* since the primary means of punishing criminals are execution and incarceration. Any criminal procedure can be scrutinized for fairness on the basis of the due process clause. While the Fifth Amendment applies to federal action, a similar clause in the Fourteenth Amendment applies to the states, subjecting state action to review by federal courts.

The defendant has a **right to a speedy and public trial**. Most state and federal jurisdictions have by statute fixed a time period in which a criminal case must be brought. If the prosecutor exceeds the time limit, the accused may not be tried. The right to a public trial is designed to prevent abuse that might occur in a closed hearing. When appropriate and with the court's approval, the defendant may waive this right and close the trial to the public.

The right to an **impartial jury** is fundamental to our criminal justice system since police and prosecutor assume an accusatorial role. Great pains are often taken to guarantee that the jury is untainted by pretrial publicity or acquaintance with the facts of the case.

The defendant must be informed of the **nature and cause of the accusation** in order to prepare a defense. This simply spells out the notice requirement that would otherwise be implied by the due process clause.

The right of the defendant to be **confronted with the witnesses against him** is a protection against anonymous accusers and ensures the right to cross-examine witnesses.

Compulsory process refers to the power of the defendant in a criminal case to force witnesses to attend trial under a subpoena issued by the court. If appearance were voluntary, the defendant would be at a severe disadvantage.

The right to effective **assistance of counsel** for the defendant has become a cherished right only in the last few decades. For many years, the right to counsel was considered applicable only to federal cases and then only when the accused could afford to pay or was accused of a capital offense (*Powell v. Alabama*, 287 U.S. 45 [1932]) until the famous exchange between Gideon and the Florida judge:

> *The Court:* Mr. Gideon, I am sorry, but I cannot appoint Counsel to represent you in this case. Under the laws of the State of Florida, the only time the Court can appoint Counsel to represent a Defendant is when that person is charged with a capital offense. I am sorry, but I will have to deny your request to appoint Counsel to defend you in this case.

The Defendant: The U.S. Supreme Court says I am entitled to be represented by Counsel.

Gideon v. Wainwright, 372 U.S. 335 (1963).

Mr. Gideon was not exactly correct when he made this statement, but after he presented his own defense and was convicted, he took the case to the U.S. Supreme Court, which agreed with him. *Argersinger v. Hamlin*, 407 U.S. 25 (1972) extended the right to petty offenses involving possible imprisonment. A defendant who cannot afford an attorney must be furnished one by the government.

The right to be free from the imposition of **excessive bail** is self-explanatory; what is excessive may be judged relative to what is usual bail under similar circumstances. This is a limitation on the judge's discretion.

The right against the imposition of **cruel and unusual punishments** is also a relative concept. This particular principle has been viewed as an evolving standard—what was not considered "cruel and unusual" fifty years ago may be considered uncivilized and barbaric by today's standards.

The **due process** clause demands fair procedure and reasonable laws; it is a standard that the courts can invoke when injustice is apparent.

The **equal protection** clause imposes a test of equality before the law against discriminatory practices. There must be no difference in treatment in the statement of the law itself or in its application, but in recent years the differential impact of the laws with regard to minorities has raised equal protection claims; for example, it has been shown statistically that blacks receive a disproportionate number of death sentences.

CASE NO. 9–1   *Self-Incrimination*

The privilege against self-incrimination in the Fifth Amendment is zealously guarded by the U.S. Supreme Court, as the following case demonstrates.

GRIFFIN

v.

CALIFORNIA

U.S. Supreme Court
380 U.S. 609 (1965)

Mr. Justice DOUGLAS delivered the opinion of the Court.

Petitioner was convicted of murder in the first degree after a jury trial in a California court. He did not testify at the trial on the issue of guilt, though he did testify at the separate trial on the issue of penalty. The trial court instructed the jury on the issue of guilt, stating that a defendant has a constitutional right not to testify. But it told the jury:

> As to any evidence or facts against him which the defendant can reasonably be expected to deny or explain because of facts within his knowledge, if he does not testify or if, though he does testify, he fails to deny or explain such evidence, the jury may take that failure into consideration as tending to indicate the truth of such evidence and as indicating that among the inferences that may be reasonably drawn therefrom those unfavorable to the defendant are the more probable. . . .

Petitioner had been seen with the deceased the evening of her death, the evidence placing him with her in the alley where her body was found. The prosecutor made much of the failure of petitioner to testify:

> . . . He would know how she got down the alley. He would know how the blood got on the bottom of the concrete steps. He would know how long he was with her in that box. He would know how her wig got off. He would know whether he beat her or mistreated her. . . .
>
> These things he has not seen fit to take the stand and deny or explain.
>
> And in the whole world, if anybody would know, this defendant would know.
>
> Essie Mae is dead, she can't tell you her side of the story. The defendant won't.

The death penalty was imposed and the California Supreme Court affirmed. . . .

. . . The question remains whether, statute or not, the comment [on defendant's refusal to testify] rule, approved by California, violates the Fifth Amendment.

We think it does. It is in substance a rule of evidence that allows the State the privilege of tendering to the jury for its consideration the failure of the accused to testify. No formal offer of proof is made as in other situations; but the prosecutor's comment and the court's acquiescence are the equivalent of an offer of evidence and its acceptance. The Court in the *Wilson* case stated: " . . . It is not every one who can safely venture on the witness stand though entirely innocent of the charge against him, . . . will often confuse and embarrass him to such a degree as to increase rather than remove prejudices against him. It is not every one, however honest, who would, therefore, willingly be placed on the witness stand. The statute, in tenderness to the weakness of those who from the causes mentioned might refuse to ask to be a witness, particularly when they may have been in some degree compromised by their association with others, declares that the failure of the defendant in a criminal action to request to be a witness shall not create any presumption against him."

. . . What the jury may infer, given no help from the court is one thing. What it may infer when the court solemnizes the silence of the accused into evidence against him is quite another. That the inference of guilt is not always so natural or irresistible is brought out in the *Modesto* opinion itself: "Defendant contends that the reason a defendant refuses to testify is that his prior convictions will be introduced in evidence to impeach him and not that he is unable to deny the accusations. It is true that the defendant might fear that his prior convictions will prejudice the jury, and therefore another possible inference can be drawn from his refusal to take the stand."

. . . We take that in its literal sense and hold that the Fifth Amendment, in its direct application to the Federal Government, and in its bearing on the States by reason of the Fourteenth Amendment, forbids either comment by the prosecution on the accused's silence or instructions by the court that such silence is evidence of guilt.

Reversed.

MR. JUSTICE STEWART, with whom MR. JUSTICE WHITE joins, dissenting. . . .

We must determine whether the petitioner has been "compelled . . . to be a witness against himself." Compulsion is the focus of the inquiry. Certainly, if any compulsion be detected in the California procedure, it is of a dramatically different and less palpable nature than that involved in the procedures which historically gave rise to the Fifth Amendment guarantee. When a suspect was brought before the Court of High Commission or the **Star Chamber**, he was commanded to answer whatever was asked of him, and subjected to a far-reaching and deeply probing inquiry in an effort to ferret out some unknown and frequently unsuspected crime. He declined to answer on pain of incarceration, banishment, or mutilation. And if he spoke falsely, he was subject to further punishment. Faced with this formidable array of alternatives, his decision to speak was unquestionably coerced.

Those were the lurid realities which lay behind enactment of the Fifth Amendment, a far cry from the subject matter of the case before us. I think that the court in this case stretches the concept of compulsion beyond all reasonable bounds, and that whatever compulsion may exist derives from the defendant's choice not to testify, not from any comment by court or counsel. . . .

CASE GLOSSARY

The Star Chamber was a special high court in England that was transformed by Henry VIII and succeeding kings into a political device to punish political opposition. It became so notorious that it was finally abolished.

THE EXCLUSIONARY RULE

The exclusionary rule is a special feature of criminal procedure that has developed from a series of U.S. Supreme Court interpretations of the Fourth, Fifth, and Fourteenth Amendments. It applies to excluding evidence illegally obtained by the government and enforces the adversarial concept in criminal proceedings. Because of the disparity between the power and resources of the government and the relative powerlessness of the criminal defendant, a number of protections, such as those enumerated in the Constitution, are afforded the defendant to equalize the respective positions in a criminal proceeding. The exclusionary rule operates to protect the defendant from abusive procedures by a more powerful opponent.

Basically, the exclusionary rule excludes from trial evidence obtained in violation of the defendant's constitutional rights. It first arose in *Weeks v. United States*, 232 U.S. 383 (1914), which held that evidence illegally obtained by federal officers could be excluded from evidence, but *Weeks* failed to apply the principle to the states. *Wolf v. Colorado*, 338 U.S. 25 (1949) held that search and seizure provisions of the Fourth Amendment were applicable to the states under the due process clause of the Fourteenth Amendment but did not exclude illegally obtained evidence from state prosecutions. *Wolf* was overruled in 1961 by *Mapp v. Ohio*, 367 U.S. 643, which held that the products of a search violating Fourth Amendment rights may not be used in state prosecutions.

Suppose the police exact a confession from a suspect through torture. Should the confession be presented to the jury and the defendant allowed to disavow the confession because it was involuntary? Should the jury be allowed to weigh the relevance of the confession in light of the circumstances under which it was obtained? Our law answers in the negative. Coerced confessions have no place in the trial. This principle needs little justification; it is a reasonable interpretation of the meaning and intent of the due process clause of the Fourteenth Amendment.

In *Miranda v. Arizona*, 384 U.S. 486 (1966), Chief Justice Warren wrote an opinion that linked the right to counsel of the Sixth Amendment and the privilege against self-incrimination of the Fifth Amendment, both applicable to the states under the Fourteenth Amendment due process clause. The four dissenters argued that the Fifth Amendment was historically unconnected to the exclusion of involuntary confessions, but Warren and his four brethren prevailed, and police have been reading Miranda rights ever since. (Warren pointed out that these rights had been FBI policy for some time.) The precise requirements were spelled out in Chief Justice Warren's majority opinion:

> Our holding will be spelled out with some specificity in the pages which follow but briefly stated it is this: the prosecution may not use statements, whether exculpatory or inculpatory, stemming from custodial interrogation of the defendant unless it demonstrates the use of procedural safeguards effective to secure the privilege against self-incrimination. By custodial interrogation, we mean questioning initiated by law enforcement officers after a person has been taken into custody or otherwise deprived of his freedom of action in any significant way. As for the procedural safeguards to be employed, unless other fully effective means are devised to inform accused persons of their right

of silence and to assure a continuous opportunity to exercise it, the following measures are required. *Prior to any questioning, the person must be warned that he has a right to remain silent, that any statement he does make may be used as evidence against him, and that he has a right to the presence of an attorney, either retained or appointed.* The defendant may waive effectuation of these rights, provided the waiver is made voluntarily, knowingly and intelligently. If, however, he indicates in any manner and at any stage of the process that he wishes to consult with an attorney before speaking there can be no questioning. Likewise, if the individual is alone and indicates in any manner that he does not wish to be interrogated, the police may not question him. The mere fact that he may have answered some questions or volunteered some statements on his own does not deprive him of the right to refrain from answering any further inquiries until he has consulted with an attorney and thereafter consents to be questioned. [emphasis added]

In most jurisdictions, a motion to suppress (evidence or a confession) is a pretrial motion that tests the applicability of the exclusionary rule to the facts of the case. If the prosecution's case relies on such evidence, the granting of the motion will be followed by a dismissal of the charges or a motion by the defense for a judgment of acquittal. A surprising majority of criminal defendants make confessions in spite of being advised of their right to remain silent and their right to an attorney. When first contacted, the criminal defense attorney's first words of advice are likely to be: "Do not say anything to the police until I get there."

The criminal courts have been inundated for many years by drug crimes. In most of these, the defense's best attack is to suppress the evidence, so search and seizure appeals abound. Search and seizure law has come to draw extremely fine lines between proper and improper searches.

PLEA BARGAINING

The criminal justice system cannot be appreciated without an understanding of the custom of plea bargaining. The prosecuting attorney and the defense attorney usually engage in a form of negotiation, which until recent years has been a largely unofficial part of criminal procedure. Nearly all convictions are the result of negotiation. The defendant agrees to plead guilty in return for beneficial treatment by the prosecution. The prosecution may agree to drop some of the charges, reduce the offense—say, from first-degree murder to second-degree murder or from burglary to criminal trespass—thereby lessening the penalty, or recommend a lenient sentence or probation, which recommendation is usually accepted by the judge.

The present system could not work without plea bargaining. If every defendant demanded a jury trial, there would not be enough courts and prosecutors to try all the cases. Less than five percent of criminal cases go to trial (the same is true of civil cases). The presumption is that in most cases a trial would result in a conviction, thus encouraging defendants to make the best deal they can. Nevertheless, the custom of plea bargaining has come under severe criticism because negotiation takes place outside of public and judicial scrutiny and suggests a degree of collusion between prosecutors and defense attorneys.

CASE NO. 9–2 Plea Bargaining Fails

A plea bargain is often treated as a contract, and like a contract, sometimes the bargain is broken. In the following case, the defendant did not fulfill his promises but is nevertheless attempting to enforce the contract with the prosecutor through a contract remedy called *specific performance*, which asks the court to order the other party to the contract to perform the contract.

STATE of Arizona, Appellee,

v.

Ricky Wayne TISON, Appellant.

Supreme Court of Arizona,
En Banc.
633 P.2d 335 (1981)

STRUCKMEYER, Chief Justice.

This appeal is by Ricky Wayne Tison from judgments of guilty and death sentences on four counts of first degree murder. He also appeals from judgments of guilty and sentences on three counts of kidnapping, two counts of armed robbery, and one count of theft of a motor vehicle. . . .

On July 30, 1978, appellant and his two brothers, Raymond and Donald Tison, assisted in the escape of their father, Gary Tison, and Randy Greenawalt from the Arizona State Prison. Both appellant's father and Greenawalt were serving life sentences for murder at the time. Appellant's convictions for crimes arising out of the prison escape and subsequent capture twelve days later were recently affirmed by this Court. [C.]

The five men fled the prison in a green Ford. Later they transferred to a Lincoln Continental. The Lincoln was discovered on August 6, 1978, in Yuma County, Arizona, near Quartzsite. In and around the vehicle were the bodies of John and Donnelda Lyons and their twenty-two-month-old son, Christopher. The body of a niece of the Lyonses, Theresa Tyson, was later found approximately one-fifth of a mile west of the Lincoln. All four had died from shotgun wounds. . . .

Appellant in his statements explained that the Lincoln became disabled with a flat tire near Yuma. The Mazda was flagged down and all five men pulled guns on the Mazda's occupants, who were taken out of that car and placed in the Continental. Both cars were then taken down another road and parked trunk to trunk. Articles were exchanged between cars, and money and weapons belonging to John Lyons were taken. The Continental was then moved a short distance further, where Gary Tison and Greenawalt shot the victims. . . .

The appellant first contends that a plea agreement which he had entered into should be specifically enforced against the State because, he asserts, he was willing to abide by the terms of the agreement. The agreement provided that appellant would plead guilty to one count of murder in the first degree for a recommended sentence of 25 years to life. In exchange, appellant would:

> "* * * appear and testify truthfully in any proceedings pertaining to criminal charges relating to an incident occurring on or about August 1, 1978, in which the John Lyons family and Theresa Tyson were killed."

Appellant thereafter gave statements describing his participation in the murders, but a dispute arose as to the scope of the testimony which he would give in subsequent proceedings. Consequently, appellant withdrew his plea of guilty. . . .

While the remedy of specific performance of the plea bargain was sanctioned in *Santobello* for the unkept bargains of a prosecutor, it has rarely been used. See Note, The Legitimation of Plea Bargaining; Remedies for Broken Promises, 11 Am.Crim.L.Rev. 771 (1973), where specific enforcement of a plea agreement was refused because the defendant failed to disclose the agreed information.

The appellant argues in spite of his failure to carry out the terms of the plea bargain that he should be entitled to specific performance. He asserts that he was compelled to withdraw from his plea of guilty because the agreement's scope had been too broadly construed by the prosecution. We disagree. By the terms of the plea agreement, appellant was to provide testimony "in any proceedings," which he has refused to do. His non-compliance with the plea agreement precludes him from the relief requested. . . .

Judgments of conviction and sentences affirmed.

THE STEPS IN PROCESSING A CRIME

The steps in criminal procedure tend to follow a more consistent routine than those of civil procedure because of legal limitations. The burden of proving guilt beyond a reasonable doubt, as opposed "a preponderance of the evidence," forces police and prosecutor to monitor cases carefully. The exclusionary rule makes evidence or confessions unlawfully obtained inadmissible at trial and thus forces a careful investigation, arrest, interrogation, and search and seizure of evidence lest the case fail for improper procedure. The constitutional right to a speedy trial forces police and prosecutor to organize investigation, charges, and trial within a limited time-frame. In addition, the constitutional protections afforded an accused require that cases be carefully prepared to avoid infringement of the accused's rights.

The following is an outline of the steps involved in the criminal process, which are followed virtually universally in criminal cases, though the terminology may differ from one jurisdiction to another:

1. Detection of crime.
   a. Report of crime.
   b. Police investigation.
2. Identification of a suspected criminal.
3. Arrest.
   a. Arrest without a warrant before the filing of a complaint.
   b. Arrest with a warrant after the filing of a complaint.
4. Initial appearance before a magistrate.
   a. Inform the accused of the charges and legal rights.
   b. Set bail or the terms of release from custody.
5. Preliminary hearing.
   a. Determine probable cause that accused committed a crime.
   b. Release accused or bind over for grand jury.
6. Indictment.
   a. Grand jury decides whether accused should be tried, or
   b. Prosecutor indicts by "information."
7. Arraignment before the court.
   a. Accused informed of charges brought.
   b. Accused enters plea.
      i. If plea of guilty or *nolo contendere*, the defendant may be sentenced.
      ii. If plea of not guilty, accused requests or waives jury.
8. Pretrial preparation.
   a. Pretrial motions.
   b. Discovery.
   c. Plea bargaining.
9. Trial.
   a. Acquittal results in release of defendant.
   b. Conviction leads to sentencing.
10. Optional posttrial motions, appeals, and habeas corpus.

Detection of Crime

The initial intervention of law enforcement officers is prompted by the report of a suspected crime by victims or witnesses or the police themselves, who may witness a crime or discover one during a police investigation into suspected criminal activities. The criminal act may be apparent from the circumstances, as when police encounter bank robbers in the act of robbing a bank, or there may simply be suspicious activities that require investigation or surveillance.

Although it may be clear that a crime has been committed, the identity of the perpetrator may not be immediately apparent. The objective of police inquiry is to establish facts to support the conclusion that a crime has been committed and that a specific person or persons committed that crime. Detection of crime is simply the first step; the police must also furnish the prosecutor with sufficient evidence to form the basis for a probable conviction of the offender.

CASE NO. 9–3 Miranda Warnings

Statements made in the absence of Miranda warnings in the course of a custodial interrogation may be excluded from evidence at trial. What exactly a *custodial interrogation* signifies has been the subject of numerous cases, including the following.

PENNSYLVANIA
v.
THOMAS A. BRUDER, Jr.

U.S. Supreme Court
488 U.S. 9, 102 L. Ed. 2d 172,
109 S. Ct. 205 (1988)

Per Curiam.

In the early morning of January 19, 1985, Officer Steve Shallis of the Newton Township, Pennsylvania, Police Department observed Bruder driving very erratically along State Highway 252. Among other traffic violations, he ignored a red light. Shallis stopped Bruder's vehicle. Bruder left his vehicle, approached Shallis, and when asked for his registration card, returned to his car to obtain it.

Smelling alcohol and observing Bruder's stumbling movements, Shallis administered field sobriety tests, including asking Bruder to recite the alphabet. Shallis also inquired about alcohol. Bruder answered that he had been drinking and was returning home. Bruder failed the sobriety tests, whereupon Shallis arrested him, placed him in the police car and gave him Miranda warnings. Bruder was later convicted of driving under the influence of alcohol. At his trial, his statements and conduct prior to his arrest were admitted into evidence. On appeal, the Pennsylvania Superior Court reversed, 365 Pa Super 106, 528 A.2d 1385 (1987), on the ground that the above statements Bruder had uttered during the roadside questioning were elicited through custodial interrogation and should have been suppressed for lack of Miranda warnings. The Pennsylvania Supreme Court denied the State's appeal application.

In Berkemer v. McCarty, supra, which involved facts strikingly similar to those in this case, the court concluded that the "noncoercive aspect of ordinary traffic stops prompts us to hold that persons temporarily detained pursuant to such stops are not 'in custody' for the purposes of Miranda" . . . .

The facts in this record, which Bruder does not contest, reveal the same noncoercive aspects as the Berkemer detention: "a single police officer ask[ing] respondent a modest number of questions and request[ing] him to perform a simple balancing test at a location visible to passing motorists." [C.] Accordingly, Berkemer's rule, that ordinary traffic stops do not involve custody for purposes of Miranda, governs this case. The judgment of the Pennsylvania Superior Court that evidence was inadmissible for lack of Miranda warnings is reversed.

Arrest and Complaint

Arrest is not an easy term to define in all circumstances and cases, but it generally refers to a detention for the purposes of answering to an allegation of a crime. The *complaint* is the formal allegation that the accused has committed a crime.

Legal process begins with a complaint. The complaint may be filed before or after arrest. When an arrest is made without a warrant during the commission of a crime, the complaint is filed at the defendant's initial appearance before the court or magistrate. When a crime has been completed and the police have information linking a person to the crime, the complaint is filed and an arrest warrant issued, which then serves as the basis for arresting the suspect.

In either case, an initial determination must be made whether there is *probable cause* to believe that a crime has been committed and that the defendant committed it. The complaint is accompanied by sworn statements, *affidavits*, which must present sufficient allegations to persuade the magistrate that a warrant should issue. If an arrest is made without a warrant, the arresting officer must have probable cause to believe the suspect has committed a crime.

The arrest powers of police are limited by constitutional and statutory requirements. When police exceed their authority in making an arrest, they may subject themselves to civil suit by the arrestee for the tort of false arrest or to a civil rights suit. An arrest made in the good faith belief that it is lawful and under the authority of a warrant and conducted with reasonable force is the ideal standard against which allegedly improper arrests are tested. There is a large body of constitutional cases on arrest since arrest commonly involves incidental searches and the discovery of evidence later used in prosecution.

Initial Appearance

State and federal statutes require that an arrestee be brought before a magistrate without undue delay, commonly within twenty-four hours. This is called *initial* or *first appearance* and is designed to protect individuals from being jailed without charges or bonds in the absence of scrutiny by an impartial magistrate. The accused will be informed of the charges and legal rights, especially the right to an attorney, and that an attorney will be appointed at state expense if the accused does not have funds to pay an attorney.

Bail will be set at the initial appearance. The purpose of bail is to assure the defendant's appearance at further hearings. The Eighth Amendment prohibits excessive bail, and the defendant may request a hearing to reduce the bail. Under federal law, the court must set the least restrictive conditions to assure appearance. Defendants are frequently released on their own recognizance if, for instance, the defendant has steady employment, a stable residence, presents little threat to society, and the nature of the crime suggests little likelihood that the defendant would flee the jurisdiction. Extreme circumstances may justify a denial of bail. The court may impose certain conditions on release, such as restrictions on travel.

Preliminary Hearing

A preliminary hearing is frequently called to examine the basis for the charges against the defendant, although this is frequently waived by the defendant. Since in the American system the prosecutor enjoys unbridled authority over whether or not to prosecute, the preliminary hearing provides a defendant the opportunity to challenge the prosecution's case before the court. The preliminary hearing does not determine guilt but examines the legal basis for the charges against the defendant. The judge determines whether there is sufficient evidence to send the case to the grand jury or whether instead to release the defendant. Since not all states require a grand jury indictment, the preliminary hearing may be the only opportunity to challenge the charges prior to trial.

Indictment and Information

Although the Constitution requires a grand jury for "infamous crimes" and many states require a grand jury indictment for felonies, many cases are brought on the basis of an "information," which is a written accusation by a public prosecutor. The practice differs from jurisdiction to jurisdiction, but the defendant must be formally charged by an indictment or information.

Grand jury hearings are not truly adversarial; they are secret hearings in which the prosecutor is given wide latitude to present the case for the guilt of the defendant. The grand jury does not decide guilt but determines whether or not probable cause exists that the defendant committed the crime. If the grand jury finds no probable cause, the defendant is discharged; otherwise, the defendant is indicted, and the case goes to trial.

Arraignment

After indictment or upon an information, the defendant is brought before the court to answer the charge. At arraignment, the defendant makes a plea. In minor crimes (misdemeanors), the arraignment may be part of the preliminary hearing—the defendant is informed of the charges and asked to make a plea. Felonies requiring a grand jury and indictment separate the preliminary hearing and the arraignment, which follows the indictment.

The defendant has three pleas available:

1. Not guilty. A plea of not guilty results in a trial. The defendant may waive a jury, but the Constitution guarantees the right to a jury trial in criminal cases.
2. Guilty. The defendant admits the commission of the crime and submits to the sentence of the court. Guilty pleas are usually the result of a plea negotiation between the prosecution and the defense attorney, with the acquiescence of the defendant.
3. *Nolo contendere. Nolo contendere*, literally "I do not wish to contest" is equivalent to a guilty plea except that it does not admit guilt. It is treated the same as a guilty plea for the purposes of sentencing, but it cannot be used in later civil or criminal cases as an admission of guilt.

The court has discretion to accept a guilty or *nolo contendere* plea. The court may require a defendant to plead guilty or not guilty rather than *nolo contendere* and may also in its discretion refuse to accept a guilty plea. If the defendant refuses to make a plea, the court will assume this refusal to be a plea of not guilty and set the case for trial.

A special plea of "not guilty by reason of insanity" is available in many jurisdictions; this subject is more fully covered in Chapter Ten. This plea admits to the commission of the acts of which the defendant is charged but negates the critical element of criminal intent on the basis of the insanity of the defendant.

Pretrial

In many respects the pretrial phase is reminiscent of civil procedure. Pretrial motions are available, such as the motion to suppress evidence. Discovery procedures are similar except for protections against self-incrimination. Plea bargaining bears some resemblance to the strategies for negotiating settlements in civil cases.

CASE NO. 9–4 Getting Away with Murder

Many states have enacted the speedy trial provision of the Sixth Amendment into statutory form, specifying a time period from arrest or charge within which a case must be ready for trial. The relevant time period in the following case was 120 days.

The STATE of Texas ex rel. Henry WADE, Criminal District Attorney, Dallas County, Petitioner,

v.

Honorable Richard MAYS, Judge, 204th District Court, Dallas County, Respondent.

Court of Criminal Appeals of Texas, En Banc.
689 S.W.2d 893 (1985)

CLINTON, Judge.

This cause seeks to invoke the original subject matter jurisdiction of the Court provided by Tex. Const. V, § 5. and is denominated an original application for writ of prohibition by the petitioner. The salient undisputed facts follow.

On March 12, 1984, one Joseph Jones was apparently killed during the course of an aggravated robbery. On the same day, Joe and Cathy Cody were arrested in connection with this offense.

Joe and Cathy Cody were subsequently, in April, indicted separately for the murder of Joseph Jones. On the last day of April the State filed an announcement of ready in Joe Cody's murder case; in the middle of May, an announcement of ready was filed in the Cathy Cody murder prosecution.

Both defendants were, in mid July, additionally indicted for the March 12 aggravated robbery of Joseph Jones. The State filed an announcement of ready in the Cathy Cody aggravated robbery case on July 31, which was 140 days after "the commencement of the criminal action" against her. An announcement of ready in the Joe Cody aggravated robbery case was filed on August 2, which was 143 days after "the commencement of the criminal action" against him.

Both Joe and Cathy Cody thereafter in August moved the court to set aside their indictments for aggravated robbery, alleging the State's failure to be ready thereon within 120 days of their arrests for the offense of murder, arising out of the same transaction, entitled them to discharge under Article 32A.02, supra, § 1.

The Honorable Richard Mays, Judge of the 204th Judicial District court and Respondent herein, granted these motions and discharged each defendant from the aggravated robbery indictments, apparently without any contest or argument from the State.

Very shortly after Respondent dismissed the aggravated robbery indictments against the Codys, each defendant moved the court in September to dismiss also the murder charges pending against them on the authority of Article 28.061, V.A.C.C.P., which provides:

> "If a motion to set aside an indictment, . . . for failure to provide a speedy trial as required by Article 32A.02 is sustained, the court shall discharge the defendant. *A discharge under this article is a bar to any further prosecution* for the offense discharged or *for any other offense arising out of the same transaction.*"

A hearing was convened on these motions at which time it was stipulated by the parties that the murder charges arose out of the same transaction as the previously dismissed aggravated robbery charges.

Respondent announced his belief that under the mandatory language of Article 28.061, supra, he had no discretion to do anything other than grant the motions and discharge the Codys. . . .

After hearing these arguments Respondent informed the parties that Article 28.061 and *Kalish,* both supra, barred prosecution of the murder cases and therefore required dismissal of the murder indictments against the Codys. He then announced his intention to enter written orders to such effect within 10 days. On request of the State, Respondent agreed to stay his ruling so that the State could seek extraordinary remedies from this Court. Respondent then admitted Joe and Cathy Cody to bail.

[There follows a lengthy discussion of the remedy of the writ of prohibition, concluding that the State is not entitled to it—the defendants may not be prosecuted.]

Trial

In most respects the criminal trial is conducted in the same way as a civil trial. The prosecutor has the burden of proving the case. Each side presents its witnesses and cross-examines witnesses for the other side. There are opening statements and closing arguments, etc. The major difference in the nature of the proceedings comes from the much higher standard that the prosecutor must meet, that of proving guilt beyond a reasonable doubt. Another major difference is that the defendant may not be compelled to testify. In one respect this right is illusory. It is human nature to expect the defendant to take the witness stand and declare innocence. If a criminal defendant declines to testify, the judge will instruct the jury that they should not draw any conclusions from this since the defendant is exercising a constitutional right, but it is doubtful that jurors can easily ignore the defendant's silence.

Sentencing

Sentencing procedures differ widely among the states. Historically, judges had wide discretion in sentencing because the range of imprisonment was broad, e.g., "one to ten years." But some states have adopted guidelines that establish customary sentences for crimes. The judge must justify imposing a sentence more severe than the guidelines or risk reversal on appeal. Some crimes in some states now call for mandatory minimum imprisonment, limiting the judge's discretion.

There are a number of alternatives to incarceration. In recent years, judges have become reluctant to send convicted criminals to jail. This is partly because our jails are full and partly because numerous studies have shown that incarceration tends to breed career criminals rather than prepare them for a return to society. It is now rare for a person on first conviction of nonviolent lesser crimes to be sent to prison.

Among alternatives to incarceration, the oldest is probation. Probation is ordered for a fixed period of time, during which the probationer is subject to stringent conditions, the violation of which may result in incarceration. The probationer is monitored by a probation officer, who ideally not only checks for violations of probation but also serves as a personal counselor to aid the probationer in obtaining employment and making appropriate choices in conduct and career.

A convicted criminal may also be sentenced to perform community service. The accused may also avoid conviction by having the judge withhold adjudication under specified conditions. Some jurisdictions allow pretrial diversion, which postpones and usually obviates the need for trial if the accused meets certain conditions, typically the performance of community service. The criminal justice system recognizes that incarceration can be detrimental not only to the criminal but also to society. In addition, the effect of conviction may be a serious impediment to a person's career, so that young first-offenders are often treated leniently.

Prison alternatives are frequently the result of plea bargaining and offer the judge considerable discretion in the treatment of offenders. This feature of the criminal justice system distinguishes it from civil procedure. In criminal cases, the court is not concerned simply with the determination of guilt and the award of penalties, but also with the regulation of conduct and the protection of society.

Appeal

In most respects criminal appeals are similar to those in civil procedure. Appellate courts, however, jealously guard infringements of basic constitutional rights in an effort to ensure fairness to the accused. The right to counsel is the subject of many appeals. Indigent defendants are appointed counsel from the Public Defender's office or private counsel. Public defenders typically have high caseloads and may not always be able to devote as much attention to each case as it deserves. Private attorneys often serve on a *pro bono* basis and are under pressure to devote their time to paying clients. Whether or not this results in neglect of criminal cases, those who are convicted often argue that it does in an effort to obtain a new trial.

While prejudicial error is the basis of reversal of rulings on the law, jury instructions, etc., as in civil cases, the test of error in fact-finding is necessarily different in a criminal trial because the test is guilt beyond a reasonable doubt. On appeal the guilty verdict is tested against the standard that asks whether "no trier of fact could have found proof beyond a reasonable doubt." Like "clearly erroneous" and "substantial evidence," this test shows great deference to fact-finding at trial and makes it difficult to challenge on this basis.

Habeas Corpus

The writ of habeas corpus provides prisoners with a remedy not available in civil cases. Since it challenges the lawfulness of detention, habeas corpus is often used as a means to obtain review of a case in addition to appeal.

SUMMARY

Criminal procedure is similar to civil procedure in the steps it follows from pretrial to trial, in the presentation of evidence, and in the adversarial nature of the proceedings. There are important differences, however, many of which are based on constitutional rights of the accused. The Bill of Rights forms a skeletal code of criminal procedure that has been elaborated through appellate decisions. Among the more important rights guaranteed an accused are the privilege against self-incrimination, the right to an attorney even for those who cannot afford one, the right to a speedy and public trial, the right to be free of cruel and unusual punishment, and the right against excessive bail.

Criminal procedure involves initial steps to assure that the accusation of crime is well grounded: the requirement of probable cause for arrest and for warrants (arrest or search warrants); of initial appearance before a magistrate after arrest; of preliminary hearing; and of grand jury indictment and arraignment.

The major differences between criminal and civil trials are the right of the accused in a criminal trial not to be compelled to testify and the burden of proof on the prosecution to prove guilt beyond a reasonable doubt.

CHAPTER QUESTIONS

1. Why do grand juries usually indict the defendants brought before them?
2. When is the privilege against self-incrimination usually exercised?
3. What is a custodial interrogation?
4. Who usually brings a petition for a writ of habeas corpus?
5. Which principle in the Bill of Rights is considered by the courts to express an evolving standard, which may be more strict as time passes?
6. The exclusionary rule has frequently been criticized because it allows guilty persons to go free merely to discipline the police. What counterarguments can you make to this charge?
7. At what point should a police officer inform persons of their Miranda rights?
8. What advantages are there to pleading *nolo contendere?*
9. Should the role of the criminal justice system be to punish or rehabilitate the offender?
10. Should plea bargaining be abolished?
11. What is the difference in the burden of proof between criminal and civil cases?

EXERCISES

1. Do the statutes in your state express a speedy trial standard? What are the time periods, and when do they start to run?
2. Find your state constitution and compare its protections for criminal defendants with those expressed in the U.S. Constitution.
3. Under what circumstances are grand jury indictments required in your state? May a criminal case be brought on an "information"?
4. What are the pros and cons of plea bargaining?
5. Who handles the criminal defense of indigents in your state?

PROFESSIONAL PROFILE

Excerpted with permission from James Publishing, Inc.,
Legal Assistant Today (September/October 1990).

Before starting her legal career, "I thought it would be like Perry Mason," Deborah Thompson remembers. "The public perception is that you're always dashing to court, but it's not like that. I didn't realize how long things would take."

In her career, Thompson has worked on cases that went to the Supreme Court, reviewed documents in a cave in Alabama, and stood on a Cleveland loading dock at 2 a.m. "Everything you do needs to be at a very high standard because it has an effect on people's lives. You read about your case in the *Wall Street Journal* and the *New York Times.* To me, that's exciting. Every day has new challenges, new situations. I've been able to grow with the firm." Thompson also appreciates the people she works with and the rewards of being part of a team. "One can now do more as a legal assistant. We have new specialties and good salaries."

Right after completing her B.A. in history at Meredith College (North Carolina), Thompson got a certificate at the National Institute for Paralegal Studies in Atlanta. She worked for a year at a Boston law firm, but missed being in the South, and moved to Washington D.C., where many of her friends lived. There she found a job at Jones, Day, Reavis & Pogue.

Deborah Thompson
Paralegal Administrator

Thompson says. "They expect you to work long hours. I used to work as much as the attorneys did. That's the nature of litigation. What that means to the legal assistants who work those hours is they're part of the team. You do get tired after a long run of fourteen-hour days. But you are really involved in the case, rolling up your sleeves."

In 1987 Thompson moved up to administrative assistant, away from paralegal tasks. Supervising legal assistants in their day-to-day work, she trained, hired, and prepared budgets, and arranged schedules. While involved in planning and designing their new 43,000-square-foot litigation center, Thompson learned about construction, lighting, etc. "The center is wonderful! We have mock courtrooms, space to do the work we need to do, and all the support we need. It's an efficient way to process documents."

On August 1, 1990, Thompson became paralegal administrator for the Atlanta, Georgia, firm of King & Spalding.

Thompson has nearly completed a graduate certificate in administrative management at George Washington University. Currently vice president of LAMA/Southeastern Region, she appreciates the change "to meet people like myself who have been in the field for a long time, and have grown with the profession. Now law firms really see a cost incentive to hire legal assistants, because it's a high-profit area for the firms, and because of growing client sensitivity to costs. A higher calibre person is now entering the field," she adds.

What kinds of earnings can you expect in America's fastest-growing profession? "Starting salaries vary with the market area," Thompson explains. "Supply and demand keeps salaries lower in Washington D.C. than in Dallas. Because more people want to go to work in Washington, the beginning range is $18,500-22,000." She's seen a great increase in the number of paralegal schools on the East Coast. "We see few people who didn't come from an ABA-approved program. There are so many here, I just expect it."

Thompson recommends, "Find out where your talents are. If it's computers, move toward litigation support. If your strengths are in public relations and public contact, recruiting may be for you. If you enjoy travel, be a legal assistant with a large national firm, in litigation or mergers and acquisitions. Lots of options exist. But you must pay your dues!"

CHAPTER 10
Criminal Law

> **The law in its majestic egalitarianism, forbids the rich as well as the poor to sleep under bridges, to beg in the streets, and to steal bread.**
>
> — *Anatole France (1894)*

This chapter discusses the **substantive law of crimes.** As already discussed in Chapter 9, the functioning of the criminal justice system is largely procedural, and very few cases go to trial. Since criminal substantive law varies from state to state, a catalog of American crimes is not possible. The discussion will concentrate on underlying issues related to criminal concepts of fault involved principally in the criminal act and especially in criminal intent.

CRIMINAL LAW AND THE PARALEGAL

Paralegals are currently underutilized in criminal work. Much of criminal work involves plea bargaining and trial work that can be done only by an attorney. Also, many criminal defense attorneys work as sole practitioners or in small firms where a large staff is not cost-efficient. The most promising area for paralegals is public employment, assisting prosecutors and public defenders. In addition, many government agencies have positions in which legal training and skills are useful. No understanding of American law is complete, however, without studying the basics of criminal law.

DEFINITION

There is no adequate substantive definition of crime. The condemnation of heinous acts against persons, such as murder, runs throughout human societies; but property crimes, crimes against the state, and regulatory crimes and penalties reflect arbitrary decisions to penalize that vary considerably from nation to nation and even from one American state to another. The criminal law as presently constituted is a compilation of specific prohibited acts. In a sense, a crime may be defined simply as an act that violates the criminal law. In the American legal system a line has been drawn between those acts that are regulated by criminal law process and those for which redress is sought through the civil law process. In many instances, a specific act may give rise to both civil and criminal legal actions.

Thus, *criminal law* may be defined as the list of crimes promulgated by the state. This list is essentially arbitrary in the sense that the state may penalize conduct that was formerly not criminal and may decriminalize conduct that was formerly criminal. Slavery was once legal in the United States; now it is not. Using cocaine was once legal; now it is not. It was once criminal to libel the President; now it is not.

Criminal law may be usefully defined by concentrating on procedural distinctions. When crime is defined as a "wrong against society," this really means that redress for that wrong is monopolized by the state. Our system has evolved to put the redress of criminal conduct wholly in the hands of public officials, so we have created agencies of police, prosecutors, and judges to accomplish

substantive law of crimes
includes not only specific crimes, such as burglary, embezzlement, and murder, but also the fundamental elements of criminal behavior, such as criminal act and criminal intent. Substantive law also covers issues of participation, such as conspiracy, accessories to crime, and attempted crimes. In general, substantive criminal law deals with culpability, while criminal procedure deals with the manner in which criminal cases are processed.

the task. A criminal case can be identified by its being brought by the public prosecutor, enforcing a criminal statute.

In short, a crime is a crime because the legislature (or in some cases the Court) says it is a crime.

CRIME AND MORALITY

There is an often repeated slogan that "You can't legislate morality." This is patently false since that is exactly what law, especially criminal law, does. However, if the statement really means that immorality cannot be eliminated by passing criminal laws, then the statement is correct.

To say that a crime is a wrong against society is to assert that it is immoral, otherwise it might merely be a wrong against a person and of little consequence to the public at large. There are certain offenses, like murder, which are virtually universally condemned in our society, and others, such as using marijuana, over which there is widespread disagreement. As social mores change, so, too, will the law. In part, the criminal law is a reflection of societal values, but it is also an effort by lawmakers to control and regulate conduct they consider politically undesirable. In the latter sense, the criminal law may impose morality rather than express it.

Mala in Se and Mala Prohibita

Some crimes, such as murder, are considered inherently wrong (*mala in se*) while others are not wrong in themselves but are nonetheless penalized, usually as a regulatory measure, such as failure to file an income tax return, and are called *mala prohibita*. The recent proliferation of the latter offenses is derived from the growth of a highly bureaucratized and regulated political organization in the form of the state.

Consider the difference in nature between driving while intoxicated and driving with an expired automobile registration. The former represents a danger to the public and is *mala in se,* while the latter is primarily designed for revenue collection and recordkeeping and is *mala prohibita.*

In simpler times, a person could rely, with good reason, on the shared values of society to avoid breaking the moral injunctions of the law. Today, the bewildering complexity of a regulated society requires its members to consult the requirements of the law at every turn. The moral basis of the penal law has become obscure.

The confusion is encouraged by rules that penalize offenses that are not criminal, a development of recent decades. Parking violations may no longer be misdemeanors (smaller crimes), as they were in the past. That ne'er-do-well who lets his auto registration expire will most certainly pay an extra fee when he renews, but why is he penalized? He was not caught, not charged, not convicted; he incurred no extra administrative expense. No doubt the late fee is called a *civil penalty*, something of a contradiction in terms. It is not labeled criminal, but it looks like a wrong and certainly not a private wrong.

In short, a crime is not a crime if the legislature says it is not a crime.

NOTE ON THE MODEL PENAL CODE

The American Law Institute, which issues the *Restatement of Torts* and the *Restatement of Contracts* is also responsible for the *Model Penal Code,* an additional attempt to encourage uniformity in state law. Some areas of criminal law present a bewildering assortment of treatments among the states, and the *Model Penal Code* is often a leader in these areas rather than merely a restatement of the law. Many state laws are a hodge-podge of custom, past practice, and reformulation of the common law of crimes. The *Model Penal Code* attempts a more consistent and coherent statement of criminal law, but it has no official standing in state law that departs from it. Nevertheless, it is perhaps the most modern American statement of criminal law and will occasionally be referred to below. It is an important research resource for those examining the law and is often quoted in judicial opinions.

punishment
or retribution and **deterrence** of crime are traditional motivations behind the criminal law. In addition, criminal law aims at incapacitation, that is, removing the criminal from society through incarceration, and rehabilitation, helping the criminal toward a productive role in society. The relative importance of retribution, deterrence, incapacitation, and rehabilitation varies depending on one's view of the ultimate goals of the criminal law and is as much of a political and social issue as a legal one.

FAULT

Fault is as much a part of public wrongs as it is of private wrongs. In criminal law, however, the element of intent to do wrong is far more important than in tort law or contract law, where the law's attention is drawn to the injured party. Criminal law is primarily concerned with the **punishment** of the criminal and the **deterrence** of crime; Anglo-American law aims at punishing those who deserve it. Traditionally, two components have been required to hold a person responsible for a crime: criminal act and criminal intent.

CRIMINAL ACT AND CRIMINAL INTENT

To find a person guilty of a crime, there first must be a criminal act or *actus reus*, conduct that the law prohibits or absence of conduct that the law requires. With most crimes there must also be criminal intent or *mens rea* (literally "criminal mind"). Before defining these requisites for a crime, consider the following cases:

1. A prostitute, knowing she has AIDS, continues to ply her trade and is charged with attempted murder.
2. Four seamen adrift in a lifeboat for twenty days decide that one of them must be sacrificed and eaten in order to save the rest. A young cabin boy in weakened condition is killed and eaten. The others are charged with murder.
3. A parent who belongs to a religious sect that believes that physical illness must be cured by prayer and faith refuses medical aid for a child suffering from leukemia. When the child dies, the parent is charged with manslaughter.
4. A young woman is kidnapped by a revolutionary gang, put in a closet for several weeks, and occasionally raped by her kidnappers. For several months she is subjected to political indoctrination and finally agrees to participate in a bank robbery with her abductors to get funds to continue the revolutionary cause. When finally found, she is charged with bank robbery.
5. A man meets a young woman in a bar; when asked by the bartender for identification proving her age, she shows a driver's license and is served a beer. She states to the man that she is twenty, and he believes it. Later they go to his apartment and have sexual relations. He is later charged with the crime of statutory rape, "sexual relations with a person under the age of 18."
6. A woman believes her husband to be dead and remarries. When her first husband reappears, she is charged with bigamy.
7. A man picks up the wrong suitcase at an airport, believing it to be his, but later finds out his mistake and returns the suitcase. He is charged with theft.
8. A physician assists a terminally ill person to commit suicide by preparing and providing the means to end her life in a painless and comfortable way. He is charged with murder.
9. A game warden makes an image of a deer and puts it in the woods. When hunters shoot at the deer, the game warden arrests them for hunting deer out of season.
10. A man shoots a person intending to kill. It later turns out the victim was already dead, although the shooting would have

killed him if he had still been alive. The man is charged with homicide.

Criminal Act

Under early English law, most crimes were treated in the courts as common law crimes. Today, most crimes are statutory, though many of these are simply statutory refinements of the old common law crimes, e.g., murder, rape, burglary, embezzlement, etc. In an earlier, settled, agricultural society, values relating to wrongs against persons and property were widely shared and understood, so that the courts could turn to customary values and religious principles to define criminal misconduct. Today, in our diverse and complex society it is not always clear exactly what should be prohibited and what should not. The underlying policy of the criminal law is that a person should not be punished for conduct not expressly prohibited by the law. This requires the articulation of criminal law by the legislatures rather than the courts. All states have criminal statutes, and most do not allow conviction for common law crimes. Judges are not supposed to impose their perceptions of wrongful conduct; they must find that the conduct falls clearly within a criminal statute in order to hold a person guilty of a crime. Ultimately, a court must determine the meaning of the statute as it applies to a particular incident; but, as already noted, criminal statutes are strictly construed.

The first question in a criminal case, whether in the decision to prosecute or in the preparation of a defense, is to look to the statutes to determine whether or not a criminal act has been committed by the accused.

Actus reus requires that the act be voluntary. While this suggests mental state akin to *mens rea*, it refers to whether or not the act was a product of free will (as distinguished from a "willful" or intentional motive). Examples of involuntary acts are those occurring during sleep, unconsciousness, or hypnosis and those caused by reflexes or convulsions.

Thoughts alone are not criminal; an act must occur. In general, speech is protected by the First Amendment, but speech is conduct and sometimes constitutes a crime, as with inciting to riot or promoting a conspiracy.

The failure to act, an omission, may also constitute *actus reus* in cases in which the law imposes a duty to act, e.g., a parent fails to provide nourishment to a child or a person with knowledge of a felony fails to report such knowledge (misprision of a felony). Failure to meet a moral obligation to act is not a crime if there is no legal duty to act. Historically, American law has not recognized a duty to rescue; a person may stand by and watch another drown, even if saving the drowning person offers no risk to the potential rescuer. A duty arises only if the rescuer was in some way responsible for the peril or enjoys a status requiring rescue, such as a lifeguard.

Since criminal act is typically shown by physical evidence, it presents far fewer problems than criminal intent, in which a mental state must usually be inferred from the circumstances of the events of the crime.

Criminal Intent

An act may be voluntarily accomplished without entailing *mens rea.* The man who mistakenly took the wrong suitcase at the airport acted voluntarily but without criminal intent. The nature of the intent required for guilt varies significantly from one crime to another, and some crimes incur strict liability, removing the need to prove criminal intent.

General Intent

The broadest form of intent is called *general intent,* as distinguished from *specific intent,* to be discussed in the next section. General intent refers to the traditional form of *mens rea* in the common law. It requires that the actor intended a harmful act, but not that the specific result was intended. This may extend to reckless and negligent acts in which the actor acted with a "conscious disregard of a substantial and unjustifiable risk of harm" (recklessness) or, without a conscious disregard, acted when a "reasonable person would have recognized a substantial and unjustifiable risk" (negligence). A person throwing a firecracker into a crowd of people would be guilty of resulting harm covered by a crime requiring only general intent.

Criminal intent is more convincingly shown if malice can be proven. General intent is a somewhat cloudy area due to the variety of harmful acts and the mysteries of the human mind and human motivation. The law and judicial decisions reflect a desire not to punish involuntary, innocent, and accidental acts unless the nature of the harm encourages a high standard of conduct, invoking the deterrence principle of the criminal law. The elements that make up a specific crime indicate the intention required.

Specific Intent

As a rule of thumb, statutes that use the words "knowingly," "willfully," or "maliciously" require *specific intent.* These statutes are most easily satisfied when the defendant intended the precise results of the wrongful act, e.g., shooting someone in the head at close range. Defendants will naturally assert a lack of intent or knowledge, but the courts are disinclined to accept such assertions. It may be enough that a knowledge of a high risk was present, as measured by what a reasonable person would know. The problem is that this is a subjective measure, that is, what the defendant knew or intended. Since only the defendant knows for certain what his knowledge and intent were, the defendant theoretically is the most reliable witness as to that intent. However, in practice the defendant's statements are highly unreliable because self-interest often overrides truth. What was intended may be inferred from defendant's conduct, and defendant's self-serving statements may be treated with skepticism.

CASE NO. 10–1 "I Didn't Know the Trunk Was Loaded"

The *Jewell* case represents the court's reluctance to accept the defendant's self-serving assertions.

UNITED STATES of America,
Plaintiff-Appellee
v.
Charles Demore JEWELL,
Defendant-Appellant

U.S. Court of Appeals, 9th Circuit
532 F.2d 697 (1976)

[This is an appeal from a conviction for violating the Comprehensive Drug Abuse Prevention and Control Act of 1970. Jewell was found to have knowingly transported marijuana in the trunk of his car from Mexico to the United States. The marijuana was concealed in a secret compartment behind the back seat of his car. Jewell insisted that he did not know the marijuana was in the secret compartment. Whether he knew or did not know was a fact question for the jury. If he knew, he was guilty of the crime; but the trial judge was concerned that even a lack of knowledge could have been the result

of "deliberate ignorance" and gave the following instruction to the jury:

The Government can complete their burden of proof by proving, beyond a reasonable doubt, that if the defendant was not actually aware that there was marijuana in the vehicle he was driving when he entered the United States his ignorance in that regard was solely and entirely a result of his having made a conscious purpose to disregard the nature of that which was in the vehicle, with a conscious purpose to avoid learning the truth.

Jewell appealed on the grounds that this instruction was not an accurate statement of the law with regard to criminal intent and that the jury should have been instructed that to find guilt, they must find that he knew he was in possession of marijuana. The Court of Appeals upheld the trial court's jury instruction with the following reasoning:]

The substantive justification for the rule is that deliberate ignorance and positive knowledge are equally culpable. The textual justification is that in common understanding one "knows" facts of which he is less than absolutely certain. To act "knowingly," therefore, is not necessarily to act only with positive knowledge, but also to act with an awareness of the high probability of the existence of the fact in question. When such awareness is present, "positive" knowledge is not required.

. . . .

. . . The *Turner* [*v. United States*, 396 U.S. 398 (1970)] opinion recognizes that in defining "knowingly" makes actual knowledge unnecessary. "[T]hose who traffic in heroin will inevitably become aware that the product they deal with is smuggled, *unless they practice a studied ignorance to which they are not entitled.*"

. . . Holding that this term [knowingly] introduces a requirement of positive knowledge would make deliberate ignorance a defense. It cannot be doubted that those who traffic in drugs would make the most of it. This is evident from the number of appellate decisions reflecting conscious avoidance of positive knowledge of the presence of contraband—in the car driven by the defendant or in which he is a passenger, in the suitcase or package he carries, in the parcel concealed in his clothing.

. . . .

The conviction is affirmed.

Kennedy, J., dissenting.

. . . the "conscious purpose" jury instruction is defective in three respects. First, it fails to mention the requirement that Jewell have been aware of a high probability that a controlled substance was in the car. It is not culpable to form "a conscious purpose to avoid learning the truth" unless one is aware of facts indicating a high probability of that truth. . . .

The second defect in the instruction as given is that it did not alert the jury that Jewell could not be convicted if he "actually believed" there was no controlled substance in the car. . . .

Third, the jury instruction clearly states that Jewell could have been convicted even if found ignorant or "not actually aware" that the car contained a controlled substance. This is unacceptable because true ignorance, no matter how unreasonable, cannot provide a basis for criminal liability when the statute requires knowledge. . . .

CASE QUESTIONS

1. Why did the majority not adopt the dissent's approach?
2. In a portion of the dissenting opinion omitted above, the dissenting judge declared his approval of the *Model Penal Code* §2.02 (7), which reads as follows:

   Requirement of Knowledge Satisfied by Knowledge of High Probability. When knowledge of the existence of a particular fact is an element of an offense, such knowledge is established if a person is aware of a high probability of its existence, unless he actually believes that it does not exist.

   Does this imply the dissent's conclusion that "true ignorance, no matter how unreasonable, cannot provide a basis for criminal liability when the statute requires knowledge . . . "?

3. Perhaps when Jewell spoke with his attorney, the attorney said, "the statute requires that you *knowingly* transported controlled substances. You didn't know that what was in the secret compartment was *actually* marijuana, *did* you?" And suppose Jewell responded, "I didn't actually *see* marijuana put in the car; I didn't actually *know* there was marijuana in there." Can attorney and client then with full conscience go to court and base their defense on lack of knowledge? Is it unethical for the attorney to lead the client in this way?

4. Is not subjective knowledge always arguable? If Jewell actually knew there was marijuana placed in the secret compartment, but he left his car for an hour, would he *know* the marijuana was still there if he did not check to see? Does this deliberate ignorance principle furnish a reasonable alternative to the philosophical problem of knowledge?

5. Does the rule in *Jewell* accord with the principle of strict construction of criminal statutes?

6. Do you think the jury would have found differently if it had been instructed as the dissent suggested?

Mens rea is a confusing area of criminal law because it attempts to define subjective knowledge, volition, and intent. To paraphrase Justice Loevinger's comments about the definition of contracts, perhaps the definition of *mens rea* consists of the totality of the cases that define it. As a practical matter this means that applying criminal intent to a given case requires fitting that case into similar cases of the past. It then becomes clear that the method of the common law prevails even in an area that ostensibly has been preempted by statute.

All the research in the world, however, means little to the jury. Through its deliberations, the jury mysteriously arrives at conclusions about the defendant's intent. The jury is likely to pay more attention to common sense and experience than the technicalities of the jury instructions. In the *Jewell* case, some jurors must have asked, "Why did he have a secret compartment in his trunk? Surely he must have known, or at least guessed there was marijuana in the secret compartment." Preparation of a jury case must pay at least as much attention to the mentality of the jury as to the law.

Specific Problems of Criminal Intent

The nature and degree of criminal intent required varies from crime to crime. In some instances, intent refers simply to the knowledge the accused must have. For example, crimes involving theft commonly require that the defendant intended to deprive someone permanently of property, knowing that the property belonged to another. Such a requirement would save our airport suitcase mistake because there was neither an intent to permanently deprive nor a knowledge of true ownership at the time of the taking. (Compare the old Army story of the soldier who went AWOL (absent without leave) and, in an apparent attempt to avoid the charge of desertion, would send to the army each year a postcard saying "I'll be back.")

Crimes against property, such as burglary, embezzlement, and larceny, are usually economically motivated so that intent can readily be inferred. Unless these involve violence or large amounts of money, they receive only modest attention in the press, which tends to focus on bizarre and violent crime.

Other crimes require special ingredients for criminal intent that make them quite distinct. Murder, rape, and conspiracy are examples.

Murder

Murder is the unlawful killing by one human being of another with malice aforethought. It is distinguished from manslaughter (also called murder in the second degree) by the requirement of "malice aforethought," often referred to as premeditation or malice prepense, depending on one's preference for Old English, new Latin, or French. The requirement of premeditation removes from this most heinous of crimes homicides that are accidental but blameworthy (i.e., caused by culpable negligence) and those occurring in a moment of passion or anger. At the very least, murder requires some reflection about what one is doing or sufficient time between the beginning of the act and its completion to provide an opportunity to desist from following through. Obviously, a planned killing satisfies premeditation. In other cases, proof of premeditation typically takes the form of showing that the accused thought about what he or she was doing and then did it.

Murder cases present a very distorted picture of the criminal law. One reason is the requirement of evil intent; another is the availability of the death penalty in most states. Because of our fear of sending an innocent person to the gallows, a mistake that can never be corrected, the propriety of conduct by the police and prosecution and the conduct of the trial are scrutinized to a degree unusual in other cases. Because of media attention to these cases, the public forms a strange picture of the criminal law and criminal procedure.

Rape

Forcible rape is the most serious of sex crimes. At present there is little uniformity either in terminology or definition among the states with regard to sex crimes. On the one hand, we have seen a strong movement to decriminalize consensual sexual relations, but different states have shown different approaches depending on whether the partners are married, heterosexual, or homosexual. On the other hand, there has been an expansion of definitions of sex crimes to protect specific categories of victims—the young, the elderly, the mentally and physically handicapped. Since this is presently a dynamic area of legislation, there is little uniformity among the states.

With regard to the mental element required for forcible rape, the problem is compounded by its nonconsensual element. Not only the defendant's mental state is at issue but also the victim's. It is a defense to forcible, as opposed to statutory, rape that the alleged victim consented to the sexual act. Since sexual relations usually occur in private without witnesses, ascertaining the mental states of perpetrator and victim presents difficult problems of proof.

An essential element of rape is the use of force. What constitutes force is problematic, and the relationship between force and consent raises additional questions. If a man holds a knife to a woman's throat and asks her if she wants to have sexual relations, is her affirmative answer consent? Surely consent under duress is not consent at all.

To illustrate problems inherent in rape, consider the following hypothetical cases, which are drawn from two actual cases but are highly embellished:

1. A woman and a man meet in a bar; the woman is scantily clad, with a hemline that barely conceals that she is wearing no underwear. She agrees to have sexual intercourse with him for money, and they go off in his van. She later charges him with rape. She has prior convictions for prostitution, and on a prior occasion charged rape against another man under roughly similar circumstances. The defendant is wanted in another state on a rape charge.

2. Man and woman meet in a singles bar. The woman is dressed provocatively and plays the temptress. After many drinks, they end up in her apartment. She puts on a nun's habit and declares she is a virgin and married to God. Then she takes her clothes off, and they have intercourse all the while she is saying "No. No. No. I'm a virgin" (which she is not). It turns out later that the woman is psychotic, with multiple personalities, and the man is of below-average intelligence.

forcible rape
is distinguished from *statutory rape*. Forcible rape has as one of its elements that force or threat of force be used. This goes further than mere lack of consent on the part of the victim. Statutory rape involves consensual sex when the victim is deemed not capable of consent because of age, mental condition, status, etc.

He acknowledges overcoming some slight efforts of physical resistance on her part.

In both of these illustrations, a rape may have occurred, but the factual issues raised would make it very difficult for a jury to convict, relying on proof of guilt beyond a reasonable doubt. Rape is a serious crime that occurs with significant frequency in our society and is likely to leave victims with permanent emotional damage, yet it is difficult to prove and usually goes unreported. The commands of the criminal law have failed to control primal urges toward violence and sex. Recently, focus has changed toward victim-oriented services and enlightened treatment of victims in court.

Conspiracy

Conspiracy presents problems for both *mens rea* and *actus reus* in that it addresses the planning of crime rather than its actual commission. From the *Model Penal Code*, §5.03 Criminal Conspiracy:

(1) *Definition of Conspiracy.* A person is guilty of conspiracy with another person or persons to commit a crime if with the purpose of promoting or facilitating its commission he:
   (a) agrees with such other person or persons that they or one or more of them will engage in conduct which constitutes such crime or an attempt or solicitation to commit such crime; or
   (b) agrees to aid such other person or persons in the planning or commission of such crime or of an attempt or solicitation to commit such crime.

   . . . .

(5) *Overt Act.* No person may be convicted of conspiracy to commit a crime, other than a felony of the first or second degree, unless an overt act in pursuance of such conspiracy is alleged and proved to have been done by him or by a person with whom he conspired.

(6) *Renunciation of Criminal Purpose.* It is an affirmative defense that the actor, after conspiring to commit a crime, thwarted the success of the conspiracy, under circumstances manifesting a complete and voluntary renunciation of his criminal purpose.

Under these rules one may effectively be charged with conspiracy for participating in the planning of a bank robbery even if one did not plan to participate in the actual bank robbery, conduct that society may appropriately condemn as criminal; but the crime of conspiracy may cast a wide net to include many persons marginally associated with others engaged in criminal conduct.

CASE NO. 10–2   The Postman Always Rings Twice

The following case involves call girls and the telephone answering service they used. One may wonder why the police and prosecutor were anxious to find the owner of the answering service guilty of conspiracy to commit prostitution. The answer may lie in an effort to find another crime against the call girls. When the conspiracy count against Lauria failed, it also failed against the call girls.

**The PEOPLE of the State of
California,
Plaintiff and Appellant
v.
Louis LAURIA et al.,
Defendants and Respondents**

California District Court of Appeal,
Second District, Division 2
251 Cal.App.2d 471, 59
Cal.Rptr. 628 (1967)

FLEMING, J.

In an investigation of call-girl activity the police focused their attention on three prostitutes actively plying their trade on call, each of whom was using Lauria's telephone answering service, presumably for business purposes. . . .

On April 1 Lauria and the three prostitutes were arrested. Lauria complained to the police that this attention was undeserved, stating that Hollywood Call Board had 60 to 70 prostitutes on its board while his own service had only 9 or 10, that he kept separate records for known or suspected prostitutes for the convenience of himself and the police. When asked if his records were available to police who might come to the office to investigate call girls, Lauria replied that

they were whenever the police had a specific name. However, his service didn't "arbitrarily tell the police about prostitutes on our board. As long as they pay their bills we tolerate them." On a subsequent voluntary appearance before the Grand Jury Lauria testified he had always cooperated with the police. But he admitted he knew some of his customers were prostitutes, and he knew Terry was a prostitute because he had personally used her services, and he knew she was paying for 500 calls a month.

Lauria and the three prostitutes were indicted for conspiracy to commit prostitution, and nine overt acts were specified. Subsequently the trial court set aside the indictment as having been brought without reasonable or probable cause. (Pen. Code, §995). The People have appealed, claiming that a sufficient showing of an unlawful agreement to further prostitution was made. . . .

Under what circumstances does a supplier become a part of a conspiracy to further an illegal enterprise by furnishing goods or services which he knows are to be used by the buyer for criminal purposes? . . .

Both the element of *knowledge* of the illegal use of the goods or services and the element of *intent* to further that use must be present in order to make the supplier a participant in a criminal conspiracy.

Proof of *knowledge* is ordinarily a question of fact and requires no extended discussion in the present case. The knowledge of the supplier was sufficiently established when Lauria admitted he knew some of his customers were prostitutes and admitted he knew that Terry, an active subscriber to his service, was a prostitute. . . .

The more perplexing issue in the case is the sufficiency of proof of *intent* to further the criminal enterprise. The element of intent may be proved either by direct evidence, or by evidence of circumstances from which an intent to further a criminal enterprise by supplying lawful goods or services may be inferred. . . .

. . . Essentially, the People argue that knowledge alone of the continuing use of his telephone facilities for criminal purposes provided a sufficient basis from which his intent to participate in those criminal activities could be inferred.

1. Intent may be inferred from knowledge, when the purveyor of legal goods for illegal use has acquired a stake in the venture. . . .

In the present case, no proof was offered of inflated charges for the telephone answering services furnished the codefendants.

2. Intent may be inferred from knowledge, when no legitimate use for the goods or services exists. . . .

However, there is nothing in the furnishing of telephone answering service which would necessarily imply assistance in the performance of illegal activities. Nor is any inference to be derived from the use of an answering service by women, either in any particular volume of calls, or outside normal working hours. Nightclub entertainers, registered nurses, faith healers, public stenographers, photographic models, and free lance substitute employees, provide examples of women in legitimate occupations whose employment might cause them to receive a volume of telephone calls at irregular hours.

3. Intent may be inferred from knowledge, when the volume of business with the buyer is grossly disproportionate to any legitimate demand, or when sales for illegal use amount to a high proportion of the seller's total business. . . .

No evidence of any unusual volume of business with prostitutes was presented by the prosecution against Lauria. . . .

With respect to misdemeanors, we conclude that positive knowledge of the supplier that his products or services are being used for criminal purposes does not, without more, establish an intent of the supplier to participate in the misdemeanors. With respect to felonies, we do not decide the converse, viz. that in all cases of felony knowledge of criminal use alone may justify an inference of the supplier's intent to participate in the crime. . . .

Under these circumstances, although proof of Lauria's knowledge of the criminal activities of his patrons was sufficient to charge him with that fact, there was insufficient evidence that he intended to further their criminal activities, and hence insufficient proof of his participation in a criminal conspiracy with his codefendants to further prostitution. Since the conspiracy centered around the activities of Lauria's telephone answering service, the charges against his codefendants likewise fail for want of proof.

In absolving Lauria of complicity in a criminal conspiracy we do not wish to imply that the public authorities are without remedies to combat modern manifestations of the world's oldest profession. Licensing of telephone answering services under the police power, together with the revocation of licenses for the toleration of prostitution, is a possible civil remedy. The furnishing of telephone answering service in aid of prostitution could be made a crime. (Cf. Pen. Code, §316, which makes it a misdemeanor to let an apartment with knowledge of its use for prostitution.) Other solutions will doubtless occur to vigilant public authorities if the problem of call-girl activity needs further suppression.

The order is affirmed.

Attempt

The attempt to commit a crime is also a crime. In its simplest form, an attempt is a crime that failed. The deterrent aspect of the criminal law should apply equally to attempts as to successful crimes, i.e., it would seem useful to deter bank robbers whether or not they are successful. The punitive aspect of the criminal law, however, has traditionally been more lenient with attempted crimes, which are usually of lesser grade or lesser sentence. The *Model Penal Code* §5.05(1) treats attempts as equal to the crime attempted, and a few states have adopted this policy. *Mens rea* can become confused in the area of attempt, as the following two cases demonstrate.

CASE NO. 10–3   A Wolf in Deer's Clothing

STATE
v.
GUFFEY et al.

Springfield Court of Appeals,
Missouri
262 S.W.2d 152 (1953)

[Missouri Conservation agents set up a stuffed deer hide in a field about fifty yards from roadside then lay in wait for "some citizen who might come that way, see the tempting bait and with visions of odoriferous venison cooking in pot or pan, decide not to wait until" the beginning of deer season. Defendants drove by with a spotlight and noticed the deer; the car stopped, followed by a shotgun blast. Defendants were arrested, and despite their testimony that they were out frog-hunting and shot at the "deer" thinking it was a wolf, were convicted of the misdemeanor of pursuit and taking of wildlife against rules and regulations, Section 252.040, V.A.M.S. and regulations of the Missouri Conservation Commission.]

VANDEVENTER, Presiding Judge.

Bearing these definitions [of "pursue"] in mind, it seems to us that the State has wholly failed to make its case when it stands upon the proposition that defendants "pursued" a deer. In the first place there was no deer. The hide of a doe long since deceased filled with boards, excelsior and rods with eyes made of a reflective scotch tape, was not a deer within the meaning of the statute and Section 33 of the "Wildlife Code of Missouri." The dummy, such as it was, was a stationary affair, it could not run, could not jump, it could not flee from the rifle slug of a hunter. It was not wild and it had no life.

. . . .

Undoubtedly the words "pursued" as used in the statute and "pursue" as used in Section 33 of the Code mean to follow with the intention of overtaking, or to chase.

. . . .

. . . The State's evidence shows that one of the defendants did shoot the dummy but did they pursue, chase or follow a *deer* by shooting this stuffed defunct doe hide? It was not a deer. If the dummy had been actually taken (it could not be pursued), defendants would not have committed any offense. It is no offense to attempt to do that which is not illegal. . . . Neither is it a crime to attempt to do that which it is legally impossible to do. For instance, it is no crime to attempt to murder a corpse because it cannot be murdered [C.].

. . . .

If the State's evidence showed an attempt to take the dummy, it fell far short of proving an attempt to take a deer. We hold that the State wholly failed to make a case.

CASE QUESTIONS

1. Did the state's case fail because of an absence of *actus reus* or *mens rea*?
2. In part of the case omitted, the court examined the meaning of the word "pursue" in great detail. Why was this necessary?

CASE NO. 10–4 Murdering a Corpse

The PEOPLE of the State of New York,
Appellant
v.
Melvin DLUGASH,
Respondent.

Court of Appeals of New York
41 N.Y.2d 725, 363 N.E.2d 1155 (1977)

[Dlugash, Bush, and Geller had been drinking until three o'clock in the morning. Several times Geller, in whose apartment the incident occurred, had demanded that Bush pay $100 toward the rent since Bush had moved in with Geller. Bush threatened to shoot Geller if he would not shut up, and on the final demand Bush fired three shots at Geller, one of which went through Geller's lung and into his heart. A few minutes later, Dlugash fired several shots into Geller's head. When the investigating detective asked Dlugash why he did this, he said at first he did not really know, but when asked the third time, Dlugash said, "well, gee, I guess it must have been because I was afraid of Joe Bush." At trial, medical experts testified that the chest wounds would have killed Geller without prompt medical attention, but it was not clear whether Geller was still alive when Dlugash fired into his head. Dlugash did not testify at trial, but after the jury found him guilty of murder, he moved to set the verdict aside on the grounds that he was certain Geller was dead before Dlugash shot him, and his shots were made because Bush held a gun on him and said he would kill Dlugash if Dlugash did not shoot the body. On appeal to the Appellate Division, it was held that the state failed to prove beyond a reasonable doubt that Geller had been alive at the time Dlugash shot him; and also held him not guilty of attempted murder. The highest court came to a somewhat different conclusion:]

JASEN, Judge.

The criminal law is of ancient origin, but criminal liability for attempt to commit a crime is comparatively recent. At the root of the concept of attempt liability are the very aims and purposes of penal law. The ultimate issue is whether an individual's intentions and actions, though failing to achieve a manifest and malevolent criminal purpose, constitute a danger to organized society of sufficient magnitude to warrant the impositions of criminal sanctions. . . . [One] concern centers on whether an individual should be liable for an attempt to commit a crime when, unknown to him, it was impossible to successfully complete the crime attempted. . . . The 1967 revision of the Penal Law approached the impossibility defense to the inchoate crime of attempt in a novel fashion. The statute provides that, if a person engages in conduct which would otherwise constitute an attempt to commit a crime, "it is no defense to a prosecution for such attempt that the crime charged to have been attempted was, under the attendant circumstances, factually or legally impossible of commission, if such crime could have been committed had the attendant circumstances been as such person believed them to be." (Penal Law, §110.10.) This appeal presents to us, for the first time, a case involving the application of the modern statute. We hold that, under the proof presented by the People at trial, defendant Melvin Dlugash may be held for attempted murder, though the target of the attempt may have already been slain, by the hand of another, when Dlugash made his felonious attempt.

[There follows a long discussion of the facts followed by the conclusion that the Appellate Division was correct in overturning the conviction for murder. The court then discusses the history of impossibility theory, concluding that legal impossibility was a defense, citing *Guffey*, "it is no crime to attempt to do that which is legal," while factual impossibility was not a defense ("Thus, a man could be held for attempted grand larceny when he picked an empty pocket."]

In the belief that neither of the two branches of the traditional impossibility arguments detracts from the offender's moral culpability [Cc.], the Legislature substantially carried the code's treatment of impossibility into the 1967 revision of the Penal Law. [C.] Thus, a person is guilty of an attempt when, with intent to commit a crime, he engages in conduct which tends to effect the commission of such crime. (Penal Law, §110.10) It is no defense that, under the attendant circumstances, the crime was factually or legally impossible of commission. . . . Thus, if defendant believed the victim to be alive at the time of the shooting, it is no defense to the charge of attempted murder that the victim may have been dead.

. . . .

The jury convicted the defendant of murder. Necessarily, they found that defendant intended to kill a live human being. Subsumed within this finding is the conclusion that defendant acted in the belief that Geller was alive. Thus, there is no need for additional fact findings by a jury. . . .

The Appellate Division erred in not modifying the judgment to reflect a conviction for the lesser included offense of attempted murder. . . .

CASE QUESTIONS

1. Consider the following fact situations:
    a. A person shoots a corpse in the head, knowing that the corpse is dead.
    b. A person shoots a corpse in the head, believing the corpse to be alive.
    c. A person intending to kill shoots at a figure in a bed, but there is no one there.
    d. A person shoots at someone, intending to kill, but misses.
    Which of these is the law of attempts intended to punish? Which of these would be attempts under the reasoning of *Dlugash*?
2. *Dlugash* refers to a New Jersey case in which the defendant agreed to perform an abortion, then illegal, upon a female undercover police investigator who was not pregnant. The defendant was found guilty, and it was "no defense that the defendant could not succeed in reaching his goal because of circumstances unknown to him." Is this reasoning sound?
3. The court cites another case in which it was held that "men who had sexual intercourse with a woman, with the belief that she was alive and did not consent to the intercourse, could be charged for attempted rape when the woman had, in fact, died from an unrelated ailment prior to the acts of intercourse." Is this reasoning sound?
4. What if the police have a sting operation and buy drugs from someone who believes the police to be drug dealers but sells them powdered sugar instead of drugs, intending to cheat the drug dealers? Has the seller committed a crime? An attempted crime?

Strict Liability

Underlying the *mens rea* requirement is the traditional legal principle in criminal law of a *presumption of innocence*. *Mens rea* imposes a burden on the prosecution to show that the defendant acted out of evil intent. In recent years, however, legislatures have imposed strict criminal liability, thereby either eliminating the burden of proving *mens rea* or shifting to the defendant the burden of proving innocent motive.

Some precedent for strict liability can be found in the common law felony-murder rule, under which a person can be found guilty of murder without proof of premeditation if a person is killed during the perpetration of a felony. Some justification in the rule can be found in an attempt to deter the use of unreasonable force in the commission of a felony, but on rare occasions the rule has been applied with peculiar results, as when one of the felons is killed by police and the others are held accountable for felony-murder. The felony-murder rule has been subject to much criticism and is severely qualified in some jurisdictions.

Another example of traditional strict liability is covered in the crime of statutory rape, in which sexual relations with a person under a certain age eliminates the defense of consent and in many states denies the defendant the defense of a good faith belief that the victim was above the prescribed age. Again, a reasonable objective of protecting young and innocent or naive girls from predatory older males is used to justify strict liability. The so-called "sexual revolution" and the apparent rampant promiscuity of American youth have caused many legislatures to tinker with a traditional age of consent, lowering the age of the victim when defenses are not allowed, providing for different grades of crime depending on the relative ages of the participants. Gender equality has also confused the issue. If a fourteen-year-old boy and a fourteen-year-old girl have sexual intercourse, who is the perpetrator and who is the victim? The states have come up with fifty different solutions to this problem.

The growth of strict liability, however, has occurred primarily in regulatory statutes. On the one hand, strict liability has been justified when a class of persons, such as the young, seem to warrant special protection, or when the danger to the public is particularly hazardous—alcohol, firearms, drugs, poisons. On the other hand, legislatures can be justly accused of relaxing the *mens rea* requirement simply to make conviction easier.

The Insanity Defense

No discussion of *mens rea* would be complete without mention of the insanity defense. A criminal defendant may plead "not guilty by reason of insanity." This plea acknowledges the commission of the criminal act but negates criminal intent because of the defendant's insanity. The policy basis for the defense is to hold accountable for crimes only those persons who freely chose to commit crimes. An additional reason for the defense is the inappropriateness of putting insane persons in with the general prison population. The insanity defense is very much like the defense of an involuntary act or of the absence of criminal intent. The difference lies in acknowledging insanity, which typically results in commitment to a mental institution if insanity is proven.

The principal problem with insanity is defining it. Understanding the subjective states of the human mind is difficult even for those psychologists and psychiatrists with extensive training and experience. While some persons may be found to be insane by almost any measure, the line between sanity and insanity cannot be drawn with accuracy, yet the law requires that the line be drawn.

The English rule originating in the nineteenth-century M'Naghten case (10 Cl. & F. 200, 8 Eng. Rep. 718 [1843]) is still followed with some modifications in many American jurisdictions. Daniel M'Naghten suffered delusions that the Prime Minister was out to get him; M'Naghten shot and killed the Prime Minister's secretary, mistakenly believing the secretary to be the Prime Minister. Public outrage over M'Naghten's acquittal ultimately led to a consideration of the insanity defense by the House of Lords (England's "Supreme Court"). Consensus resulted in what is often called the "right-wrong test," namely, whether the accused suffered from a defect of mind such that he did not understand the nature of his act or did not know that it was wrong. This is a difficult test to meet since it requires a very serious mental imbalance.

The fields of psychology and psychiatry in the twentieth century have shown that we are much less in control of our minds and actions than was formerly believed, so other insanity tests have been adopted that lower the threshold of insanity for legal purposes. The issue of legal accountability for acts committed by someone with diminished mental capacity is very murky at present.

Insanity defenses frequently involve several highly paid expert witnesses. Prosecution witnesses testify that the defendant was sane at the time of the act, while defense witnesses argue precisely the opposite; the jury must attempt to arrive at the "truth" of defendant's mental state as described by experts who reconstruct that mental state after the fact.

The satisfactory resolution of these and other problems related to the insanity defense does not appear to be forthcoming.

SUMMARY

While the practice of criminal law tends to focus on problems of proof and other procedural issues, the substantive law of crimes is largely the concern of legislative enactments. There is considerable variability in the definitions of specific crimes from state to state. A general definition of crime is difficult to state, but crime may be identified procedurally by recourse to statutes that define crimes and delegate authority to police and prosecutors for the resolution of misconduct so labeled.

The criminal law penalizes conduct that offends the moral sentiments of the people. However, in our diverse society, moral commands are not always a matter of consensus. In addition, lawmakers provide criminal and civil penalties to encourage people to conform to an increasingly regulated state.

Traditionally, a crime requires both a criminal act and criminal intent on the part of the actor. The criminal act is defined by the elements of specific crimes, and it is up to the courts to determine whether a particular act falls within the prohibitions of the law.

Criminal intent, or *mens rea,* requires that the defendant in a criminal case be shown to have a specific state of mind at the time of the commission of the criminal act. Since subjective states of mind are difficult to ascertain, the intent of the defendant is a frequent issue in trials. Specific crimes often require or infer a specific state of mind. Questions of motivation, willfulness, premeditation, accident, knowledge, and intent are fact questions for the jury that may be quite confusing to resolve. The insanity defense is particularly problematic because of the inconsistency of legal and psychiatric definitions of insanity.

CHAPTER QUESTIONS

The following questions are designed both to test your understanding of the key points in the chapter and to make an initial inquiry into the substantive crimes of your state jurisdiction. Typically, statutory law is found in one long section or sections on the subject and is readily found from the index. The statutes themselves may be examined, but answers to the difficult questions presented would usually call at least for resort to the statute or code annotations, which give brief summaries of the rules found by the courts.

1. A prostitute, knowing she has AIDS, continues to ply her trade and is charged with attempted murder. Such charges have actually occurred in this situation. It can be a crime to attempt a crime. What does the law of your state say about attempts? What is the likely outcome of this case? Is there a criminal act? Is there *mens rea?*

2. A parent who belongs to a religious sect that believes that physical illness must be cured by prayer and faith refuses medical aid for a child suffering from leukemia. When the child dies, the parent is charged with manslaughter. Would it make a difference if the leukemia were medically incurable, though the child's life might have been prolonged with medical treatment? Does the parent's action fit into any definition of homicide found in your state's statutes? How does the First Amendment's freedom of religion fit into the case?

3. A young woman is kidnapped by a revolutionary gang, put in a closet for several weeks, and occasionally raped by her kidnappers. For several months she is subjected to political indoctrination and finally agrees to participate in a bank robbery with her abductors to get funds to continue the revolutionary cause. When finally found, she is charged with bank robbery. This hypothetical case is based on the famous Patty Hearst case, in which she was convicted and went to prison. There was a serious question as to whether Patty Hearst was acting voluntarily or intentionally. What do you think?

4. A man meets a young woman in a bar; when asked by the bartender for identification proving her age, she shows a driver's license and is served a beer. She states to the man that she is twenty, and he believes it. Later they go to his apartment and have sexual relations. He is later charged with the crime of statutory rape, "sexual relations with a person under the age of 18." What is the age (or ages) for statutory rape in your state? Does the defendant have a defense with regard to his reasonable belief in the age of the girl?

5. A woman believes her husband to be dead and remarries. When her first husband reappears, she is charged with bigamy. Bigamy has traditionally been a strict liability crime. What is it in your state? Should it be in this case?

6. A physician assists a terminally ill person to commit suicide by preparing and providing the means to end her life in a painless and comfortable way. He is charged with murder. Depending on state law, the physician could be an accomplice or conspirator in the crime of suicide. Does your state have a law covering "causing or aiding suicide"? Are the elements of murder or some lesser homicide present in the case?

PROFESSIONAL PROFILE

"The most rewarding aspect of my work is the knowledge that I have used all my talents, education, and company's resources to the benefit of our clients. To see an account proceed from referral to payment in full and knowing that your hard work and diligence made it happen is truly rewarding," says Janet Norris.

Married with two teenage children, Norris is employed by Overton, Russell and Doerr Law Offices in Albany, New York. In 1983 she originally applied for a clerical position at the firm to supplement the family income. At that time, being a paralegal was the furthest thing from her mind. "I'm not sure I really understood what a paralegal actually did," she says. After two years as a supervisor of the file department, an opportunity to join the paralegal department became available. "I applied, was accepted, and loved the job immediately. I soon enrolled in college, and have attended evening paralegal classes for the past year," Norris explains.

Norris's paralegal training has been a combination of on-the-job training by attorneys and supervisory personnel as well as formal education received in the paralegal program at Schenectady County Community College. Her on-the-job training has helped her to see the material learned in class applied to practice every day.

Norris states, "I am employed by a firm specializing in collections, and am involved with medical collections exclusively. This includes daily contact with over a dozen business offices of various hospitals and medical groups. A typical day includes making telephone calls or responding to correspondence from attorneys wishing to clarify or settle their clients' accounts. Other duties include the gathering of information necessary to pursue collection, determining correct court venue, proper legal service, entering judgments, and income executions. "Specific knowledge of jurisdiction and legal procedure is needed to correctly secure the clients' interests," Norris emphasizes.

Norris comments, "In my position there is a great dependency on teamwork. All team members are working toward the same goal. With this goal in mind, our legal team is very conscious of one another and is always available to support everyone's efforts."

"I wish, before entering this field, I had been more aware of the great diversity in the paralegal field. The opportunities for employment tend to be found in certain specific fields (real estate, collections, etc.). Yet, I feel an effective paralegal should have a sound basic education and then be offered further specialized education in a chosen area of the law. This would be a definite advantage for the paralegal who is pursuing a career in specialized legal work," says Norris. Her advice to those embarking on a paralegal career would be to research the avenues of possible employment available, to get a good educational base, and then to pursue the area of the law that is personally interesting. "Be aware that there are endless opportunities to learn and that none should be missed," Norris concludes.

Janet M. Norris
Medical Collections Paralegal

CHAPTER 11
Torts, Personal Injury, and Compensation

The right of personal security consists in a person's legal and uninterrupted enjoyment of his life, his limbs, his health, and his reputation.
— *Wm. Blackstone*, **Commentaries** *(1st Ed. 1765)*

241

The traditional term for the field of personal injury and compensation law is *torts*. Generally, torts have specific legal labels, each considered a different cause of action, such as **trespass**, **slander**, **negligence**, and **products liability**. They often seem to have little in common except that the law recognizes that private interests can be subject to injury, the remedy of which is typically compensation if responsibility for the injury can be attributed to another party. The difference in terminology reflects a difference in attitude. "Torts" suggests a set of fixed, labeled causes of action, while "compensation for injuries" reflects a more flexible approach that recognizes the open-ended quality of tort law in that new interests are protected as tort law evolves. For example, electronic eavesdropping has come to be recognized as an impermissible intrusion on privacy subsumed under the cause of action **invasion of privacy**. Despite the more descriptive and realistic "compensation for injuries," "torts" continues to be favored for saving seven syllables or twenty keystrokes.

DEFINITION

In the word torts we have a rare example of legal custom providing a doctrinaire but reliable definition: "A tort is a private wrong not arising out of contract." Unfortunately, the definition states what a tort is *not* without stating exactly what it *is*. It is not a public wrong, that is, it is not a crime and it is not based on a contract.

Tort versus Crime

Legal scholars have argued whether in ancient times crime and tort were separable. In modern times, the distinction between the two is clear because the rise of the modern state resulted in the assumption of authority by the state over misconduct it deemed "criminal." Public wrongs are often characterized as "wrongs against society." It is doubtful that the victim of a rape or robbery meditates on the social impact of the crime. Nevertheless, in our legal system the public has a legitimate interest in preventing such crimes.

Distinguishing tort from crime is clearest from a procedural standpoint. If the public prosecutor seeks a remedy (usually punishment) for misconduct, the wrong is public—it is a crime. If the victim sues in his or her own right for compensation, the wrong is private, a cause of action in tort. If conduct constituting a public

trespass
originally covered a wide variety of wrongs, one species of which, trespass *quare clausum fregit* constituted "trespass to land," which is a wrongful intrusion on land (real property). Also, an injury to a person's right of exclusive possession (e.g., where a neighbor builds a shed that encroaches on another's property).

slander
is an injury to reputation ordinarily caused by the communication of lies to third parties that result in a loss of good reputation. Slander is the spoken form of defamation, while *libel* is the written form. Rules governing slander and libel are considerably more complex than this definition suggests.

negligence
is a cause of action based on a failure to meet a reasonable standard of conduct that results in an injury.

products liability
pertains to strict liability for injuries caused by defective products. See page 262 for fuller explanation.

wrong causes injury to person or property, there is nearly always a private action in tort available to the injured party in addition to prosecution available to the state. The public and private actions are independent of each other and are procedurally distinct. In some cases the causes of action may have similar names—battery is a criminal offense as well as a civil cause of action in tort. The crime of rape, on the other hand, fits best into the civil cause of action called battery (some states have renamed the crime "sexual battery").

Not all torts involve criminal conduct. Since crimes ordinarily require intentional conduct, unintentional infliction of injuries, such as through negligence (e.g., causing an auto accident, medical malpractice), and liability for unsafe products (products liability) are usually not criminal even though the wrongdoer, a **tortfeasor**, may be subject to severe financial liability in tort.

Civil cases can be distinguished from criminal cases by the titles of the cases. *Montagu v. Capulet, Hatfield v. McCoy* are civil cases, while *Commonwealth v. Ripper, People v. Samson, State v. Miranda* (when defendant appeals to the U.S. Supreme Court, it becomes *Miranda v. Arizona, Ripper v. Massachusetts*) are criminal cases, though this distinction is not infallible since states may be involved in civil cases as well.

Tort versus Contract

Private wrongs fall into two categories: tort and contract. Since torts are "private wrongs not arising out of contract," non-contract actions based on wrongful conduct are necessarily torts. The reason for defining tort by what it is *not* can be attributed to the fact that the field of torts consists of a number of causes of action that have little in common, while contract actions are predicated on the existence of a valid contract.

The legal significance of this distinction rests on the source of the duty imposed on the defendant. In contract cases, the duties are created by the agreement between the parties and do not exist without it. If a young man offers to mow a neighbor's lawn for ten dollars and the neighbor agrees, the neighbor is obligated by this contract under the law to pay the ten dollars if the man mows the lawn. On the other hand, if the young man simply mows the lawn in the neighbor's absence without any agreement and then demands payment, the neighbor has no obligation to pay; there was no contract. In fact, going on the neighbor's land without consent could technically constitute the tort of trespass.

Rights and duties in tort action, by contrast, are based on obligations imposed by law. For example, our law recognizes an

invasion of privacy actually is composed of four different forms of misconduct that harm a person's reasonable expectations of privacy, including the wrongful use of another's name, likeness, or private history, as well as unreasonable intrusion into another's private life and affairs.

tortfeasor is a person who engages in tortious conduct.

individual's right to a good reputation and a corresponding duty on others not to spread lies that injure an individual's reputation. If such an injury occurs, the injured party may sue in tort under a cause of action for **defamation**. Liability is based on the breach of duties established by law (statutes and cases) rather than on an agreement between the parties found in the terms of a contract.

In a cause of action for breach of contract, the court looks to the contract to determine whether it is valid and enforceable under contract law and then, if valid, to the terms of the contract to determine precisely what obligations were created. If one party failed to fulfill promises made in the contract, liability may be imposed for a resulting injury to the other party. In principle this is simple, but life is complex, so a large body of law has developed to fit this principle to a variety of circumstances, which we will discuss fully in the next chapter. It should be kept in mind that the law sets the rules for the enforcement of contracts, but the specific duties on which suits are based are to be found in the private agreement of the parties, the contract itself. In a sense, the duty imposed by the law of contracts simply embodies a policy that the law favors the fulfillment of promises made between private parties.

In a cause of action for tort, duties to be enforced must be found in the law. A basic policy of protecting person, property, reputation, etc., is not sufficient. The Court needs guidance to determine whether liability should be imposed under the unique circumstances that a given case presents. This is the reason that the common law has been extremely important in the development of tort law. Whenever possible, the Court will look to similar cases from past decisions to determine how the duties have been defined. If duties have been established by statute, these may serve as the basis for judicial enforcement in tort. In fact, legislatures often create or redefine tort actions. For example, Congress provided in **42 U.S.C. §1983** (Civil Rights Act of 1871) for private actions to be brought against state officials who wrongfully deprive individuals of their civil rights.

Often tort actions will arise between persons who have relations such that the cause of action may appear to be a contract action. For example, medical malpractice cases arise in a contract relation—a physician agrees to furnish medical services in return for payment, a rather typical exchange of promises between parties to a contract. If the physician negligently treats a patient, thereby causing injury, the patient may sue for malpractice in tort based on the duties imposed by law on the physician rather than based on the terms of the contract. While this seems to be a wrong arising out of contract, in fact, the court looks to the law rather

defamation
is an injury to reputation (slander and libel are forms of defamation).

42 U.S.C. §1983
"Every person who, under color of any statute, ordinance, regulation, custom, or usage, of any State or Territory, subjects, or causes to be subjected, any citizen of the United States or other person within the jurisdiction thereof to the deprivation of any rights, privileges, or immunities secured by the Constitution and laws, shall be liable to the party injured in an action at law, suit in equity, or other proper proceeding for redress." (Civil Rights Act of 1871)

than the contract to determine the duties between the parties. There is also a tort called "wrongful interference with contractual relations," which occurs when a person *not* a party to a contract improperly disrupts the contractual relationship of others, as when a theater owner persuades a singer to break a contract at another theater. Obviously the tort is predicated on a contract, but in this case the contract is not one between the plaintiff and defendant.

Elements of Tort

As suits for personal injury developed over the centuries, the courts distinguished types of wrongful conduct. It seemed clear that the intentional infliction of physical injury, for example, was quite different in nature from an injury to reputation, so each required its own definition. Even the *threat* of physical injury (**assault**) was distinguished from the *infliction* of injury (**battery**). The definitions of specific causes of action in tort were framed in terms of elements (crimes are also defined by elements). In order to succeed in a tort action, the plaintiff must allege sufficient facts in a complaint to satisfy each element of a particular cause of action. If the plaintiff fails to do this, the complaint may be dismissed for failure to state a cause of action (the defendant would make a motion to dismiss "for failure to state a claim upon which relief can be granted"). Of course, the plaintiff must prove these allegations at trial in order to win the case.

Battery provides a time-tested example of the elements of a tort. It has been defined traditionally as an "unconsented, unprivileged, offensive contact." The definition contains the elements of battery as well as the defenses to battery.

Elements:
1. Intent
2. Bodily contact (extended to clothing, etc.)
3. Offensive in nature

Defenses:
1. Consent to the contact
2. Privilege

Battery is rooted in injury caused by fists or weapons but has been extended generally to offensive bodily contacts, such as sexual touching. It must be intentional and not simply accidental or careless, which might constitute a cause of action for negligence. There must be a contact and not merely a threat of contact (assault). The contact must be offensive. While a particular form of

assault
is putting someone in apprehension of a battery. The actor must have the ability to carry out the threatened battery.

battery
is an unconsented offensive contact.

defenses
In addition to defending by challenging the allegations and proof of the plaintiff, the defendant has available specific defenses in specific torts to prevent plaintiff from recovering anything. For example, while defamation represents an injury to reputation, truth is an absolute defense; i.e., even though plaintiff's reputation may have suffered, if the statement that caused the injury is true, the plaintiff does not recover damages.

contact may ordinarily constitute a battery, consent may prevent recovery, as with prizefighters and football players. The contact may be privileged, as when a parent strikes a child as a reasonable disciplinary measure or a policeman subdues a criminal with reasonable force.

Tort Law: An Evolving Field

Preparation of a tort suit begins with the search for an appropriate cause of action and an examination of whether or not a client's case fits comfortably within the elements of one or more torts. Tort law has experienced and continues to experience an evolution in its definition and the definition of specific causes of action. Not only does our notion of appropriate conduct change, but opportunities for injury change as well.

For example, the tort labeled "intentional infliction of mental distress" is a product of the twentieth century, undergoing considerable growth and refinement. While courts of the past were reluctant to compensate for emotional suffering unless accompanied by some physical injury, modern courts have come to recognize emotional injuries as compensable when caused intentionally by malice or outrageous conduct. Harassing telephone calls, unscrupulous bill collectors, impersonal public and private bureaucracies and perhaps even the lowering standards of courtesy on many fronts have all contributed to a recognition that the potential for serious harm to one's emotional well-being is a fact of modern life. The courts have come to impose a legal duty on conduct that custom has always disapproved but not legally condemned. The recognition of intentional infliction of mental distress is not designed to compensate for every insult or affront nor to encourage the overly sensitive to sue. Nevertheless, some individuals engage in conduct aimed at causing suffering in ways that the courts feel compelled to condemn. (Example: A man was held liable when he jokingly told a woman her husband was in a serious accident and persuaded her to rush down to the hospital.)

Each new tort must start with a dispute before a judge, who will be inclined to recognize right and duty when faced with a compelling set of facts. Tort law has evolved to be highly individualized, based on a recognition of an individual's right to be free from unjustified intrusions on person, personality, personal dignity, and private property. Establishment of a new right of action occurs when an appropriate case demands the redress of a harm that is socially acknowledged and fits within the basic policy of general tort law. In short, the court is unwilling to refuse an injured party a remedy even if the case does not fit precisely into the elements of some traditional cause of action. Whether this will give rise to a cause of action depends on whether other courts agree and allow the precedent to stand or whether they criticize it, thus cutting short its life.

CASE NO. 11-1   Creating a New Tort

The *Singer* case below arose out of the Wall Street scandal involving a number of financiers and brokerage houses in the late 1980s, commonly associated with the investigation and ultimate incarceration of Ivan Boesky. As the facts disclose, Mr. Singer apparently was an innocent victim of the events in which he was unwittingly embroiled. He lost his job, and his reputation was tarnished through the fault of others. The facts of the case, however, do not fit neatly into any of the ready-made causes of action in tort.

New York was the leader in developing the concept of **prima facie** tort, under which a cause of action was recognized even if it did not fit into a traditional label. Essential to plaintiff's case is the proof of bad motives (originally described as "disinterested malevolence" by Justice Oliver Wendell Holmes) on the part of defendant, who in turn may defend on the grounds of justification. The concept was eventually drafted in the following form as §870 of the *Restatement (Second) of Torts*:

One who intentionally causes injury to another is subject to liability to the other for that injury, if his conduct is generally culpable and not justified under the circumstances. This liability may be imposed although the actor's conduct does not come within a traditional category of tort liability.

The *Singer* case demonstrates that tort law is still evolving.

**Michael C. SINGER,
Plaintiff-Respondent,**

v.

**JEFFERIES & COMPANY, INC. et al.,
Defendants-Appellants.**

Supreme Court, Appellate Division,
First Department
553 N.Y.S.2d 346 (1990)

MEMORANDUM DECISION.

In essence, defendants contend that plaintiff's claim is solely for injury to reputation; is governed, and barred, by one year statute of limitations, CPLR §215(3); and, in any event, fails to state a cause of action because, *inter alia*, any harm suffered by plaintiff was unforeseeable. A discussion of the facts giving rise to the instant action is therefore an indispensable prerequisite for determining the merit of defendants' assertions.

[The issues of statute of limitations and foreseeability, concerning which the court held in plaintiff's favor, are omitted.]

Plaintiff, Michael G. Singer, was employed as a Senior Vice President in the corporate finance department of the corporate defendant, Jefferies & Co., from 1983 until early September 1986. The individual defendant, Boyd Jefferies, was the Chief Executive Officer of the corporate defendant.

In March 1985, individual defendant Jefferies telephoned plaintiff and instructed him to dictate an invoice, in the amount of $3,000,000.00, for services rendered, to Ivan F. Boesky Corporation. This plaintiff dutifully did, signing his name on the subject invoice.

In September 1986, plaintiff left defendants' employ, joining Salomon Brothers as a Vice President. On November 14, 1986, a federal subpoena of plaintiff, related to the Ivan Boesky insider trading investigation was issued by the SEC. This was delivered to Salomon Brothers, who accepted service of the subpoena in plaintiff's absence. Counsel for Salomon Brothers legal staff apparently reviewed the subpoena, which specifically asked about the subject invoice and the reason behind any payments made to Boesky by Jefferies.

Action by Salomon Brothers was swift. In a matter of days, on November 18, 1986, plaintiff's resignation was requested, allegedly with the assurance that he would be rehired were it determined that he had committed no wrong. The international press, including the New York Times, Wall Street Journal and Financial Times featured articles on November 19–21, detailing the relationship between Jefferies and Boesky, the subpoenas served upon Singer and Jefferies, and the circumstances surrounding Singer's abrupt departure from Salomon Brothers.

Plaintiff, who was never personally accused of any improprieties, fully cooperated with the government in its investigations. Indeed, in 1987, he received a commendation from the then US Attorney for the Southern District of New York, Rudolph Guiliani, for his cooperation. In sharp contrast, defendant Boyd Jefferies resigned his position, and, on or about March 19, 1987 entered a plea of guilty to two felony counts under federal securities law; these concerned aiding and abetting one of Boesky's entities in making false entries on its books. In a subsequent press release, Jefferies accepted sole responsibility for the false invoice he had instructed plaintiff to prepare and deliver to Boesky.

Although vindicated, plaintiff sustained a prolonged period of unemployment in 1987. Salomon Brothers declined to rehire him. Plaintiff thereafter had a less than enthusiastic response to his job search, and ultimately accepted a position at which his earnings were a fraction of those at Salomon Brothers.

. . . .

We find the facts herein state a cause of action sounding in tort. That we are unable to precisely categorize this tort is of no import, since "[i]t is axiomatic that the simple fact that [a plaintiff's] action does not fit into a nicely defined or established 'cubby-hole' of the law does not in itself warrant the denial of relief to him." *Seidel v. Greenberg*, 108 N.J.Super. 248, 260 A.2d 863, 868 (Law 1969). Indeed, as Dean Prosser has written:

> There is no necessity whatever that a tort have a name. New and nameless torts are being recognized constantly, and progress of the common law is marked by many cases of first impression, in which the court has struck out boldly to create a new cause of action, where one has never been recognized before.

Prosser and Keeton on Torts, 5th Ed., p. 3.

Defendants' contention on appeal that plaintiff's claim should be narrowly construed as one for defamation is unavailing. They make much of the fact that "unlike most torts, defamation is defined in terms of the injury, damage to reputation, and not in terms of the manner in which the injury is accomplished," *Morrison v. National Broadcasting Co.*, 19 N.Y.2d 453, 458, 280 N.Y.S.2d 641, 227 N.E.2d 572 (1967). However, unlike the plaintiff in *Morrison*, the plaintiff herein is not seeking recovery for damages solely because of injury to his reputation. . . .

Our view is, instead, that the claims asserted by plaintiff may be analogized to a variety of torts including, but not limited to, fraud and misrepresentation, malicious prosecution and breach of contract. We do not, however, disregard the possibility of a defamation-type claim, in view of the unquestioned injury to plaintiff's reputation. [Cc.] As a matter of policy, justice and fairness, plaintiff should not be precluded from having his day in court simply because the hornbook index does not list the tortious acts herein involved. [Cc.]

. . . .

Accordingly, the order appealed from is affirmed.

CASE GLOSSARY

Prima facie is Latin for "at first sight." It is used in law to refer to something that appears true or proven until evidence can be shown to the contrary. A prima facie tort is one that appears on its face to be tortious, intentional, wrongful conduct causing an injury, as distinguished from a tort that fits into one of the established causes of action.

EXTRANEOUS FACTORS INFLUENCING TORT LAW

The law develops in a social, economic, and political context. As Oliver Wendell Holmes declared in 1881, "[t]he life of the law has not been logic; it has been experience." Lawmaking is not simply a process of refining abstract rules, nor is the process of deciding disputes controlled by the simple expedient of applying abstract rules to concrete events. Tort law has a strong component of logic and common sense. The rights represented by tort law generally reflect what most Americans consider their rights should be (e.g., a person can use force against another person in self-defense). In a sense, tort law more than any other area of law reflects our social values with regard to interpersonal conduct. Nevertheless, there are some special factors that play a large part in actual tort suits and influence actual outcomes independent of the values expressed in substantive principles.

The Doctrine of Respondeat Superior

The English legal historian Plucknett attributes the birth of this doctrine to Lord Holt, who in deciding a case in 1691 stated: "Whoever employs another is answerable for him, and undertakes for his care to all that make use of him." Until that time, the doctrine of *respondeat superior*, which places liability on the employer for injuries caused by an employee, had only been applied to certain public officials when their underlings could not pay damages. There is nothing inherent in tort law that requires this principle, which is a peculiarity of Anglo-American common law. It contradicts a fundamental principle of tort law, namely, that fault should be the basis for liability. Nonetheless, an employer may be liable without acting wrongfully.

The influence of *respondeat superior* on modern tort litigation is great. Personal injury cases are costly to litigate, and it is futile to sue a defendant who has few resources. If, however, a person is injured by someone working on the job for a large corporation, the suit becomes economically feasible. The resources of employees are generally far less than those of their employers. As a practical matter, juries may be less concerned about the pocketbooks of large businesses than they are about those of workers.

As a result, the availability of compensation may depend more on who may be liable than on the legal merits of the case. When we read in the newspapers of unusually high awards, we can be relatively certain that some "deep pocket" was available to be sued. *Respondeat superior* creates many deep pockets.

Insurance

The rise of the modern insurance industry has abetted tort litigation. The basic principle of insurance is pooling risk. A homeowner who buys fire insurance contributes a small amount to a large pool for protection against the possible but unlikely prospect of a fire. Although the risk of fire is small, the result if it occurs is likely to be financial catastrophe for the uninsured. The insurance company is the pooling agency, collecting payments and maintaining funds from which the unlucky are reimbursed for their losses. The homeowner usually has a homeowner's policy that includes protection against suits from those who may in some way be injured on the homeowner's property. While loss from a fire may be a simple economic loss that can be fairly easily established, it is quite different when the child next door wanders over and drowns in the swimming pool. The value of that child's life is not easy to fix and will likely produce a protracted negotiation between the insurance company and the bereaved parents (through their attorneys). Insurance companies differ greatly in their willingness to make reasonable settlement offers, so the threat of lawsuit is often necessary; when a settlement cannot be reached, the dispute may be resolved by trial.

The presence of insurance encourages lawsuits for the very reason *respondeat superior* does—the insurance company has great financial resources. The economic costs of this system are great—attorneys reap large rewards, insurance companies make handsome profits, and injured parties suffer through long delays to receive their (presumably) just compensation.

Given the realities of the economic system and tort law, however, alternative choices are often too dangerous. For example, physicians commonly pay enormous premiums for malpractice insurance. One might think that a competent, diligent physician need not carry insurance since the likelihood of suit is minimal. But dedicated, ethical physicians are more concerned with treatment than with liability. Under the law they are held to a high standard of professional care. A simple error of judgment may result in death or serious permanent injury. The potential injuries are so severe that a physician practices without insurance at the peril of financial ruin. The alternative is to practice medicine with the primary purpose of avoiding liability, something neither the medical profession nor the public finds desirable.

Contingency Fees

The prominence of personal injury lawsuits in the practice of law is encouraged by the custom of contingency fees. This is a contract between the lawyer and the client under which the lawyer receives compensation measured by the settlement negotiated with the defendant or the award determined by the court. Rather than charging an hourly fee or a fee fixed in advance, the attorney agrees to represent the client for a percentage of the award. Typically the minimum fee is one third for a settlement, forty percent if the case goes to trial.

Ethically, contingency fees have always been suspect. They not only encourage suits if the potential award is great, but they also give the attorney an interest in the lawsuit, which presents a temptation for the attorney to act on the basis of personal gain rather than in the interests of the client or the law. The contingency fee arrangement is a peculiarly American institution and is not allowed in most countries. The justification for the arrangement most often given is that most injured parties could not afford to pursue a lawsuit if they were forced to pay attorneys as the case proceeds. They would be forced by economic circumstances to settle for much less than their injuries are worth. The individual of limited resources suing an insurance company or a large corporation with sufficient funds to pay attorneys to delay awards indefinitely is necessarily at a great disadvantage. The contingency fee arrangement somewhat equalizes the disparity between the parties. One must question, however, whether this is a natural or artificial product of the tort law.

Contingency fees encourage some sorts of lawsuits and discourage others. If an injury is severe and permanent, especially if it is disabling or disfiguring, compensation may be very great and thus justify the costs of litigation. If the defendant has no financial resources, a lawsuit is unlikely.

Contingency fees do not include the litigation costs incurred beyond the attorney's services, such as expert witness fees, cost of reproducing transcripts, etc. The attorney may not ethically underwrite the lawsuit; litigation costs must be paid by the plaintiff regardless of the outcome of the suit. The ABA *Model Rules of Professional Conduct* insist that the client be aware of the obligation to pay such costs.

FAULT

The concept of fault is central to the development of legal theories of tort. Ultimately the resolution of a tort suit involves the question of a transfer of wealth from the defendant to the plaintiff. If someone suffers an injury or a loss, should there be a source of compensation? The law looks to the cause of the injury. If caused by an "act of God," as when someone is struck by lightning, the law cannot allocate compensation since there is no party at fault.

On the other hand, if the cause of the injury can be attributed to human forces, liability may be appropriate. At that point a question of fairness arises. Would it be fair for this person or this organization to surrender some of its resources to the injured party? An affirmative answer to this question is easiest when the injury can be shown to have been caused directly by wrongful conduct of another party, while the injured party is utterly blameless. Unfortunately, causation and blameworthiness are frequently obscure or difficult to prove. What should be the result, for example, when a commercial airline crashes killing all aboard, but the cause of the crash cannot be determined? Should a widow of one of the passengers be compensated for her loss by the airline? Our sympathies are naturally with the widow, but should the airline compensate her even though she cannot prove fault on the part of the airline? The famous case of *Cox v. Northwest Airlines, Inc.*, 379 F.2d 893 (7th Cir. 1967) resolved this issue through the often-criticized principle of *res ipsa loquitur* ("the thing speaks for itself"). *Res ipsa* is used to infer negligence, specifically a failure of due care, when it would appear that the injury would not have occurred with due care. An airplane does not crash without some fault attributable to those in control of it (is this really true?). In this case the principle could be applied without pangs of con-science. The deceased was clearly blameless. The airline was in control of the airplane. In other words, it seems fair that the airline should pay, essentially making the airline the insurer of its pas-sengers; but the fact that fault was established in the absence of proof is troubling to those demanding logic and consistency in the law. Put another way, would it not be better simply to charge air-lines (and other common carriers) with the duty to insure the safety of their passengers rather than apply the questionable principle of *res ipsa loquitur*? Practically speaking, the doctrine of *res ipsa loqui-tur* is merely a device to get the issue of negligence to the jury.

A different problem of fault was encountered in another famous case, *Summers v. Tice*, 33 Cal.2d 80, 199 P.2d 1 (1948). Summers was injured in a hunting party when two of his compan-ions fired simultaneously at a quail, hitting Summers in the eye. It was not possible to determine which hunter's shot was respon-sible for Summers's injury. Logically one was at fault, while the other was not, but the California Supreme Court held both liable since both were negligent in firing in Summers's direction, even though only one could have been the actual *cause* of the injury. "To hold otherwise would be to exonerate both from liability, although each was negligent, and the injury resulted from someone's negli-gence." The Court refused to make Summers suffer the burden of his injuries simply because he could not prove which companion fired the shot that hit his eye.

A similar problem is encountered in the DES (diethylstilbes-trol) cases in which an antimiscarriage drug has been alleged to be the cause of cancer in the later life of children born to women who took the drug while pregnant. Assuming the truth of the alle-gations and assuming that the several drug companies who marketed the drug were legally responsible for the later injuries, who should pay when the medical records, prescriptions, and the mother's memory do not establish which company sold the drug that caused the cancer? One solution proposed to this problem is *enterprise liability*. Since several companies produced the drug, li-ability could be pooled among the companies according to their shares of the market for the drug (if one company sold fifteen percent of the drug, it would pay fifteen percent of the damages).

While enterprise liability is still controversial, it reflects the capacity of tort law to find novel remedies for unusual situations.

Enterprise liability also represents the modern trend in tort law away from the technicalities of finding fault toward emphasizing the search for compensating the innocent victim. The courts and legislatures have been increasingly sensitive to the plight of the consumer, the workforce, the motorist, the homemaker, the man on the street. Unfortunately, the principles that have arisen do not correct the inequities of the legal system itself. Compensable injuries go uncompensated when the economics of litigation prove an impediment. If there is no "deep pocket," or the injuries are less than the costs of litigation, personal injury attorneys will decline to pursue a case.

The legal profession has the ethical responsibility to provide services to the public in general, not just in cases in which legal fees are readily obtained. The American Bar Association has shown concern for this very problem, but it is up to the attorneys to shoulder the responsibility or assist in finding a solution. One promising alternative in this regard is in the growing body of well-trained paralegals. Many of the services provided by attorneys could be provided by paralegals at a much lesser cost—not only do paralegals provide their services at a lower fee, they can operate within restricted areas with lower overhead. Thus, full utilization of paralegals by lawyers can significantly reduce costs to clients. Economic necessity together with ethical obligation should result in a growth area for paralegals. This would serve the public and enhance the image of the legal profession. For paralegals this would be a welcome development; helping the nonwealthy may be more personally rewarding than protecting rich and corporate America. And no one will ever say "Let's kill all the paralegals."

CASE NO. 11–2   Whose Fault Is It?

Should a business enterprise be liable for the intentional torts of a third party on its premises? That is the question in the *Goggin* case. It represents both the search for fault and the plaintiff's search for an affluent defendant.

One of the defenses to negligence is "assumption of risk," where the plaintiff voluntarily encounters a known risk (e.g., someone employed to detonate explosives). In the case below the court not only finds the defendant free of negligence for the harm caused by a third party but suggests the plaintiff knew what he was getting into. At the same time the court acknowledges that the owners of premises open to the public have duties with regard to the safety of patrons. The case raises interesting issues with regard to the assignment of fault.

Harold J. GOGGIN

v.

NEW STATE BALLROOM

Supreme Judicial Court of
Massachusetts,
Suffolk
355 Mass. 718, 247 N.E.2d 350 (1969)
REARDON, Justice.

On March 17, 1960 [St. Patrick's Day, a holiday of great revelry in Boston], the plaintiff accompanied by a lady companion, entered the New State Ballroom in Boston at approximately 8:45 P.M. in anticipation of an evening with Terpsichore. Having paid the admission of $2 each and checked clothing, they commenced dancing when the music began. At this time there were approximately 900 people in the hall. The dance floor was waxed and polished and was about 125 feet long with a width of 90 feet. By 9:30 P.M. the crowd had grown to 1,200, and by 10 P.M. it had increased to the point where there were 1,800 to 1,900 people on the dance floor. These dancers were "noisy and boisterous, kicking their feet, bumping into people and doing some real kicking." This kicking occurred in connection with the execution of such dances as the "cha cha and jitterbug," and was accompanied by "bumping." The plaintiff, however, "only danced the waltz and refrained from the cha cha or the jitterbug." The record is silent relative to the problem of how one can negotiate a waltz when the music bein performed is geared to a cha cha or a jitterbug. It does disclose that in addition to the band which was on hand to render fox trots and waltzes there was a second orchestra designated as an "Irish band for Irish figure dancing which is rather fast music." While the plaintiff's partner claimed she saw no attendants, there was testimony from the defendant's

manager that two police officers, plus a sergeant, were on duty "along with two employees of the Ballroom who were on the dance floor." This detail was evidently insufficient to aid the plaintiff, for at 10 P.M. "he was dancing the waltz with his partner in a corner as there was one fellow he was trying to keep away from. When it is crowded like that you really can get bumped." He and his partner remained in the corner "but this fellow kept coming and all of a sudden, bang! 'We were pushed right over!'" The plaintiff went down, his head hit the floor, and his partner fell on top of him and ripped her dress in the descent. The plaintiff had been no stranger to the physical activity which took place at the ballroom for he was a regular attendant there on every Saturday evening between March 17, 1959, and March 17, 1960. He also repaired to the ballroom during that period on any holiday nights that fell on a weekday.

On this evidence the defendant moved for a directed verdict on a count in an action of tort brought by the plaintiff wherein he alleged that he was on the defendant's premises by invitation, that he had paid an admission, and that he was injured by reason of the defendant's negligence in its failure to conduct its establishment in an orderly manner and in compliance with statutes, ordinances and rules relating to it. The motion was denied, there was a verdict for the plaintiff, and the defendant is here on an exception to that denial.

The law in these circumstances has been often stated. The defendant, which opened its ballroom to the public in furtherance of its business, owed the duty to the plaintiff, who paid to enter, of reasonable care that no injury occur to the plaintiff through the actions of a third person whether such acts were accidental, negligent or intentional. . . . Restatement 2d: Torts, § 344. The defendant, however, was not an insurer of the plaintiff's safety. . . . Its liability in this instance must arise from its knowledge, or the fact that it should have known of or anticipated, in the exercise of reasonable care, the disorderly or rowdy actions of third persons which might lead to injury to the plaintiff. . . . Furthermore, where in a ballroom such as this conditions existing at the time of the accident are open and obvious to any person of ordinary intelligence, the defendant is under no duty to warn the plaintiff even where a substantial crowd has gathered. . . .

The plaintiff in this case chose on an evening not noted for restraints on exuberance in the city of Boston to go with his lady to a public dance hall where he knew the patrons were lovers of the cha cha and the jitterbug. He knew these dances involved muscular contortions and a degree of abandon not associated with a minuet. A certain amount of innocent bumping in a large crowd would be unavoidable. That the bump which floored the plaintiff may have been deliberate was, in our view, not such a happening that the defendant was bound to anticipate it. It was unusual and not reasonably to be apprehended and affords no basis for treating the defendant as negligent. . . . The vagaries of fashions in the dance and their consequences are better left subject to the judgment of those who engage in them or frequent establishments where they may be found, absent circumstances which may in the light of the principles herein discussed provide a basis for liability. . . .

Exceptions sustained. Judgment for the defendant.

FAULT AND THREE AREAS OF TORT LAW

Tort law covers a variety of areas of injury to person and property, but three areas constitute the bulk of tort litigation:

1. Intentional torts
2. Negligence
3. Strict liability (represented primarily by the booming area of products liability)

The oldest is intentional torts; negligence flowered in the nineteenth and twentieth centuries; and products liability has come to fruition only in recent decades. It is not possible here to discuss any of these in sufficient detail to suggest a mastery of them, which must be left for later study. They are discussed primarily with regard to the different ways in which they relate to concepts of fault in its historical legal evolution.

Intentional Torts

A number of causes of action are lumped together as intentional torts. Many of them are quite ancient, such as battery, assault, trespass, false imprisonment, etc. Some are recent in origin, such as invasion of privacy and intentional infliction of mental distress. Their common bond is the essential element of intent. Intent to do some harm (sometimes the intent to do specific harm) must be alleged and proven in order for the plaintiff to prevail. Neither malicious motive nor criminal intent is required for an intentional tort, though **malicious prosecution** specifically requires a showing of malice. Absence of malice may in some cases be a defense against libel.

The requirement of intent demands a proof of fault against the defendant and requires a willful act on the part of the defendant. The law of intentional torts assumes that human beings act from free will and can conform their conduct to societal rules. When they fail to do so, resulting in harm to others, they will be held responsible for their acts to the injured party. If a harmful act was intended, punitive damages are often awarded in addition to compensation. Punitive damages ordinarily are not available for nonintentional torts.

The plaintiff must prove intentional conduct, but the defendant has the opportunity to rebut intent. Intent is commonly inferred from the events that gave rise to the injury. In the colorful case of *Katko v. Briney*, 183 N.W.2d 657 (Iowa 1971), an Iowa farmer protected his wife's often-vandalized, unoccupied farm house by wiring a shotgun to a bedroom door to go off when someone opened the door. Katko, a trespasser looking for old bottles, had the misfortune of opening the door and suffered permanent injury to his leg. Briney's attempt to negate intent by stating on the witness stand that he "did not intend to injure anyone" was not believed by the jury, which found that he had acted maliciously and awarded Katko $20,000 in compensatory and $10,000 in punitive damages.

Conversely, when a five-year-old child pulled a lawn chair out from under a woman about to sit in it, the Supreme Court of Washington held that it was insufficient that the child's act was intentional and incurred a risk and remanded the case back to the trial judge to determine whether the child realized with a "substantial certainty" that the harmful contact would result (*Garrett v. Dailey*, 46 Wash.2d 197, 279 P.2d 1091 [1955]). Liability was thus

malicious prosecution occurs when someone initiates or causes a groundless suit to be brought out of malice. It is essential that the original suit be terminated in favor of the person later suing for malicious prosecution.

predicated on the knowledge and understanding of a five-year-old. (On remand the trial court found that the child did in fact have such knowledge.)

In addition to intent, plaintiff must allege and prove all the other elements of the specific cause of action as discussed earlier.

Negligence

The Industrial Revolution of the nineteenth century and the automobile of the twentieth both caused a marked increase in serious personal injuries. These injuries were caused by machines and the human beings that control them. Injury was rarely intentional but usually accidental so that traditional notions of intentional fault required significant elaboration.

A complete listing of the names of the causes of action in tort would be dominated by intentional torts, but the cases brought for personal injuries would be dominated by the single cause of action called *negligence.* Most people are injured accidentally and not intentionally. In negligence law, liability arises through a different notion of fault than intent. In a sense negligence is simply culpable carelessness. Poor judgment, momentary inattention, and lack of foresight often result in injury. Negligence law sought and found a measure by which the failure to exercise due care could be categorized as fault and could therefore incur liability.

The standard of care is embodied in the *reasonable man* test. Tradition uses the generic male for the standard, but today the test is more properly put as "what a reasonably prudent *person* would have done under the circumstances." Whether someone should be found at fault and held liable is measured by a standard of care based on reasonableness rather than subjective mental state or intent.

Negligence has four elements:

1. Duty (standard of care)
2. Breach of the duty (conduct falling below the standard of care)
3. Causation (the breach must be the cause of the injury)
4. Injury

The breach of the duty establishes fault. Since negligence applies to the myriad injuries incurred daily through oversight and carelessness, it is not possible to cover in the elements the precise circumstances that give rise to liability; they are simply too numerous. The reasonable man standard acknowledges that what may be prudent conduct in one situation may not be prudent in another. (The *Cordas* case below suggests that the apparently unreasonable conduct of a driver leaving a running car may not always be unreasonable.) The test must be applied on a case-by-case basis with the standard of care determined by the jury. The "reasonable man" is a hypothetical person of ordinary understanding but prudent in conduct so that individuals are not expected to exercise extraordinary care, nor are they excused by the fact that most people are often careless. It would undoubtedly be negligent not to fence in a swimming pool in a neighborhood full of small children but perhaps not imprudent not to do so on a country estate with no neighboring children; it is up to the jury to decide what is reasonable and prudent.

The standard of care for negligence may vary from the reasonable man standard. Thus, if a statutory standard fits the case, it usually serves for the standard of care. For example, if a motorist runs a stop sign and causes an accident, the breach of the standard of care is satisfied by a statute that requires a full stop at stop signs, so the jury need not question whether a reasonably prudent person stops at stop signs.

For professionals the standard of care is measured by professional standards in the community in which the professional practices or by a national standard for specialists. It would hardly do for a jury to decide what a reasonably prudent person would do when performing brain surgery. At present paralegals are not professionals in this legal sense, so negligence on their part ordinarily would result in a suit against the supervising attorney. Should a paralegal who has been certified as a legal assistant by NALA be subject to suit if the paralegal represents himself as a "Certified Paralegal"? At present many states are questioning whether paralegals should be licensed, which would presumably make them professionals and subject to suit for their negligent mistakes.

CASE NO. 11-3 "The Reasonable Man"

The "reasonable man" is a rather colorless person who takes few chances, always looks out for others, and exercises a prudent degree of caution in all his endeavors. He has been the butt of jokes by those of legal persuasion, but perhaps never so much as in the case below. Judge Carlin, when called upon to set a standard of care under very unreasonable circumstances, treated the matter with a humor rarely seen today. Fortunately, the injuries incurred were "slight."

CORDAS et al.

v.

PEERLESS TRANSPORTATION CO.
et al.

City Court of New York, New York County
27 N.Y.S.2d 198 (1941)

CARLIN, JUSTICE.

This case presents the ordinary man—that problem child of the law—in a most bizarre setting. As a lonely chauffeur in defendant's employ he became in a trice the protagonist in a breath-bating drama with a denouement almost tragic. It appears that a man, whose identity it would be indelicate to divulge, was feloniously relieved of his portable goods by two nondescript highwaymen in an alley near 26th Street and Third Avenue, Manhattan; they induced him to relinquish his possessions by a strong argument ad hominem couched in the convincing cant of the criminal and pressed at the point of a most persuasive pistol. Laden with their loot, but not thereby impeded, they took an abrupt departure, and he, shuffling off the coil of that discretion which enmeshed him in the alley, quickly gave chase through 26th Street toward 2d Avenue, whither they were resorting "with expedition swift as thought" for most obvious reasons. Somewhere on that thoroughfare of escape they indulged the stratagem of separation ostensibly to disconcert their pursuer and allay the ardor of his pursuit. He then centered on for capture the man with the pistol, whom he saw board the defendant's taxicab which quickly veered south toward 25th Street on 2d Avenue, where he saw the chauffeur jump out while the cab still in motion, continued toward 24th Street; after the chauffeur relieved himself of the cumbersome burden of his fare the latter also is said to have similarly departed from the cab before it reached 24th Street.

The chauffeur's story is substantially the same except that he states that his uninvited guest boarded the cab at 25th Street while it was at a standstill waiting for a less colorful fare; that his "passenger" immediately advised him "to stand not upon the order of his going but go at once," and added finality to his command by an appropriate gesture with a pistol addressed to his sacroiliac. The chauffeur in reluctant acquiescence proceeded about fifteen feet, when his hair, like unto the quills of the fretful porcupine, was made to stand on end by the hue and cry of the man despoiled, accompanied by a clamorous concourse of the law-abiding who paced him as he ran; the concatenation of "stop thief," to which the patter of persistent feet did maddingly beat time, rang in his ears as the pursuing posse all the while gained on the receding cab with its quarry therein contained. The hold-up man sensing his insecurity suggested to the chauffeur that in the event there was the slightest lapse in obedience to his curt command that he, the chauffeur, would suffer the loss of his brains, a prospect as horrible to an humble chauffeur as it undoubtedly would be to one of the intelligentsia.

The chauffeur, apprehensive of certain dissolution from either Scylla, the pursuers, or Charybdis, the pursued, quickly threw his car out of first speed in which he was proceeding, pulled on the emergency, jammed on his brakes and, although he thinks the motor was still running swung open the door to his left and jumped out of his car. He confesses that the only act that smacked of intelligence was that by which he jammed the brakes in order to throw off balance the hold-up man, who was half-standing and half-sitting with his pistol menacingly poised. Thus abandoning his car and passenger the chauffeur sped toward 26th Street and then turned to look; he saw the cab proceeding south toward 24th Street, where it mounted the sidewalk. The plaintiff-mother and her two infant children were there injured by the cab, which, at the time, appeared to be also minus its passenger, who, it appears, was apprehended in the cellar of a local hospital where he was pointed out to a police officer by a remnant of the posse, hereinbefore mentioned. He did not appear at the trial. The three aforesaid plaintiffs and the husband-father sue the defendant for damages, predicating their respective causes of action upon the contention that the chauffeur was negligent in abandoning the cab under the aforesaid circumstances. Fortunately the injuries sustained were comparatively slight. . . .

Negligence has been variously defined but the common legal acceptation is the failure to exercise that care and caution which a reasonable and prudent person ordinarily would exercise under like conditions or circumstances. . . . Negligence is "not absolute or intrinsic," but "is always relevant to some circumstances of time, place or person." . . . The learned attorney for the plaintiffs concedes that the chauffeur acted in an emergency, but claims a right to recovery upon the following proposition taken verbatim from his brief: "It is respectfully submitted that the value of the interest of the public at large to be immune from being injured by a dangerous instrumentality such as a car unattended while in motion is very superior to the right of a driver to abandon same while it is in motion, even when acting under the belief that his life is in danger and by abandoning same he will save his life."

To hold thus under the facts adduced herein would be tantamount to a repeal by implication of the primal law of nature written in indelible characters upon the fleshy tablets of sentient creation by the Almighty Law-giver, "the supernal Judge who sits on high." There are those who stem the turbulent current for bubble fame, or who bridge the yawning chasm with a leap for the leap's sake, or who "outstare the sternest eyes that look, outbrave the heart most daring on the earth, pluck the young sucking cubs from the she-bear, yea, mock the lion when he roars for prey" to win a fair lady, and these are the admiration of the generality of men; but they are made of sterner stuff than the ordinary man upon whom the law places no duty of emulation. . . .

. . . .

Kolanka v. Erie Railroad Co., 215 App.Div. 82, 86, 212 N.Y.S. 714, 717, says: "The law in this state does not hold one in an emergency to the exercise of that mature judgment required of him under circumstances where he has an opportunity for deliberate action. He is not required to exercise unerring judgment, which would be expected of him, were he not confronted with an emergency requiring prompt action." The circumstances provide the foil by which the act is brought into relief to determine whether it is or is not negligent. If under normal circumstances an act is done which might be considered negligent, it does not follow as a corollary that a similar act is negligent if performed by a person acting under an emergency, not of his own making, in which he suddenly is faced with a patent danger with a moment left to adopt a means of extrication.

The chauffeur—the ordinary man in this case—acted in a split second in a most harrowing experience. To call him negligent would be to brand him coward; the court does not do so in spite of what those swaggering heroes, "whose valor plucks dead lions by the beard", may bluster to the contrary. The court is loathe to see the plaintiffs go without recovery even though their damages were slight, but cannot hold the defendant liable upon the facts adduced at the trial. Motions, upon which decision was reserved, to dismiss the complaint are granted, with exception to plaintiffs. Judgment for defendant against plaintiffs dismissing their complaint upon the merits.

Contributory Negligence/Comparative Negligence

With the rise of negligence suits in the nineteenth century, the requirement of fault (breach of the standard of care) also gave rise to a defense based on fault. It did not seem just to allow a recovery if the plaintiff shared some responsibility for causing the injury. Plaintiff's fault was called *contributory negligence* and constituted a complete defense to a suit for negligence. The courts soon realized that the result of using this doctrine was not always just. In some cases the minor fault of the plaintiff would not allow recovery. Railroad workers, for example, often worked under dangerous conditions in which a moment's inadvertence could result in serious injury or death. It was not sufficient for the widow and children to prove the employer had been responsible for the dangerous conditions; if the employee had not been careful, there was no recovery.

workers' compensation
is a statutory
scheme whereby
fixed awards are
made for
employment-related
injuries. Commonly
this takes the form
of state-regulated
employers' insurance arrangements.
A claimant does not
need to show negligence, nor is contributory negligence
a defense.

§402A
The *Restatement of
Torts* (Second) §402A
covers products liability as follows:
  Special Liability of
Seller of Product for
Physical Harm to
User or Consumer

Legislatures responded to dangers in the workplace with **workers' compensation**, and many courts and legislatures responded with *comparative negligence*. Under comparative negligence schemes, many of which are statutory, fault is apportioned; that is, if the plaintiff is negligent as well as the defendant, the plaintiff's award is reduced by plaintiff's percentage of fault. Thus, if the jury, under the judge's instructions, determines that eighty percent of the fault rests with the defendant, while twenty percent is the fault of the plaintiff, the plaintiff is entitled only to eighty percent of the amount of the injuries. If the jury values plaintiff's injuries at $50,000, plaintiff would receive $40,000. The percentages are arbitrary approximations, but the jury must estimate them if it finds fault on both parties. Many states will not allow the plaintiff to recover if the jury assigns fifty percent or more of the fault to the plaintiff. Automobile accidents often involve injuries to both drivers, each of whom claims the other was at fault. The final award can differ greatly depending on whether the jurisdiction uses contributory negligence or comparative negligence ("pure" or modified).

Strict Liability/Products Liability

The Age of Technology has confounded the concept of fault in tort. The American consumer acquires a bewildering assortment of machines, appliances, and pharmaceutical drugs as well as other products that pose unseen dangers. Manufacturers may exercise reasonable precautions to make their products safe and certainly do not intend to injure their customers, so it is difficult to assign fault under theories of negligence or intentional tort. The purchase of products creates a contractual relationship, but ordinary contract remedies do not contemplate compensation for personal injury.

Earlier in the twentieth century judges were troubled by innocent victims of defective products who could not prove fault on the part of the producer. As America became a mighty industrial power, courts became less concerned about protecting business from ruinous lawsuits and more concerned about the hapless victims of their products. It did not seem just that a company could reap large profits from the sales of their products without compensating those injured by them. A number of cases strained at the concept of fault to protect innocent parties, and in 1963 Justice Traynor of the California Supreme Court wrote the opinion in *Greenman v. Yuba Power Products, Inc.*, 59 Cal.2d 57, 377 P.2d 897, which announced the birth of products liability. Greenman had purchased a combination power tool for his home workshop that one day inexplicably ejected a piece of wood, striking him in the forehead. Justice Traynor reasoned that traditional requirements of proof of fault were no longer tenable and set the standard for the plaintiff in the case as follows:

> To establish the manufacturer's liability it was sufficient that plaintiff proved that he was injured while using the Shopsmith in a way it was intended to be used as a result of a defect in design and manufacture of which plaintiff was not aware that made the Shopsmith unsafe for its intended use . . .

Perhaps no case in the common law has had a more immediate and far-reaching effect on American law. The *Restatement of Torts* responded two years later with **§402A**, which elaborated on the *Greenman* decision. 402A was adopted in some form by state after state in rapid succession. In a few short years numerous cases served to refine the principles of products liability. Never has such a vast body of law so quickly fixed a cause of action so firmly in the law.

This was a revolution in tort law waiting to happen. Traynor could appeal to precedent in **implied warranty** theory, which held sellers responsible for the fitness for use of the products they sell. The consumer reasonably relied on the seller to deliver a product fit for use. Implied warranties were in addition to the express warranties given by the seller. The advent of the automobile made

---

(1) One who sells any product in a defective condition unreasonably dangerous to the user or consumer or to his property is subject to liability for physical harm thereby caused to the ultimate user or consumer, or to his property, if

(a) the seller is engaged in the business of selling such a product and

(b) it is expected to and does reach the user or consumer without substantial change in the condition in which it is sold.

(2) The rule stated in Subsection (1) applies although

(a) the seller has exercised all possible care in the preparation and sale of his product, and

(b) the user or consumer has not bought the product from or entered into any contractual relation with the seller.

implied warranty is a promise imposed by law, as distinguished from an *express warranty* stated in the contract. Of particular importance is the implied warranty of merchantability or fitness (for the use seller knows to be required) in the sale of a product.

implied warranties important because the purchaser was rarely in a position to determine whether the product was properly designed or assembled.

The adoption of the cause of action for products liability was justified on policy grounds, which were stated succinctly by Judge Jacobson in a concurring opinion in *Lechuga, Inc. v. Montgomery,* 12 Ariz.App. 32, 467 P.2d 256:

> It is apparent from a reading of the Restatement, and the leading cases on this subject, that the doctrine of strict liability has evolved to place liability on the party primarily responsible for the injury occurring, that is, the manufacturer of the defective product. This, as Justice Traynor stated in his concurring opinion in *Escola v. Coca Cola Bottling Co. of Fresno,* 24 Cal.2d 453, 150 P.2d 436 (1944), is based on reasons of public policy:
> "If public policy demands that a manufacturer of goods be responsible for their quality regardless of negligence there is no reason not to fix that responsibility openly." 150 P.2d, at 441.
> These public policy considerations have been variously enumerated as follows:
>
> (1) The manufacturer can anticipate some hazards and guard against their recurrence, which the consumer cannot do. Restatement, *supra,* comment c.
> (2) The cost of injury may be overwhelming to the person injured while the risk of injury can be insured by the manufacturer and be distributed among the public as a cost of doing business. *Greenman v. Yuba Power Products, Inc.* [59 Cal.2d 57], 27 Cal.Rptr. 697, 377 P.2d 897 (1962).
> (3) It is in the public interest to discourage the marketing of defective products. *Escola v. Coca Cola Bottling Co. of Fresno, supra.*
> (4) It is in the public interest to place responsibility for its reaching the market. *Greenman v. Yuba Power Products, Inc., supra.*
> (5) That this responsibility should also be placed upon the retailer and wholesaler of the defective product in order that they may act as the conduit through which liability may flow to reach the manufacturer, where ultimate responsibility lies. *Vandermark v. Ford Motor Co.* [61 Cal.2d 256], 37 Cal.Rptr. 896, 391 P.2d 168 (1964).
> (6) That because of the complexity of present day manufacturing processes and their secretiveness, the ability to prove negligent conduct by the injured plaintiff is almost impossible. *Escola v. Coca Cola Bottling Co. of Fresno, supra.*

(7) That the consumer does not have the ability to investigate for himself the soundness of the product. *Santor v. A and M Karagheusian, Inc.*, 44 N.J. 52, 207 A.2d 305 (1965).

(8) That this consumer's vigilance has been lulled by advertising, marketing devices and trademarks. Concurring opinion, *Lockwood, J., Nalbandian v. Byron Jackson Pumps, Inc.*, 97 Ariz. 280, 399 P.2d 681 (1965).

Inherent in these policy considerations is not the nature of the transaction by which the consumer obtained possession of the defective product, but the character of the defect itself, that is, one occurring in the manufacturing process and the unavailability of an adequate remedy on behalf of the injured plaintiff.

In addition to implied warranty as a ground for products liability, the principle of **absolute liability** for extrahazardous activities furnished precedent. Under this principle, parties engaged in especially dangerous activities, such as the use of explosives, were held to liability regardless of fault. The policy grounds were similar. It appeared to the courts unjust that innocent parties could be injured through the direct cause of other's activities and be left without a remedy simply because those engaged in the activities had exercised due care.

Behind liability for dangerously defective products and extrahazardous activities lies a foreseeability issue. Clearly, engaging in activities that present a significant risk to the public makes injury foreseeable in a general sense, even if neither the victim nor the manner of occurrence is precisely foreseeable. And when a manufacturer makes products that are potentially dangerous, the risk of injury has a degree of foreseeability. The law now holds that those who incur risks should bear the cost of the injuries that result. Foreseeability lurks everywhere in tort law. Because of the nature of lawsuits, the foreseeability issue always arises from hindsight—what may seem foreseeable in looking back on the course of events may not have been remotely foreseen at the beginning. Foreseeability is an issue that is both argued and ignored, but further study is beyond the scope of our present discussion.

DAMAGES

A person who loses an arm, a leg, or an eye or is left paraplegic suffers a loss of lifestyle as well. The courts have long considered a reduction in earning potential as recoverable, but recently attorneys have argued, sometimes successfully, that injured

absolute liability
is liability without fault or negligence, often used interchangeably with *strict liability*, though many would contend there is a difference.

parties should collect for "hedonic" losses, meaning essentially a decrease in enjoyment of life. Imagine an artist made blind by another's wrongful conduct. The artist may lose not only a career and earnings but also much of the meaning and enjoyment of life. The next few years will tell how far courts are willing to go in recognizing such losses as compensable.

CASE NO. 11-4   Loss of Consortium

The *Gates* case represents a loss that has been long recoverable, by husbands, at least. The loss is to the spouse of the physically injured party. The Supreme Court of Florida here rectified the sexism of the earlier common law principles.

Hilda I. GATES, Petitioner
v.
Harry Edwin FOLEY, Jr., Respondent

Supreme Court of Florida
247 So.2d 40 (Fla. 1971)

ADKINS, J.

. . . .

Plaintiff, Hilda I. Gates, sued the Defendant, alleging that the Defendant negligently operated his automobile causing a collision with an automobile operated by the husband of Plaintiff. It is further alleged that as a result of the accident Plaintiff's husband was rendered totally disabled and the Plaintiff claimed damages for "the loss of consortium and other services from her said husband."

. . . .

At common law the wife could not maintain such an action. . . .

It should be specifically noted that the suit is for "loss of consortium" and not loss of support or earnings which the husband might recover in his own right. We are only concerned with loss of consortium, by which is meant, the companionship and fellowship of husband and wife and the right of each to the company, cooperation and aid of the other in every conjugal relation. Consortium means much more than mere sexual relation and consists, also, of that affection, solace, comfort, companionship, conjugal life, fellowship, society and assistance so necessary to a successful marriage. [C.]

. . . .

The recent changes in the legal and societal status of women in our society forces us to recognize a change in the doctrine [that a wife could not recover for loss of consortium at common law].

. . . .

The rule that we now recognize is that the wife of a husband injured as a proximate result of the negligence of another shall have a right of action against that same person for her loss of consortium. We further hold that her right of action is a derivative right and she may recover only if her husband has a cause of action against the same defendant. This means that the tortfeasor was negligent and the husband was free from contributory negligence.

In such actions by the wife, the trial court should carefully caution the jury that any loss to the wife of her husband's material support is fully compensated by any award to him for impairment of his lost earning and that the wife is entitled to recover only for loss of consortium as defined in this opinion.

CASE QUESTIONS

1. Can you think of the reasons why in earlier times a husband was able to collect for injuries to his wife that interfered with their relationship?
2. Why were wives unable to be compensated in the same way that their husbands were?
3. Why does the court take pains to point out that consortium is not merely concerned with sexual relations?
4. Should someone be able to receive compensation when someone else is injured? See N.Y. *Times,* August 31, 1990, "2 Can Sue Over Something Horrible They Saw," telling the story of passengers on a park aerial tram, which was struck by part of the tramway system, killing another of the passengers. The plaintiffs were unrelated to the decedent but claimed emotional injuries for the incident and sued for "negligent infliction of emotional distress." A California Court of Appeals reversed the trial court and held the plaintiffs had stated a cause of action.

Punitive (or Exemplary) Damages for Intentional Tort

If compensatory damages aim at returning the plaintiff to the condition enjoyed before the wrongful injury by way of monetary compensation, punitive damages are reserved to punish the outrageous conduct of the defendant. They have nothing to do with compensation and are a windfall to the plaintiff (after paying thirty or forty percent of the award to plaintiff's attorney, the windfall is likely to be erased).

CASE NO. 11–5 Punitive Damages

The following case explains most of the important features of punitive damages. It also presents a case in which the appellate court is very unhappy with the jury's award of compensatory damages as well as the jury's refusal to award punitive damages. The court was apparently far more outraged by the defendant's conduct than was the jury and rather adeptly makes an end run around the jury (and perhaps the law).

Three intentional torts are claimed: Assault, battery, and intentional infliction of mental distress. Battery, as discussed above, is an unconsented, unprivileged, offensive contact. The essence of assault is putting someone in fear of a battery, usually by threat of a battery. Intentional infliction of mental distress is somewhat self-explanatory, except to add that the courts have generally required outrageous conduct that would create severe emotional distress under the circumstances of the case.

Susan MICARI, Jyll Johnstone, Joan Field,
Karyn Wohl, Cynthia Greco, Elizabeth Jackson, Corrinne Collett and Bridget Fidler, Plaintiffs,
v.
Paul MANN and Paul Mann Actors Workshop, Inc. Defendants.

Supreme Court, Trial Term,
New York County, Part XI-B
126 Misc.2d 422, 481 N.Y.S.2d 967
(1984)
EDWARD H. LEHNER, Justice.

The novel legal issue presented on this motion pursuant to CPLR 4404 is whether the court may direct a new trial solely on the issue of punitive damages when the jury declined to award such damages.

FACTS

Plaintiffs, students in defendant's acting school, instituted this action to recover damages based on allegations of sexual abuse and harassment.

At trial the moving plaintiffs (all of whom were in their early twenties at the time of the incidents complained of) testified that defendant (who was then in his mid sixties) caused them to perform at school various sexual acts with him or in his presence, including fellatio upon him and masturbating and engaging in lesbian acts in his presence. Plaintiffs

acknowledged that no physical force was employed or threatened by defendant to cause them to perform these acts. They asserted, however, that defendant individually told them that this sexual activity was intended to release their inhibitions and thus improve their acting skills. They indicated that, in light of defendant's outstanding reputation as an acting teacher who had taught many famous members of the profession, they trusted him, although they each professed doing so with a certain amount of trepidation.

Defendant denied that any of the alleged sexual activity occurred except for one instance of fellatio which he stated was initiated by one of the plaintiffs.

. . . .

THE JURY VERDICT

The jury found in favor of each of the moving plaintiffs in the sum of $2,000; $500 was granted on the claim of assault, $1,000 on the battery cause of action, and $500 for intentional infliction of mental distress. No award of punitive damages was made to any plaintiff on any cause of action.

THE JURY NOTE

Together with its verdict the jury handed up a note in which it was stated that "minimal damages" were awarded because "the defendant has suffered sufficiently in terms of stress, damaged reputation and financial distress" and "as a result of the findings of guilt by the jury, the defendant will continue to suffer by result of a damaged reputation in the acting/teaching field." The note concluded as follows: "Hopefully, our decision will serve as a future deterrent in sexual abuse and harassment behavior of teacher against student."

. . . The legal question presented by the note is whether its contents may be considered in the determination of the motion before the court.

. . . .

Thus, although no explanation was sought of the jury, and explanations should not be encouraged, as they could result in confusion and uncertainty, the court nevertheless believes that in the case at bar there is no valid reason to disregard the note in considering the issue before it.

COMPENSATORY DAMAGES

Although the court would have been inclined to award higher compensatory damages than were awarded by the jury, a court may set aside a verdict only if the award is found to be "so grossly inadequate as to be unconscionable" [Cc.]. . . .

Here there was very little proof presented at trial on the issue of damages sustained by plaintiffs. Therefore, in light of the foregoing guidelines, the court may not overturn the jury award of compensatory damages, and the request that it do so is denied.

PUNITIVE DAMAGES

Punitive damages may be awarded "where the wrong complained of is morally culpable, or is actuated by evil and reprehensible motives, not only to punish the defendant but to deter him, as well as others who might otherwise be so prompted, from indulging in similar conduct in the future." *Walker v. Sheldon,* 10 N.Y.2d 401, 404, 223 N.Y.S.2d 488, 179 N.E.2d 497. The award is "to serve as a warning to others" and "as punishment for gross behavior for the good of the public." *Toomey v. Farley,* 2 N.Y.2d 71, 83, 156 N.Y.S.2d 840, 138 N.E.2d 221.

Here the wrongs which the jury found defendant to have committed are most reprehensible. The jury, by rendering a verdict for plaintiffs on each of the three causes of action submitted to it, determined that defendant misrepresented the reason he requested the performance of the sexual acts about which the plaintiffs testified. Thus, defendant, a person with a distinguished reputation as an acting teacher, abused the relationship which he, as a teacher with overpowering influence over his students, possessed.

In this connection the court observes that the jury in its note intended its decision to "serve as a future deterrent in sexual abuse and harassment behavior of teacher against student." The court does not believe that the verdict accomplished this result. Although there was testimony elicited during presentation of defendant's counterclaim for prima facie tort (dismissed after defendant's case) that indicated that defendant's teaching career had suffered (which may have convinced the jury that defendant had "suffered sufficiently"), there was no evidence presented with respect to his financial condition. It has been held that a jury is entitled to consider such condition after an award has been made for compensatory damages.[Cc.]

MODIFYING AN AWARD OF
PUNITIVE DAMAGES

Although "the power of the trial court to grant a new trial on the ground that the verdict is inadequate or excessive, is undisputed" as to compensatory damages, *O'Connor v. Papertsian,* 309 N.Y. 465,471, 131 N.E.2d 883, the court has found no authority in this state with respect to the power of a trial judge to grant a new trial after a jury fails to award exemplary damages, or awards an inadequate sum.

[The Court then discusses cases from other states which held that the court could overturn or reduce excessive awards of punitive damages but could not order a new trial on grounds that punitive damages were inadequate arguing that plaintiff only had a right to compensation, punitive damages being designed to punish the defendant.]

. . . .

Since the authority of trial courts to review damage awards is now generally recognized as far broader than previously, it is only fitting that the power to raise such awards be now recognized as to punitive damages as well. A court should not stand by idly when it is apparent that a verdict is shockingly inadequate. "A jury's verdict must have some relation to reality and it is the court's duty to keep it so." *Faulk v. Aware Inc.*, 19 A.D.2d 464, 470. 244 N.Y.S.2d 259.

"There is no rigid formula by which the amount of punitive damages is fixed, although they should bear some reasonable relation to the harm done and the flagrancy of the conduct causing it." *I.H.P. Corp. v. 210 Central Park South Corp.*, 16 A.D.2d 461, 467, 228 N.Y.S.2d 883. In order to accomplish its goals, the amount of the award depends upon the degree of culpability of the wrongdoer, the situation and sensibilities of the parties concerned, and the extent to which such conduct offends a public sense of justice and propriety. In addition, "if the purpose of punitive damages is to punish and to act as a deterrent . . . unless it is of sufficient substance to 'smart,' . . . In light of the discretion granted trial judges in New York pursuant to CPLR 4404 to set aside verdicts, the court declines to follow the aforementioned out of state cases and holds that the same power a court possesses to increase an inadequate or nominal award of compensatory damages exists with respect to punitive damages.

Clearly such discretion should be exercised only in the rare situations where the failure of the jury to award punitive damages, or the award of an inadequate sum, shocks the conscience of the court.

Here the testimony indicated that defendant, playing upon the emotional needs of his insecure students, actively sought to be ensconced as their trusted father figure—indeed, one of the plaintiffs described defendant's behavior after a sexual experience as "fatherly." It is this studied effort at domination under the guise of acting in loco parentis, coupled with both his actual and apparent ability to affect plaintiffs' dearest aspirations, that renders defendant's actions so heinous. This gross violation was not merely of their bodies but of their trust as well, an invasion so reprehensible as to cry out for the imposition of a sanction expressing the moral outrage of society. Under these circumstances one would be hard pressed to find a situation where punitive damages were more warranted.

Thus, considering the deplorable and outrageous conduct which the jury found was committed by defendant upon these young women under his tutelage, the court believes that the foregoing discretion should be exercised in the case at bar. Accordingly, the court hereby orders a new trial solely on the issue of punitive damages unless defendant shall, within 30 days from the date hereof, stipulate to an award of $5,000 punitive damages for each movant.

SUMMARY

Tort has traditionally been defined as "a private wrong not arising out of contract." This definition distinguishes between public wrongs, which are classified as crimes, and private wrongs, which are designed to redress wrongful conduct causing injury to a private party. The public prosecutor is responsible for bringing actions in criminal cases; private parties bring actions on their own behalf to redress a wrong. The definition also distinguishes between torts and contract causes of action. In contract, the legal obligations are created by mutual agreement of the parties; the law of contracts simply establishes the requisites for enforcement. In tort law, obligations are imposed by law. Tort law establishes protected private interests relating to person, property, reputation, etc., that are not premised on a contractual relationship, though one may exist, e.g., doctor–patient in medical malpractice.

There are numerous causes of action in tort, each having "elements," each of which must be present for the court to accept a lawsuit based on a specific cause of action. However, tort law is a continually evolving field. New causes of action arise with some regularity, and courts exercise some flexibility in allowing cases that do not fit into textbook definitions if conduct is clearly wrongful and injury is apparent.

Many factors influence the course of tort law independent of the interest sought to be protected. New law cannot be made by the courts unless disputes are brought, yet the economics of litigation usually influence which suits may be economically rewarding for a plaintiff.

Among the factors facilitating suit is the doctrine of *respondeat superior,* which holds an employer liable for the wrongful acts of an employee, thus making feasible suits when the wrongdoer/employee has limited funds while the employer has substantial resources. Similarly, the widespread use of insurance presents the opportunity for collecting full compensation for injuries sustained, which might not be possible if the defendant were uninsured and without assets.

In personal injury cases, customary practice includes the use of contingency fee arrangements whereby attorneys receive as their compensation a percentage of the settlement or award at the termination of the case. A great many cases could not be brought if the injured party were required to provide compensation to a lawyer as the case progressed.

Although these factors address practical questions, they effect the development of tort law since certain sorts of cases are frequently pursued while others remain impractical.

Traditionally, the basis for requiring a defendant to compensate an injured plaintiff was fixing fault on the defendant for a wrongful act. The degree of fault required for a particular tort distinguishes between major categories of tort. The common element of intentional torts is an intentional act, while in negligence the standard is not what defendant intended but the failure to act in a reasonable and prudent manner, the so-called "reasonable man" standard.

The relatively new field of products liability establishes liability without the necessity of proving fault. Manufacturers, in particular, are held liable for distributing dangerously defective products despite a lack of intent to harm or care in production. Although products liability has developed primarily over the last three decades, its roots can be found in much older theories of implied warranty and absolute liability for extrahazardous activities.

An important aspect of tort law is damages, or monetary compensation. Determining the amount of compensation depends on what can be included, but the object is to put the injured party in the position occupied before the wrongdoing occurred, that is, compensation for the difference in plaintiff's life that the injury imposed. In some cases punitive damages may be available to punish the wrongdoer. These go beyond actual compensation and require malicious or outrageous conduct on the part of the defendant.

CHAPTER QUESTIONS

1. In the aftermath of a barroom brawl, two lawsuits arise. One is titled *State v. Holmes* and the other *Gonzalez v. Holmes*; the defendant is the same in both. Which is a criminal case and which a civil case? Several stages later, one of the cases is retitled *Holmes v. California*. Which case name has changed, and why has it changed?

2. At a New Year's Eve party, Beau Jangles attempts the Mexican Hat Dance blindfolded and bumps into a guest, causing physical injuries. Would Beau be more likely to be liable for battery or negligence? Why?

3. Why is it necessary in medical malpractice cases for plaintiff to call a physician as a witness even though the witness may have no firsthand knowledge of the events of the case?

4. Why are contingency fee arrangements allowed in personal injury cases but not in divorce cases?

5. Black's Law Dictionary defines "champerty" as "a bargain by a stranger with a party to a suit, by which such third person undertakes to carry on the litigation at his own cost and risk,

in consideration of receiving, if successful, a part of the proceeds or subject sought to be recovered." Champerty was originally a crime. Is a contingency fee arrangement different from champerty?

6. Which of the policy grounds for products liability enumerated in *Lechuga, Inc. v. Montgomery* do you find most persuasive?

7. The most common form of legal advertising falls in the area of personal injury cases. The ABA and state bar associations for many years restricted advertising as unethical. What arguments can you make for and against advertising legal services in the personal injury field?

8. One state recently passed a law to prevent attorneys from free access to police accident reports after police complained that attorneys were searching reports for potential clients. How does this practice differ from advertising (soliciting clients versus advertising)?

9. Mental state may be considered an important feature of torts. The measure of the difference between intentional torts and negligence is sometimes stated as that between an objective and a subjective measure of mental state. Which uses an objective and which uses a subjective measure?

10. If a pharmacist negligently fills a prescription for birth control pills with tranquilizers, should the pharmacist pay for the costs of raising the child born nine months later?

EXERCISES

1. Go to a law library, preferably one used by practitioners rather than an academic law library, and locate materials on torts. What areas are represented, and what proportion does each area comprise, e.g., how many texts or manuals are there on products liability, negligence, malpractice, etc.? To what extent can coverage be explained by extraneous factors influencing tort litigation?

2. Find out if your state follows a contributory or comparative negligence principle. If it follows the comparative negligence principle, determine what formula applies. Then determine what the award would be in your state for the following:

   In *Hadley v. Baxendale*, the jury determines that defendant Baxendale was forty percent responsible for the auto accident on which the suit was based, while plaintiff Hadley was sixty percent at fault. Hadley's injuries were determined to be $50,000.

What would be the award if the apportionment of fault were reversed (Baxendale sixty percent and Hadley forty percent)?

3. The California Supreme Court in *Cronin v. J.B.E. Olson Corp.,* 8 Cal.3d 121, 104 Cal.Rptr. 433, 501 P.2d 1153 (1972) rejected *Restatement (Second) of Torts,* §402A definition of products liability as a departure from Justice Traynor's original statement of products liability. Compare the two rules (Justice Traynor's rule in *Greenman* as stated in the text and §402A on page 262) to find what the court found different; then find *Cronin* to see how the California Supreme Court distinguished them.

4. Under the doctrine of *respondeat superior,* an employer may be liable for the negligence of an employee while the employee is acting in the scope of his employment. "An employee acts in the scope of his employment when he is doing something in furtherance of the duties he owes to his employer and where the employer is, or could be, exercising some control, directly or indirectly, over the employee's activities."

   In an interview with a new client, she tells you that she was injured in an accident by the driver of a United States Telephone and Telegraph truck at 8:00 P.M. on October 31. The driver was wearing a U.S. T & T uniform; sitting inside the truck beside the driver were two children dressed as clowns.

   An oral deposition has been scheduled for the driver. Make up ten questions you would ask to determine whether *respondeat superior* would be applicable.

5. After you have filed suit against the driver and U.S. T & T, you are to formulate written interrogatories to be sent to U.S. T & T. List five questions you would ask, knowing that the answer would likely be framed by U.S. T & T's attorneys.

6. Your client, Joe Minnesota, is the quarterback for the Albuquerque Roadrunners football team. His back was broken by Bubba Bruto in a game with the Metro Muggers, known for their disregard for the rules. In contemplating a suit for battery, you realize that consent or privilege may be used as a defense. Make up ten questions you would ask Joe that might assist you in countering the defenses.

PROFESSIONAL PROFILE

"Being a paralegal is rewarding. While there are still a lot of unsettled issues within the profession, it is very young. A career as a paralegal can be exciting, stressful, frustrating, and exhilarating all at the same time," says Roxane MacGillivray, the senior commercial litigation paralegal at Akerman, Senterfitt & Eidson, a large commercial law firm with offices in Orlando, Miami, Tampa, and Tallahassee. She is thirty-four years old, married, and has a three-year-old daughter.

MacGillivray admits, "My entry into the paralegal field was an accident." She says, in hindsight, it is clear that she did things a little backward. MacGillivray began her career at the age of sixteen, working part time for Sears, Roebuck & Co. in the credit department. After a few internal transfers, she found herself in the legal department.

MacGillivray's job as legal representative required her to be Sears' primary contact with its local counsel, who handled all litigation claims too large to be heard in small claims court. As a result of her constant contact with the local counsel in Orlando, MacGillivray developed a great rapport with several attorneys at Akerman, Senterfitt &

Roxane MacGillivray
Commercial Litigation Paralegal

Eidson. When an opening occurred at that firm, she was offered a job.

The original position was that of legal secretary, but the opportunity for advancement was present. Shortly after being hired, a paralegal position became available in the litigation department. Akerman required that all paralegals have a bachelor's degree in paralegal studies. "At that time I was working on my degree," says MacGillivray, "but they made an exception in my case because of my background with Sears." MacGillivray studied at the University of Central Florida's legal studies program and worked as a paralegal. In the interim, she was awarded the University's Legal Assistant Award of Distinction and obtained her certification from the National Association of Legal Assistants.

MacGillivray explains, "To become certified, you must take a two-day examination. The exam includes sections on legal terminology, judgment, analytical ability, ethics, witness interviewing, communications, research and writing, and a five-part substantive law section." In order to pass the exam, a candidate must score at least 70 percent on each section.

MacGillivray's job as a commercial litigation paralegal defies precise description: "I essentially perform the same function as a junior-level associate attorney, except that I am ethically prohibited from giving legal advice and I am legally prohibited from representing a client in court or in a deposition," she said.

The cases MacGillivray handles are varied and exciting. In one day, she can work on a commercial foreclosure of an apartment complex or a suit related to rusted elevators in a condominium complex. She may also coordinate the levy of heavy equipment. In one instance, she coordinated and attended the levy of 2,000-dozen T-shirts with the Orange County Sheriff's Department. While looking for the T-shirts, they uncovered a counterfeiting operation. Apparently, the company sued was making counterfeit Bart Simpson, Mickey Mouse, and Reebok T-shirts. They went to the company's store in Daytona Beach, the Sheriff's Department's sirens blaring all the way. Eventually, a deal was struck with the president of the company and they were able to recover the T-shirts. Just another typical day in the life of a paralegal.

CHAPTER 12

Contracts and Commercial Law

FAILURE OF THE CLASSICAL MODEL
THE FIELD OF COMMERCIAL LAW
   The Uniform Commercial Code
   Commercial Paper
   Secured Transactions
   Business Organizations
SUMMARY

Only in the nineteenth century did judges and jurists finally reject the longstanding belief that the justification of contractual obligation is derived from the inherent justice or fairness of an exchange. In its place, they asserted for the first time that the source of the obligation of contract is the convergence of the wills of the contracting parties.

— *Morton J. Horwitz*, **The Transformation of American Law, 1780–1860 (1977)**

The quotation from Horwitz expresses two fundamental, conflicting conceptions of contractual obligations. The earlier, pre-nineteenth century conception embodied equitable principles emphasizing fairness and concepts of property, especially relying on transfer of title. The nineteenth century, according to Horwitz, gave rise to the modern law of contracts in which the obligations of contracts were cast in the light of the agreement itself, the bargain relationship, and the intent of the parties.

The title theory of exchange works well for the simultaneous exchange of things of fixed value, as when one pays for groceries at the supermarket. The will theory is more effective for **executory contracts**, that is, contracts relying on promises of future performance. For example, if a food processor contracts with farmers to buy crops for delivery at a fixed price in the future, principles of transfer of property rights at the making of the contract prove very awkward, while an examination of the bargain and the intent of the parties usually provides a basis for the enforcement of promises. The will theory is far more suitable for merchants and manufacturers in a commercial society and was gradually adopted by nineteenth-century courts, which viewed the encouragement of commerce and manufacturing as an important instrument of national growth.

A mechanical adherence to the will theory, however, encourages ruthless competition, so many of the adjustments to contract law in the twentieth century have been designed to ensure fairness in the market and protection against unfair exploitation. Equitable concepts of fairness are used by the courts to prevent the excesses of the unscrupulous. In addition, legislatures have been active in

executory contracts
An executed contract is one that has been performed, completed by both sides; an executory contract is one that still has some obligation to be performed.

passing laws, such as recent consumer-oriented legislation, to protect a vulnerable public.

CONTRACT LAW AND THE PARALEGAL

Most contract obligations are discharged by performance of the parties according to the terms of the agreement. When full performance is not feasible, the parties usually compromise their differences without recourse to law or litigation. Except for the specialist in commercial litigation, lawyer and paralegal alike are most often concerned with making, rather than breaking, contracts. Aiding contract negotiation and drafting contracts consumes most of the work. Precision and clarity of language are the skills most needed for drafting and should be taught as part of a legal writing course (but often are not).

It may appear that we devote an inordinate amount of space in this chapter to contract formation and the conflicting principles that surround it. The reason for this concentration is twofold:

1. Paralegals are generally more concerned with the formation of contracts than any other aspect.
2. The law governing contract formation is complex and confusing, despite being commonly presented in business law texts as consistent and logical.

While the approach here may seem unduly theoretical for a text for practitioners, the object is to avoid the morass of confusion presented by comprehensive contract texts and the omissions and simplifications of texts on business law.

DEFINITION

Like so many legal concepts, contract is not easily defined. If, as Grant Gilmore has persuasively argued, contract is dead and is being reabsorbed into tort, present definitions may look silly to future generations. Nevertheless, there is a difference between tort and contract in determining obligations from mutual agreements of the parties as opposed to obligations imposed by the law of torts. Even this distinction becomes seriously blurred when a court imposes terms or conditions on parties that they never bargained for and never agreed to.

The important feature of contract law is not the contract but contractual relations, and it is the regulation of relationships that is the subject of this chapter. If a court declares a contract void because one of the parties was coerced into agreement, it is saying something not about the nature of contracts but about the nature of contractual relationships. With this caveat in mind, let us look at some definitions of contract.

> A contract is a promise or set of promises for the breach of which the law gives a remedy, or the performance of which the law in some way recognizes as a duty. *Restatement (Second) of Contracts*, §1 (1981).

> "Contract" means the total legal obligation which results from the parties' agreement as affected by this Act and any other applicable rules of law. *Uniform Commercial Code* §1-201(11).

The *Restatement* takes the traditional view of contract as an exchange of promises (e.g., "I promise to pay you $10,000 if you promise to give me title to your automobile") that the law recognizes as enforceable. The *UCC* avoids promissory language and describes a contract as an enforceable agreement. At any rate, it is clear that individuals may make promises or agreements, some of which are legally enforceable and are called contracts.

The *Restatement* definition of contract reflects the will theory mentioned above, which will henceforth be referred to as the *classical* approach to contracts, reflecting developments in contracts in the nineteenth and early twentieth centuries. It comprises what most paralegals and lawyers need to know about contracts (along with the *UCC*) in order to draft contracts. Classical contract theory treats the essentials of contract formation in terms of discrete elements necessary to make a valid contract, namely, offer, acceptance, and consideration. It attempts to treat contract law as logical, precise, and self-contained.

Unfortunately, when the promises made at the formation stage are not fulfilled, issues of fairness and morality arise that are not so neatly resolved. A body of law that conflicts with classical theory has evolved to deal with contractual relations. This approach might be called the *moral* or *reliance theory* and is embodied in the somewhat obscure language of Section 90 of the first *Restatement:*

> A promise which the promisor should reasonably expect to induce action or forbearance of a definite and substantial character on the part of the promisee and which does induce such action or forbearance is binding if injustice can be avoided only by enforcement of the promise.

In many cases, this principle allows the court to weigh the fairness of enforcement or nonenforcement of contract claims. While theories of reliance and moral obligation may be of little significance in drafting contracts, they are important once a contract dispute arises. Failure to appreciate that there are two competing theories of contract inevitably leads to confusion. The classical model will be addressed with the issue of contract formation, and the reliance model will be introduced in connection with breach of contract and contract remedies.

CONTRACT FORMATION: THE CLASSICAL MODEL

The requirements of contract formation established in the nineteenth century cast the bargain relationship in idealized form. Parties to contracts were seen as individuals negotiating from equal positions of power, freely arriving at a "meeting of the minds," in which the agreement that constituted the contract was complete and its subject matter and terms were understood by both parties. Where such was the case, if one of the parties failed to fulfill contractual promises, it would be necessary only for the Court to apply the appropriate remedy for the injured party. Under this scheme, the court inquired into whether the elements of offer, acceptance, and consideration were present and then interpreted the terms of the contract.

Offer

Contract negotiations typically begin with an offer; the party making the offer is the *offeror*. The contract is not complete until an offer has been accepted by an *offeree*. An offer requires:

1. Intent to make an offer on the part of the offeror,
2. Definite terms,
3. Communication to the offeree.

The failure of any of the requisites of an offer may nullify contract formation.

What appears to be an offer may fail because it lacks intent on the part of the offeror. Offers are often distinguished from "invitations to negotiate" or even solicitations for offers. "No reasonable offer refused," "would you go as high as $1000?," or "I might sell it for as little as $500" are illusory offers in this category. The circumstances of the offer may also indicate that intent is lacking, as when the offer is made in jest, anger, or intoxication ("I'd sell that money-sucking car for two cents!"). The offeror's post hoc claim that a serious offer was not intended is not sufficient to avoid the contract; the test is whether a reasonable person would conclude that a serious offer was made under the circumstances.

The offer may be made in terms so indefinite as to render the contract unenforceable; no meeting of the minds was present. Indefiniteness of price, for example, is usually fatal ("just pay me a fair price"). [The *UCC* takes exception to the indefinite price rule in the sale of goods when certain conditions are met. See *UCC* 2-305.]

A valid and intended communication must be made to the offeree. The classic example in this category is the offer of a reward. Someone not aware of a reward offer who returns a lost dog is not legally entitled to the reward.

Acceptance

An offer does not bind the offeror until it is accepted by the offeree. Prior to acceptance, the offeror may revoke the offer, so acceptance subsequent to revocation does not bind the offeror. Acceptance requires:

1. Communication to the offeror
2. Acceptance of the terms of the offer.

Since a valid acceptance creates a contract, it is essential that the acceptance be communicated to the offeror. Acceptance has traditionally been classified in two forms:

1. Acceptance by a return promise ("I will pay the $4000 you are asking for your car").
2. Acceptance by performance required by the offer (acceptance of the offer of a reward for lost property is made by returning the property, not by promising to return the property).

Where an offer calls for a return promise, it is called a *bilateral contract*. Where the offer calls for acceptance in terms of performance, it is called a *unilateral contract*. Since most contracts are bilateral, it is important for the offeror who insists on performance (rather than a promise to perform) to make this condition quite clear. To "I will pay you $500 to clear my lot by Thursday, October 20" should be added "If you cannot finish by the end of Thursday, do not undertake the job because I will not pay."

The offeror is *master of the offer* and may set specific terms or manner of acceptance. Where the offer is silent as to the manner of acceptance, the law has developed a complex set of rules governing the communication of acceptance, to which the *UCC* has made exceptions with regard to sales of goods.

A valid acceptance requires that the offeree agree to the specific terms of the offer. This is the so-called *mirror image rule,* which has been changed drastically for sales of goods covered by the *UCC.* If the offeree attempts to change the terms of the offer, the attempted acceptance will be treated as a counteroffer rather than an acceptance, and the offeror and offeree change places. If the offeror offers to sell "my first edition of *Moby Dick* for $500," offeree's response of "I'll pay $400" is a counteroffer rather than an acceptance, and the purchaser has become the offeror and the owner the offeree ("I accept your offer of $400" would constitute acceptance and create a contract). Similarly, "I will pay $500 if you furnish a certificate of authenticity" is a counteroffer because it has added a term not present in the original offer.

The meeting-of-the-minds/mirror-image formula is technically simple, but transactions in the real world often defy its application. For example, in something as simple as the first edition sale, when the offeree appears with the personal check for $500, the offeror may insist on cash or a cashier's check. When they agreed on $500, did this mean "cash"? Can the offeror insist on cash? Does the offer to clear land "by" Thursday mean "before" Thursday (midnight Wednesday) or "on" Thursday (before Friday). An apparent meeting of the minds rarely includes every last detail of performance, and the courts do not require perfection in offer and acceptance; but those who draft contracts must be particularly careful in the precision of their language and use their imaginations to include essential terms and conditions of the contract.

The goal of the attorney may conflict with that of the contracting parties. The attorney aims at protecting a client and providing a contract, the terms of which are sufficiently clear that litigation can be avoided, or if litigation is necessary, the Court could apply the contract terms as originally intended. The contracting parties, on the other hand, are interested in a mutually satisfactory result. Professor Stewart Macaulay has noted that businesspersons are often more concerned about flexibility, cooperation, and continuing good relations than they are about technical problems of contract law. A good legal team should not assume that contracting parties are adversaries since contract relations are ordinarily created because both sides have found a mutual benefit in working together.

CASE NO. 12-1 The Contract Was No Joke

If a contract is formed by a "meeting of the minds," what happens when one of the parties later claims the intentions were different? If anyone could avoid a contract simply by asserting a secret intent at the time of making the contract, no contract could be reliable. The courts have developed an "objective" standard for assessing the intent of the parties similar to the reasonable man standard of torts: What would a reasonable person have inferred from the circumstances and conduct of the parties? Such a standard is applied in *Lucy v. Zehmer*.

W.O. LUCY and J.C. Lucy
v.
A.H. ZEHMER and Ida S. Zehmer

Supreme Court of Appeals of Virginia
196 Va. 493, 84 S.E.2d 516 (1954)

BUCHANAN, JUSTICE.

This suit was instituted by W.O. Lucy and J.D. Lucy, complainants, against A.H. Zehmer and Ida S. Zehmer, his wife, defendants, to have specific performance of a contract by which it was alleged the Zehmers had sold to W.O. Lucy a tract of land owned by A.H. Zehmer in Dinwiddie county containing 471.6 acres, more or less, known as the Ferguson farm for $50,000. J.C. Lucy, the other complainant, is a brother of W.O. Lucy, to whom W.O. Lucy transferred a half interest in his alleged purchase.

The instrument sought to be enforced was written by A.H. Zehmer on December 20, 1952, in these words: "We hereby agree to sell to W.O. Lucy the Ferguson Farm complete for $50,000, title satisfactory to buyer," and signed by the defendants, A.H. Zehmer and Ida S. Zehmer.

The answer of A.H. Zehmer admitted that at the time mentioned W.O. Lucy offered him $50,000 cash for the farm, but that he, Zehmer, considered that the offer was made in jest; that so thinking, and both he and Lucy having had several drinks, wrote out "the memorandum" quoted above and induced his wife to sign it; that he did not deliver the memorandum to Lucy, but that Lucy picked it up, read it, put it in his pocket, attempted to offer Zehmer $5 to bind the bargain, which Zehmer refused to accept, and realizing for the first time that Lucy was serious, Zehmer assured him that he had no intention of selling the farm and that the whole matter was a joke. Lucy left the premises insisting that he had purchased the farm.

. . . .

The defendants insist that the evidence was ample to support their contention that the writing sought to be enforced was prepared as a bluff or dare to force Lucy to admit that he did not have $50,000; that the whole matter was a joke; that the writing was not delivered to Lucy and no binding contract was ever made between the parties.

It is an unusual, if not bizarre, defense. When made to the writing admittedly prepared by one of the defendants and signed by both, clear evidence is required to sustain it.

In his testimony Zehmer claimed that he "was high as a Georgia pine," and that the transaction "was just a bunch of two doggoned drunks bluffing to see who could talk the biggest and say the most."

That claim is inconsistent with his attempt to testify in great detail as to what was said and what was done. It is contradicted by other evidence as to the condition of both parties, and rendered of no weight by the testimony of his wife that when Lucy left the restaurant she suggested that Zehmer drive him home. The record is convincing that Zehmer was not intoxicated to the extent of being unable to comprehend the nature and consequences of the instrument he executed, and hence that instrument is not to be invalidated on that ground. [C.] It was in fact conceded by defendants' counsel in oral argument that under the evidence Zehmer was not too drunk to make a valid contract.

The evidence is convincing also that Zehmer wrote two agreements, the first one beginning "I hereby agree to sell." Zehmer first said he could not remember about that, then that "I don't think I wrote but one out." Mrs. Zehmer said that what he wrote was "I hereby agree," but that the "I" was changed to "We" after that night. The agreement that was written and signed is in the record and indicates no such change. Neither are the mistakes in spelling that Zehmer sought to point out readily apparent.

The appearance of the contract, the fact that it was under discussion for forty minutes or more before it was signed; Lucy's objection to the first draft because it was written in the singular, and he wanted Mrs. Zehmer to sign it also; the rewriting to meet that objection and the signing by Mrs. Zehmer; the discussion of what was to be included in the sale, the provision for the examination of the title, the completeness of the instrument that was executed, the taking possession of it by Lucy with no request or suggestion by either of the defendants that he give it back, are facts which furnish persuasive evidence that the execution of the contract was a serious business transaction rather than a casual, jesting matter as defendants now contend.

. . . .

If it be assumed, contrary to what we think the evidence shows, that Zehmer was jesting about selling his farm to Lucy and that the transaction was intended by him to be a joke, nevertheless the evidence shows that Lucy did not understand it but considered it to be a serious business transaction and the contract to be binding on the Zehmers as well as on himself. The very next day he arranged with his brother to put up half the money and take a half interest in the land. The day after that he employed an attorney to examine the title. The next night, Tuesday, he was back at Zehmer's place and there Zehmer told him for the first time, Lucy said, that he wasn't going to sell and he told Zehmer, "You know you sold that place fair and square." After receiving the report from his attorney that the title was good he wrote to Zehmer that he was ready to close the deal.

Not only did Lucy actually believe, but the evidence shows he was warranted in believing, that the contract represented a serious business transaction and a good faith sale and purchase of the farm.

In the field of contract, as generally elsewhere, "We must look to the outward expression of a person as manifesting his intention rather than to his secret and unexpressed intention. The law imputes to a person an intention corresponding to the reasonable meaning of his words and acts.'" [C.]

. . . .

" . . . The law, therefore, judges of an agreement between two persons exclusively from those expressions of their intentions which are communicated between them. . . . " Clark on Contracts, 4 ed., §3, p. 4.

. . . the law imputes to a person an intention corresponding to the reasonable meaning of his words and acts. . . . it is immaterial what may be the real but unexpressed state of his mind. [C.]

So a person cannot set up that he was merely jesting when his conduct and words would warrant a reasonable person in believing that he intended a real agreement.[C.]

Whether the writing signed by the defendant and now sought to be enforced by the complainants was the result of a serious offer by Lucy and a serious acceptance by the defendants, or was a serious offer by Lucy and an acceptance in secret jest by the defendants, in either event it constituted a binding contract of sale between the parties.

. . . .

The complainants are entitled to have specific performance of the contract sued on. . . .

Reversed and remanded.

CASE QUESTIONS

1. Zehmer had bought the farm eleven years before for $11,000 and had refused an offer seven years prior by Lucy for $20,000. If the contract had been for $10,000, would the court have enforced it?
2. What if Lucy had known the contract was a joke but proceeded as if it had not been? Would the facts have been any different?
3. Could Zehmer have succeeded if he argued that he was drunk at the time, claiming intoxication as a defense?

Consideration

Consideration is a somewhat anomalous requirement for contract formation. It is the symbolic proof that the contract was the result of bargaining. In its broadest conception, consideration is represented by the exchange of something of value. Many form contracts include a recital of consideration, typically one dollar or ten dollars, in order to satisfy the consideration requirement. Although this is artificial and often illusory (no money actually changes hands), many courts developed the doctrine that the sufficiency of consideration is not to be questioned.

The bargain aspect of consideration is exemplified by §71 of the *Restatement:* "To constitute consideration, a performance or a return promise must be bargained for." The "something of value" may simply be a return promise. The original purpose of consideration appears to have been the refusal to enforce promises of gifts where the promisee does nothing in return. If Grandmother says to Grandson, "When you reach 25, I'll give you $10,000," and Grandson replies, "I'll be glad to receive it," the appearance is that of acceptance; but when Grandmother's junk bonds become worth twenty cents on the dollar, the Court is loath to enforce the agreement, arguing that Grandson neither conferred a benefit on Grandmother nor suffered a "detriment" by forbearing to do something he was entitled to do so that there was no consideration on his part for the contract. On the other hand, where Uncle promised Nephew $5,000 on his twenty-fifth birthday if until that time Nephew would refrain from drinking and smoking, the Court may find consideration in that Nephew suffered a legal detriment by forbearing doing something he had a legal right to do. Courts have on occasion found consideration based on "love and affection" to support the promise of a gift where a relative has provided aid and support. It would seem that the courts have attempted to avoid unfairness by invoking consideration or its absence and have stretched logic to justify their conclusions. Any other explanation suggests a logic and consistency to the concept of consideration that is not corroborated by the cases.

Consideration is an artificial legal concept rarely of concern to those engaged in the bargaining relationship. Gilmore traces the rise of the concept to Holmes' *The Common Law,* where it appears mysteriously without authority. The effect of the consideration requirement is to negate many contracts that would be enforceable without it. It is a device that can be used by a court to declare that contract formation was flawed and therefore unenforceable. It is probably of little practical importance to the attorney except as a strategy on behalf of a client trying to avoid enforcement of a contract. Nevertheless, where custom dictates a recital of consideration, it is wise to follow established practice.

Consideration is important in option contracts. Since offers may be revoked prior to acceptance, one way to keep an offer open is to pay for it. A person may purchase an option on land, for example—by paying $1,000 for an option to purchase land for $50,000 before January 1. In this way, the offer to sell the land may not be revoked until the expiration of option (January 1). Since consideration has been paid, a contract has been formed. Of course, if January 1 passes without action, the contract ends along with the duties of the parties.

CASE NO. 12–2 Forbearance as Consideration

Consideration can be constituted not only by a promise to do something but also by a promise not to do something one is legally entitled to do (forbearance). *Palmer v. Dehn* involved forbearance from a lawsuit. This is very common, considering that when a settlement is reached in tort or for breach of contract, the plaintiff agrees not to sue or to dismiss a suit already filed, which is the consideration for the settlement contract. But negotiated settlement contracts are precise in their terms and reflect the intentions of the parties. *Palmer v. Dehn* is quite different.

PALMER

v.

DEHN

Court of Appeals of Tennessee,
Eastern Section
198 S.W.2d 827 (1947)

BURNETT, Judge.

This suit is based on a two count declaration. The first count is to recover damages for personal injuries due to the negligence of the **plaintiff in error**. The second count is for breach of contract based on a promise of the plaintiff in error to compensate the **defendant in error** for the personal injuries received in the accident set forth in the first count. [At trial, the defendant moved for a directed verdict on each count, the denial of which was the basis for this appeal.]

The facts and legitimate inferences to be drawn therefrom, as viewed from the plaintiff's (defendant in error's) standpoint, are: On October 31, 1944 . . . , Mr. Dehn, a skilled mechanic and travel-

ing representative of Transit Bus Sales Company of St. Louis, Missouri, made one of his quarterly trips to Knoxville. On this trip he contacted Mr. Palmer who had formerly purchased a motor bus from the company Mr. Dehn represented. On being informed that Mr. Palmer was having mechanical trouble with his bus, Dehn went with him to the place the bus was parked. Dehn inspected the bus and told Palmer a belt was too loose. Palmer s driver went away and got the belt tightened. When the driver returned with the tightened belt, the three, Palmer, Dehn and the driver, discussed the matter at length. Dehn was then attempting to show Palmer how tight it should be when the driver started the motor cutting off two of Dehn's fingers. Dehn thought all the time that the driver was out of the car and that no one was inside that could start the motor. Before putting his fingers in their position of peril Dehn did not throw a safety switch which he knew was there so as to prevent injury to him. His explanation for not using this safety switch was that it was to be used when men were working at opposite ends of the bus and since he thought the driver was with him he did not deem it necessary to take this precaution.

Palmer immediately rushed Dehn to a local hospital. On the way to the hospital Palmer said: "I am awful sorry this happened, but don't worry a minute. I will see you are compensated for the loss of your finger, take care of your expenses for the loss of your finger, and all." Later Palmer made a similar assurance.

It is very earnestly and ably argued that the trial judge should have directed a verdict on behalf of the defendant as to the second count (one based on above contract) because there is no consideration for said promise or contract.

For there to be a consideration in a contract between parties to the contract it is not necessary that something concrete and tangible move from one to the other. Any benefit to one and detriment to the other may be a sufficient consideration. The jury may draw any reasonable and natural inference from the proof and if by inference a benefit to the promisor and detriment to the promisee might be inferred this will constitute a valid consideration. In the instant case the jury was justified in inferring that the promisee accepted this promise if it were performed within a reasonable time was a good consideration moving to the promisor; they were clearly justified in inferring that the basis of the promise of the promisor was for forbearance in bringing suit. By forbearing he might have readily borne a detriment. The promisor might easily have gained a benefit by such a forbearance. See 12 Am.Jur., Sec. 85, page 580.

"An agreement to forbear, for a time, proceedings at law or in equity, to enforce a well-founded claim, is a valid consideration for a promise. . . . " *Beasley v. Gregory,* 2 Tenn.App. 378, 382, opinion by Faw, P.J., in which he cites ample authority for the statement.

The result is all **assignments** must be overruled and the judgment below affirmed.

HALE, J., concurs.

McAMIS, JUDGE (dissenting).

I am unable to follow the majority in holding that an enforceable contract arises from the circumstances of the case or the language quoted in the majority opinion.

I cannot think there was any intention to make a binding contract but, if so, there was no consideration moving from plaintiff to defendant. There was no detriment to plaintiff and no benefit to the defendant. The plaintiff had the same right to sue in tort after the promise was made that he had before as indicated by the fact that he is still asserting his tort action in the first count of the declaration and it follows that defendant was not benefitted by being relieved of tort liability.

I can find no basis for holding that there was an inference of a forbearance to sue which would furnish a sufficient supporting consideration. There is no suggestion that this was a condition of the promise and the tort action was not lost to plaintiff as a result of being induced to delay bringing suit beyond the limitation period.

CASE GLOSSARY

plaintiff in error refers to the appellant, who was the defendant at trial, and **defendant in error** refers to the appellee, who was the plaintiff at trial. Note that the original title of the case was *Dehn v. Palmer.*

assignments here refers to assignments of error, the grounds for the appeal.

CASE QUESTIONS

1. When Palmer made the promise, did Dehn agree? Or did he merely rely on the promise?
2. Dehn sued in contract as well as in tort. What is the weakness of Dehn's cause of action in tort?
3. Was this contract bargained for?

LIMITATIONS ON CONTRACT FORMATION

Even when offer, acceptance, and consideration are present, the law will not recognize a contract if the bargaining process was flawed by misconduct (fraud, misrepresentation, duress, and undue influence), defect in agreement (mistake), the incapacity of one of the parties (minority or mental incompetence), or illegal purpose. In addition, the law requires that certain contracts must be in writing to be enforceable (Statute of Frauds). Each of these is treated in summary fashion below.

Contract Induced by Misconduct of One of the Parties

Although parties have great latitude in the promises they exchange in a bargaining relationship, the absence of a bargain may be found because one of the parties was deceived as to the bargain or deprived of free will in bargaining.

rescind
To rescind a contract is to annul or cancel it, putting the parties back in the position they were in before, as if no contract had been made. This is the basis for the equitable remedy of rescission, which in some cases is an alternative to suing for damages for breach of contract.

Fraud and misrepresentation are generally distinguished on the basis of intentional false representations (fraud) and innocent false representations (misrepresentation). If a used car dealer sells a 1979 model as a 1980 model knowing it to be a 1979 model, it would be fraud, while if the dealer believed it to be a 1980 model it would be misrepresentation. In either case, the innocent party should have the option to accept the contract or to **rescind** it, returning the car and receiving the return of payments made. Such contracts are *voidable*, meaning the innocent party may avoid the contract by returning to the conditions prior to the agreement. This is distinguished from contracts that are void (see "Illegality," below).

A contract is also voidable if it can be shown that one of the parties could not exercise free will in the bargaining process.

Duress occurs when one party is threatened with harm to induce agreement. The threatened harm is ordinarily physical or emotional harm directed against the party, the party's family, or the party's property. Usually economic pressure is not sufficient to constitute duress, nor is the threat to bring lawsuit ("If you don't sell, I'll foreclose").

Undue influence occurs when relentless pressure so weakens a party's will that the bargain is not freely obtained. Undue influence also occurs when the parties have a confidential relationship such as close family relations, attorney/client, physician/patient, etc.

Mistake

Mutual, or bilateral, mistake of fact makes the contract voidable by either party. For example, in one famous case, the violinist Efrem Zimbalist purchased two violins believed by the purchaser and seller to have been made by Guarnerius and Stradivarius. Zimbalist was able to void the contract when the violins proved to be nearly worthless. This example somewhat oversimplifies the complex and confusing area of mistake.

Lack of Capacity to Form a Contract

Lack of capacity may be due to lack of legal competence based on status (minors), lack of mental capacity to form contracts, or temporary incapacitation (intoxication).

In most states, the age of majority is eighteen. Until reaching the age of majority, persons are not legally competent, which includes an incapacity to bind themselves contractually. Exceptions are sometimes made for **emancipated minors**. Contracts with minors may be avoided by the minor, but can be **ratified** upon reaching the age of majority. Contracts for "necessaries" such as food and clothing are usually enforceable against minors.

The invalidity of contracts involving lack of mental capacity are based on the notion that lack of capacity prevents an individual from understanding the bargain. A person may display peculiarities that indicate mental illness yet understand fully the subject matter and obligations entered into by contract, in which case the contract may not be avoided. A person determined to be mentally incompetent by legal authority is not legally competent, and contracts with such persons are in some states void from their inception.

Inability to understand the nature and purpose of contractual obligations may also be established by the intoxication of one of the

emancipated minor is a person under the age of majority who is totally self-supporting or married, the definition varying from state to state.

ratified A contract is ratified when one suffering a disability approves the contract after the disability has terminated, as when a minor reaches the age of majority and subsequently agrees to the provisions of the contract.

parties at the time the contract was formed. Intoxication includes all drugs that affect one's mental state and ability to understand the consequences of the bargain. The intoxicated person may later affirm or disaffirm the contract. There is significant variation among jurisdictions as to proof and legal effect of intoxication.

CASE NO. 12–3   Horse Medicine Is a Crazy Business

There is a story about Sophocles, the great dramatist of ancient Athens, who had amassed significant wealth from prizes for his plays. When he reached the ripe old age of eighty, his children, then in their fifties, grew tired of waiting for their inheritance and brought Sophocles before the court of Athenian citizens to have him declared senile so that they could manage his wealth. As his only defense, Sophocles read to those assembled a play he had just written. The jury found him to be of sound mind, and his children had to wait another ten years to collect their inheritance.

Sophocles would undoubtedly have enjoyed the result in the following case.

HANKS
v.
McNEIL COAL CORPORATION et al.

Colorado Supreme Court
114 Colo. 578, 168 P.2d 256 (1946)

STONE, Justice.

Lee A. Hanks, who was a prosperous farmer and businessman in Nebraska, came to Colorado with his family in 1918, at first settling on a farm in Weld county, which included the coal lands involved in this proceeding; then, in 1920 moving to Boulder where he purchased a home, engaged in the retail coal business, and thereafter resided. . . . Shortly after 1922 Lee Hanks discovered that he was afflicted with diabetes, and members of his family noticed a progressive change in his physical and mental condition thereafter. He became irritable and easily upset, very critical of his son's work, and increasingly interested in the emotional type of religion. He began to speculate in oil and other doubtful ventures with money needed for payment of debts and taxes. About 1934 he sent his son what he denominated a secret formula for the manufacture of medicine to cure fistula in horses, which was compounded principally of ground china, brick dust, burnt shoe leather and amber-colored glass. If the infection was in the horse's right shoulder, the mixture was to be poured in the animal's left ear, and if on the left shoulder then in the right ear. In 1937 Mr. Hanks started to advertise this medicine through the press under the name of Crown King Remedy. Thereafter he increasingly devoted his efforts and money to the compounding and attempted sale of this concoction, his business judgment became poor and he finally deteriorated mentally to the point that on May 25, 1940, he was adjudicated insane and his son was appointed conservator of his estate.

[Before being adjudicated insane, in 1937, Hanks sold property to the coal company, which he had learned was hauling coal over his lands. His son, the conservator of his estate brought this suit to avoid the contract.]

. . . The legal test of Hanks' insanity is whether "he was incapable of understanding and appreciating the extent and effect of business transactions in which he engaged."

. . . One may have insane delusions regarding some matters and be insane on some subjects, yet capable of transacting business concerning matters wherein such subjects are not concerned, and such insanity does not make one incompetent to contract unless the subject matter of the contract is so connected with an insane delusion as to render the afflicted party incapable of understanding the nature and effect of the agreement or of acting rationally in the transaction.

. . . Patently Hanks was suffering from insane delusion in 1937 with reference to the efficacy of the horse medicine, but there is no evidence of delusions or hallucinations in connection with this transaction or with his transaction of much of his other business at that time; there is no basis for holding voidable his sale here involved on the ground of his insanity. . . .

Illegality

Agreements to do an unlawful act, including tortious as well as criminal acts, or for an unlawful purpose are deemed void by the courts and will not be enforced. A number of problems, such as what exactly is unlawful and how to handle a contract that is in part unlawful and in part lawful, have had different results in different jurisdictions.

Statute of Frauds

An oral contract binds the parties as much as a written one, though a written contract provides a more certain evidence of the terms of a contract than personal recollection of what was orally agreed. In 1677 the Statute of Frauds was enacted, making certain contracts unenforceable unless written. In 1677 the law of contracts was poorly developed, as were the laws of evidence and proof; the Statute was an attempt to prevent fraudulent abuse of legal process. The Statute of Frauds remained largely intact in American jurisdictions, often with merely minor modifications. Although the Statute identified five categories in which a written contract was required, two remain of major importance in the practice of law: (1) contracts for the conveyance of interests in land; (2) contracts not to be performed within one year. The *UCC* has created its own version of the Statute of Frauds, requiring certain contracts be in writing, the most notable of which covers the sale of goods for more than $500 and the sale of other forms of personal property valued at more than $5000.

Today the Statute of Frauds can actually invite fraud, as, for instance, when a person attempts to avoid an obligation by invoking the Statute while at the same time benefitting from another's performance. The courts have displayed considerable creativity in getting around the Statute where the interests of justice are not served by strict adherence to the Statute.

COMPENSATORY DAMAGES FOR BREACH OF CONTRACT

Since contract law is premised largely on business relations and obligations created by the contract itself, the remedy for breach of contract is quite different from that in tort. Injuries that are not foreseeable or not within the contemplation of the parties are not a usual element of compensatory damages. Physical or emotional injuries are not recoverable except where tort principles have invaded contract territory (e.g., malpractice and products liability).

The overriding policy in compensatory damages for breach of contract is to put the "nonbreaching party in the position he would have been in had the contract been performed." This may include lost profits if they are roughly ascertainable and within the contemplation of the parties. It may mean paying the cost of completion, as with unfinished construction contracts, or cost of replacement, or the difference between contract price and market price. Damages are often rephrased as "giving the nonbreaching party the benefit of his bargain." Several different measures of damages have developed for different categories of contracts, and the *Uniform Commercial Code* provides its own special rules. The diversity of rules is designed to ensure that the nonbreaching party does not suffer a loss or enjoy a windfall. While breach represents the fault aspect of contract law, the breaching party is to be protected rather than penalized (punitive damages are rare in contract cases).

This brief summary of damages ignores numerous complicating factors, such as **anticipatory breach**, **substantial performance**, and cases in which both parties breach, which

anticipatory breach occurs when one party to a contract expresses an intention not to perform; the other party may then treat the contract as breached and sue for appropriate remedies rather than wait for the time performance is due under the contract.

substantial performance occurs when one party has attempted to complete performance in good faith, but a minor variance from the specific terms of the contract has occurred. This equitable principle can be applied by the Court to enforce the contract, though it is common to reduce the obligation to pay by the value of the variance. This applies particularly to construction contracts in which performance varies in a minor way from the specifications and the cost of remedying the variance would be extreme, e.g., moving a wall two inches.

are normally covered in some detail in contract and business law texts.

PROBLEMS WITH THE CLASSICAL MODEL

Classical contract theory, which developed during the period before and after the turn of the century, constructed a logical set of rules based on offer, acceptance, and consideration for the formation of contract and compensatory damages for the resolution of contract disputes. This scheme is satisfactory for a great many contracts, but the diversity of contract relationships creates a variety of situations that defy mechanical solutions:

1. *A person promises to make a gift.* A brother offers his sister the free use of his second home on a permanent basis. She sells her house, moves her belongings and family. Brother later gets a good offer on the house and reneges on his promise. Under classical consideration principles, the sister has no enforceable contract rights.
2. *Charitable pledges.* A church solicits pledges from its parishioners to build a new annex, then enters a building contract. Was there consideration to support enforcing the pledges?
3. *Confidential professional relationships.* Doctor and patient enter a contract for treatment, but the treatment is negligently performed. Compensatory damages for breach of contract do not compensate for the injuries sustained.
4. *Indefinite oral contracts.* Buyer and seller agree to transfer title to an automobile, but time and place of performance are not mentioned.
5. *Unilateral contracts requiring performance as acceptance where promisee has begun to perform and promisor revokes the offer.* Property owner offers $2500 to roofer when roof is completed to "owner's satisfaction." Roofer moves trucks and men out to do the work only to find owner has hired someone else.
6. *Contracts in which the parties leave the details to be worked out later.*
7. *Performance without a contract.* Contractor blacktops the wrong driveway while the owner stands by and watches silently, later disclaiming any liability in the absence of a contract.
8. *Contracts for which compensatory damages create an unfair result.* Seller of house lot refuses to deliver deed as required by contract because a second buyer has offered a higher

price. First buyer's costs attributable to the breach of contract are minimal.

9. *Inducements to contract cause a party to incur costs relying on the inducement, but the contract is never completed.* Offer of hardware franchise induces potential franchisee to sell business at loss and work as manager/trainee to learn business. Franchisor later refuses to enter contract.

10. *Strict adherence to the Statute of Frauds will have grossly unfair results.* Seller and buyer agree orally to transfer land for a fixed price. Buyer clears the land and puts in a foundation for a house, and seller decides not to sell. Under the Statute, the contract is unenforceable.

11. *Manufacturer claims no responsibility for person injured by a product since purchaser bought the product from a dealer and had no contractual relation with manufacturer.*

Fault

Historically, judges were naturally reluctant to leave an innocent injured party without a remedy. This presented no problem if the contract was clearly enforceable and one party had breached. If a damages remedy fully compensated the injured party, an easy and just result was available. The breaching party was at fault under contract law, and liability was fixed. In many cases, such as those listed above, contract principles were unavailing. Judges employed a number of devices to avoid unjust results, some of them old, notably equitable remedies and principles, some of them new, and some of them fictitious.

When fault under common law contract theory was unworkable, the Court frequently resorted to the developing law of torts. Negligence theory provided a ready remedy for professional malpractice, especially medical malpractice, where compensatory contract damages were inappropriate since the injury was not loss of profits but disability, death, or pain and suffering. The duty of due care was imposed by law rather than by contract so that these cases jumped the fence from contract to tort at an early date without much resistance from the courts. The foreseeability of serious injury from medical malpractice, viewed either from a contract or tort law perspective, gives strength to the imposition of liability. A high standard of professional care also places the burden on the physician in the doctor–patient relationship.

The shift of products liability from contract to tort was more tortuous (forgive the pun). Although Justice Traynor finally justified the imposition of tort liability for defective products on policy grounds (see Chapter Eleven), his landmark decision in *Greenman v. Yuba Power Products* rested on a line of cases developed from Judge Cardozo's opinion in *McPherson v. Buick Motor Co.*, 217 N.Y. 382, 111 N.E. 105 (1916) dispensing with the **privity of contract** requirement and holding the manufacturer as well as the dealer liable. Products liability ultimately rested on the principle of implied warranty, the law imposing duties beyond the express terms of the contract. Although products liability is said to be strict liability without the need to prove fault, the plaintiff must show that the product was "dangerously defective when it left the manufacturer" and that the user was using the product in the manner for which it was designed. In many cases, plaintiff's burden of proof is not significantly less than showing manufacturer's negligence.

In other cases, fault in the sense of a legal wrong (e.g., breach of contract, tortious conduct) may be absent, but concepts of commercial morality, such as "good faith," present convenient analogies.

EQUITABLE REMEDIES

When compensatory damages are inadequate, equitable remedies may be available. Some exist as alternative remedies if certain defects in contract formation can be shown (rescission and reformation), while others ask for something other than money (specific performance and injunctive relief).

Rescission and Reformation

Rescission aims at destroying the contract and its obligations and putting the parties back in their positions prior to the agreement. Grounds for rescission are defects in formation already mentioned: illegality, undue influence, insanity, etc. Reformation aims at correcting the contract to reflect the actual intent of the parties, usually where mutual mistake exists.

Specific Performance

Specific performance asks the court to order the breaching party to perform rather than compensate, to deliver the goods or the deed to real property. This is available where goods are unique, such as a Stradivarius violin (land is always considered unique, hence the availability of specific performance for enforcing real property sales contracts). This remedy, however, is premised on a

privity of contract is the relationship created between contracting parties; only the parties to the contract can sue based on it. This has largely been abrogated in cases of implied warranty and products liability where it was formerly used as a defense by manufacturers who did not sell directly to the consumer.

valid contract and does not remedy formation and consideration problems.

Injunctive Relief

Injunctive relief is sometimes available to order someone not to do something that is prohibited by a contract, e.g., to prevent someone from building a carport in a development where deed restrictions require garages and prohibit carports. Such relief also is premised on valid contractual obligations.

LIBERAL CONSTRUCTION OF CONSIDERATION

One means of avoiding the arbitrariness of the classical model of contract formation was to construe consideration in the broadest possible terms in order to create a contract. This method was especially used by Judge Cardozo of the New York Court of Appeals. Cardozo enforced a father's promise to pay an annuity to his daughter following her marriage by finding consideration in her forbearance from breaking off the engagement. *DeCicco v. Schweizer*, 221 N.Y. 431, 117 N.E. 807 (1917). In another case he found consideration for a pledge to a college endowment campaign in an implied duty of the college to memorialize the donor. *Allegheny College v. National Chatauqua Bank*, 246 N.Y. 369, 159 N.E. 173 (1927). In both of these cases, classical theory should have found a promise to make a gift without consideration on the part of the promisee.

When consideration was designed to deny contracts even where offer and acceptance were present, the liberal construction of consideration undercut its importance. When a powerful moral, as opposed to legal, obligation was present or when a promisee changed position in reliance on a promise, judges at first strained to find consideration.

MORAL OBLIGATION AND RELIANCE THEORY

Consider the following examples taken from those listed earlier:

A. Contractor makes a contract with Thomas to blacktop Thomas' driveway at 116 Spring Street for $2000. Contractor mistakenly blacktops Henry's driveway at 114 Spring Street (the two houses are in an urban subdivision where the houses bear a striking similarity to each other). Variations on the facts might be: Henry is away on vacation while the blacktopping occurs and has no knowledge of it until he returns; Henry watches through his window but remains silent, all the while knowing that Thomas was planning to blacktop and that contractor was mistaken.

B. Owner of a small business opens negotiations with a national hardware chain for a franchise. Franchisor insists that George get experience as manager/trainee in one of the branches and assures George that training plus $25,000 will result in franchise, although no guarantees are made. George sells store, moves to another city, and works as trainee. Franchisor increases cost of franchise to $35,000. George sells his house to raise the money, but the franchisor decides not to grant the franchise.

Moral Obligation: Quasi-Contract

In example A, there was no contract, but Henry has received a benefit at Contractor's expense. There was no contract, no offer, no acceptance, no consideration on Henry's part; but it would seem unfair for Henry to retain the benefit, particularly if he failed in his moral obligation to inform Contractor of his mistake. In such a situation the Court may impose contractual obligations in the name of *quasi-contract,* which is not an actual contract but a "non-contractual obligation that is to be treated procedurally as if it were a contract." *Continental Forest Products, Inc. v. Chandler Supply Co.,* 95 Idaho 739, 518 P.2d 1201 (1974).

Quasi-contract is also called *contract implied in law* (distinguished from a **contract implied in fact**) and is based on the concept of unjust enrichment and **restitution**. Unjust enrichment is an equitable principle asserting that one receiving a benefit at another's loss owes restitution to the other. Since fairness is the goal of equity, the imposition of contractual obligations depends on the specific circumstances of each case and cannot easily be reduced to mechanical rules. Typically, quasi-contract requires that the recipient of the benefit have the opportunity to decline the benefit and yet fail to do so. In the example above, the Court might imply such failure since Henry sat idly by and watched the work. It is doubtful that the Court would impose the same obligation if Henry had no knowledge of the work (for example, if he was on vacation).

contract implied in fact is a contract that can be inferred by the conduct of the parties in the absence of a verbal or express contract—enrolling in college and paying tuition creates a contractual relationship even though no words are exchanged. A contract implied in fact reflects the unspoken intentions of the parties to create a contract, whereas a contract implied in law arises when intent is lacking but the Court treats the relation as having contractual obligations in order to avoid unjust enrichment.

restitution means the restoration of a party to the position enjoyed before a loss, applied in contract law to the equitable remedy of rescission.

Reliance: Promissory Estoppel

estoppel
is a principle used by the courts to prevent someone from making an assertion inconsistent with prior words or conduct that led another to act, which action would be to his detriment if the later assertion were allowed. For example, if an imposter posing as a physician negligently treats a patient, the imposter should be estopped from later avoiding a malpractice suit on the grounds of never having had a license to practice medicine.

Example B presents a different problem. Although a contract was never complete, George's course of action was determined by assurances made in the course of contract negotiations. George incurred significant costs in reasonably relying on those assurances. The national chain received no benefit at George's expense, so unjust enrichment/quasi-contract is not available, but George has certainly suffered because of the chain's conduct. To impose liability on the chain, the court may resort to another equitable principle called equitable **estoppel**, under which liability is incurred if one by language or conduct leads another to do something he would not otherwise have done. This is the basis for the mysterious language of the first *Restatement* §90:

> A promise which the promisor should reasonably expect to induce action or forbearance of a definite and substantial character on the part of the promisee and which does induce such action or forbearance is binding if injustice can be avoided only by enforcement of the promise.

This section applies to George's plight; it is a concise statement of *reliance theory*. Promises were made on which George relied to his detriment. Although a contract never quite passed the negotiation stage, it would be unjust for George to go without some compensation.

CASE NO. 12–4   Contract by Promissory Estoppel

The following is a classic case of promissory estoppel. Plaintiff was induced into a course of conduct by the defendant with the promise of a forthcoming contract that never came. Good faith and reliance on one side was met with vacillation and chicanery on the other. Nevertheless, promissory estoppel is not the same as breach of contract, and the case was ultimately set for new trial on the issue of the amount plaintiff should receive. Omitted from the excerpts below is the following quotation from Corbin, one of the leading contributors to the *Restatement of Con-*

tracts, the supreme master of reliance theory, showing just how elusive promissory estoppel can be:

Enforcement of a promise does not necessarily mean Specific Performance. It does not necessarily mean Damages for breach. Moreover the amount allowed as Damages may be determined by the plaintiff's expenditures or change of position in reliance as well as by the value to him of the promised performance. Restitution is also an "enforcing" remedy, although it is often said to be based upon some kind of a rescission. In determining what justice requires, the court must remember all of its powers, derived from equity, law merchant, and other sources, as well as the common law. Its decree should be molded accordingly.

Joseph HOFFMAN
v.
RED OWL STORES, INC.,
a foreign corp., et al.
Appellants

Supreme Court of Wisconsin
26 Wis.2d 683, 133 N.W.2d 267 (1965)

[An agent for Red Owl Stores engaged in continuing negotiations with Hoffman, who operated a bakery but wanted to run a Red Owl supermarket. Negotiations took over two years, during which Hoffman sold his bakery at the agent's request and bought and worked in a small grocery store. During this period, the price of the franchise was raised from $18,000 to $24,000 to $26,000. When Red Owl insisted that $13,000 put up by Hoffman's father-in-law be agreed by the father-in-law as a gift, Hoffman balked.]

. . . .

Applicability of Doctrine to Facts of This Case

The record here discloses a number of promises and assurances given to Hoffman by Lukowitz in behalf of Red Owl upon which plaintiffs relied and acted upon to their detriment.

Foremost were the promises that for the sum of $18,000 Red Owl would establish Hoffman in a store. After Hoffman had sold his grocery store and paid the $1,000 on the Chilton lot, the $18,000 figure was changed to $24,100. Then in November, 1961, Hoffman was assured that if the $24,100 figure were increased by $2000 the deal would go through. Hoffman was induced to sell his grocery store fixtures and inventory in June, 1961, on the promise that he would be in his new store by fall. In November, plaintiffs sold their bakery building on the urging of defendants and on the assurance that this was the last step necessary to have the deal with Red Owl go through.

We determine that there was ample evidence to sustain the answers of the jury to the questions of the verdict with respect to the promissory representations made by Red Owl, Hoffman's reliance thereon in the exercise of ordinary care, and his fulfillment of the conditions required of him by the terms of the negotiation had with Red Owl.

There remains for consideration the question of law raised by defendants that agreement was never reached on essential factors necessary to establish a contract between Hoffman and Red Owl. Among these were the size, cost, design, and layout of the store building; and the terms of the lease with respect to rent, maintenance, renewal, and purchase options. This poses the question of whether the promise necessary to sustain a cause of action for promissory estoppel must embrace all essential details of a proposed transaction between promisor and promisee so as to be the equivalent of an offer that would result in a binding contract between the parties if the promisee were to accept the same.

Originally the doctrine of promissory estoppel was involved as a substitute for consideration rendering a gratuitous promise enforceable as a contract. See Williston, *Contracts* (1st ed.), p. 307, sec. 139. In other words, the acts of reliance by the promisee to his detriment provided a substitute for consideration. If promissory estoppel were to be limited to only those situations where the promise giving rise to the cause of action must be so definite with respect to all details that a contract would result were the promise supported by consideration, then the defendants' instant promises to Hoffman would not meet this test. However, sec. 90 of Restatement, 1 Contracts, does not impose the requirement that the promise giving rise to the cause of action must be so comprehensive in scope as to meet the requirements of an offer that would ripen into a contract if accepted by the promisee. Rather the conditions imposed are:

(1) Was the promise one which the promisor should reasonably expect to induce action or forbearance of a definite and substantial character on the part of the promisee?

(2) Did the promise induce such action or forbearance?

(3) Can injustice be avoided only by enforcement of the promise?

We deem it would be a mistake to regard an action grounded on promissory estoppel as the equivalent of a breach of contract action. As Dean Boyer points out, it is desirable that fluidity in the application of the concept be maintained. 98 University of Pennsylvania Law Review (1950), 459, at page 497.

While the first two of the above listed three requirements of promissory estoppel present issues of fact which ordinarily will be resolved by a jury, the third requirement, that the remedy can only be invoked where necessary to avoid injustice, is one that involves a policy decision by the court. Such a policy decision necessarily embraces an element of discretion.

We conclude that injustice would result here if plaintiffs were not granted some relief because of the failure of defendants to keep their promises which induced plaintiffs to act to their detriment.

. . . .

. . . Plaintiffs contend that in a breach of contract action damages may include loss of profits. However, this is not a breach of contract action.

The only relevancy of evidence relating to profits would be with respect to proving the element of goodwill in establishing the fair market value of the grocery inventory and fixtures sold. Therefore, evidence of profits would be admissible to afford a foundation for expert opinion as to fair market value.

Where damages are awarded in promissory estoppel instead of specifically enforcing the promisor's promise, they should be only such as in the opinion of the court are necessary to prevent injustice. Mechanical or rule of thumb approaches to the damage problem should be avoided.

. . . .

"The wrong is not primarily in depriving the plaintiff of the promised reward but in causing the plaintiff to change position to his detriment. It would follow that the damages should not exceed the loss caused by the change of position, which would never be more in amount, but might be less, than the promised reward." Seavey, Reliance on Gratuitous Promises or Other Conduct, 64 Harvard Law Review (1951), 913, 926.

. . . .

At the time Hoffman bought the equipment and inventory of the small grocery store at Wautoma he did so in order to gain experience in the grocery store business. At that time discussion had already been had with Red Owl representatives that Wautoma might be too small for a Red Owl operation and that a larger city might be more desirable. Thus Hoffman made this purchase more or less as a temporary experiment. Justice does not require that the damages awarded him, because of selling these assets at the behest of defendants, should exceed any actual loss sustained measured by the difference between the sales price and the fair market value.

Since the evidence does not sustain the large award of damages arising from the sale of the Wautoma grocery business, the trial court properly ordered a new trial on this issue.

FAILURE OF THE CLASSICAL MODEL

Out of the chaos of contract law in the nineteenth century, an effort was made by scholars, particularly Langdell and Holmes in this country, to reduce contract law to logical principles in the common law. The effort was doomed from the start because of the nearly infinite variety of promissory situations and bargaining relations. Judges were disinclined to apply mechanical formulas when the results were clearly unjust. The concepts of fairness and good faith in principles of equity provided alternative remedies in some cases, and in other cases alternatives were found in the foundations for quasi-contract and promissory estoppel. The result has been an uneasy coexistence of two contradictory conceptions of contract.

Evidence of the demise of the classical model can be found in the *Uniform Commercial Code,* which departs from that model at every turn. The UCC *assists* contract formation rather than restricts it. Consideration is transformed, the mirror image rule is banished, indefinite terms may be implied or determined by the custom of the marketplace, and so on.

For the practitioner, the classical model of offer, acceptance, and consideration must be kept in mind in constructing contracts, but the full range of principles must be appreciated when agreement fails.

THE FIELD OF COMMERCIAL LAW

Contract law is the starting point for the study of commercial law since most commercial relationships are contractual in nature. Just as the intricacies of contract law are beyond the scope of this book, so too are the various specialized areas of commercial law, each of which deserves a course by itself in law school curricula. While they are very important to the paralegal, only a brief introduction to the subject matter of the major subfields of commercial law is presented in order to acquaint the paralegal with topics covered more fully elsewhere.

The Uniform Commercial Code

The *Uniform Commercial Code* was designed to establish a set of rules governing commercial transactions, modernizing the concepts of contract and commercial law to suit the marketplace. The *UCC* encouraged uniformity in state law regarding commercial transactions, and in this it has been largely successful, having been adopted with only minor variations in all states except Louisiana, which has adopted only four of its articles. Separate sections (articles) of the *UCC* cover the following subjects:

> Sales
> Commercial Paper
> Bank Deposits and Collections
> Letters of Credit
> Bulk Transfers
> Warehouse Receipts, Bills of Lading, and Other Documents of
>   Title
> Investment Securities
> Secured Transactions; Sales of Accounts, Contract Rights,
>   and Chattel Paper

Except for the specialist, the key sections of the *UCC* concern sales, commercial paper, and secured transactions. Of these, Article 2 (Sales) is extremely important since it clarifies and modifies existing principles of contract law, some of which have been noted earlier. The one transactional area *not* covered in detail by the *UCC* is real property transactions, in which long-standing principles differ widely among the states, defying attempts at unification. The *UCC* as incorporated in state law should be consulted on any question that comes within its coverage.

Commercial Paper

Commercial paper, or "negotiable instruments," consists of substitutes for cash used to facilitate commercial transactions. **Checks, drafts, promissory notes**, and **certificates of deposit** constitute commercial paper. Commercial paper is thus a signed writing representing an unconditional promise to pay money. It is regulated by Article 3 of the *UCC*.

---

draft
is an order to pay money. A drawer orders a drawee to pay money to a payee. A **check** is a draft on a bank payable on demand.

promissory notes
are promises by the *maker* of the note to pay money to a payee, usually involved in loans or debts.

certificates of deposit
are promises by banks to pay money deposited with the bank, ordinarily with interest.

collateral
is property pledged to pay a debt; it is a security interest.

mortgage
is a written instrument creating an interest in land as collateral for the payment of a debt. Originally a mortgage transferred legal title to the mortgagee (creditor) and returned to the mortgagor when the debt was paid, but most states now hold that the mortgagee has only a lien on the property rather than legal title. Similar security interests on personal property are called chattel mortgages but are usually now covered by the *UCC* provisions on secured transactions.

Secured Transactions

A secured transaction takes place when the payment of a debt is protected by **collateral**. The most common secured transactions are (1) real property **mortgages**, in which the purchaser or owner of land borrows money, pledging interests in real property to satisfy the debt in case of default and (2) purchase money installment contracts for personal property, such as an automobile, in which the seller retains rights of repossession in case of default. Article 9 of the *UCC* covers secured transactions of personal property except for interests arising by operation of law, such as **mechanic's liens**. Secured interests in real property fall outside the *UCC*, so the law of each state must be consulted for applicable rules.

Obligations to pay money that are unsecured are covered by the state law of debtor and creditor. Discharge of debt through bankruptcy falls within federal jurisdiction under the U.S. Constitution.

Business Organizations

Business organizations consist of variations on three forms: **corporations, partnerships,** and **sole proprietorships**. Attorneys are regularly called upon to advise clients on the choice of business organization that will best suit its needs. Personal liability, tax consequences, and financing are major considerations that affect the choice, but size of the organization, its structure, and its long-range goals are also important considerations. Paralegals frequently draft the documents that create and control business organizations. Once formed, businesses must not only conform to their own rules but also are subject to numerous requirements of state and federal law with which the commercial lawyer and the paralegal must be familiar.

SUMMARY

The law of contracts is concerned with private agreements that the law recognizes as enforceable. Unlike torts, the obligations to be enforced are established by the agreement rather than the law. Under the classical model of contract formation, the requisites of making an enforceable contract consisted of offer, acceptance, and consideration. In its simplest form, consideration is an exchange of promises to perform agreed upon obligations. The contract is not complete until offeror and offeree agree upon

---

mechanic's lien
A lien arises when property is burdened by an obligation to pay money, as in a mortgage transaction. A mechanic's lien arises when someone (an auto mechanic, a carpenter working on a building) is not paid for work or improvements to property. Mechanic's liens are normally created by the operation of law (rather than agreement of the parties) under state statutes.

corporations
are business entities registered with a state and conforming to state requirements. They are considered by the law as "persons" and can sue or be sued. A major feature of corporations is *limited liability*—ordinarily the owners may not be sued for their private assets when the corporation is sued.

partnerships
are unincorporated business associations and as such do not have limited liability; suits that cannot be satisfied by partnership property may go after the personal assets of the partners. Most states have partnership statutes modeled on the Uniform Partnership Act.

sole proprietorships
are unincorporated businesses owned by one person.

identical terms; an attempted acceptance of an offer that alters a term of the contract is considered a counteroffer rather than acceptance.

Even when offer, acceptance, and consideration are present, contract formation is corrupted by misconduct of one of the parties, mistake, lack of contractual capacity, or illegality. Certain kinds of contracts are required to be in writing by the Statute of Frauds and the *Uniform Commercial Code*, the latter making significant changes in the model of offer, acceptance, and consideration.

When a contract is not fulfilled, compensatory damages are available to put the nonbreaching party in the position she would have been in if the contract had been performed. Punitive damages and recovery for emotional damages are not ordinarily available in contract, but the lines between contract and tort have become increasingly blurred, as witnessed by medical malpractice and products liability.

Strict adherence to the classical model provides little flexibility in the nearly infinite variety of contractual situations, so the courts have devised a number of ways around what appear to be unjust results. The classical model based on the common law must compete with traditional concepts of fairness emanating from equity. A number of equitable remedies are available that depart from monetary compensation. In addition, equitable principles have given rise to enforcement of moral obligations in the form of quasi-contract, whereby the law imposes a contract to avoid unjust enrichment, and promissory estoppel, whereby a party suffers a detriment in relying on inducements made by another where a contract is not enforceable under common law principles. Although common law contract principles and theories of moral obligation and reliance in equity exist side by side, they are intrinsically contradictory, resulting in inconsistency in contract law.

The field of commercial law covers a number of subfields such as commercial paper, secured transactions, and business organization. Much of the law in this area is statutory, including the *Uniform Commercial Code*, which has been adopted by most states and which provides uniformity in interstate commercial transactions.

CHAPTER QUESTIONS

1. Why is specific performance available to enforce contracts for sale of real property?
2. Why is a promise to make a gift usually unenforceable?
3. When may a contract with a minor be enforced?

4. Why is a promise to return a lost dog for which a reward has been offered not a contract?
5. If a contractor discovers that the completed contract for building a motel has itemized five chandeliers for $1000 each rather than $10,000 each as he quoted them to his secretary, what is his best remedy for correcting the mistake and still continuing the contract?
6. As an incentive to win a case, a criminal client offers his attorney a bonus of $5,000 if an acquittal is obtained. Can the attorney sue successfully for the bonus if an acquittal is in fact obtained?
7. Does the definition of a contract as "a promise or set of promises for the breach of which the law gives a remedy, or the performance of which the law in some way recognizes as a duty" give the Court discretion to decide arbitrarily what is a contract and what is not a contract?
8. Professor Corbin comments that "the chief purpose underlying the law of contract is not to carry out the will of the promisor . . . the chief purpose of enforcement is the avoidance of disappointment and loss to the promisee." Is this reflected in the cases included in the chapter?
9. Does the quote from Corbin in Question 8 sound more like the classical model of contract or promissory estoppel? Why?
10. Client tells attorney he is guilty of crime charged against him. Can the attorney ethically make a contract aimed at gaining an acquittal for the client?

EXERCISES

1. Law firms sometimes create a form of business organization called a professional association, abbreviated as P.A. Does your state allow such an association? What advantages does it have over the traditional law firm partnership?
2. How is a certified check different from a personal check? How are these different from a cashier's check? Find the answers to these questions in a business law or other text.
3. Find the definition of an emancipated minor in your state.
4. Is an attorney–client contract confidential (in a lawsuit)?
5. Father promises to make a gift to son on son's twenty-fifth birthday. Son wants to go to college but must borrow heavily to do so. Son asks you to write father's promise in such a way as to make it legally binding so that son can pay back college loans. Write out the contract to make it legally enforceable.

6. You advertise your car for sale, and a buyer offers $5000, which is acceptable to you, but the buyer, a stranger to you, will not have the money for a week. Draft a simple agreement that will allow you to continue to negotiate with others in case the buyer does not come up with the money.

7. Assume you are the buyer in Question 6. Draft a contract that will hold the car for you for a week for $5000.

8. Look in the newspaper for advertisements that present "illusory" offers, i.e., advertisements that appear to make offers but are not capable of acceptance.

9. Find an advertisement on television that constitutes an offer for a unilateral contract. A bilateral contract.

10. Go to a store that sells big-ticket items such as camcorders or furniture and ask for their installment contracts. Analyze the clauses to see if you would object to any. Are there any clauses that are needlessly confusing? Ask the salesperson to explain the provisions of the contract and make a record of the answers. Does the explanation correspond to your reading of the contract?

11. By now you should be aware that the author's implied promise of a definition of contract was an illusory promise. If you still do not know exactly what a contract is, perhaps the following statement by Justice Loevinger in *Baehr v. Penn-O-Tex Oil Corp.*, 258 Minn. 533, 104 N.W.2d 661 (1960) will explain why:

> Unfortunately, contract, like most of the basic terms constituting the intellectual tools of law, is conventionally defined in a circular fashion. By the most common definition, a contract is a promise or set of promises for the breach of which the law gives a remedy or the performance of which the law recognizes as a duty. This amounts to saying that a contract is a legally enforceable promise. But a promise is legally enforceable only if it is a contract. Thus nothing less than the whole body of applicable precedents suffices to define the term "contract."

Put this in your own words as if you were preparing to explain to Mr. Hoffman in *Red Owl Stores* the uncertainty of winning his case.

PROFESSIONAL PROFILE

A resident of suburban St. Paul/Minneapolis, Angela Schneeman received her paralegal certificate from the University of Minnesota six years ago. She completed her internship at the law firm where she had been working as a legal secretary. Subsequently, Schneeman convinced the attorneys of that firm to hire her on a full-time, permanent basis as a paralegal. "I was the first paralegal the law firm had ever hired, and when I first started, neither the attorneys nor I had a very clear idea of how my time and skills could best be utilized by the firm. Fortunately, the attorneys I worked for were very busy and willing to delegate any work that could possibly be done by a paralegal," Schneeman says. Within two years there were two other paralegals working for the firm, and the attorneys were very convinced of the benefits of working with paralegals.

The firm Schneeman worked for specialized in corporate law, mergers and acquisitions, qualified plans, estate planning, probate, and real estate. Originally she worked in all of those areas, but corporations became her specialty. Most of her workdays were fast-paced and unpredictable. On a "typical" day, she would spend most of her time meeting with several attorneys, calling and/or meeting with clients, and drafting legal documents and correspondence. Some of the legal documents that she prepared were articles of incorporation, bylaws, and other corporate documents. It was also her responsibility to keep the clients' corporate-minute books up to date by preparing the necessary annual minutes and other documentation.

One of the most interesting and exciting aspects of Schneeman's job involved mergers and acquisitions. She was often responsible for drafting and organizing the numerous documents required for large closings, which she usually attended. "It was very exciting and rewarding to me to be an integral part of a multi-million dollar transaction," Schneeman says. Although she found that working on mergers and acquisitions was very interesting, it also involved working long hours under a lot of pressure. It was not uncommon for her to work late into the night, and in some cases, early into the next morning, to prepare for a large closing.

The group of attorneys who employed Schneeman understood the importance of a good team effort and recognized that every member of the law firm staff is essential. Typically, when the firm was about to undertake a large project, the attorneys would decide on a team to handle the work. This team would usually consist of a partner of the firm, an associate attorney, a paralegal, and a secretary. The team would meet to discuss how the project would be handled, and then work together to see the project through to its successful conclusion.

"I left my first paralegal position two years ago and began working as a freelance author," Schneeman recalls. She has taken the knowledge and practical experience she gained as a paralegal and wrote a corporate reference book to assist paralegals and attorneys. Currently, she is working on a corporate law textbook for paralegals that will be published by Delmar/Lawyers Cooperative Publishing.

"My advice to anyone considering a career as a paralegal is to explore several different opportunities. The field is very diverse, and job descriptions and position qualifications can vary greatly depending on the size of the firm or corporation and the type of law being practiced. I think it is important to find a position with the challenges and rewards that will match your personality," Schneeman advises.

Angela Schneeman
Corporate Paralegal

CHAPTER 13
The Law of Property

OUTLINE

   . . . there is no such thing as natural property . . . it is entirely the work of law.
   . . . .
   Property and law are born together, and die together. Before laws were made there was no property; take away laws and property ceases.

                                        —Jeremy Bentham (1748–1832)

> The institution called property guards the troubled boundary between individual man and the state. It is not the only guardian; many other institutions, laws, and practices serve as well. But in a society that chiefly values material well-being, the power to control a particular portion of that well-being is the very foundation of individuality.
>
> — *Charles Reich (1964)*

trespass
is a cause of action based on an invasion of one's right of exclusive possession, e.g., where a neighbor builds a shed that encroaches on other property.

nuisance
A private nuisance is basically a continuing trespass, as when one discharges polluting effluents that seep into a neighbor's pond.

ejectment
is a cause of action designed to return rightful possession. Its common name in modern landlord and tenant law is *eviction* to remove a tenant who no longer has a right to stay on the property, but ejectment has application to persons wrongfully occupying land without any prior relation to the owner.

foreclosure
is the process whereby real property is sold to satisfy a mortgage. Foreclosures are strictly governed by state law.

capitalism, socialism, and communism
nations typically call themselves democratic. The major difference between them is the extent to which property is privately and publicly held.

The previous chapters have probably given the impression that disputes and litigation form the core of the law, but this is a false impression of the practice of law. Particularly in the area of property, litigation is rare because good "lawyerly" work prevents the need for litigation. A properly drafted and executed will should avoid all but unreasonable challenges. A carefully executed real estate transaction transfers title without loose ends and settles all important future questions about ownership.

Property law is extremely important for paralegals because it involves a great deal of work that does not require an attorney except as legal advisor and supervisor. Within the area of property law are a number of important subfields, such as real estate transactions, landlord and tenant law, estates and trusts, estate planning, planning and zoning, environmental law, and commercial leases. Other areas present specialized property law aspects, such as community property, equitable distribution, and marital estates in family law, and leases and real property transactions in contract law. Taxation is an important consideration in legal advising on all aspects of property law. There are specific causes of action in tort to protect property interests: **trespass**, **nuisance**, **ejectment**. In recent years government regulation of property by planning, zoning, and environmental law has placed severe restrictions on land use and created a need for legal specialization in these areas. Bankruptcy, **foreclosure**, mortgages, and mechanic's liens concern rights of third parties in property. In short, all of private law that is not concerned with wrongful misconduct (and much that is) revolves around property law. Perhaps in no other field of law is a more comprehensive knowledge of law required for legal advisement, even on what may appear to be a relatively simple problem or transaction, as in the area of real property law.

Bentham's dictum that property is the core of law is sound. Political systems are founded upon different ideologies of property—e.g., **capitalism**, **socialism**, **communism**. The **due process** clauses of the U.S. Constitution in the Fifth and Fourteenth Amendments protect the citizens' property rights. In the civil law, virtually all rights are either characterized in property terms or measured by property, for example, in money, which is a form of property.

PROPERTY IS AN ABSTRACTION

Bentham is correct in stating that natural property does not exist. From a legal point of view, a mountain is not property, nor a lake, nor a book. Until we assign legal rights in a thing, it is not property. When a person building a new home says, "I am going out to the property," we understand a building site, a piece of land, in its natural or altered state, but we also understand that the statement asserts rights of ownership over something that has been defined on a map with boundaries, the title to which has been transferred from one hand to another and recorded in the records of the county in which it is situated. But the most important, albeit often unconscious, assertion in this use of the word *property* is that the owner has rights that the law will defend. The definition, determination, and allocation of these rights are the subject matter of property law.

The abstract nature of property may be illustrated by a few examples:

1. A retailer builds up a profitable business over many years and then decides to sell it and retire. Not only may the retailer sell the premises and the inventory of the store, but a major part of the sales price may be for "good will," which is valuable property.
2. A professional basketball player may be paid a very large sum of money just to have his name associated with a line of sneakers. He has property rights in his name.
3. A person buys a fifth-story condominium on the beach before it is built. Until constructed, ownership is of a piece of air.
4. Someone pays for a franchise to operate a fast-food restaurant.
5. An inventor registers an invention with the Patent Office, thus acquiring an exclusive property right.
6. A state university professor receives tenure, granting a right to permanent employment at the college.
7. An Hispanic employee sues an employer for discriminating in promotions.
8. A physician challenges abortion statutes on the grounds that the right to practice medicine has been unconstitutionally restricted.

That differences in ownership of property have resulted in very different lifestyles for the people living under these regimes lends credence to the quotation from Reich about the relation between property rights and individuality. Our Founding Fathers were very much concerned about protecting private ownership of property.

due process
The Fifth Amendment to the Constitution provides: "Nor shall any person . . . be deprived of life, liberty, or property, without due process of law. . . " Since this was construed only to apply to action by the federal government, in 1868 the Fourteenth Amendment was ratified, applying the same principle to action by the states. The very breadth of these provisions has allowed a great variety of lawsuits asserting property rights and challenging government restrictions on them.

9. A state halts building construction on private land because Indian artifacts have been unearthed that suggest an important archeological site may be located on the land.

All of these examples express valuable property rights of which the law takes cognizance. Note that the government not only restricts property rights (examples 8 and 9), but also creates them (examples 5 and 6). In fact, the government through its laws can create or destroy property rights subject only to due process of law and just compensation for property taken for a public purpose.

The law may recognize something as property for one purpose but not for another. In New York, for example, a professional license may be "marital property," the value of which can be divided in a divorce, but it is not property for the purposes of sale or gift. And in *Community Redevelopment Agency v. Abrams*, 15 Cal.3d 813, 543 P.2d 905, 126 Cal.Rptr. 423 (1975), the California Supreme Court held that good will in a pharmacy that was taken in order to redevelop an urban center was not property, even though it would be property for the purposes of a private sale of the pharmacy. In relation to this last example, Professor Berger asks the unanswerable question, "Did the pharmacist lose because he had no property or did he have no property because he lost?" Good will is an abstract concept, but good will as property raises it to an even higher level of abstraction. Property itself is an abstraction of the rights that the law recognizes.

REAL PROPERTY'S "BUNDLE OF RIGHTS" MODEL

In an effort to simplify the abstraction of property, legal scholars refer to a *bundle of rights* that a person may enjoy. This model is used to explain the complex laws of real property ownership. Real property consists of land and its improvements (buildings, fences, wells, etc.—those valuable changes that humans inflict on their land). Other things that may be owned, such as money, goods, stock and bonds, etc., are called *personal property* and have a much smaller bundle of rights.

The rights in real property to which we commonly attach the word *ownership* entail numerous rights, of which the most important are rights of **possession**, use, and transfer. Each of these includes other rights. The right of possession allows one not only to be present on the land but also to exclude others. The causes of action for trespass, ejectment, and nuisance are based on this right. Use rights include the right to improve the land, to exploit it for agriculture, mining, cut timber, and so on. The right

possession includes more than physical possession. With land, occupancy and use constitute *actual possession* while the exercise of dominion and control may constitute *constructive possession* where direct physical control is absent. Conduct and intent are important evidence tending to prove possession.

dower and curtesy were interests in property held by wife (dower) and husband (curtesy), the primary purpose of which was to guarantee real property interests for the surviving spouse at death of the other. Since in early common law these interests favored the husband, they do not comport with the equal protection clause of the Fourteenth Amendment (they discriminate against wives). Most states have statutorily changed the marital estates to make them equal or have provided a modern substitute to protect surviving spouses.

of transfer or conveyance includes the right to sell, lease, or give away real property. Real property is also transferred at death by will or intestate succession; these are important rights of ownership.

The nature and duration of these rights are restricted by a number of features of property law and property rights. Consider a married couple that "owns" a home. If they acquired the home after they were married, it is likely that they have a form of co-ownership called a *tenancy by the entirety,* whereby if one of them dies, the surviving spouse will own the entire property. Even if title to the home is held in only one name, the other may have a marital interest based on **dower** or **curtesy** or on community property rights in some states. If there is a **mortgage** on the home, some other party has a right to sell the property in foreclosure if they default on the payments, and their capacity to sell the property may be severely restricted by the terms of their mortgage.

What they can do with their land may be subject to many limitations (**restrictive covenants**) placed in their deed if the home was part of a housing development. The use of their land is limited by local, state, and federal law—they may not be able to cut down a tree or have a garage sale without a permit. If their house is on a city street, the city has an **easement** along the street that gives the city a number of rights and the owners little but duties. The electric company has an easement for lines across the property, as does the city water department. There could be other private easements allowing other persons a right of way across their land. They might not own the mineral rights below the surface of their land. The city, county, state, or federal governments could take away their property to build a highway or for other public use, only providing them with just compensation. Despite these restrictions, they are taxed on the value of the entire property, which could be sold for nonpayment of the taxes.

The duration of property rights may also be limited. If possession is held by a lease, the right of possession is subject to limitations of time as well as any other conditions the lessor includes in the lease agreement. A title may be limited in duration, such as for life (life estate) or until the fulfillment of a condition. When title has a limited duration, someone other than the present possessor has a future interest in the property, so that the present possessor has duties and limitations on use for the benefit of the future interest.

The bundle of rights may be viewed as the totality of rights and restrictions on rights held by a person with regard to real property. In view of the complexities of property rights, the term ownership has limited usefulness in the field of real property. The law deals with rights, and the extent of a person's ownership depends on how much of the bundle a person has.

mortgage
is a pledge of personal or real property to pay a debt. It is a secured transaction in which the mortgagee (the creditor) may force a sale of the property to satisfy the debt if the mortgagor (debtor/owner) defaults on the payment of the debt.

restrictive covenants
take many forms including minimum square footage, architectural approval before building, grass cutting, size of "for sale" signs, and even the length of time a garage door may be left open. In modern residential developments, restrictive covenants are commonly used to maintain upscale housing. Racially restrictive covenants and other discriminatory practices have long been held unconstitutional.

easement
is a right of use in another's property as, for example, when someone has a right of way to cross another's land. Cities and counties ordinarily have easements adjacent to streets and highways, allowing them control over drainage, road shoulders, etc.

ESTATES IN LAND

In a highly commercial society such as ours, real estate is often perceived as a commodity to be bought and sold for investment or speculation. But it is not a commodity like pencils, where monetary payment and delivery of the goods passes title from one hand to the next without either side considering problems of title. Even the simplest real estate sale involves lawyers, title companies, tax stamps, recording at the court house, realtors, closing agents, mortgage companies, etc. The need for all of these has a lot to do with the ancient law of estates.

The law of tort and contract is a model of common sense compared to property law. Law based on private wrong must adapt to changing values and daily life, whether personal or commercial. Property law, on the other hand, reflects the accumulation of technical principles establishing ownership rights. Land law is conservative; many basic principles have changed little over the centuries.

The conservatism of land law is partly due to concern on the part of those who have property that their rights remain secure; and since over the centuries those with wealth in property have either made the law or had extraordinary influence over those who make the law, tinkering with the rules of property rights has been disfavored. Another reason for the conservatism can be attributed to the very law that has given us the bundle-of-rights principles. Title to land, as we have seen, is a complex matter. Intrusions into ownership rights may take place at any time—a second mortgage, a tax lien, a lease or marriage or divorce can occur during the course of possession and will affect how various rights are distributed and limited. When someone sells real estate, the buyer will want to know the status of all rights pertaining to the property in question. The current status of a piece of real property depends upon its history. A search of the history (**chain of title**) of the property may even reveal that the seller's claims of ownership are much in doubt, or that someone else claims to be the owner, or that there are restrictions that make the property unsuitable for the purchaser's intended use.

chain of title
refers to the history of the transfer of title to real property. It is essential that a seller be shown to be the true owner by virtue of a documented chain of transfer of title up to the present owner.

To many our land law is simply a cumbersome relic of the past, but it is self-perpetuating—its technical complexity makes it difficult to change. What may appear to be a minor change may turn out to require adjustments through the entire system, and anything that potentially casts doubt on ownership is unfavorably viewed by property owners, lawyers, and those who make the law. Modernization of land law would be a monumental task and an agonizing ordeal that few seem ready to undertake.

The result of this conservatism is land law based on an ancient system that bears little relation to present realities. At the core of land law are the common law estates, which were developed in the first centuries following the Norman Conquest in 1066. These came into being during England's feudal period when a person's status in society depended almost entirely on rights in land. Society and government were built on a military model with the king at its apex. Technically all land was held by the king but was divided among his subjects, who thereby owed the king certain fees and military service. Thus, a certain baron might control a certain area of land and the peasants working the land and be required to furnish his overlord with fees and a specified number of knights and soldiers in time of conflict. The overlord, in turn, was similarly responsible to his overlord, and so forth up to the king. At the base of the pyramid were the peasants who worked the land, providing a portion of their crops and personal service to the landlord, who was their protector. While no one owned the land in the modern sense of the word, the status attached to the land passed from father to eldest son (primogeniture) as long as the son was acceptable to the lord and swore fealty to him. A baron's (or count's) land was inherited by his son (land could not be passed by will until the Statute of Wills in 1540), who then became the baron.

While the system of primogeniture and certain other features of aristocratic land ownership were not adopted in the United States, the system of common law estates continues to this day. The estates were divided between freehold and nonfreehold estates; freeholders were free men, while nonfreeholders were called "villeins." Except for the last term, which has come to mean something quite different, the terms have been preserved intact. It is more common to call a nonfreehold a leasehold estate with a **lease**, a **lessor**, and a **lessee**.

Fee Simple Absolute

The inheritable freehold estates were called fees; the most important one, then and today, was the *fee simple absolute*. This estate represents the maximum bundle of rights with the fewest strings attached. Among its important features are that it is *alienable* (it can be sold or given away), inheritable, and devisable (it can be passed by will). A fee simple absolute is unconditional and potentially lasts forever. Standard real estate sales contracts call for a fee simple absolute, and that is what purchasers want and expect whether or not they are familiar with its name. Such an

lease
   is an agreement by
   an owner of
   property (**lessor**)
   with a renter
   (tenant or **lessee**)
   whereby the lessee
   pays for the right of
   possession and use
   but does not
   acquire title.

estate still represents what it did several hundred years ago: the complete bundle of rights to possession, use, and transferability.

Life Estate

Contrast fee simple absolute with *life estate,* which is a freehold estate that is not inheritable. A life estate is created to last for a person's lifetime. It cannot be inherited or passed by will because it ends immediately upon the death of the owner or *life tenant.* Otherwise, it has the attributes of a fee simple absolute. It can be sold, leased, given away; of course, the life tenant cannot transfer more than he has—the purchaser gets an estate that lasts only as long as the original life tenant is alive. A life estate always creates a future interest; someone must have title after the life tenant dies, which imposes a duty on the life tenant to preserve the estate or be liable for "waste." For example, a father conveys real property "to my son Michael for life, and then to my grandson George." If no other limiting language is included, when Michael dies, George will hold the property in fee simple absolute (while Michael is alive, George's future interest is called a *remainder*).

CASE NO. 13–1 Interpreting the Language of a Deed

Saltzman v. Ahern presents the problem of an owner of property, here the *grantor,* delivering two deeds to the property to two different *grantees.* The first grantee, Ahern, brought a suit to quiet title, an appropriate action requesting the Court to determine who has title. The Saltzmans challenged Ahern's deed, claiming it did not pass title but was an attempt to pass title at grantor's death, grantor having reserved a life estate in the property in the deed. In other words, the Saltzmans are treating the deed as if it were a will. Since a will can be revoked at any time prior to death, the subsequent deed to the Saltzmans served as a revocation. Revocation may in fact have been the grantor's intention; but if it was, he certainly chose the wrong means for

accomplishing his purpose and compounded the problem by the subsequent grant to the Saltzmans.

The Saltzmans' argument at first sight seems to strain logic, but the history of property law shows a concern for technicality that lends some support to their challenge. They make much of the fact that the terms "warranty" and "in fee simple" were deleted from the standard printed form. At common law, the words "and his [her, their] heirs" were required for conveying a fee simple absolute since the phrase meant the conveyance of a heritable estate; without the inclusion of this phrase, only a life estate was conveyed. In Florida, as in most states, this technicality has been dispensed with, and a fee simple absolute is presumed when other qualifying language is absent. Grantor's deletion of the phrase "in fee simple" might suggest some other estate was intended, but the grantor did not delete "and their heirs and assigns." The deletion of words of warranty might suggest the grantor intended something other than a warranty deed, which warrants title and promises to defend it, but there is nothing in the deed to suggest that it is anything but a warranty deed.

**Herman SALTZMAN and
Irene P. Saltzman,
his wife, et al., Appellants,**
v.
Lacey N. AHERN, Appellee

District Court of Appeal of Florida,
First District
306 So.2d 537 (1975)

BOYER, Judge.

Both appellants and appellee claim title to a parcel of real estate, each claiming under separate conveyances from a common grantor, one James M. Dudley. Appellee filed a complaint to quiet title and appellants counterclaimed. The trial judge granted a motion for summary judgment, quieting title in appellee and appellants appealed.

. . . .

The questioned deed was executed by Dudley on August 24, 1953. A standard printed form was utilized, but the grantor deleted the word "warranty" and the "warranting clause" as well as the words "in fee simple", causing the deed to read (in material part) as follows:

"WITNESSETH, that the said grantor, in consideration of Ten ($10.00) dollars and other valuable consideration, the receipt whereof is hereby acknowledged, does give, grant, bargain, sell, alien, remise, release, enfeoff, convey and

confirm unto the said grantees and their heirs and assigns the lands situate in Duval County, State of Florida, described as follows:

[The legal description of property is here omitted]

"BUT RESERVING, HOWEVER, unto the said grantor a life estate in said above described lands for the period of his natural life.

"TO HAVE AND TO HOLD the same together with the hereditaments and appurtenances, unto the said grantees, and their heirs and assigns forever, subject, however, to the estate for the life of the said grantor therein."

. . . Appellants' sole contention is that the grantor, by making the changes in the deed form above mentioned, and by subsequently conveying the identical property to appellants' predecessors in title thereby evinced an intention that the subject deed not take effect during his lifetime but be considered instead as an attempted testamentary disposition.

In order to resolve the issue, there being no question as to execution, consideration or delivery, we must examine the deed itself. When the language of a deed is clear and certain in meaning and the grantor's intention is reflected by the language employed, there is no room for judicial construction of the language nor interpretation of the words used. . . . The recitation of consideration in an instrument raises a presumption thereof and when a person executes and delivers a deed for consideration there is raised a presumption that the words employed in the deed were intended to be effective in accordance with their ordinary meaning. If a deed is, by virtue of execution, delivery, consideration and language employed, impervious to attack by the grantor executing same, then it may not be successfully collaterally attacked by another.

. . . .

The judgment appealed is accordingly Affirmed.

CASE QUESTIONS

1. In its opinion, the Court does not delve into the circumstances of the making of the deed. What is more important here, the grantor's intent or the interpretation of his intent from the language of the deed?
2. Does the treatment here conform to contract law with regard to consideration?
3. What is the status of the Saltzmans' deed?
4. Why did the grantor deed the property twice? Is that relevant?

Nonfreehold Estates

Nonfreehold estates are also called *leasehold estates* and are most commonly represented by formal leases, commercial or residential, which spell out rights, duties, commencement, and termination as well as rental terms. Since these are contractual in nature and do not pass title, problems are resolved under contract law and state landlord and tenant law. Oral and informal arrangements present special problems that are usually handled in small claims court since most rentals involving substantial amounts of money are evidenced by written contracts that are the products of professional legal advice.

Co-Ownership

Title may be held by more than one owner. Mention has been made of tenancy by the entirety, which is a species of co-ownership that can be held only by husband and wife. It includes a right of survivorship, as does *joint tenancy,* which can be held by two or more people as equal owners with equal rights of use and possession. Under the right of survivorship, if one co-owner dies, the share of the deceased is owned equally by the survivors. Sale or gift prior to death defeats the right of survivorship, but an attempted gift by will fails since death terminates all property interests in a joint tenancy or tenancy by the entirety. A remaining form of co-ownership is *tenancy in common,* which does not have a right of survivorship and which can provide unequal shares among the co-owners.

An important example of co-ownership today is the condominium, in which owners of individual housing units are also tenants in common with regard to common areas—stairs, walkways, parking lots, etc.—and are equally obligated for their maintenance. Time-share arrangements are a relatively new phenomenon commonly associated with a condominium-like land use. Under time-share, owners are tenants in common but restricted in their use to certain time periods during the year. States in which condominiums and time-share are common have adopted comprehensive statutes governing them.

CASE NO. 13–2 The Kindly Mother-in-Law

Charles and Lillian bought a ranch in the country but decided not to live there. Charles' mother gave them $20,000 to pay the balance due on the ranch. Later Charles persuaded his wife to sign a quit-claim deed (a deed relinquishing her interest in the property) made out to Charles' mother, Mrs. Hill, so that in the event that Charles and Lillian died, Mrs. Hill could own the property. In 1964, Charles recorded the deed without informing his wife. Charles and Lillian later divorced, and the lower court held that the delivery of the deed was without Lillian's consent and held that Lillian's interest in the land remained community property subject to distribution in divorce. Charles appealed.

In community property states, property acquired during the marriage is presumed to be owned equally by husband and wife.

In the case below, one imagines that the mother-in-law's gift was made during a happier period in the marriage. Later events look suspiciously like an attempt on the part of the husband and his mother to get the gift back and perhaps more. In the divorce, Lillian received property valued at $17,600 and her car, while Charles received property worth $500 and his truck, which shows that community property is not necessarily split fifty-fifty at divorce. The disproportionate award may have been influenced by the court's reaction to Charles' misconduct.

**Charles C. ARMER and Gertrude Hill,
Appellants,
v.
Lillian ARMER, Appellee**

Supreme Court of Arizona
105 Ariz. 284, 463 P.2d 818 (1970)

HAYS, Justice.

. . . .

It has long been the law in Arizona that property acquired by either spouse during **coverture**, whether taken in the name of the husband or wife, is prima facie community property. In re Torrey's Estate, 54

Ariz. 369, 95 P.2d 990 (1939). Such a presumption is rebuttable, but only by clear and convincing evidence. Smith v. Smith, 71 Ariz. 315, 227 P.2d 214 (1951). When the character of property is once fixed, the property retains such character until changed by agreement of the parties or by operation of law. [C.]

. . . .

Lillian's complaint alleged that "the defendant Charles Armer, fraudulently induced and coerced plaintiff to sign a quit claim deed conveying the (Coon Creek) property to Gertrude Hill." We do not find it necessary, however, to determine whether Lillian proved the nine elements of fraud at trial. For whether or not fraud was sufficiently proved, we hold that Charles, acting as agent for both the community and for his mother, performed an unauthorized delivery of the Coon Creek deed when he had the quit claim deed notarized, delivered to Mrs. Hill, and recorded without his wife's consent.

As previously indicated, all property acquired by either spouse during coverture is presumed to be community property. Since Charles and Lillian purchased the ranch as husband and wife, and since nothing was done subsequently to change the character of the property, the Coon Creek ranch was part of the community estate of Charles and Lillian. In Arizona, the husband is recognized as the head of the family, and its agent in control and management of the community estate. [C.] While the husband has the entire management of the community during coverture, he may not encumber or dispose of community realty without his wife's consent and signature, and must act at all times for the benefit of the community. [C.] There is no statutory or implied agency on the part of the husband to dispose of community realty. [C.] Charles, as agent of the community, had no authority to alienate any interest in the Coon Creek property without Lillian's consent. Lillian had affixed her signature to the quit claim deed only on the representation by Charles that the deed would not be notarized, that it would be put in their safe deposit box, and that it would only be delivered to Mrs. Hill in the event that Lillian and Charles were killed in a common accident. The subsequent notarization of the deed, its delivery to Mrs. Hill, and the deed's recordation were unauthorized, nor did Lillian ever ratify such actions by her husband. . . .

We cannot agree with the trial court's findings of fact, conclusions of law, and judgment in one other respect, wherein the court concluded that Charles and Lillian held the Coon Creek property as "tenants in common," and that therefore either party could convey his or her interest to a third party. . . . We hold that the entire quit claim deed conveying the Coon Creek ranch to Mrs. Hill is null and void, and that the Coon Creek ranch remains part of the community estate of Charles and Lillian. We further hold that Mrs. Hill has no interest in the property, except that she presently holds the entire ranch in trust for Charles and Lillian. . . .

CASE GLOSSARY

coverture refers to the period of time during which a couple is married.

CASE QUESTIONS

1. Did Charles come out better, worse, or the same by appealing this case?
2. Does this case suggest when title passes? At the signing of the deed or its delivery?

Implications

Clearly the holder of a life estate is missing some of the rights enjoyed by the owner in fee simple absolute. There are other less frequently used freehold estates that will not be described here, but keep in mind that in a sale of land, the purchaser ordinarily expects a fee simple absolute, and it is the responsibility of the person examining the land's past to determine whether the asserted owner does in fact have a clear title with the full bundle of rights.

The purchaser must be informed of any encumbrances. Attorneys are called upon to search titles, i.e., examine the records to establish the present owner and the extent of ownership. If there are any of the numerous intrusions on ownership mentioned previously, the purchaser should know of these and their legal ramifications—for instance, the significance of a utility easement that allows the electric company to cross the land to serve other properties. Inconsistencies and questions should be resolved—has an old mortgage been satisfied even though satisfaction of mortgage has not been recorded? what was the effect of the divorce of a prior owner? An attorney may be retained not only to help conduct the transaction but also to provide a title opinion describing the current status of the title. Title insurance companies, which maintain extensive records on land within the territory they cover, offer additional protection to the prudent buyer.

Title searches, title opinions, and title insurance are made necessary by the system of estates that has been inherited over the centuries. Land sales call for a methodical approach that typically follows an orderly checklist to prepare for a smooth closing at which the purchase price is exchanged for delivery of a deed to the property. Much of the work in real property transaction can and should, for reasons of cost, be done by paralegals. In fact, a person who specializes in such transactions, or even one who specializes in residential or commercial sales or leases, is preferable to a general practitioner. Experience develops an awareness of the myriad problems that may arise.

TITLE

The word *title* has been used frequently thus far; its definition cannot be postponed. It is an important concept but one that is often misunderstood. The definition of title is curiously absent from or cursorily treated in law texts covering real property. The concept of title is abstract to the point of mystery.

In its beginnings it was embodied in the concept of *seisin,* which originally meant possession but gradually came to signify possession under the right to claim a freehold estate. Seisin originally referred to what seems today to have been a rather mystical relationship between an owner and his land; seisin was passed from one man to another by a ritual called *livery of seisin,* symbolized by handing over a twig or a clump of dirt from the land. When seisin passed, so did the right of possession.

The concept of title is similar. Its definition takes three forms:

1. The right to ownership and possession of land
2. The means whereby an owner of land has just possession
3. The evidence of ownership of land.

Title is not a document, such as a deed, though the term is often loosely used in such a reference. A deed is simply one of many bits of evidence of title. In a sense, title is held by the one who holds the greatest number of the bundle of rights that constitute a freehold estate; a lessee does not have title despite having the right of possession.

The three definitions of title treat different aspects of title. As evidence of title, there are numerous documents that, combined in a somewhat mystical union, tell us who has title. Documents alone may not be sufficient. One in wrongful possession for a sufficient period of time may acquire title (**adverse possession**). Treating title as a means of claiming possession refers to the need on occasion for one holding title to prove title against other claimants for title or possession. Finally, the right of ownership represented by the concept of title is its most common meaning, especially when ownership is not in question. "Right of ownership" must remain abstract since the law is normally concerned with acknowledging and enforcing specific rights.

If the concept of title is still obscure, it is because it is relative and abstract. It is used in preference to ownership because it signifies the application of all the rules that identify ownership. Perhaps it is best explained by the barb, "I don't own the house, the bank owns it." This is an obvious reference to the lender on a mortgage, who usually puts up a far greater portion of the purchase price than the actual purchaser. In most states, however,

adverse possession is a means of acquiring title by occupying and using land for a certain length of time even though the occupier does not have title. The period required by the common law was traditionally twenty years, which has been shortened in most states. Several other requirements must be met, which are spelled out in state statutes.

the bank merely holds a lien on the property and no part of the title. Nevertheless, the title to the land in question is encumbered by the mortgage, and no prudent purchaser would buy the land without resolving the mortgage question. (A mortgage may not prevent a sale of land, but since the mortgage is secured by the land, a failure to pay the mortgage could result in foreclosure no matter who has title.)

bailment
occurs when the owner of personal property delivers possession without intent to pass title, as when one leaves an automobile with an auto mechanic. The bailee in possession may or may not have authority to sell the property for the owner (bailor). The bailee may retain the property under certain circumstances, as when the owner does not pay the auto mechanic, who may keep the auto until the repair bill is paid (this is covered by the law governing "mechanic's liens").

Personal Property

Title to personal property does not usually raise the complex problems associated with chain of title to real property. Since tangible personal property is commonly exchanged by sale or gift, mere possession is significant evidence of exchange of title. Most problems arise with **bailments** and lost, stolen, or abandoned property, which is usually covered by well-established legal rules. The *Uniform Commercial Code* gives specific guidance on sale of goods and intangible personal property in the form of negotiable instruments.

CASE NO. 13–3 The Engagement Ring Problem

What happens to an engagement ring when the marriage does not take place? Devising fair principles is not as easy as it may seem. The problem is complicated by the intersection of several fields of law:

1. Contract law. Is an engagement a contract? If the contract is breached, is restitution in the form of return of the engagement ring an appropriate remedy?
2. Tort law. There was at one time an action at common law called "breach of promise to marry" with a consequent suit for damages. Many states have abolished this cause of action. Could the engagement ring be an element of damages? Does

abolishing the cause of action put the ring beyond reach?
3. Family law. Should the marriage (and engagement) contract be treated like any other contract, or should the state's interest in the sanctity of the family treat this contract specially, including the right to the engagement ring? If the state's public policy is not to force incompatible couples to marry, how should the court decide on the ring?
4. Property law. Is the engagement ring a gift? Consideration for a contract? A pledge? Has title passed?

The basic principles that developed concerning return of the ring were as follows: (1) If donee breaks off the engagement without fault on the part of the donor, the donor is entitled to its return. (2) If the donor breaks off the engagement, the donee keeps the ring. (3) An engagement broken by mutual consent obliges the return of the ring.

In the state of New York, these common law rules applied until 1935 when the legislature abolished actions for breach of promise to marry, which was interpreted by the courts to bar an action for recovery of engagement rings. In 1965, the legislature enacted law to allow recovery of engagement rings where "justice so requires."

This moral tone is echoed in the next case in which the fiance was killed in an auto accident shortly before the wedding and the personal representative of his estate attempted to recover the ring.

COHEN
v.
BAYSIDE FEDERAL SAVINGS AND LOAN ASSOCIATION

Supreme Court of New York
62 Misc.2d 738, 309 N.Y.S.2d 980
(1970)

TESSLER, J.

. . . .

. . . Some courts have propounded a pledge theory. Other courts state that principles of unjust enrichment govern and the most popular rationale is that the ring is given as a gift on condition subsequent. It is not always clear, however, whether it is the actual marriage of the parties or the donee's not performing any act that would prevent the marriage that is the actual condition of the "transaction."

Thus a confusing body of law has grown up around the engagement ring and, after careful consideration of these principles, this court has decided that Carol should keep the ring because that result is equitable and because "justice so requires" . . . .

. . . .

I cannot believe that the age-old ritual of giving an engagement ring to bind the mutual premarital vows can be or is intended to be treated as an exchange of consideration as practiced in the everyday market place. Can it be seriously urged that the giving of this ring by the decedent "groom" to his loved one and bride-to-be can be treated as the ordinary commercial or business transaction requiring the ultimate in consideration and payment? I think not. To treat this special and usually once in a lifetime occasion, one as requiring quid pro quo, is a mistake and unrealistic.

[Carol Cohen's ring was worth only one thousand dollars. In *Lowe v. Quinn* the ring was valued at $60,000, which explains why she wanted to keep it and he went to the highest state court to get it back. Although she broke off the engagement, he was in a special dilemma—he was still married.]

Edwin S. LOWE, Appellant
v.
Jayne D. QUINN, Respondent

Court of Appeals of New York
27 N.Y.2d 397, 267 N.E.2d 251 (1971)

Fuld, C.J.

. . . .

An engagement ring "is in the nature of a pledge for the contract of marriage" [C.] and, under the common law, it was settled—at least in a case where no impediment existed to a marriage—that, if the recipient broke the "engagement," she was required, upon demand, to return the ring on the theory that it constituted a conditional gift. [Cc.] However, a different result is compelled where, as here, one of the parties is married. An agreement to marry under such circumstances is void as against public policy [Cc.], and it is not saved or rendered valid by the fact that the married individual contemplated divorce and that the agreement was conditioned on procurement of the divorce. [Cc.] Based on such reasoning, the few courts which have had occasion to consider the question have held that a plaintiff may not recover the engagement ring or any other property he may have given the woman. . . .

[The court goes on to argue that the legislative reenactment of the right to recover an engagement ring did not apply to a situation in which either of the parties is married at the time of the gift of the ring.]

A somewhat similar case had occurred in Massachusetts a few years before with different results. In *De Cicco v. Barker*, 339 Mass. 457, 159 N.E.2d 534 (1959), a married man gave several rings to a woman, at least one of which, a six-carat diamond ring, was apparently an engagement ring. His wife was in the hospital at the time, and the engagement was conditioned on her death, which occurred two months later. Subsequent to the wife's death, the fiancee bought him an engagement ring but several months later broke the engagement.

She relied on the Massachusetts' legislative abolishment of the cause of action for breach of promise to marry, but the court gave him the six-carat ring, stating:

> . . . It is a proceeding not to recover damages, either directly or indirectly for breach of the contract to marry but to obtain on established equitable principles restitution of property held on a condition which the defendant was unwilling to fulfil. It seeks to prevent unjust enrichment.

ESTATE PLANNING

An important area of law practice concerns estate planning, which deals with the orderly distribution of assets in case of death. If no provision is made in advance, the property of a deceased person, called the *estate* or *decedent's estate*, will pass by intestate succession as ordered by state law. Most persons would distribute their property somewhat differently than will the state and should so provide in advance by will and/or trust. The estate planner not only assists in preparing the documents of distribution but also advises clients on tax and other legal consequences of different distributions. Advice is not merely legal and financial but can be very personal as well.

Wills

The primary purpose of wills is the distribution of the financial assets of the deceased according to directions provided prior to death in the will itself. Many persons wish to control the use of their property long after death or want to specify in great detail how everything they own will pass to intended beneficiaries. All this can be accomplished through a will, but unnecessary complexity not only makes administration of the estate cumbersome, it also tends to anger and frustrate beneficiaries and encourage suits to contest the validity of the will. When specific problems, such as a spendthrift child or spouse, warrant limitations on the distribution or use of property, a trust is often the more appropriate solution.

Will drafting is often left to paralegals, who can use the language and form of past models to express the intent of the testator, to be reviewed by the responsible attorney prior to signing by the testator and witnesses. Today drafting wills can be greatly facilitated by computers programmed with standard clauses and paragraphs that reflect the requirements of state law. In some instances an attorney or paralegal may simply follow a checklist of questions, the answers to which are entered into a computer and a will is printed. If the computer program is comprehensive, the possibility of human error is minimized.

Each state requires specific formalities for the signing and attesting of wills that must be strictly adhered to in order to create a valid will. The legal advisor's goal should be to give force to the intent of the testator in a form that will discourage and overcome legal challenge.

Working with clients who wish to have wills drafted calls for delicacy, tact, common sense, and a basic understanding of human nature. Contemplation of death is unpleasant at best, and letting go of the acquisitions of a lifetime is not easy.

A special note is warranted here. Making a will for a client usually results in the attorney and staff acquiring a detailed knowledge of the client's finances and personal relationships. All of this information is strictly confidential, and all members of the legal staff must scrupulously avoid revealing any knowledge thus acquired.

Trusts

A trust is a device dating back to the fourteenth century, when it was used to avoid certain features of the ownership of common law freehold estates. It was enforced in the courts of equity and is still governed by equity today. A trust involves a transfer of title of real or personal property to a trustee who is charged with a duty to hold the property for the benefit of another, a beneficiary (*cestui que* trust). The trust instrument provides instructions for the trustee to follow in distributing property to the beneficiary.

By setting up a *living (inter vivos) trust,* a person can put property into the trust that will go to named parties immediately or when the donor dies. In this way it can be used as a will substitute and has the advantage of making possible detailed instructions on the distribution of property at the same time that it avoids probate of the property. When a trust is used as a will substitute, the donor can make herself trustee and beneficiary for her lifetime and thereby both control and benefit from the property. Trusts can also be used to transfer property without regard to death, as with a trust fund to send one's children to college; the donor may relinquish any control (*irrevocable trust*).

The advantage of a trust over a will is that it names a trustee to carry out the wishes of the donor. Without such an arrangement, future decisions would be based on interpretations of the intent of the testator, which might prove inappropriate as times and situations change. The donor may provide for flexibility that would not be possible in an outright distribution. Also, the trustee has a fiduciary duty toward the beneficiary that can make the trustee more accountable than someone who misuses distributed property. For someone with minor children or others who cannot properly take care of their affairs, a trust can be established that provides temporarily for financial needs while preserving assets for later distribution. In short, the trust can be tailored to very special problems that would be very awkward to handle in a will.

A good deal of the work involving trusts can be efficiently done by paralegals.

GOVERNMENT REGULATION OF REAL PROPERTY

Ownership of real property today is subject to many intrusions on the part of government. Most of these take the form of restrictions on use. In addition, governments may take property under the power of eminent domain, and the federal government has authority over navigable waters. Former rights over airspace above an owner's property have been restricted primarily because of the advent of the airplane.

Eminent Domain

The Fifth Amendment to the U.S. Constitution, the repository of basic rights in criminal law, ends with the clause, "nor shall private property be taken for a public use, without just compensation." This along with similar language in state constitutions is the basis for the power our governments exercise called *eminent domain.* This power is used to take property for highways, parks, urban redevelopment, and protection of the environment. "Public use" has been broadly defined to cover laws allowing private railroads to acquire property for their routes, electric utilities to obtain rights of way, and so forth.

Compensation for the taking of property is often subject to dispute, but state and federal governments have procedures designed to determine fair market value and to give the opportunity to challenge assessments. The major issue in litigation has been the interpretation of the word "taking." When government takes title to an entire piece of property, the problem may be simple—pay fair market value. If, however, the state builds a new highway, reducing traffic on an old highway and thereby making a filling station unprofitable, there is no "taking"—it is considered *damnum absque injuria,* a harm without a legal injury, and not compensable. Thus, some effects of government action constitute taking and some do not. The issue arose early in this century with planning and zoning.

Planning and Zoning

The most direct intrusions into a private property owner's rights have come from government attempts to regulate land use. For both residential and commercial owners, planning and zoning have resulted in severe restrictions on property owners' rights. The classic example of planning that is still to be found everywhere is the comprehensive zoning ordinance. Starting in the 1920s, cities and counties throughout the country adopted the practice of mapping land use zones, which restrict areas to categories of use such as residential, professional, commercial, and industrial. Generally these zones reflect contemporary uses but restrict future development. The object of zones is to diminish the effects of urban blight, save agricultural and green areas, and prevent the intrusions of incompatible uses in adjacent areas. Since zoning clearly represents the government depriving property owners of use rights they would otherwise enjoy, it was challenged as a taking under eminent domain for which no compensation was provided.

The U.S. Supreme Court in *Euclid v. Ambler*, 272 U.S. 365, 47 S.Ct. 114, 71 L.Ed. 303 (1926) upheld comprehensive zoning in the village of Euclid, Ohio, under the state's power to regulate health, safety, and welfare but found a taking in *Nectow v. City of Cambridge*, 277 U.S. 183, 48 S.Ct. 447, 72 L.Ed. 842 (1928), where zoning effectively deprived the owner of any economically feasible use of his property (property zoned residential, though adjacent properties were occupied by industrial enterprises), the judgment relying on the Fourteenth Amendment's prohibition of deprivation of property without due process of law. Subsequent constitutional history has affirmed the resulting balancing test between the rights of communities to control land use and the rights of individual property owners to make a reasonable use of their land.

Today planning has taken on additional tasks. Zoning maps are only a temporary solution to the problems that intensive growth has created in many areas. Comprehensive, long-range planning prevails in populous states along with environmental concerns. Residential and commercial development are frequently carried out on a grand scale, and federal and state laws have been enacted to require exhaustive studies of the impact of such development on the environment and the capacity of local resources to support new building. Government has taken a serious role in controlling and directing growth. Major projects, airports, shopping malls, large residential developments, etc., are subject to intense scrutiny to assure compliance with the law, and it is unlikely that legal requirements will decrease in the future.

Lawyers find much work in this area in advising, negotiating, and facilitating cooperation between developers and local governmental bodies. Paralegals can be invaluable in the process.

SUMMARY

Property is an abstract concept, not a natural or physical object or feature. It is best explained in terms of legal rights, such as rights to possess, exclude, and transfer. Rights can also be limited in time, such as a lease or a life estate, and in the nature of use and transferability. Rights may be restricted by a deed, by zoning ordinances, and by rights of others, such as utility easements and rights of way.

Property is divided into real and personal property. Real property, which consists of land and its improvements, is based on common law estates, which have endured for many centuries because of the basic conservatism of real property law. Under this system a person owns rights in land, the bundle-of-rights concept, rather than owning the land itself. When a person owns the maximum bundle of rights, the estate is called a fee simple absolute and corresponds to what we casually refer to as ownership. Lesser estates may be held, of which the most common is the life estate, which allows the life tenant to exercise rights over the property while alive. Upon death, the rights automatically transfer to a person who until that time held only a future interest.

Leasehold (or nonfreehold) estates involve the temporary transfer of the right of possession and are regulated by landlord and tenant laws of each state.

Title is an important concept in property law. It is not a document like a deed but an abstraction based on the history of the ownership of property that describes the extent of rights and limitations on rights and that can be determined by examining the records of transactions dealing with a particular piece of land. Title to personal property is generally much simpler, especially where physical property is directly exchanged for cash or a cash equivalent—title passes instantaneously.

An important aspect of the practice of property law involves estate planning, preparing for the distribution of a person's estate (the totality of one's property, real and personal). The most common devices used in estate planning are wills and trusts. A will provides for the distribution of property at death. A trust may distribute property at death or during one's lifetime; it establishes a trustee who distributes property to a beneficiary according to instructions in the trust instrument.

Today property is extensively regulated by government. Particularly affecting real property are restrictions on land use covered by local government planning and zoning, but state and federal governments have become more and more active in limiting land use, especially in the area of environmental law.

CHAPTER QUESTIONS

1. Why would the owner of a vacant city lot vehemently object to the city rezoning the lot from commercial to residential?
2. What is equal ownership with right of survivorship called?
3. Why have we preserved the ancient law of estates?

4. Why is it necessary to examine the chain of title prior to a sale of real estate?
5. Where does the state's power of eminent domain come from?
6. Are stocks and bonds personal property or real property?
7. Why are real property transactions so much more complicated than personal property transactions?

EXERCISES

1. All states have Recording Acts, the purpose of which is to have a record of real estate transactions. When a deed is delivered upon the sale of real property, the purchaser ordinarily records that deed, usually with a clerk of the court. Once recorded, anyone searching the title of the land involved should discover the deed as part of the process of establishing who has title. Recording acts do not require recording but provide for the consequences of the failure to record. Recording acts are designed to protect those who rely on the official records. Suppose, for instance, that in *Saltzman v. Ahern* the first grantee, Ahern's predecessor in title, did not record the deed until *after* the Saltzmans received their deed (from the original grantor as well) and recorded it. The Saltzmans' deed would be the first deed in the record. Who has title? The answer varies among the states. Check your recording statute to answer this question. Does it make a difference if the Saltzmans knew about the prior deed, that is if they had "notice" of the prior deed?

2. The civil law (continental Europe) does not use the concept of estates of the common law (England) but describes ownership by the concept of *dominium*. Look up "estate" and "*dominium*" in a comprehensive law dictionary (e.g., Black's) and try to determine the difference in the concepts. It may help to look at "title," "ownership," "fee," and "usufruct" as well. Try to put the difference in your own words—this may help to understand the concept of common law estates.

3. What property transactions in your state must be in writing? Check the Statute of Frauds and the *Uniform Commercial Code*.

4. Is your state a title state (mortgagor/debtor holds title) or a lien state (mortgagee/creditor holds title until debt is paid)?

5. Imagine you are sixty years old, worth two million dollars, and have two sons and a daughter. Under what circumstances would you want to set up trusts for your children rather than simply distributing your property at death? What would be better to put in a will than in a trust?

"Winning cases!" says Eric Selin, is the most rewarding aspect of his work as a legal assistant at the Environmental Protection Bureau of New York State's Department of Law. He obtained this position five years ago after scoring high on a civil service examination. His chief responsibilities include drafting pleadings and documents, legal research, and answering citizen complaints. "On a typical day," Selin says, "I am asked by attorneys to find cases that support the arguments they will make."

Born in Provo, Utah, Selin is married with three children. He attended Brigham Young University and Schenectady County Community College, where he received his A.A.S.—paralegal degree. He has served on the paralegal advisory committee to the college for four years.

Selin says a good educational background includes developing organizational skills, writing proficiency, and research skills. "In addition, it is very helpful to be able to narrow a question of law and avoid wasting time researching outside the scope of inquiry," he says. However, he emphasizes, "It should be well understood by prospective paralegals that the most valuable training you will receive is the training you give yourself."

Selin wishes that he had learned more about basic research skills other than merely legal research. "I wish I had learned more about legislative intent and how inflexible judicial schedules can be. The latter is responsible for many late hours of working, long after others go home."

"Choose a field of law that you enjoy and agree with philosophically," Selin says. He admonishes paralegals to avoid jobs where they must work with people who hold ideals, values, morals, or politics that are contrary to the goals of your company or agency. "You won't be happy," he says. "Learn to be good at what you do because once you land the job, the learning just begins. An academic degree only demonstrates that you *can* be taught," advises Selin.

Eric Selin
Environmental Protection Legal Assistant

CHAPTER 14
Administrative Law and Procedure

> If you have ten thousand regulations you destroy all respect for the law.
>
> — *Winston Churchill*

Administrative law refers to the law that governs administrative action by government. It regulates the relationship between the citizen and the government. Although it is poorly understood by laypersons and many practitioners, it has a greater impact on

335

the daily lives of Americans than any other area of law. Most people have few, if any, brushes with criminal law; few are often involved in personal injury law; contract and property law are matters of occasional concern for the nonbusinessperson. But the rules and regulations of government agencies are encountered throughout a lifetime. The water we drink, the air we breathe, the places we work, the schools we attend, the social security system, and a host of other facets of our lives are subject to regulations by agencies governed by administrative law.

THE FIELD OF ADMINISTRATIVE LAW

Administrative law is a phenomenon of the twentieth century. In theory, it can be traced back for centuries, but the field as it is defined today emanates principally from the U.S. Constitution as it has come to be interpreted in this century. The federal Administrative Procedure Act, first enacted in 1946, represents the major addition to administrative law, although its provisions drew heavily on prior case law. Since administrative law is relatively new, it is still dynamic and changing. Our **bureaucracy** has expanded and blossomed, particularly in the years since the New Deal. The greatest expansion has come in social services agencies, such as social security, the Veterans Administration, Medicare, and the social welfare agencies. The new agencies and the expanding scope of government activities have presented numerous problems that have encouraged the growth of administrative law and the litigation that often shapes it. Charting new ground for law has left a confusing array of cases and rules that makes administrative law a great challenge.

bureaucracy
The executive branch of government as a whole is referred to as the bureaucracy. The term comes from the French word "bureau," referring to bureaus or agencies of government, and the Greek -cracy, referring to rule (e.g., democracy), implying that the modern state is ruled by the government agencies.

Substantive Law

The study of administrative law is generally confined to procedural law because of the impossibility of learning the substantive law. Each agency has its own set of substantive rules and regulations, sometimes a product of the legislature and sometimes the legislative product of the agency itself. The regulations of the Social Security Administration bear little resemblance to those of the Securities and Exchange Commission or the Environmental Protection Agency, and their regulations are collected in the *Code of Federal Regulations*, which is a huge compendium that no one has ever mastered. It would be a major undertaking simply to gain a relatively complete understanding of the rules and regulations of the Social Security Administration.

Procedural Law

Administrative procedural law encompasses most of what is usually meant when the term administrative law is used. There are certain principles governing administrative action regardless of the agency concerned. Administrative agencies pose a special problem for the law because most agencies engage in all three governmental functions. Although part of the executive branch of government, most agencies engage in rulemaking, which is the administrative agency equivalent of legislation; and most large agencies (and many small agencies) have an adjudicatory function as well.

Administrative procedure is particularly concerned with the legislative (rulemaking) and adjudicatory functions of agencies. Since these involve state or federal action, they are constrained by the due process clauses of the Fifth and Fourteenth Amendments requiring fundamental fairness in substance and procedure. What makes administrative procedural law different from the procedural principles that apply in suits between private parties derives from the nature of the parties involved.

Every administrative law case potentially involves weighing the important interests of the individual against the interests of society as represented by government. A prime example is sovereign immunity from suit. In the nineteenth century, the courts and some state legislatures concluded that it made no sense for a private citizen to sue the government. At that time, of course, government was small, offered few services, and intruded very little into private affairs. A democratic government was perceived as benevolent, as representing the people, so it was illogical for the people to sue themselves. By the 1960s and 1970s, it had become apparent that a democratic government could indeed be intrusive and abusive so that sovereign immunity was often viewed as a license for government to run roughshod over private interests.

ADMINISTRATIVE LAW AND THE PARALEGAL

The study of administrative law is a worthwhile endeavor for the paralegal student for a number of reasons. Only by studying administrative law can a person gain a deep understanding of the basic process of upholding the rights of the citizen against the intrusions of government. It is also a rewarding education into constitutional law. But the study of administrative law can be very practical. Litigation against the government increases as the scope of government activities increases, and there seems to be no end to this increase. Administrative law cases frequently involve lengthy litigation with copious amounts of research that should be done by paralegals for reasons of cost efficiency. In addition, many agencies, such as the Social Security Administration and other social service agencies, permit the claimant to be represented by anyone of their choosing. The California Bar Association in 1989 issued an opinion allowing paralegals employed by law firms to represent the firm's clients in administrative hearings. This affords paralegals an opportunity to do trial work. Many legal aid offices employ paralegals to represent indigents at administrative hearings. Administrative law thus presents a promising area for employment of paralegals. Although many, perhaps most, paralegals will never handle administrative law work, many others will be administrative law specialists.

INDEPENDENT REGULATORY AGENCIES

Administrative law questions ultimately concern the power of government to regulate and the right of private parties to challenge regulation. Most of the major principles of the law of administrative procedure grew out of challenges to government regulation of business against government agencies established for the purpose of regulating business.

The discussion of administrative law in this chapter uses federal administrative procedure as its model. Most states have adopted comprehensive administrative procedure statutes, modeled on the federal act with modifications. Nevertheless, administrative law at the federal level has tended to lead the way—the federal Administrative Procedure Act (APA) predates state acts by two, three, and four decades. Congress and the federal courts naturally became involved at an earlier stage because of the creation of independent regulatory agencies with national authority and great power.

Independent regulatory agencies were originally created to control the devastating effects of cutthroat competition in certain industries.. The first great agency to be created was the Interstate Commerce Commission, created in 1887. Since that time Congress has periodically created new agencies; there now exist a dozen major independent regulatory agencies with over fifty smaller ones. Regulating an industry is essentially anticompetitive and counter to a pure market model of free enterprise. Even a cursory review of world history will demonstrate that free enterprise unregulated by government probably never existed, though the United States may have come closest to the model at one time or another.

In a legal sense, we have been more committed to a *fair* market than a *free* market. It is the nature of government to allocate and distribute power and wealth, which makes it inevitable that business will be taxed and regulated.

The Interstate Commerce Commission (ICC) is a good illustration of the rationale of regulation. The ICC was formed to serve the railroad industry and the public. Vicious competition combined with monopolistic practices often undermined individual companies on the one hand and allowed excessive rates on the other. The industry was unstable at a time when the railroads were a major vehicle for economic growth of the country. Railroads are different from some other businesses in that they must operate on fixed routes—the investment in land and track must result in a level of use that will repay the investment. If one hundred railroads build tracks from Chicago to St. Louis, none of them will make money until most have abandoned the route. The ICC was charged with regulating routes and rates in such a way that the railroads could make a reasonable profit charging rates that business and the public could afford so that everyone would benefit. Regulatory schemes are not perfect—sometimes they benefit the country and sometimes they are a burden—but the fact remains that some business activities are so central to the national economy that the government is unlikely to relinquish control.

Some activities must be controlled because they are by nature monopolistic. Public utilities are the prime example. The furnishing of water, sewer, gas, and electricity is an activity that can only be accomplished efficiently by one company serving a community, locality, or region. In fact, these activities are often performed by government. Where they are not, public service commissions monitor their activities and particularly their rates. Since these activities provide absolutely essential services to the community, government does not allow the utilities a free reign.

Independent agencies may be distinguished on the federal level by the following rule of thumb: an independent agency is one whose head cannot be removed by the president without cause. By contrast, cabinet chiefs (the secretary of state, labor, defense, etc.) occupy their positions at the pleasure of the president. While the president must obtain Congress' approval for appointment, he can remove a cabinet secretary at any time. The president may remove the chiefs or commissioners of the independent regulatory agencies only upon showing just cause for their removal.

Since the Roosevelt New Deal era, Congress has moved away from creating new industry-regulating agencies toward the establishment of social service agencies such as the Social Security Administration, the Occupational Safety and Health Review

Commission, established by the Occupational Safety and Health Act (OSHA), and the Consumer Product Safety Commission (CPSC).

The importance of independent regulatory agencies for administrative law is twofold. First, the creation of these agencies brought into question the authority of Congress to delegate its legislative powers granted by the Constitution. Second, authority was delegated to administrative agencies with a degree of independence from the executive branch of government of which they were a part. Since the agencies often regulated national industries and activities, the regulations they promulgated, the enforcement procedures they used, and their activities were frequently challenged by business interests that could afford to pursue their remedies all the way to the U.S. Supreme Court. Since the initial legal issues were basic constitutional questions, many of the fundamental principles of administrative procedure were formulated in the context of the regulation of business.

Thus, many of the landmark cases in administrative law seem remote from daily life. For example, *United States v. Morgan,* 313 U.S. 409 (1941), involved the fixing of rates for buying and selling livestock at the Kansas City Stock Yards, but it went to the U.S. Supreme Court four times and ultimately set standards for the extent to which litigants could inquire into the decisionmaking of high level policymakers. *Abbott Laboratories v. Gardner,* 387 U.S. 136 (1967), concerned Food and Drug Administration regulation of drug labeling but set forth the fundamental interpretation of judicial review under the APA, namely, that agency action is presumptively reviewable by the courts.

Research and argument in administrative procedural law differ from other areas of law because the cases deal with a myriad of agencies. Whereas in most private law cases, especially substantive questions of law, the researcher looks for cases with a similar fact pattern (argument in a slip-and-fall case will usually revolve around prior slip-and-fall decisions), administrative procedure arguments are constructed from a line of precedent-setting cases that bear no fact resemblance other than the procedural issue raised.

THE DELEGATION OF LEGISLATIVE AUTHORITY

In the nineteenth century, the courts frequently repeated the doctrine that Congress could not delegate its legislative authority, on the grounds that the Constitution restricted this authority to Congress. In actual fact, Congress from the very beginning delegated its authority to administrative agencies, but the courts did not strike down such delegation until 1935 when a broad delegation of authority under the National Industrial Recovery Act was held by the U.S. Supreme Court to be unconstitutional in two cases. Since that time the nondelegation doctrine has been all but dead, though it was partially resurrected in *Immigration and Naturalization Service v. Chadha,* 462 U.S. 919 (1983). The principle is still occasionally raised in administrative law cases with state agencies.

JUDICIAL REVIEW OF AGENCY ACTION

Critical topics in the field of administrative law are judicial review and the scope of judicial review. These issues address basic questions concerning whether a dispute over agency action is a matter for the courts, who may bring such an action, and what exactly the courts should consider. These problems are constitutional ones. Since the U.S. Constitution establishes the doctrine of separation of powers, it was thought in the nineteenth century that the courts had no authority to question actions by the executive branch of government. An opposing constitutional premise, however, is that the executive branch may not violate the Constitution; and since the federal courts are responsible for interpreting the Constitution, logically the courts should be the forum for preventing the executive branch from exceeding its constitutional authority.

The demise of the doctrine of nonreviewability was signaled by *American School of Magnetic Healing v. McAnnulty,* 187 U.S. 94 (1902), in which the postmaster general prohibited the school from using the mail. It was clear that the postmaster general did not have such authority, and the court was faced with either dismissing the case for nonreviewability, thereby allowing the postmaster general unbridled authority, or reviewing the case and limiting the postmaster general to his legal authority. There really was no choice; our democratic legal principles could not allow a public official to act unlawfully. The postmaster general lost, and judicial review took on respectability. Thereafter, the doctrine of judicial review was formulated in a series of cases that culminated in the enactment of Chapter 7 of the APA, which states in relevant part:

§ 701. Application; definitions

(a) This chapter applies, according to the provisions thereof, except to the extent that—

    (1) statutes preclude judicial review; or

(2)   agency action is committed to agency discretion by law.

§ 704.   Actions reviewable

Agency action made reviewable by statute and final agency action for which there is no other adequate remedy in a court are subject to judicial review.

What exactly these two sections mean in combination has been the subject of much commentary and will undoubtedly continue to require clarification. What is clear, in theory if not always in fact, is that §701(a)(1) means that Congress may specifically exempt some agency action from court review by statute, but when review is specifically authorized by statute, review is available. If Congress states that action cannot be reviewed, it cannot be reviewed; if Congress states action can be reviewed, it can be reviewed. This is simple enough except that Congress is usually silent with regard to review. In that case §704 would seem to indicate that review is available, except where "agency action is committed to agency discretion by law," a proviso that is less than crystal clear. *Abbott Laboratories v. Gardner,* 387 U.S. 136 (1967), resolved the issue by ignoring the lack of clarity in the language of the APA, stating that the APA expresses a "presumption of reviewability." The courts and Congress seem content with that principle and have left the debate over the nuances of the APA to legal scholars.

Scope of Review

The reluctance of the early courts to review administrative action was due in part to a desire to avoid retrying the facts. Where an agency had made a determination of rights, especially if a hearing had been provided, the courts saw no need to conduct another hearing. Where facts were found by the agency, the courts did not want to engage in a new round of fact-finding. In addition, the agency was presumably better at finding facts because it employed experts in the field for which it was established. It was reasoned, for example, that the ICC was better able to understand the intricacies of the railroad business than ordinary judges and juries, so the courts were reluctant to interfere with policymaking by the agencies entrusted with that function.

The resolution of this problem came about through the gradual transformation of judicial review into an appellate procedure with the agencies serving in the place of trial courts, conducting the hearings, finding fact, and applying rules and the court of appeals reviewing agency determinations much like an appellate court reviews an appeal from a trial court. Today, nearly all judicial review in both state and federal courts takes place at the appellate level.

In this way, the courts have limited the scope of judicial review to the legal questions with which appellate judges are competent and comfortable. Issues of jurisdiction, the interpretation of statutes, and due process raise questions that the courts treat on a daily basis. When fact-finding is questioned, the courts borrow the substantial evidence test used for appellate review of jury fact-finding. By limiting the scope of review, the courts remove themselves from making policy decisions and assume responsibility for monitoring the fairness of procedure.

A celebrated example of this was *Environmental Defense Fund, Inc. v. Ruckelshaus*, 439 F.2d 584 (D.C. Cir. 1971), in which the secretary of agriculture was sued by an environmental group in an effort to ban the pesticide DDT. Judge Bazelon separated the questions of fact from the questions of law. He declined to examine the conclusion of the secretary that DDT did not present an "imminent hazard," which would warrant summary suspension—this was a fact question left to the determination of the agency. However, the issue raised by EDF concerning whether the standard of proof used by the secretary conflicted with legislative intent in the applicable statute was a legal question appropriate for judicial determination. In this way, the court avoided making policy as to whether DDT should or should not be banned and restricted the scope of review to whether the agency acted properly within the statute.

RULEMAKING

The major innovation made by the APA was §553, "Rule Making." With acceptance of Congress' authority to delegate its legislative powers, a standard was needed to ensure that those powers were exercised with procedural fairness. Rulemaking is simply the name applied to the agency's legislative function. In some cases, Congress specifically charges an agency with rulemaking authority; sometimes Congress is silent, but rulemaking authority is implied from the agency's statutory mission; and occasionally Congress denies an agency rulemaking authority (the Federal Trade Commission, for example, is an investigatory rather than a regulatory agency).

When an agency engages in rulemaking, it must follow the procedure of the APA, or the rule is invalid and unenforceable. The steps required by the APA are simple:

§ 553. Rule Making

(b) General notice of proposed rule making shall be published in the Federal Register, unless persons subject thereto are named and either personally served or otherwise have actual notice thereof in accordance with law. The notice shall include—
  (1) A statement of the time, place, and nature of public rule making proceedings;
  (2) reference to the legal authority under which the rule is proposed; and
  (3) either the terms or substance of the proposed rule or a description of the subjects and issues involved.
    . . . .

(c) After notice required by this section, the agency shall give interested persons an opportunity to participate in the rule making through submission of written data, views, or arguments with or without opportunity for oral presentation. After consideration of the relevant matter presented, the agency shall incorporate in the rules adopted a concise general statement of their basis and purpose. . . .

(d) The required publication or service of a substantive rule shall be made not less than 30 days before its effective date [with exceptions].

Although §553 presents some burden to the agencies, the steps are not cumbersome. Basically it requires public notice of proposed rules and an opportunity for public input. Legally there is nothing to prevent an agency from making rules despite major opposition as long as it follows the procedure. The innovation of §553 is in requiring that the process be public and provide for public participation. The weaknesses and unpopularity of a proposed rule may be brought into the open. An agency cannot long defy the public interest without a response from Congress and the president, who ultimately control the power that the agency exercises.

Section 553 has some significant exceptions. Internal housekeeping rules, those concerning personnel and internal management, are not covered by it. So-called "interpretative rules" need not go through §553 procedure. In a loose sense, interpretative rules are those that carry out the meaning of a statute, interpreting it rather than adding to it. The distinction between interpretative and legislative or substantive rules is far from clear—a technical question that several cases have confused rather than clarified. The question seems purely academic until an agency attempts to make an interpretative rule without going through §553 procedure, only to find a complaining party asserting that the rule is substantive and therefore invalid for lack of proper procedure. If the Court agrees with the complaining party and concludes that the rule is substantive (legislative), the failure to follow §553 procedure makes the rule invalid.

When Congress specifically authorizes an agency to make rules under §553, those rules are said to have the "binding force of law," meaning that the courts will accord them the same respect as if the rules had been passed by Congress. Interpretative rules do not enjoy this stature, though as a practical matter they will ordinarily be enforced by the courts.

THE RIGHT TO BE HEARD

Section 553 leaves to the agency the authority to allow oral presentation and argument and its scope, and some rules call for more than the opportunity for written submission of argument. Some questions are better left to an adjudicatory process by the agency.

As discussed in earlier chapters, legislation and adjudication are different processes appropriate to different situations. In the administrative field, two cases arising in Colorado have been used repeatedly as examples of this distinction. In *Bi-Metallic Investment Co. v. State Board of Equalization,* 239 U.S. 441 (1915) the state had increased the valuation of all real estate in Denver by forty percent. The court denied a suit for an injunction by the company, holding that no hearing was necessary. The court distinguished the earlier case of *Londoner v. Denver,* 210 U.S. 373 (1908), in which it had required a hearing ("by argument however brief, and, if need be, by proof, however informal") on the assessment of plaintiff's land for the cost of paving a street. The distinction was made on the difference between policy that treated the entire community equally (*Bi-Metallic*) and a decision in which a few persons were affected individually (*Londoner*). In other words, the decision to set valuations in general is a legislative question, while assessing costs individually and differentially is an adjudicative question since the individual may have special reasons why the assessment is unfair. Highly particularized disputes of this sort call for a hearing.

What Kind of a Hearing?

The right to a hearing in administrative law does not necessarily mean an "on-the-record," trial-type or "evidentiary" hearing. Such events present a significant burden to an agency, which may devote significant resources and time when the full complement of rights and procedures must be respected. The extent of a person's rights in a hearing run the gamut of extremely informal meetings to hearings that are virtually indistinguishable from a trial. The extremes are represented by *Goss v. Lopez,* 419 U.S. 565 (1975), and *Goldberg v. Kelly,* 397 U.S. 254 (1970). *Goss* involved the ten-day suspensions of high school students. The U.S. Supreme Court held that they were entitled to a hearing, but the rights of the students were limited to (1) notice of the charges against them; (2) explanation of the evidence against them; and (3) the opportunity to present their side of the facts. By contrast, *Goldberg* concerned the right of a welfare recipient to a hearing prior to termination of benefits. The court held she was entitled to a hearing before termination, including the following rights in connection with the hearing:

1. Notice with reasons for the termination
2. Confrontation of witnesses against her
3. Oral argument
4. Cross-examination of adverse witnesses
5. Disclosure of evidence for the other side
6. Representation by an attorney
7. Determination on the record
8. Statement of reasons relied on for decision
9. Impartial decision maker

Practically speaking, this is a catalog of the rights ordinarily enjoyed in a civil trial.

Administrative Hearings

Most agencies provide procedural steps within the agency for processing grievances and complaints. Judicial review is premised on "final agency action," which requires some authoritative determination of rights; the APA allows the agencies to require that a claimant exhaust some or all of these steps prior to seeking judicial review. Prior to the APA, claimants were required to exhaust all administrative remedies before judicial review, and many states still require this.

Agencies are hierarchical bureaucracies and typically provide aggrieved parties the opportunity to pursue review of determinations from lower levels all the way to the top of the bureaucratic pyramid. Someone once counted thirty-three steps in the social security system that would have to be completed in order to fully exhaust the administrative remedies available. It is unrealistic to think that the reviewing court would reverse a consistent determination through all these steps except on the grounds that the procedure itself was constitutionally defective.

Hearings at the highest level are held by hearing officers called *administrative law judges,* who are employed by the government to hold recorded hearings, and make findings of fact, and recommend action to the highest level of the agency. In most instances, the agency will follow the recommendations of the administrative law judge.

CASE NO. 14–1 Exhaustion of Administrative Remedies

The doctrine of "exhaustion of administrative remedies" is based on the rationale that judicial review of agency action is principally appellate review of findings and conclusions of the agency. The reluctance of the courts to act as trial courts for agency disputes is rationalized with the argument that the agency is better suited to find the facts in a case within its expertise than are judges. The doctrine also encourages an orderly process within the agency and discourages a multiplicity of suits in court by disgruntled citizens.

Despite the policy reasons for the doctrine, the exhaustion of administrative remedies often inflicts a serious burden on aggrieved parties, and there is always the danger that the agency will decide on a partial basis in its own favor. The agency may also design its remedies in such a way as to unfairly impede resolution of a just complaint. As a result, the courts must examine agency procedure and refuse to require exhaustion if it appears to deny aggrieved parties due process of law. The Administrative Procedure Act has severely curtailed the exhaustion doctrine in federal agencies.

The following case is a good example of the balance the courts attempt to make between the legal rights of citizens and the need for government to conduct its business without unreasonable interference of litigation.

BOWEN v. CITY OF NEW YORK
476 U.S. 467 (1986)
United States Supreme Court

Justice POWELL delivered the opinion for the unanimous Court.

. . . .

On February 8, 1983, respondents, the City of New York, the New York City Health and Hospitals Corporation, and two state officials, suing on their own behalf and as *parens patriae,* together with eight named individuals, brought this class action against the Secretary and the Commissioner of S[ocial S[ecurity] A[dministration]. They sought relief on behalf of all individuals residing in the State who had applied for or received SSD or SSI benefits on or after April 1, 1980, who had been found by petitioners to have a severe mental impairment, and whose applications for benefits either had been or were to be denied, or whose benefits had been or were to be terminated, based on petitioners' determination that the claimants were capable of substantial gainful employment.

. . . .

Petitioners also contend that the District Court erred in including in the class those members who failed to obtain a "final decision" from the Secretary as required by §405(g). To obtain a final decision from the Secretary a claimant is required to exhaust his administrative remedies by proceeding through all three stages of the administrative appeals process. Only a claimant who proceeds through all three stages receives a final decision from the Secretary. At the outset, we note that by the time this lawsuit was filed, it was too late for a large number of class members to exhaust their claims, since expiration of the 60-day time limits for administrative appeals barred further access to the administrative appeals process. . . . Since "[m]embers of the class could not attack a policy they could not be aware existed," it would be unfair to penalize these claimants for not exhausting [their remedies] under these circumstances.

At the time the suit was filed, however, some claimants may still have had time to exhaust their administrative remedies. The question remains whether it was permissible to include these claimants in the class. . . .

Finally, application of the exhaustion doctrine is "intensely practical." Eldridge, 424 U.S., at 331, n. 11. In *Salfi*, we explained:

> Exhaustion is generally required as a matter of preventing premature interference with agency processes, so that the agency may function efficiently and so that it may have an opportunity to correct its own errors, to afford the parties and the courts the benefit of its experience and expertise, and to compile a record which is adequate for judicial review. 422 U.S., at 765.

The ultimate decision of whether to waive exhaustion should not be made solely by mechanical application of the Eldridge factors, but should also be guided by the policies underlying the exhaustion requirement. The purposes of exhaustion would not be served by requiring these class members to exhaust administrative remedies. This case is materially distinguishable from one in which a claimant sues in district court, alleging mere deviation from the applicable regulations in his particular administrative proceeding. In the normal course, such individual errors are fully correctable upon subsequent administrative review since the claimant on appeal will alert the agency to the alleged deviation. Because of the agency's expertise in administering its own regulations, the agency ordinarily should be given the opportunity to review application of those regulations to a particular factual context. Thus, our holding today does not suggest that exhaustion is to be excused whenever a claimant alleges an irregularity in the agency proceedings.

These claimants stand on a different footing from one arguing merely that an agency incorrectly applied its regulation. Rather, the District Court found a systemwide, unrevealed policy that was inconsistent in critically important ways with established regulations. Nor did this policy depend on the particular facts of the case before it; rather, the policy was illegal precisely because it ignored those facts. The District court found that the policy was being adhered to by state agencies due to pressure from SSA, and that therefore exhaustion would have been futile. Under these unique circumstances, there was nothing to be gained from permitting the compilation of a detailed factual record, or from agency expertise.

. . . [T]he Secretary had the capability and the duty to prevent the illegal policy found to exist by the District Court. The claimants here were denied the fair and neutral procedure required by the statute and regulations, and they are now entitled to pursue that procedure. The judgment of the Court of Appeals is affirmed.

It is so ordered.

LIABILITY OF GOVERNMENT AND ITS OFFICERS

Recent decades have seen a major change in liability for agency action. When sovereign immunity was in its heyday, the only remedy for a person injured by official action was a suit against the public employee who caused the injury. Even at that, the Court developed a doctrine of official immunity for injuries caused by "discretionary" acts within the scope of the employee's duties. Policy makers and planners were thus immunized for most of their acts.

The death knell of sovereign immunity for tort suits came with the enactment of the Federal Tort Claims Act (FTCA) in 1947. The FTCA continued the judicial doctrine of discretionary immunity and exempted a number of intentional torts but held the federal government "liable, respecting the provisions of this title relating to tort claims, in the same manner and to the same extent as a private individual under like circumstances." This formally enacted a judicial doctrine that had developed to disallow governmental immunity where the activities were the same as those performed by private enterprise, the so-called "governmental-proprietary function test." The states gradually followed suit, though they did so with a variety of statutes, many of which retained varying degrees of immunity.

With the availability of suits against the government, the courts became more protective of government officers. Not only was the discretionary immunity expanded, but a form of "qualified immunity" was invented that immunized from suit officers acting in good faith and reasonable belief that their actions were proper. This was a logical result of the dilemma in which public officers, especially police, found themselves when acting under statutory authority, only to find the court holding the statute unconstitutional. For example, a police officer makes an arrest under a state statute, but the statute is found by the court to be unconstitutional, so the arrest was illegal and the officer subject to suit for false arrest and false imprisonment. If the standards of the doctrine are met, the officer enjoys qualified (as distinguished from "absolute") immunity.

42 U.S.C. §1983

In order to protect former slaves from abuse at the hands of white authorities following the Civil War, Congress passed the Civil Rights Act of 1871, from which 42 U.S.C. §1983 reads:

> Every person who, under color of any statute, ordinance, regulation, custom, or usage, of any State or Territory, subjects, or causes to be subjected, any citizen of the United States or other person within the jurisdiction thereof to the deprivation of any rights, privileges, or immunities secured by the Constitution and laws, shall be liable to the party injured in an action at law, suit in equity, or other proper proceeding for redress.

The broad provisions of this act were rarely used until 1961 when a suit brought against Chicago police officers and the City of Chicago was successful (*Monroe v. Pape*, 365 U.S. 167). *Monroe* held, however, that the city was not a "person" under the act and could not be sued; but in 1978 the U.S. Supreme Court overruled *Monroe* and allowed a suit against the City of New York in *Monell v. Department of Social Services of City of New York*, 436 U.S. 658. Since *Monell*, §1983 suits have proliferated and are a constant concern of local governments, especially for the conduct of their police; a §1983 suit was even brought against the governor of Ohio over the National Guard shootings of Kent State University students during antiwar demonstrations in 1970. The U.S. Supreme Court held that the governor had qualified immunity. The broad scope of the language of §1983 and its expanding application have made it a frequent basis for litigation.

CASE NO. 14–2 *Judicial Immunity*

Although the scope of 42 U.S.C. §1983 has been greatly expanded with regard to suing state and local governments, suits against government officials have confronted an increasing recognition of absolute and qualified immunities. The courts have been steadfast in upholding absolute immunity of judges acting in their judicial capacity. *Stump v. Sparkman* expresses the most extreme applica-tion of judicial immunity. The mother of a "somewhat retarded" daughter petitioned Judge Stump of an Indiana Circuit Court for an order permitting the daughter to be sterilized. Judge Stump met with the mother in chambers and wrote and signed the order. The sterilization procedure was performed, the daughter being told that her appendix was being removed. When the daughter married two years later, she soon discovered what had happened. She sued Judge Stump under §1983. The U.S. District Court held the judge enjoyed immunity from suit, but the Court of Appeals reversed and the case reached the U.S. Supreme Court on certiorari.

STUMP
v.
SPARKMAN

U.S. Supreme Court
435 U.S. 349 (1978)

Mr. Justice WHITE delivered the opinion of the Court. . . .

The governing principle of law is well established and is not questioned by the parties. As early as 1872, the Court recognized that it was "a general principle of the highest importance to the proper administration of justice that a judicial officer, in exercising the authority vested in him, [should] be free to act upon his own convictions, without apprehension of personal consequences to himself." *Bradley v. Fisher*, [13 Wall. 335], at 347. For that reason the Court held that "judges of courts of superior or general jurisdiction are not liable to civil actions for their judicial acts, even when such acts are in excess of their jurisdiction, and are alleged to have been done maliciously or corruptly." 13 Wall., at 351. Later we held that this doctrine of judicial immunity was applicable in suits under §1 of the Civil Rights Act of 1871, 42 U.S.C.A. §1983, for the legislative record gave no indication that Congress intended to abolish this long-established principle. *Pierson v. Ray*, 386 U.S. 547, 87 S.Ct. 1213, 18 L.Ed.2d 288 (1967).

. . . .

Perhaps realizing the broad scope of Judge Stump's jurisdiction, the Court

of Appeals stated that, even if the action taken by him was not foreclosed under the Indiana statutory scheme, it would still be "an illegitimate exercise of his common law power because of his failure to comply with elementary principles of procedural due process." 552 F.2d at 176. This misconceives the doctrine of judicial immunity. A judge is absolutely immune from liability for his judicial acts even if his exercise of authority is flawed by the commission of grave procedural errors. . . .

. . . Disagreement with the action taken by the judge, however, does not justify depriving that judge of his immunity. Despite the unfairness to litigants that sometimes results, the doctrine of judicial immunity is thought to be in the best interests of "the proper administration of justice . . . [, for it allows] a judicial officer, in exercising the authority vested in him [to] be free to act upon his own convictions, without apprehension of personal consequences to himself." *Bradley v. Fisher*, 13 Wall., at 347. The fact that the issue before the judge is a controversial one is all the more reason that he should be able to act without fear of suit. . . .

Mr. Justice STEWART, with whom Mr. Justice MARSHALL and Mr. Justice POWELL join, dissenting.

It is established federal law that judges of general jurisdiction are absolutely immune from monetary liability "for judicial acts, even when such acts are in excess of their jurisdiction, and are alleged to have been done maliciously or corruptly." *Bradley v. Fisher*, 13 Wall. 335, 351, 20 L.Ed. 646. It is also established that this immunity is in no way diminished in a proceeding under 42 U.S.C.A. §1983. *Pierson v. Ray*, 386 U.S. 547, 87 S.Ct. 1213, 18 L.Ed.2d 288. But the scope of judicial immunity is limited to liability for "judicial acts," and I think that what Judge Stump did on July 9, 1971, was beyond the pale of anything that could sensibly be called a judicial act.

. . . .

When the Court says that what Judge Stump did was an act "normally performed by a judge," it is not clear to me whether the Court means that a judge "normally" is asked to approve a mother's decision to have her child given surgical treatment generally, or that a judge "normally" is asked to approve a mother's wish to have her daughter sterilized. But whichever way the Court's statement is to be taken, it is factually inaccurate. In Indiana, as elsewhere in our country, a parent is authorized to arrange for and consent to medical and surgical treatment of his minor child. Ind.Code §16–8–4–2 (1973). And when a parent decides to call a physician to care for his sick child or arranges to have a surgeon remove his child's tonsils, he does not, "normally" or otherwise, need to seek the approval of a judge. On the other hand, Indiana did in 1971 have statutory procedures for the sterilization of certain people who were

institutionalized. But these statutes provided for *administrative proceedings* before a board established by the superintendent of each public hospital. Only if after notice and an evidentiary hearing, an order of sterilization was entered in these proceedings could there be review in a circuit court. See Ind.Code §§16–13–13–1 through 16–13–13–4 (1973).

. . . .

Mr. Justice POWELL, dissenting.

While I join the opinion of Mr. Justice STEWART, I wish to emphasize what I take to be the central feature of this case—petitioner's preclusion of any possibility for the vindication of respondent's rights elsewhere in the judicial system.

. . . .

But where a judicial officer acts in a manner that precludes all resort to appellate or other judicial remedies that otherwise would be available, the underlying assumption of the *Bradley* doctrine is inoperative. . . . The complete absence of normal judicial process foreclosed resort to any of the "numerous remedies" that "the law has provided for private parties."

. . . .

CASE QUESTIONS

1. Was Judge Stump's order a "judicial act"?
2. Judicial immunity was again tested in the U.S. Supreme Court in 1988 in *Forrester v. White*, 108 S.Ct. 538, where a female probation officer was fired by Judge White, who was responsible for hiring and firing probation officers. Ms. Forrester sued under §1983 on the grounds that she had been discriminated against because of her sex. Writing the opinion of the Court, Justice O'Connor applied the "judicial function" test that asserts absolute immunity for a judge's actions while exercising a judicial function. Justice O'Connor concluded that Judge White's authority over personnel was an administrative function separate from his judicial function, rendering him amenable to suit for improper actions in his administrative function, and the suit was allowed to proceed. Can you reconcile *Forrester* with *Stump*?

SUMMARY

Administrative law covers the rules relating to legal action taken against the administrative agencies of the government. While each agency has its own substantive rules and regulations, procedural law has evolved, and is still evolving, first from the Constitution and more recently from the enactment of federal and state administrative procedure legislation.

The last one hundred years have witnessed reversals in the major areas of administrative law. In the nineteenth century sovereign immunity was doctrine throughout the United States—officers could be sued but not the government. It was presumed that Congress could not delegate its legislative authority to other government agencies. There was a presumption of nonreviewability of administrative action by the courts. All of these doctrines have met their demise in the twentieth century. Rather than challenging legislative delegation, the courts have concentrated on the question of whether the agencies adhere to legislative intent. Rather than refusing to review, the courts have limited the scope of review along lines similar to appellate review. With the erosion of sovereign immunity, the courts have expanded the liability of government and narrowed the liability of public officers.

The enactment of the Administrative Procedure Act in 1946 put administrative law on a firm footing. The major innovation of the APA was its provisions for rulemaking, requiring public notice and the opportunity for public input prior to the promulgation of agency rules.

Administrative law was forced to change as government changed from performing relatively few services into an immense bureaucracy regulating every aspect of our daily lives. Administrative law changed to hold government more accountable to the public.

CHAPTER QUESTIONS

1. What determines whether an agency of government is an independent regulatory agency?
2. Why do courses on administrative law concentrate almost exclusively on administrative procedure?
3. What is the legal source for federal rulemaking?
4. Where may the substantive rules of federal administrative agencies be found?
5. Why are public utilities subject to regulatory agencies?

6. What special role can the paralegal play in administrative law that is not available in private law cases?
7. Where does the "presumption of reviewability" come from?
8. What is meant by "judicial review" in administrative law?
9. When is oral argument available in §553 rulemaking?
10. Can a person sue a city under 42 U.S.C. §1983?

EXERCISES

1. Does your state have a comprehensive statute for administrative procedure? How do its rulemaking provisions compare to Chapter VII of the federal Administrative Procedure Act?
2. Locate the rules and regulations of a state or federal agency and determine the steps necessary to exhaust its administrative remedies.

PROFESSIONAL PROFILE

"I suppose my career as an editor is indicative that paralegal experience is a good springboard to other exciting opportunities," Whitney says. For five years he worked as a law clerk at bankruptcy and family law firms. Whitney was also the law office administrator in charge of complete case management and staff. "One year we filed over 100

Jay Whitney
Paralegal Textbook Editor

decrees of divorce aside from all the ancillary proceedings (custody and support matters) that arose from those actions." One of his duties included accompanying a client, with a court order and the police in tow, as she reclaimed her children from an estranged spouse. The husband had simply refused to return their children following his regular weekend visitation.

"The best part of the job was helping people who were truly appreciative of my efforts, while the worst part was serving someone with a summons," Whitney says. "But, as distasteful as that may have been, I think it makes one somewhat fearless and willing to take on nearly anything without hesitation."

Whitney joined a major legal publisher at Albany, New York, in 1984. He was a legal products specialist in marketing before moving to Delmar/Lawyers Cooperative Publishing as the paralegal editor. "I think I am the only textbook editor who was a paralegal in a law firm—researching the law, drafting pleadings, communicating with clients, and running the office." He believes that experience allows him the unique perspective to guide authors as they write their manuscripts, including the content, features, and pedagogy so important to paralegal students' understanding of the law.

Married to an attorney who teaches paralegal classes, Whitney is the father of two young daughters. The family lives in Niskayuna, New York. He attended DePauw University and Western New England College.

CHAPTER 15
Law in the Age of Computers

Predicting the future is a hazardous occupation at best, but when dealing with computer applications, clairvoyance is particularly difficult to come by. Nevertheless, any person preparing to become a paralegal must look into the future. Much of the paralegal's work is decidedly technical, and technicians who do not prepare themselves for changes in technology can become as obsolete as the machines that are sent to the junkpile each year. Paralegal employment in the near future will unquestionably increase at a startling rate, but the number of paralegal training programs has already multiplied significantly. There will be many opportunities, but the competition will be stiff. In this context, those with the most credentials will take the lead. It behooves the paralegal-in-training to keep abreast of developments in the field and in office technology.

FUTURE TRENDS FOR PARALEGALS

In her recent book, *Paralegal,* Barbara Bernardo predicts ten future trends in the paralegal field. Several of these warrant discussion:

1. "Greater emphasis will be placed on education." The paralegal field appears headed inevitably toward recognition as a profession, and professional status inevitably requires educational credentials. This is supported by the fact that lawyers have both a bachelor's degree and a law degree and the fact that legal problems reflect the full diversity of our complex society. Paralegals will be expected to be more than technicians; they will be educated professionals.

2. "More sophisticated and substantive legal work will be performed by paralegals." Anyone who has been in the legal field over the past two decades cannot help but have noticed a radical change in lawyers' attitudes toward paralegals. Twenty years ago, most lawyers doubted that a person without law school training could adequately conduct legal research or draft legal documents. Tens of thousands of paralegals have convinced them otherwise. Many lawyers now see paralegals as essential members of the legal team who perform most of the same tasks as lawyers—and perform them just as well. As legal specialization increases, paralegal specialization increases; the result is that paralegals become virtually indispensable. Imagine an attorney specializing in workers' compensation with a paralegal who has assisted for five years and understands every facet of the specialization, as well as the attorney's work routine and strategies. Losing that paralegal is like a death in the family. This increased dependence on paralegals will result not only in increased status for the paralegal, but increased compensation as well.

3. "Recognition of the paralegal profession by the general public will continue to increase." Twenty years ago, very few people, even some lawyers, were familiar with the term paralegal. This has changed dramatically; paralegal is a commonly considered career choice for those seeking careers and is known to every career counselor. Tens of thousands of legal clients have dealt directly with paralegals and have gained respect for them. Some businesses have begun to question high legal fees with, "Couldn't this have been done by a paralegal?"

4. "New career alternatives." In business and government, a great many tasks call for an understanding of the law. In many cases hiring a paralegal is cost-effective, where hiring an attorney would not be feasible. Those with paralegal

training are employed as insurance adjustors, real estate appraisers, bank trust department employees, office managers, etc. As the field becomes more appreciated, employers of all sorts will come to consider paralegals as valuable alternatives to those with more general education.

5. "More paralegals will start their own businesses." The California movement toward permitting or licensing independent paralegals has spread to all regions of the country. Given the Bar's stated mission of providing legal services to all sectors of the society, the inevitable conclusion is that some services can be provided economically only by paralegals who can charge less and keep overhead down. Rosemary Furman proved that a variety of legal services can be provided at minimal cost to clients; perhaps she was simply ahead of her time—the problems her activities raised could have been minimized by licensing and regulation. As far as paralegals are concerned, unauthorized practice of law is currently being redefined.

THE NEW TECHNOLOGY OF THE LAW OFFICE

Since lawyers excel in the art of verbal dialogue, persuasion, and negotiation, it is not surprising that this profession was slow to acquire the new technology that has proliferated in science and business. Today the law office staff must be computer literate. How much knowledge is needed is difficult to say. Presumably one can never know enough about computers and technology, but the investment in time can be enormous. The discussion that follows is not designed to teach computer literacy—this is gained both through formal training and self-motivated extracurricular effort. Rather, the following pages are intended to describe where we are and where we are headed.

Why Use Computers?

In the next edition of this book, the question that heads this section will be obsolete; computers will be as essential to the law office as electricity. Computers have certain features that make them extremely useful in legal work:

1. Computers can store vast amounts of data and information in a very small space and can access that information very

quickly. Something as simple as retrieving a file can be done with a few keystrokes instead of searching a file cabinet. While this may mean five seconds as opposed to a minute, when multiplied over and over again, the savings in time and convenience becomes very great.

2. Computers can conduct searches with lightning speed. Two dramatic examples of this are *Westlaw* and *Lexis,* two legal databases that contain all the reported appellate decisions of American courts as well as the federal district court opinions. In an actual search, in less than two minutes *Westlaw* searched every state and federal case for the terms "homosexual marriage" and "same-sex marriage." The speed was partially due to the extreme rarity of cases—there were only three—but such a search conducted manually would take hours for even the most adept researcher. Intraoffice files can be searched with comparable time savings.

3. Computers eliminate many human errors. With unusual exceptions, computers do not make mistakes, though the human beings who program them and the users who enter information and data on them can make mistakes. More and more, computers are being programmed to anticipate human error in data entry. A simple example is spell checking—some programs will check the spelling of each word as it is typed. There are also programs to check whether the legal citations in a document are in the correct form. Ultimately computer software will check to see if a named case and the citation that follows it are correct, i.e., a case dictionary that includes the correct citation for the case.

4. Computers as word processors are now indispensable in the law office. Long-time practitioners can remember when letters and documents were constantly retyped because of typographical errors or a need to change a phrase or a sentence on rereading. Editing a document is now child's play by comparison. Word processing software now has so many features that few users are even aware of all the things that can be done. Indexing and outlining can be done with speed and accuracy.

5. Standard forms have taken on a new meaning with computers and word processors. Lawyers have always relied on forms for drafting simple documents, but now the forms can be put on computer. In some instances drafting can be accomplished simply by filling in the blanks. In other cases, for example drafting a will, programs have been devised in which the attorney or paralegal may simply run through a set of questions and enter information into the computer, which can then print out a will. The will can be printed immediately,

even relatively complex wills if the will-drafting program is truly sophisticated. When the program is error-free, the result is error-free, eliminating major and minor mistakes that might inadvertently occur otherwise.

6. Computers are at their best when dealing with numbers. For example, there are numerous tax programs that are error-free if the correct numbers are entered; figures can be changed, and the entire tax form will be recalculated.

7. Computers are orderly, and they force the workers in the law office to be orderly. Recordkeeping becomes a simple and mechanical process. Billing programs abound and have made a traditionally sloppy process an orderly one, which has made firms more profitable. A positive side-effect has been to protect attorneys from accusations of excessive charges. For instance, a large firm can install a program that mechanically times telephone calls and records them in a client's file, thus providing an unassailable record for billing purposes.

8. Computers are indispensable in support of complex litigation, which collects massive documentation that may be indexed, filed, tracked, and accessed with an efficiency that was unthinkable a few years ago. Computers are not only faster and more efficient than manual filing systems, they have retrieval capacities not possible with manual filing. For example, the computer can quickly find every document in a file that contains the name of a witness or a business entity; it can order any set of documents chronologically, alphabetically, or numerically.

COMING EVENTS IN LAW OFFICE AUTOMATION

The law office library as it presently exists will soon disappear. Those venerable rows of the reporter series will be replaced by compact disks, which can store enormous amounts of text in a very small space. The compact disks can be read by the computer so that the law library becomes part of the working files of the law office.

When technology improves and the price plummets, optical character readers (OCRs) will be universally used. These permit text in written form (hardcopy) to be scanned and entered into the computer files for retrieval or editing without the need to type in text. Preparation of reports, legal memoranda, and trial and appellate briefs will be accomplished with unimaginable speed and enhanced accuracy.

The combination of computer and telecommunications will revolutionize many aspects of practice. Computers can exchange data and information with each other; fax machines may become a relic of the past. It is conceivable that court reporters may simply monitor a device that translates the spoken word into print that can be sent by telephone to the firm's computer. A copy of a deposition or a trial could be available within hours of its completion.

SPECIALIZATION

Recent decades have witnessed increasing specialization among lawyers, and there is no end to this trend in sight. The largest law firms have doubled and tripled in size and even created branches in different cities. This enables lawyers to specialize in very restricted fields where the market provides a sufficient number of clients. Where in the past a lawyer might simply have specialized in property law, there are now lawyers who specialize in government defense contracts, commercial leases, and condominiums. Even smaller firms may develop narrow specialties once they have developed a client base and may form informal referral arrangements with other firms that have different specialties. The advantage of narrow specialization is that an attorney may acquire a nearly total grasp of the field, keeping abreast of each new case and every statutory revision.

Paralegals have tended to be even more specialized than lawyers. In a small firm, a single paralegal may serve a few lawyers, but in larger firms, paralegals specialize in restricted fields and in restricted tasks. A paralegal may be assigned exclusively to real estate closings or deposition analysis if the volume of work warrants. From a business standpoint, this specialization is very effective since it encourages efficiency, accuracy, and speed. Paralegals are better able to concentrate on one task at a time than lawyers, who must frequently interrupt their work to respond to client requests.

Unless there is a continuing local market for a particular specialization, it is difficult for paralegal training programs to offer significant specialized training. Law firms often train their paralegals to perform specialized tasks, but some will actively recruit specialists when a vacancy occurs. It is difficult for the paralegal-in-training to prepare for an employment requiring specialization. Perhaps the best way to prepare for such a market is to be up-to-date with law office technology.

ALTERNATIVE DISPUTE RESOLUTION

Litigation is a costly and cumbersome process. Disputing parties are turning to more efficient forms of dispute resolution. In commercial cases, disputes often arise between parties who wish to resolve their differences without injury to their business relationship. Litigation tends to drive the parties apart because the process is adversarial and expensive. Two frequently used alternative means for resolving disputes are arbitration and mediation. Both of these suggest rich opportunities for paralegals in the future.

Arbitration

Arbitration has traditionally been linked to labor–management disputes, but it is fast becoming a commonly used method to settle commercial disputes. If the disputing parties agree, a third party or parties can be chosen to hear both sides and render a decision on the merits of the dispute. Many contracts provide for arbitration in lieu of litigation in case of a breach. The ground rules can minimize the costs commonly associated with discovery and delays in settlement. If the original contract does not provide for arbitration, parties may nevertheless agree once a dispute has arisen to settle the differences through arbitration. The American Arbitration Association is composed of retired judges who serve as arbitrators. The arbitration procedure may imitate a trial-type hearing, but a lesser degree of formality and technicality can make arbitration faster and cheaper than a trial. It is essential in arbitration that the parties waive their rights to trial by agreeing to be bound by the decision of the arbitrator. Occasionally nonbinding arbitration is employed; this is really a form of mediation, which will be discussed below. It is important to remember that private parties may agree to any mutual rights and duties that are lawful. Theoretically, disputing parties could agree to pick the first person they meet in the street to arbitrate their dispute. In this context, the opportunities for using paralegals are self-evident at all levels, but their use in minor disputes clearly would be cost-effective.

Mediation

Mediation is not binding on the parties; it has a very different design than arbitration. The function of a mediator is to assist disputants in working out their problems. The mediator does not take sides but works to minimize unproductive hostilities and to maximize means of cooperation. Mediation is nonadversarial. It has been used extensively in divorce and child custody problems, helping the parties to learn to cooperate to settle the terms of their break-up. Since it is not binding, it is not always successful, but the advantage of mediation in divorce cases is that it empowers the parties to take control of their lives. It may even establish a method for future cooperation that is essential if the parties must continue to deal with each other with regard to their children.

Mediation is appropriate in a multitude of other situations in which the goal is long-term cooperation despite the present dispute. Public institutions such as schools and school boards may avail themselves of mediation in order to open lines of communication with their constituents and avoid the adversarial role that litigation promotes. Mediation in commercial disputes can also be a much more comfortable procedure than the adversarial process.

Many states have encouraged mediation and have established mediation training programs. The various states differ on licensing or qualifying mediators. Many lawyers engage in mediation, and some have even forsaken the practice of law in favor of a career as a mediator. Psychologists and other mental health professionals have entered the mediation field as well. Neither the practice of law nor mental health training fits the mediation model precisely since the role of the mediator is neither to solve individual emotional problems nor to take sides in an adversarial role. The paralegal as mediator has not yet been recognized, but the paralegal would seem to be an obvious choice since the paralegal has or can easily acquire the knowledge of the law necessary for mediating a dispute. (In divorce mediation, for example, a marital settlement agreement cannot be attempted without some understanding of its tax consequences.) The paralegal, while working for an advocate, does not take on the role of advocate but is more likely to assume the role of liaison between client and attorney. It might well be that the ideal mediator would be a paralegal with counseling and mediation training.

LEGAL DATABASES

Discussion of legal technology would not be complete without mention of legal databases. Although there are a number of specialized databases, the most commonly used, broad-based databases are *Westlaw* and *Lexis*. There are some differences between these, which their marketers are only too happy to point out, but their primary use is similar. Every month, each adds some new materials, but the advantage of these databases is that cases and statutes are stored in very powerful systems that permit quick access to legal materials.

Aside from the time they save finding and searching through books, they have one major advantage over traditional library research: the computer can quickly scan huge numbers of cases for quite specific words and phrases. For example, suppose the researcher is involved in a case in which a defective ball-joint is the alleged cause of an auto accident. *Westlaw* or *Lexis* could collect reported decisions that include the word "ball-joint." Since ball-joint is not a legal term, it will not be found in any of the indexes for cases. When the researcher is looking for cases with factual similarities, such a tool is invaluable. A search can be further narrowed to finding "ball-joint" in the same sentence or paragraph with "Chevrolet" or "defective." These legal databases can quickly provide materials that would be difficult and time-consuming to find through traditional manual searches.

To put this in perspective, a note must be added about legal research, a subject otherwise left to other texts and courses. Much of legal research aims at building a legal argument based on decided cases bearing some resemblance to the present case. While legal arguments are based on legal, rather than factual, issues, the more similar a cited case is in its fact situation to the case at hand, the more compelling is the precedent. Legal materials are extensively cross-indexed so that often the first task of research is to find a pertinent case, then pursue the leads that case presents until a full complement of cases bearing on the issues is assembled. With unlimited time, anyone with a modicum of instruction can find all the pertinent cases; the problem is finding them with the least waste of time. The legal databases are unbeatable in this respect. At present the cost (per minute) of using these databases is fairly high, but for the researcher who knows how to use them efficiently, a two-minute search can easily save two hours in the law library, a considerable savings for the client.

SUMMARY

In the late 1980s employment estimates for the paralegal field placed it at the very top of occupations, and these projections did not even take account of the possibilities for new and expanding opportunities for paralegals. Paralegals will be employed in many areas not clearly foreseen. Legal specialization and expanding law office technology will require expansion of legal staff in directions only vaguely discernible at present. The prospects for paralegals appear more promising in number than those for lawyers. It is essential that a person preparing for the paralegal profession take notice of new developments in the practice of law and in the law office and be prepared for the many changes that will inevitably occur.

APPENDIX A

How to Read a Case

Reported judicial decisions have a style and format all their own. The following discussion is designed to acquaint readers with the form and the nature of judicial decisions. While judges have considerable freedom in how they write opinions, some uniformity of pattern comes from the similarity of purpose for decisions, especially decisions of appellate courts, which frequently serve as authority for later cases.

Similarity is also a product of custom. The influence of West Publishing Company, which publishes the regional reporter series as well as the federal reporters, has been great. Some of the material below repeats discussions in the first chapters of the book, but this appendix is designed to be read at almost any point during the book—the sooner, the better, since judicial decisions are interspersed throughout the text.

WHICH COURT?

Knowing which court issued the opinion is extremely important. As a general rule, the higher the court, the more compelling is its authority. The binding nature of precedent depends on the court from which it comes and the court using the opinion as authority. A decision of the Iowa Supreme Court has no precedential power over courts in Tennessee because each state has its own laws and legal system. Iowa courts may not dictate to Tennessee what Tennessee law is or should be. On the other hand, decisions of the Supreme Court of Tennessee, the highest court of that state, are binding precedent on other state courts in Tennessee—lower courts must follow the law as stated by a higher court in their jurisdiction.

Federal and State Courts

The United States has two parallel legal structures. Each state has its own set of laws and courts. In addition, the federal government has a separate legal authority through courts located in every state. Federal courts are not superior to state courts but parallel to them, having authority over different types of cases. For example, the U.S. Constitution restricts authority over patents and copyrights to the federal government. Thus, a patent case will be heard in federal court but not in a state court. On the other hand, there are both federal and state civil rights laws, so a particular case might be filed in one or the other. Where federal and state courts have concurrent jurisdiction of this sort, exercise of authority is governed by custom or law; but when state and federal law overlap and conflict, state law must yield to federal law.

Trial and Appellate Courts

State and federal courts are divided into trial and appellate courts. Most cases originate in trial courts, where evidence is presented, witnesses are questioned, and a judgment determining the rights of the parties is entered. If one of the parties to the case is dissatisfied with the result, the case may be appealed; an appellate court is petitioned to review the proceedings of the lower, or trial, court to determine if errors were made that would justify changing the outcome of the case.

The federal system provides a model followed in general terms by a majority of state systems. The U.S. District Court is the primary federal trial court. The next higher federal court is the United States Court of Appeals. It is an intermediate appellate court since it is subordinate to the highest court, the U.S. Supreme Court.

Most states name their highest court Supreme Court, New York being a notable exception, calling its highest court the Court of Appeals and using the designation Supreme Court for lower courts. Some states do not have intermediate appellate courts. There is also considerable variety in state trial courts and the names applied to them.

The careful researcher always takes note of the court issuing a decision because the higher the court, the greater the force of its decision. The decision of a court is binding on lower courts within its jurisdiction, meaning that the rules it lays down must be followed by lower courts when faced with the same issue.

FOR WHOM ARE JUDICIAL OPINIONS WRITTEN?

In evaluating any written material, the reader should assess the audience the writer is addressing and the writer's goals. Judges write decisions for two reasons. The first is to inform the parties to the dispute who won and who lost, giving the rules and reasoning the judge applied to the facts. The second is to inform the legal profession, attorneys and judges, of the rules applied to a given set of facts and the reasons for the decision.

Attorneys and Judges Read Judicial Opinions

Very few laypersons ever enter a law library to find and read cases. The people found in the county law library are usually lawyers, paralegals, and judges. Cases are rarely intended to be entertaining, and judges are not motivated to make their cases "reader-friendly." Their tasks are quite specific. Since any case may serve as precedent, or at least form a basis for subsequent legal arguments, judges are especially concerned with conveying a precise meaning by carefully framing the rules and providing the reasoning behind them. The higher the court, the greater this concern will be. Imagine writing an opinion for a highly skilled, highly intelligent readership that critically analyzes every word and phrase, an opinion that may well affect important right of citizens in the future.

Judicial writing is different from most other kinds of writing in that its goal is neither simply to pass on information nor persuade the reader of the author's point of view. Persuasion is past; the judge is stating the law, making a final judgment, but must do so with caution so that the statements are not misinterpreted or misused. An appreciation of the judge's dilemma is essential to critical evaluation of cases.

The Effect of Setting Precedent

The cost of litigation is great, and appeal of a decision incurs significant additional cost. It makes sense to appeal if the losing party legitimately concludes that the lower court was incorrect in its application of the law. It would be quite foolish to spend large sums of money to go to the higher court if the chances of winning were slim and the stakes were small. This means that the cases we read from appellate courts, and especially from the highest courts, generally involve questions that have strong arguments on both sides. The judges of these courts are faced with difficult decisions and must respect the reasonable arguments of both sides in deciding which side will prevail.

Clarity versus Confusion

Judicial writing is often difficult and obscure, but such criticism of judicial writing often neglects to recognize that not only are the issues difficult to present with clarity but also that often the importance of narrowing the application of the decision encourages a tortuous reasoning. For example, when faced with a landmark case of reverse discrimination (a white applicant for medical school was denied admission, while less-qualified minority students were admitted), the U.S. Supreme Court was expected to lay down a rule concerning the constitutionality of such admissions programs. Those expectations were disappointed. The justices wrote divergent opinions that made it very difficult to discover exactly what the rule was. At the time the issue was quite controversial, and the decision potentially could have affected efforts by the Administration and Congress to help the position of disadvantaged minorities. Any precedent of the court would have far-reaching consequences. Although the plaintiff won and subsequently entered medical school, there was some confusion as to why he won. The effect of the decision was to stifle future efforts to pursue reverse discrimination cases. Each justice of the court viewed the problem in a different light, and the result was a resolution of the dispute without a clear picture of the rule to be applied in such cases.

Thus, the reader of cases should be aware that the complex reasoning of a judge's writing is not always due to the complexity of the issues but may also be caused by the judge's desire to narrow the effect of the precedent.

Doing Justice to the Parties

It is a mistake to assume that judges are dispassionate, totally rational, and objective interpreters of the law. The notion that judges reason directly from the facts to the law in a rather automatic fashion neglects the obvious fact that judges are human beings doing their best to dispense justice. We must suspect that in any given case, the judge or judges form an opinion as to which side in the interest of fairness should win and then select rules and arguments to support that side.

Sometimes a strict application of the law will cause a very undesirable result. The Kentucky Court of Appeals was faced with such circumstances in *Strunk v. Strunk,* 445 S.W.2d 145, in which a man was dying of a kidney problem and his brother was the only appropriate donor for a life-saving kidney transplant. The problem was that the brother with the healthy kidneys was severely mentally retarded and therefore legally incompetent to consent to the operation. The issue facing the court was whether the mother of the two brothers could consent to the operation, acting as the guardian of the retarded brother. Kentucky precedents (cited by the dissenting judges, but ignored by the majority) seemed to show clearly that a guardian's authority did not extend to making such a decision. Faced with a heart-rending life-or-death decision, four of seven judges deciding the case ignored prior precedents. Three of the judges disagreed, and one wrote a vigorous dissenting opinion. The reasoning of the majority opinion was weak, but it is difficult to fault the judges in light of the circumstances.

THE FORMAT FOR A REPORTED DECISION

The cases found in the reporters generally follow a uniform format with which researchers must become familiar. The first part of the case has no official authority. Authoritative statements begin with the actual text of the opinion.

Format Preceding the Opinion

West Publishing Company publishes the reporter series and has established a quite uniform format. To illustrate this format, the first page of *United States v. National Lead Co.,* 438 F.2d 935 (8th Cir. 1971) (Figure A-1) provides all the elements necessary.

The Citation

The heading of the page indicates the citation **"UNITED STATES v. NATIONAL LEAD COMPANY"** and "Cite as 438 F.2d 935 (1971)." This is the name of the case and where it can be found, namely, on page 935 in Volume 438 of the Federal Reporter, Second Series. Note that this differs from the official citation, *United States v. National Lead Co.,* 438 F.2d 935 (8th Cir. 1971), that would be used in legal texts and opinions. The official citation indicates that the case was decided by the U.S. Court of Appeals for the Eighth Circuit.

UNITED STATES v. NATIONAL LEAD COMPANY
Cite as 438 F.2d 935 (1971)

**UNITED STATES of America,
Plaintiff-Appellant,**

v.

NATIONAL LEAD COMPANY, a Corporation, and Chemical Workers' Basic Union Local 1744, AFL-CIO, Defendants-Appellees.

No. 20427.

United States Court of Appeals,
Eighth Circuit.

Feb. 26, 1971.

Action by government against company and union for alleged violations of Civil Rights Act of 1964. The United States District Court for the Eastern District of Missouri, Roy W. Harper, Senior District Judge, 315 F.Supp. 912, denied government's motion for preliminary injunction, and government appealed. The Court of Appeals, Bright, Circuit Judge, held that although, under facts, some of vestiges of employer's past discrimination seemed preserved in employer's transfer and promotion procedures, in view of fact that actual impact of this discrimination upon black employees possessing seniority dating back prior to end of discrimination was unclear, and in view of fact that an appropriate solution was not readily apparent from partial development of facts, denial of relief by way of a preliminary injunction was not error.

Affirmed and remanded.

1. Civil Rights   3

Employment policies which appear racially neutral but build upon bias that existed prior to enactment of 1964 Civil Rights Act to produce present discrimination are actionable. Civil Rights Act of 1964, § 701 et seq., 42 U.S.C.A. § 2000e et seq.

2. Civil Rights   3

Policy of 1964 Civil Rights Act is not fulfilled by a showing that black employees may enjoy substantially equal pay with others in similar capacities; the test is whether all employees possess an equal opportunity to fully enjoy all employment rights. Civil Rights Act of 1964, §§ 703(h), 706(g), 42 U.S.C.A. §§ 2000e–2(h), 2000e–5(g).

3. Injunction   137(4)

Although, under facts, some of vestiges of employer's past discrimination seemed preserved in employer's transfer and promotion procedures, in view of fact that actual impact of this discrimination upon black employees possessing seniority dating back prior to end of discrimination was unclear, and in view of fact that an appropriate solution was not readily apparent from partial development of facts, denial of relief by way of a preliminary injunction was not error. Civil Rights Act of 1964, §§ 701 et seq., 707(a) 42 U.S.C.A. §§ 2000e et seq., 2000e–6(a).

4. Injunction   147

In view of evidence disclosing that in recent years blacks had filled three of six vacancies for guard positions and that employer planned no immediate expansion of present guard force or filling of any existing vacancies, no need for preliminary injunction was shown with respect to guard force. Civil Rights Act of 1964, §§ 701 et seq., 707(a), 42 U.S.C.A. §§ 2000e et seq., 2000e–6(a).

◆

Jerris Leonard, Asst. Atty. Gen., Daniel Bartlett, Jr., U. S. Atty., David L. Rose, Stuart P. Herman, Attys., Dept. of Justice, Washington, D. C., for plaintiff-appellant.

Edward Weakley, Howard Elliott, Boyle, Priest, Elliott & Weakley, St. Louis, Mo., for National Lead Co.

Harry Moline, Jr., Thomas, Busse, Cullen, Clooney, Weil & King, St. Louis, Mo., for Chemical Workers' Basic Union, Local 1744, AFL-CIO.

Before GIBSON and BRIGHT, Circuit Judges, and McMANUS, Chief District Judge.

BRIGHT, Circuit Judge.

The United States by its Attorney General brings this action seeking in-

FIGURE A-1

UNITED STATES of America,
Plaintiff-Appellant,

v.

NATIONAL LEAD COMPANY, a Cor-
poration, and Chemical Workers'
Basic Union Local 1744, AFL-
CIO, Defendants-Appellees.

No. 20427.

United States Court of Appeals,
Eighth Circuit.
Feb. 26, 1971.

FIGURE A-2

The Caption

Figure A-2 shows the caption of the case, which names the parties. Note that the citation names only one party for each side, while the caption includes a codefendant, a union local of the AFL-CIO. The caption also indicates the status of the parties with regard to the suit as "Plaintiff-Appellant" and "Defendants-Appellees." We can surmise from this that the United States brought the original suit as plaintiff and then also the appeal, apparently having lost the original suit.

Commonly the caption simply states "appellant" and "appellee," and the reader must discover from the text who brought the suit originally. It is important to note who is appellant and who is appellee because many opinions refer to the parties by those terms. In *National Lead*, Judge Bright refers to "the government" and "National Lead," which makes reading much less confusing.

Below the parties we find "No. 20427," the docket number, which is a number assigned to the case upon initial filing with the clerk of the court and by which it is identified prior to assigning it a volume and page number in the reporter series. This number is important when attempting to research the case prior to its official publication. Below the docket number is the name of the court issuing the decision and the date of the decision.

The Syllabus

Following the caption is a brief summary of the case called the *syllabus* (Figure A-3). While this is sometimes written by the court or a reporter appointed by the court, it is a narrow condensation of the court's ruling and cannot be relied upon as the precise holding of the court. The syllabus can be useful in obtaining a quick idea of what the case concerns—a summary of

Action by government against company and union for alleged violations of Civil Rights Act of 1964. The United States District Court for the Eastern District of Missouri, Roy W. Harper, Senior District Judge, 315 F.Supp. 912, denied government's motion for preliminary injunction, and government appealed. The Court of Appeals, Bright, Circuit Judge, held that although, under facts, some of vestiges of employer's past discrimination seemed preserved in employer's transfer and promotion procedures, in view of fact that actual impact of this discrimination upon black employees possessing seniority dating back prior to end of discrimination was unclear, and in view of fact that an appropriate solution was not readily apparent from partial development of facts, denial of relief by way of a preliminary injunction was not error.

Affirmed and remanded.

FIGURE A-3

the issue and the holding of the court. Frequently legal researchers follow leads to cases, which upon reading prove to be unrelated to the issue of the research. Reading the syllabus may make reading the entire opinion unnecessary. On the other hand, if the syllabus suggests the case may be important, a careful reading of the entire text of the opinion is usually necessary.

Headnotes

Figure A-4 illustrates the *headnotes*, which are statements of the major points of law discussed in the case. With limited editing, the headnotes tend to be nearly verbatim statements lifted from the opinion. The headnotes are listed in numerical order, starting at the beginning of the opinion, so that the reader may look quickly for the context of a point expressed by a headnote. For example, the part of the text that deals with a particular point made in the headnote will have the number of the headnote in brackets, e.g., [4], at the beginning of the paragraph or section in which it is discussed. This is very helpful when researching lengthy cases in which only one issue is of concern to the researcher.

To the right of the headnote number is a generic heading, such as "Civil Rights," and a *key* number. Since this reporter is published by West Publishing Company, it uses an indexing title and number that can be used throughout the many West indexes, reporters, and encyclopedias.

Attorneys for the Parties

Figure A-5 illustrates the *attorneys for the parties* as well as the judges sitting on the case. These are listed just above the beginning of the opinion, shown in Figure A-6.

3. Injunction   137(4)

Although, under facts, some of vestiges of employer's past discrimination seemed preserved in employer's transfer and promotion procedures, in view of fact that actual impact of this discrimination upon black employees possessing seniority dating back prior to end of discrimination was unclear, and in view of fact that an appropriate solution was not readily apparent from partial development of facts, denial of relief by way of a preliminary injunction was not error. Civil Rights Act of 1964, §§ 701 et seq., 707(a) 42 U.S.C.A. §§ 2000e et seq., 2000e-6(a).

4. Injunction   147

In view of evidence disclosing that in recent years blacks had filled three of six vacancies for guard positions and that employer planned no immediate expansion of present guard force or filling of any existing vacancies, no need for preliminary injunction was shown with respect to guard force. Civil Rights Act of 1964, §§ 701 et seq., 707(a), 42 U.S.C.A. §§ 2000e et seq., 2000e-6(a).

FIGURE A-4

Jerris Leonard, Asst. Atty. Gen., Daniel Bartlett, Jr., U. S. Atty., David L. Rose, Stuart P. Herman, Attys., Dept. of Justice, Washington, D. C., for plaintiff-appellant.

Edward Weakley, Howard Elliott, Boyle, Priest, Elliott & Weakley, St. Louis, Mo., for National Lead Co.

Harry Moline, Jr., Thomas, Busse, Cullen, Clooney, Weil & King, St. Louis, Mo., for Chemical Workers' Basic Union, Local 1744, AFL-CIO.

Before GIBSON and BRIGHT, Circuit Judges, and McMANUS, Chief District Judge.

FIGURE A-5

BRIGHT, Circuit Judge.
The United States by its Attorney General brings this action seeking in-

FIGURE A-6

FORMAT OF THE OPINION

Following the names of the attorneys and a list of the judges sitting on the case, the formal opinion (that is, the official discussion of the case) begins with the name of the judge writing the opinion, for example, "Bright, Circuit Judge," in *National Lead*. The author of the opinion has considerable freedom in presentation. Some opinions are written mechanically, while a few are almost poetic. The peculiarities of any particular case may dictate a special logical order of its own. Nevertheless, the majority of opinions follow a standard format. When this format is followed, reading and understanding are simplified, but no judge is required to make an opinion easy reading. The following format is the one most frequently used.

Procedure

Most opinions begin with some reference to the outcome of the trial in the lower court and the basis for appeal. In a criminal case, for example, the opinion may state that the defendant was found guilty of aggravated assault and the defendant is appealing the judge's ruling to admit certain evidence over defendant's objections that the evidence was prejudicial to the defendant's case. Often the remarks about procedure are brief and confusing, especially if the reader is not familiar with procedural rules. If the procedure is important to the opinion, a more elaborate discussion is usually found in the body of the opinion. Many things in the opinion become clear only upon further reading; and many opinions must be read at least twice for a full understanding. An opinion is like a jigsaw puzzle—the reader must put the parts together to see the full picture.

The Facts

Most of the text of an opinion in appellate decisions is concerned with a discussion of the law, but since a case revolves around a dispute concerning events that occurred between the parties, no opinion is complete without some discussion of the events that led to the trial. Since trials generally explore these events in great detail and judge or jury settle the facts, appellate opinions usually narrow the fact statement to the most relevant facts. In an interesting case, the reader is often left wanting to know more about what happened; but the judge is not writing a story. The important element in the opinion concerns the application of law.

The Issue

Following a summary of relevant facts, many writers describe the questions of law that must be decided. Rarely, this is made quite clear: "The only issue presented to the court is . . . " Unfortunately, few writers pinpoint the issue in this fashion, so the reader must search the text for the issue. At this point it is appropriate to introduce a favorite term used by attorneys: *caveat*. This means "warning" or, literally, "Let him beware."

Caveat: The issue is the most important element in an opinion. If the issue is not understood, the significance of the rule laid down by the court can easily be misunderstood. This point cannot be emphasized too strongly. Law students study cases for three years with one primary goal: "Identify the issues." Anyone can fill out forms, but a competently trained person can go right to the heart of a case and recognize its strengths and weaknesses.

The Discussion

The main body of the text of an opinion, often ninety percent of it, discusses the meaning of the issue(s) and offers a line of reasoning that leads to a disposition of the case and explains why a certain rule or rules must apply to the dispute. This part of the opinion is the most difficult to follow. The writer has a goal, but the goal is often not clear to the reader until the end. For this reason, it is usually helpful to look at the final paragraph in the case to see whether the appellate court affirmed (agreed with the lower court) or reversed (disagreed with the the lower court). Many judges seem to like to hold the reader in suspense, but there is no reason the reader needs to play this game. By finding out the outcome of the decision, the reader can see how the writer of an opinion is building the conclusion. By recognizing the issue and knowing the rule applied, the reader can see the structure of the argument. The discussion section is the writer's justification of the holding.

The Holding

The holding states the rule of the case, that is, the rule the court applies to conclude whether or not the lower court was correct. The rule is *the law*, meaning that it determines the rights of the parties until reversed by a higher court. It binds lower courts faced with a similar dispute in future cases. It is best to think of the holding as an answer to the issue.

Let us give a real-life example. A woman is suing for wrongful death. Her husband was killed in an auto accident, and she is attempting to collect damages based on the income her husband would have received if he had lived, in which income she would have shared. Since the death, however, she has married an affluent man, and her lifestyle has not diminished. The issue is whether the jury can be informed of her remarriage. The court holds that the fact of her remarriage may not be kept from the jury. The court also holds that evidence of her new husband's earnings may *not* be presented to the jury. In this instance the holding goes a bit beyond the issue and clarifies it. (This particular issue has been answered quite differently in different states.) The reasoning for the holding is as follows: There is no justification for deliberately deceiving the jury about the woman's marital status. On the other hand, her current husband's earnings are irrelevant to the damage she suffered in losing her former husband. Fairness on this issue is difficult.

EVALUATING CASES

Once the purpose, style, and structure of appellate decisions are grasped, mastering the content is a matter of concentration and experience. Researching cases generally has one or more of the following three goals:

1. Finding statements of the law.
2. Assessing the law in relation to the client's case.
3. Building an argument.

Finding the Law

Research of cases is done for a number of reasons. The principles that apply to a dispute may be unknown, unfamiliar, or forgotten. With experience, legal professionals come to develop a knack for guessing how a dispute will be decided and can even predict what rules will be applied. Once the issues of a case are recognized, a reasonable prediction of a fair outcome can be made. This is, however, merely tentative; the researchers must check their knowledge and memory against definitive statements of the law. In some instances a statute will clearly define the rights and duties that pertain to the case at hand; in others the elaboration of the law in the cases will leave little room for doubt. Frequently, however, the issue in a client's case will be complex or unique, and no case can be found that is directly "on point." Ideally, research will result in finding a case that contains a fact situation so similar to that of the client that an assumption can be made that the same rule will apply. A case with a factual background identical to that of the client is said to be *on point*, which is illustrated in the following example.

Suppose Laura Lee, while waiting for a bus, was hit and injured by an automobile. The driver had lost control because of a defective steering mechanism. Since Laura was seriously injured and the driver has minimal insurance (and may not have been at fault), the issue is whether the manufacturer of the automobile is liable. The owner could sue the automobile manufacturer, but can a bystander sue as well? In searching the cases, several involved a bystander who was injured by defective brakes and was able to sue the manufacturer for products liability. While the facts are not identical, these cases are on point since the issue is not what kind of defect caused the accident but whether a bystander can sue.

Distinguishing Cases

In some instances the facts of a dispute are used to *distinguish* it from similar cases. For example, in researching Laura Lee's case, a case is encountered in which a bystander was injured by an automobile with a defective steering mechanism. In that case, the bystander did not collect damages from the manufacturer. The case was distinguishable because the driver was intoxicated. The driver's negligence was not merely passive, such as procrastinating in obtaining repairs, but was actively caused by his intoxication. The intoxication was the true cause of the injury, so it would have been unfair to place liability on the manufacturer. (The manufacturer would probably be sued anyway simply because it has the resources to compensate for the injury.)

Only experience and knowledge of the law will develop the keen sense it takes to separate cases that are on point from those that are distinguishable. It is often the advocate's job to persuade on the basis of threading a way through a host of seemingly conflicting cases.

SUMMARY

Judicial opinions are unique as a literary form in that their statements of law as defined by the court become precedent for future legal arguments and decisions. Judges must not only do justice to the parties but must also remain aware that their decisions determine rights of other parties in the future. Complex issues often result in opinions that are difficult to follow. Controversial issues may cause judges to be evasive in their conclusions.

A standard publishing format is followed in reported judicial decisions. In addition, custom has dictated a format for the text of the opinion itself. Judges are under no requirement to follow this format, and it is up to the reader to ferret out the issues and follow the reasoning.

APPENDIX B

Exercise in Legal Analysis—
Evolution of a Legal Principle

This appendix requires an application of the principles covered in the chapters on cases and legislation. It should be clear by now that no case can be read in isolation, no statute out of context, and no rule on its own. Cases take on meaning from similar cases, from the history of the principles they express, from the impact of applicable statutes. The greater context of cases is the law as a whole and the values of society. In none of the three cases presented in this chapter could the outcome have been predicted with any certainty. Collectively they reveal a struggle between legal principles, individual rights and social justice, and the desire to preserve an orderly legal process.

This appendix presents the vicissitudes of the doctrine of sovereign immunity in the Commonwealth of Pennsylvania. While the applicability of that principle may be important to individual litigants, the three cases that are presented in their entirety (except for the omission of numerous footnotes and citations) illustrate points made in Chapters Three and Four and call upon skills outlined in Appendix A.

Lest it appear that the cases represent peculiarities of Pennsylvania legal history, it should be noted that Pennsylvania followed in footsteps made by Colorado a few years before (see Comment, *The Colorado Governmental Immunity Act: A Judicial Challenge and the Legislative Response*, 43 COLO. L. REV. 449 [1972]). Following the pattern it established in abolishing charitable immunity (see Case No. 4–2), the Supreme Judicial Court of Massachusetts in 1977 warned that it would abolish sovereign immunity in the next case to raise the issue unless the legislature took action (which it did in 1978).

These cases have been selected to demonstrate several points that are essential for an understanding of American law. Law is not merely a set of rules but a system and process that must be understood if one is to function effectively within the legal profession. Some of the points to be noted in the cases are:

1. The law is changing and dynamic.
2. The courts as well as legislatures make law.
3. Courts may change the common law but not statutes.
4. A state constitution is superior to all other state law.
5. The interpretation of constitutions is much like the interpretation of statutes.
6. The language of a constitution (or a statute) may lead to two opposite but reasonable interpretations.

> **Note:** For ease of reading, although the texts of the decisions have been reprinted in their entirety, nonessential citations and footnotes have been omitted. The numbering of footnotes does not correspond to the original decisions; the majority opinion in *Mayle,* for example, contains eighty-two footnotes.

SOVEREIGN IMMUNITY

Much of the early history of sovereign immunity and its adoption in Pennsylvania is outlined in the first case, *Mayle v. Pennsylvania Dept. of Hwys.,* and need not be repeated here. Suffice it to say that Pennsylvania, like the other states, borrowed the principle from England, albeit with considerable criticism from some quarters. In essence the doctrine states that the sovereign cannot be sued without its consent. Perhaps, some have argued, the American states after the Revolutionary War were fearful of additional burdens on their already depleted financial resources and readily adopted this principle despite its undemocratic association with royal prerogative. It was inevitable that immunity from suit would be seriously challenged in a nation that prided itself on its democratic laws and institutions, where political philosophy identified the people and not the king or the state as sovereign.

Tort law presented the testing ground for immunities of all sorts. Since compensation for injury was traditionally based on fault, the law was inconsistent when it relieved the wrongdoer of liability. If a private organization like a corporation could be sued for harm caused by its agents, why not the state? In the twentieth century, most states have responded to this question with the abolition or severe limitation of the doctrine of sovereign immunity. There was an underlying discomfort with the notion that citizens could suffer damage at the hands of the state without any recourse to the law.

There is an ancient maxim of English law that no one "shall suffer a wrong without a remedy." This principle, in somewhat different form, appears in many state constitutions very much like Article I, §11, of the Pennsylvania Constitution:

> All courts shall be open; and every man for an injury done him in his lands, goods, person or reputation shall have remedy by due course of law, and right and justice administered without sale, denial or delay.

Alone, this sentence would suggest no immunity from suits for injuries. However, the sentence immediately following has caused much dispute:

> Suits may be brought against the Commonwealth in such manner, in such courts and in such cases as the Legislature may by law direct.

Justice Roberts of the Pennsylvania Supreme Court steadfastly interpreted the second sentence of Article I, §11, to mean that the Commonwealth of Pennsylvania could be sued as long as the legislature did not provide otherwise.

Justice Pomeroy just as steadfastly interpreted the same provision to mean that the commonwealth could be sued only when the legislature provided for such suit.

Both interpretations are reasonable in the sense that the Pennsylvania Constitution appears to allow suits against the state at the same time that it gives the legislature the power to restrict such suits. Until 1978, when the Supreme Court in *Mayle* abolished sovereign immunity (Justice Roberts writing for the majority), the legislature had remained silent on this issue. Two months after *Mayle*, the legislature reinstated sovereign immunity with eight important exceptions. Legislative silence, however, must be considered in light of the fact that the Supreme Court of Pennsylvania had for more than one hundred years approved the Pomeroy interpretation that the state was immune from suit. Under the circumstances, the legislature needed to act only if it desired to subject the state to suit.

GOVERNMENTAL IMMUNITY

While sovereign and governmental immunity are frequently treated as interchangeable, the Pennsylvania Supreme Court distinguished them on the basis of the language of the Pennsylvania

Constitution. In two cases in 1973, the Court distinguished between suits against the Commonwealth, specifically referred to in the Constitution, Article I, §11, and suits against political subdivisions. In *Brown v. Commonwealth*, 453 Pa. 566, 305 A.2d 868 (1973), the Court disallowed a suit against the state based on injury to a passenger in a National Guard Jeep driven by a Pennsylvania National Guardsman on the grounds that the Constitution prohibited such suits. Justice Pomeroy, writing for the majority, distinguished between the commonwealth and local governmental bodies (Roberts, Nix, and Manderino dissented). *Ayala v. Philadelphia Board of Public Educ.*, 453 Pa. 584, 305 A.2d 877 (1973), the case reported after *Brown*, held that sovereign immunity did not apply to political subdivisions and abolished the doctrine of governmental immunity in Pennsylvania. In *Ayala* a high school student was suing for injuries received when his arm was caught in a shredding machine in an upholstery class; his arm was later amputated. In both cases the vote was split 4–3 among the justices.

In 1975, the Pennsylvania Supreme Court further distinguished the commonwealth from state-level agencies that were not specifically part of the commonwealth (namely, the Pennsylvania Turnpike Commission) in *Specter v. Commonwealth*, 462 Pa. 474, 341 A.2d 481 (1975). *Specter* did not abolish sovereign immunity but inadvertently set up the problem of distinguishing between a person injured on the Turnpike and one injured on a state highway maintained by a department of the commonwealth, exactly the question brought in *Mayle*.

Brown, Ayala, and *Specter* revealed a majority of the Court to be antagonistic to governmental immunity and one less than a majority to be ready to read sovereign immunity out of the Pennsylvania Constitution.

CASE NO. B–1 The Pennsylvania Supreme Court Abolishes Sovereign Immunity: Mayle v. Pennsylvania Dept. of Hwys.

The Pennsylvania Supreme Court had on several occasions expressed disfavor on sovereign immunity and urged the legislature to address the issue. Ironically, as *Mayle* was being decided, the legislature was in the process of enacting a law abrogating sovereign immunity in specific areas, a fact mentioned by the dissent but not the majority. Under the law that was passed by the legislature two months after *Mayle* was decided, plaintiffs in Mayle's situation would have been able to sue the Commonwealth of Pennsylvania.

MAYLE V. PENNSYLVANIA DEPT. OF HWYS.

479 Pa. 382, 388 A.2d 709 (1978)
Supreme Court of Pennsylvania
Argued March 6, 1978.
Decided July 14, 1978.
Rehearing denied and Dissenting
Opinion Aug. 31, 1978.
See 390 A.2d 181.

Before EAGEN, C.J., and
O'BRIEN, ROBERTS, POMEROY,
NIX, MANDERINO and LARSEN, JJ.

OPINION OF THE COURT

ROBERTS, Justice.

Appellant Jimmy Mayle brought an action in trespass against appellee Pennsylvania Department of Highways in the Commonwealth Court for damages incurred as a result of injuries allegedly caused by appellee's negligent maintenance of Legislative Route 79, a public highway. Appellee asserted that the "sovereign immunity" of the Commonwealth prohibited any court in the Commonwealth from hearing the suit. The Commonwealth Court dismissed the complaint. We reverse.

The question before us is whether the Commonwealth is immune from tort liability except where a legislative act expressly or implicitly authorizes suit. This rule of "sovereign immunity" has been recently upheld by this Court. We today abrogate this doctrine of "sovereign immunity." We conclude that the doctrine is unfair and unsuited to the times and that this Court has power to abolish the doctrine.

I

Whatever justification ever existed for the doctrine that the Commonwealth is immune from liability for tortious conduct unless the Legislature has consented to suit, the doctrine's day has long since passed. Under the doctrine, plaintiff's opportunity for justice depends, irrationally, not upon the nature of his injury or of the act which caused it, but upon the identity or status of the wrongdoer. Three times in recent years we have repudiated as unfair similar status-based immunities of parties.[1] A majority of the states has rejected sovereign immunity at least to some degree, and commentators oppose it nearly unanimously.

The most popular theory of the origin of sovereign immunity of the American states is that it is a carryover from the English doctrine that "the King can do no wrong." Although this maxim may originally have been a misstatement of the early English law, by the time of Henry III (mid-13th Century), it was settled feudal law that the King could not be sued in his own courts without his consent.[2] By the mid eighteenth century, the doctrine that the crown, as the embodiment of the modern state, could not be sued without its consent had become part of the Blackstonian canon.[3] The first case in Pennsylvania adopting sovereign immunity asserted that the immunity of American states is an attribute to the

---

[1] *Ayala v. Philadelphia Board of Public Educ.*, 453 Pa. 584, 305 A.2d 877 (1973) (local government immunity); *Falco v. Pados*, 444 Pa. 372, 282 A.2d 351 (1971) (parental immunity); *Flagiello v. Pennsylvania Hospital*, 417 Pa. 486, 208 A.2d 193 (1965) (immunity of charities).

[2] . . . The maxim may originally have meant that the King was not privileged to do wrong. [Cc.]

[3] . . . Yet even Blackstone admitted that the crown would, as a matter or course, permit itself to be sued. . . .

English crown which the states took on themselves at independence, but which they might better have left behind with King George:

> "At the declaration of American independence prerogatives which did not concern the person, state, and dignity of the King, but such as had been held by him in trust for his subjects, were assumed by the people here and exercised immediately by themselves; among the rest, unwisely, we think, the prerogative refusing to do justice on compulsion."[4]

Thus, in Pennsylvania, the doctrine of sovereign immunity was criticized at its very inception as an unwise remnant of English political theory. As the Supreme Court of Illinois stated:

> "in preserving the sovereign immunity theory, courts have overlooked the fact that the Revolutionary War was fought to abolish that 'divine right of Kings' on which the theory is based."[5]

Moreover, the immunity accorded Pennsylvania as "sovereign" has been far greater than that claimed by any English king or queen at least since the restoration of the monarchy in 1660. Since that time, the crown has been subject to suit in equity in the Court of Exchequer for "it would derogate from the King's honour to imagine that what is equity against a common person should not be equity against him." Nonetheless, in Pennsylvania, the immunity of the Commonwealth grew to include suits in equity and petitions for declaratory judgment as well as actions at law. No explanation was ever offered for this extension of the doctrine and the English history of the doctrine does not support it.

The second reason offered for the growth of sovereign immunity is that without such a doctrine many, if not most, of the states would have gone bankrupt soon after the American Revolution. While it is true that many states would have faced bankruptcy during that period without insulation from suit on obligations, Pennsylvania constantly allowed claims against it to be made in the office of the Comptroller General for "services performed, monies advanced, or articles furnished by order of the legislature," with a right of appeal to the Supreme Court of Pennsylvania. Indeed, the Pennsylvania Legislature failed to approve a resolution calling for a constitutional amendment which would shield the states from suits on the obligations in federal court, and when this amendment was proposed by Congress, Pennsylvania refused to ratify it. Further, before adoption of the Constitution of the United States, Pennsylvania had paid interest on certificates issued to former soldiers by the Continental Congress and, after a bitter public controversy, assumed over $5,000,000 of the national debt. Pennsylvania did not feel the need, as certain other states did, to protect itself from liability through sovereign immunity.

Two cases in this Court from the Post-Revolutionary period, *Respublica v. Sparhawk*, and *Black v. Rempublicam*, are nonetheless read by some as adopting the doctrine of sovereign immunity. In *Sparhawk*, the plaintiff sought to recover from the Comptroller General the value of goods seized during the Revolution by

---

4 *O'Connor v. Pittsburgh*, 18 Pa. 187, 189 (1851). . . .

5 *Molitor v. Kaneland community Unit District No. 302*, 18 Ill.2d 11, 163 N.E.2d 89,94 (1959) (relying on without citing the Supreme Court of Florida).

agents of the Congress. The goods had been seized to prevent them from falling into the hands of the British, but the enemy captured and used them anyway.

On appeal, this Court stated that "[t]he transaction . . . happened flagrante bello; and many things are lawful in that season, which would not be permitted in a time of peace." Far from stating that the sovereign can do no wrong, the Court stated that the original taking by the Commonwealth would have been a trespass in time of peace.

The Court then stated a rule which has occasionally been used to justify sovereign immunity: "[I]t is better to suffer a private mischief, than a public inconvenience. . . . " "Public inconvenience" has sometimes been interpreted as the demand on the public purse made by tort victims. However, the examples of inconveniences the public may avoid without liability which the Court cited in denying Sparhawk's claim do not demonstrate public immunity for torts, but merely show that in exigent circumstances, the public may use private property. Thus this maxim was interpreted in Pennsylvania not as a limitation of the liability of government for tortious conduct, but as a limitation on the private interest a citizen could claim in land and chattels against either other citizens or the government.

This Court held in the alternative that the Comptroller General had no jurisdiction to hear Sparhawk's claim because the claim was not for "services performed, monies advanced, or articles furnished." Despite the Commonwealth's direct assertion that it was an immune sovereign, the Court refused to hold that if the Commonwealth's taking had been a trespass committed in peacetime, no court would have had jurisdiction to hear the claim absent consent of the Legislature.

In *Black v. Rempublicam*,[6] another Revolutionary War case, the plaintiff attempted to demonstrate his goods were taken under a contract with agents of the state. Failing that, his claim was dismissed on the same jurisdictional ground. Once again, this Court declined to treat the Commonwealth as an immune sovereign, and did not discuss the Commonwealth's argument that subjecting it to Revolutionary War claims would bankrupt it. Thus, fear of bankruptcy did not compel the adoption of sovereign immunity in post-Revolutionary Pennsylvania.[7]

The eighteenth century also gave birth to the argument that liability of the government for torts of its agents would result in "an infinity of actions." But as early as 1851, this Court recognized that a properly formulated jurisdictional scheme could provide orderly and adequate compensation for "every damage to private property . . . by the state or [municipal] corporation that occasioned it."[8]

The Commonwealth now argues both that tort liability could overburden the courts and either bankrupt the Commonwealth or endanger its financial stability. Significantly, however, the Commonwealth has shown no evidence that tort liability of a government or a public authority has ever resulted in either undue clogging of the courts or destabilization of

---

[6] 1 Dall. (1 U.S.) at 360. . . .

[7] In *Ford v. Kendall Borough School District*, 121 Pa. 543, 548-49, 15 A.2d 812, 815 (1888), this Court expressed concern that liability for personal injury caused by torts of their agents would threaten the financial stability of "weak and poor" school districts, although we had previously suggested that all state and local governments ought to be liable for all injuries to private property. *O'Connor v. Pittsburgh*, 18 Pa. 187, 190 (1851).

[8] *O'Connor v. Pittsburgh*, 18 Pa. at 190. . . .

government finances. Indeed, the Commonwealth admits it does not know what, if anything, will happen to court dockets and public finances if the immunity of the Commonwealth from tort liability is abolished. This sort of speculation cannot support a doctrine so "plainly unjust . . . to persons injured by the wrongful conduct of the State [and which] [n]o one seems to defend . . . as fair."

If anything, the information before us suggests that making governments liable for their torts will not substantially raise the costs of government or upset governmental financial stability.[9] Certainly, the greatest threats to the financial stability of state and local governments to recent years have not concerned tort liability, but limitations on taxing authority and liability on contractual obligations such as bonds and labor agreements. Further, because negligence involves the reasonableness of the actor's conduct, unreasonably expensive protective measures will not be required of governments any more than they are required of private parties. Welfare economics analysis suggests that government, if suable in tort, may become more efficient, although this improvement may not appear on its balance sheets as added assets or reduced liabilities.

We recently rejected the government-bankruptcy and flood-of-litigation arguments when we abolished local governmental immunity:

> "We must also reject the fear of excessive litigation as a justification for the immunity doctrine. Empirically, there is little support for the concern that the courts will be flooded with litigation if the doctrine is abandoned. ' . . . [M]ore compelling than an academic debate over the apparent or real increases in the amount of litigation, is the fundamental concept of our judicial system that any such increase should not be determinative or relevant to the availability of a judicial forum for the adjudication of impartial individual rights. "It is the business of the law to remedy wrongs that deserve it, even at the expense of a 'flood of litigation'; and it is a pitiful confession of incompetence on the part of any court of justice to deny relief upon the ground that it will give the courts too much work to do." Prosser, Intentional Infliction of Mental Suffering: A New Tort, 37 Mich.L.Rev. 874 (1939). We obviously do not accept the "too much work to do" rationale. We place the responsibility exactly where it should be: not in denying relief to those who have been injured, *but on* the judicial machinery of the Commonwealth to fulfill its obligation to make itself available to litigants.' "[10]

In rejecting the financial burden argument in the context of government immunity, we noted we had rejected

> "the [financial burden] argument as it applied to the immunity of charitable institutions, [saying]: 'The voluminous arguments advanced by the defendant hospital and the amicus curiae, on the subject of the financial problems of hospitals today, are, while interesting and enlightening, wholly irrelevant to the issue before us. We have a duty to perform and that is to see that justice, within the framework of law, is done. Our function is to decide cases as they come before us on the pertinent facts

---

[9] See David, Tort Liability of Local Government: Alternatives in Immunity from Suit or Liability, 6 U.C.L.A.L.Rev. 1, 6-17 (1959). . . .

[10] *Ayala v. Philadelphia Board of Public Educ.*, 453 Pa. at 595, 305 A.2d at 882. . . .

and law. What could happen in the event the plaintiff obtains a verdict is not an issue here. The pleadings in this litigation require that we decide whether the defendant hospital should answer the charges brought against it by the plaintiff.' "[11]

The financial burden argument is no more compelling now than it was in 1790, and no more so in the context of State government than in the context of local governments or charities. We continue to reject it.

Nonliability of governments for the torts of their agents may have arisen because courts were reluctant to use the doctrine of respondeat superior or to attribute the misdeeds of officers to the sovereign. Eighteenth and nineteenth century English and Pennsylvania cases reflect this concern. In *Elliott v. Philadelphia*,[12] this Court stated:

> "It is not conceivable," says Kennedy, J., "how any blame can be fastened upon a municipal corporation because its officer, who is appointed or elected, for the purpose of causing to be observed and carried into effect the ordinances duly passed by the corporation for its police, either mistakenly or willfully, under color of his office, commits a trespass; for in such a case it cannot be said that the officer acts under any authority given to him, either directly or indirectly, by the corporation, but must be regarded as having done the trespass of his own will. . . . It is like the familiar case of master and servant; where the latter wilfully does an act without the consent or authority of the master, by

which a third person is injured, the servant alone is answerable."

Negligent performance of an act within the scope of the agent's duties was at the time of *Elliott* attributable to any private corporate master.[13] Thus the analogy drawn in *Elliott* between nonliabilities of municipal and private corporations for acts of their agents was not applicable; the Court was simply unwilling to apply the doctrine of respondeat superior to most governmental and public authorities. Any justification for this attitude has of course long since disappeared, and the attitude itself was crumbling as early as 1888. Thus, this basis for Commonwealth immunity from tort liability is invalid today.

Finally, it was formerly asserted, both in Pennsylvania and elsewhere, that government should not be liable for its torts in the absence of legislative consent to suit because otherwise there is "no fund out of which [a government] can pay damages resulting from [its] own misconduct or that of [its] officers." We recently rejected this argument as an archaic and inadequate conceptualization of the reasons for which general appropriations of public funds are made:

> "[The argument has been advanced] that immunity is required because governmental units lack funds from which claims could be paid. It is argued that funds would be diverted to the payment of claims and the performance of proper governmental functions would be obstructed. Initially, we note our disagreement with the assumption that the

---

[11] Ayala, 453 Pa. at 597, 305 A.2d at 883. . . .

[12] 75 Pa. 347, 348-49 (1874).

[13] 75 Pa. at 349. Thus, failure to apply respondeat superior to government in Pennsylvania was not, as Jaffe, supra note 7 at 232-33, asserts, due to a general unwillingness to accept respondeat superior at all.

payment of claims is not a proper governmental function. 'As many writers have pointed out, the fallacy in [the no-fund theory] is that it assumes the very point which is sought to be proved, i.e., that payment of damage claims is not a proper purpose.' "[14]

Thus, all the historic arguments made for sovereign immunity either have never been accepted in Pennsylvania or reflect obsolete legal thinking. None has continuing vitality.

II

The argument the Commonwealth advances most vigorously is that article I, section 11, of the Constitution of Pennsylvania deprives any court of jurisdiction to hear a case brought against the Commonwealth absent an act of the Legislature permitting the suit. This section reads:

> "All courts shall be open; and every man for an injury done him in his lands, goods, person or reputation shall have remedy by due course of law, and right and justice administered without sale, denial or delay. Suits may be brought against the Commonwealth in such manner, in such courts and in such cases as the Legislature may by law direct."

This section first entered the Pennsylvania Constitution in 1790, and was adopted verbatim in the Constitutions of 1838 and 1873, all three times as part of the Declaration of Rights. Despite recent cases in which a majority of this Court accepted the Commonwealth's interpretation of article I, section 11, as the sole reason for retaining the rule of sovereign immunity, we now believe that this constitutional provision does not forbid judicial abrogation of the doctrine. Rather,

> "The Constitution is . . . neutral—it neither requires nor prohibits sovereign immunity. It merely provides that the presence or absence of sovereign immunity shall be decided in a non-constitutional manner. . . . The [Commonwealth's argument] mistakenly concludes that since the framers recognized the need for resolution of these issues they thereby mandated the doctrine itself. . . . [I]t is an unwarranted conclusion to assume from the grant of the power of consent [to suit] to the legislative branch that this was implicitly an abrogation of the court's traditional powers to abolish common law principles when they no longer meet the needs of the time."[15]

The history of the adoption of this section indicates that the framers of 1790 intended to allow the Legislature, if it desired, to choose cases in which the Commonwealth should be immune, but did not intend to grant constitutional immunity to the Commonwealth.

As section I, supra, establishes, Revolutionary and post-Revolutionary Pennsylvania was hostile to the notion that the Commonwealth should have the prerogatives of the English crown or that it should be immune from paying its just debts. For example, in 1782, before the end of the Revolutionary War, the Legislature passed a statute allowing all contract and bond claims against the Commonwealth to be presented for adjudication. Likewise, in the 1788 case of *Respublica v. Sparhawk*, this Court agreed that the plaintiffs' allegations would have alleged a trespass had the Commonwealth not

---

[14] [Quoting *Ayala*]

[15] *Biello v. Pennsylvania Liquor Control Board*, 454 Pa. at 189, 301 A.2d at 854. . . .

been acting in wartime to keep goods out of the hands of the enemy.

Article IX, section 11 of the Pennsylvania Constitution was originally proposed to the 1790 Convention in the following form:

> "That all courts shall be open, and every [free]man, for an injury done him in his lands, goods, person, or reputation, shall have remedy by the due course of [the] law, and right and justice administered [to him,] without denial, or delay."[16]

James Wilson, a known opponent of sovereign immunity,[17] persuaded the Convention to add the following sentence:

> "Suits may be brought against the Commonwealth as well as against other bodies corporate and individual."

This section, subjecting the Commonwealth to suit in all cases in which private parties could be sued, would constitutionally have abolished sovereign immunity and precluded the Commonwealth's liability. Shortly after this section was approved, however, a motion was made to reconsider, and the convention substituted the following:

> "Suits may be brought against the Commonwealth in such manner, in such courts and in such cases as the legislature shall, by law direct."

Thus, although no debate concerning any of the versions has been preserved, it appears that the 1790 Convention adopted this section in that form to preserve for the Legislature the opportunity, denied by Wilson's amendment, to make Pennsylvania immune in certain cases. There is no evidence that this sentence was added to make sovereign immunity the constitutional rule unless the Legislature decides otherwise. Indeed, one would not expect such evidence to exist in 1790 in a state with such a strong history of opposition to this privilege of the crown.

Three years after the adoption of the Pennsylvania Constitution of 1790, the United States Supreme Court in *Chisholm v. Georgia,* announced that states would be subject in federal court to suits on their obligations by citizens of other states. The Court gave no indication that the states would not also be subject to suit for their torts. Nonetheless, the Legislature refused both to recommend a constitutional amendment, to deprive federal courts of this jurisdiction and to ratify the eleventh amendment when proposed by Congress.[18] Had the Pennsylvania Legislature of the 1790's seen immunity of the state, absent its consent, as an integral part of the Constitution of the Commonwealth, it surely would have opposed destruction of that doctrine in the federal courts.

Further, the judicial history of sovereign immunity indicates that it

> "has a judicial origin and has been judicially modified. The constitutional basis for this doctrine has been a more recent judicial construction. When other

---

[16] Francis Shunk, Minutes of the Convention that Formed the Present Constitution of Pennsylvania 223 (1825). James Wilson successfully urged the Convention to change "freeman" to "man."

[17] At the Pennsylvania convention which ratified the Federal Constitution, Wilson asserted that Article III of the Federal Constitution of 1787 made states liable to suit by citizens of other states, . . . and later acted on this belief as a member of the United States Supreme Court majority in *Chisholm v. Georgia,* 2 Dall. (2 U.S.) 419, 453–66 (1793). . . .

[18] . . . . The 11th amendment, passed by over 3/4 of the other states, reads: "The Judicial power of the United States shall not be construed to extend to any suit in law or equity, commenced or prosecuted against one of the United States by Citizens of another State, or by Citizens or Subjects of any Foreign State."

grounds have failed, the state constitutional provision has been thrown into the breach to sustain a crumbling legal concept."[19]

Pennsylvania courts did not unequivocally adopt sovereign immunity until 1851. *O'Connor v. Pittsburgh*, the seminal case, relied upon neither the Constitution of Pennsylvania nor upon legislative acts. This Court thus adopted a "common law" rule in the sense that that term has been used in both the nineteenth and twentieth centuries. For example, in 1855 it was said:

> "The 'common law' consists of those principles, maxims, usages, and rules of action which observation and experience of the nature of man, the constitution of society, and the affairs of life have commended to enlightened reason as best calculated for the government and security of persons and property. Its principles are developed by judicial decisions as necessities arise from time to time demanding the application of those principles to particular cases in the administration of justice. The authority of its rules does not depend on any express legislative enactment, but on the principles they are designed to enforce. . . . "[20]

In *O'Connor*, this Court stated that "the prerogative of refusing to do justice on compulsion" was one of the attributes of sovereignty the American states took on themselves at the declaration of American independence. The court saw sovereign immunity as predating, and unaffected by, the Constitution of 1790, and even the Constitution of 1776, and as inherent in the Anglo-American notion of the state, without need for legislative or constitutional enactment. Thus when this Court adopted sovereign immunity in 1851, it viewed the doctrine as part of the common law.

The first judicial statement that article I, section 11 of the Constitution embodies the doctrine that the state may not be sued without its consent did not occur until 1934, more than 140 years after the Constitution of 1790, and more than 80 years after judicial adoption of sovereign immunity in Pennsylvania. In the years since 1934, this Court has frequently referred to article I, section 11 as the source of sovereign immunity. Indeed, in those years, it has advanced no other substantial justification for retaining the doctrine. Nonetheless, as late as 1963, this Court was deciding cases in which neither the Constitution, nor any case relying on the Constitution was used to support the proposition that the Commonwealth is immune from suit absent legislative consent. Only in the past fifteen years has this Court regularly stated that article I, section 11, compels the doctrine of sovereign immunity. This interpretation of the Constitution is certainly "a recent judicial construction . . . thrown into the breach to sustain a crumbling legal concept."[21]

Once the "errors of history, logic and policy"[22] which underly [sic] both

---

[19] *Kitto v. Minot Park District*, 224 N.W.2d 795, 799 (N.Dak.1974) (abolishing doctrine of local government immunity despite a constitutional provision similar to Pa.Const. art. I, §11, and cases holding that immunities of the state and of local governments are constitutionally based).

[20] *People v. Randolph*, 2 Parker Cr.R. 174, 176 (N.Y.1855), as quoted in 8 Words and Phrases "Permanent Edition", Common Law, at 109. . . .

[21] *Kitto v. Minot Park District*, 224 N.W.2d 795,799 (N.Dak.1974).

[22] *Morris v. Mt. Lebanon Twp. School Dist.*, 393 Pa. at 635–36, 144 A.2d at 738–39.

sovereign immunity and the Commonwealth's constitutional interpretation have been laid bare, we see no reason to perpetuate them. Significantly, the people, the source of power to make the Constitution of this Commonwealth, have not ratified this erroneous interpretation of article I, section 11. The interpretation was not made until long after the plebiscite enacting the Constitution of 1873, and article I was not submitted to the people for reconsideration by the Constitutional Convention of 1968–69. Further, other states have rejected this reading of state constitutional provisions analogous to our article I, section 11.

We therefore hold that article I, section 11 of the Pennsylvania Constitution does not preclude this Court from abrogating the doctrine of sovereign immunity.

III

Finally, the Commonwealth argues that sovereign immunity is so deeply imbedded in our judicial history that principles of *stare decisis* require that we continue to adhere to it. We need only repeat what this Court has stated many times in the past:

> "the doctrine of stare decisis is not a vehicle for perpetuating error, but rather a legal concept which responds to the demands of justice and, thus, permits the orderly growth processes of the law to flourish."[23]

Stare decisis should not be invoked to preserve a rule of law when "[there is] no better reason for [it] than [that] it was laid down in the time of Henry IV. It is . . . revolting if the grounds upon which it

was laid down have vanished long since, and the rule persists from blind imitation of the past."[24] Were we to continue to adhere to the doctrine of sovereign immunity in light of its manifest unfairness and of our current knowledge that the doctrine is non-constitutional, we would be blindly imitating the past for no reason better than that this was the way justice was administered in the feudal courts of Henry III.

We therefore abolish the doctrine of sovereign immunity and overrule all inconsistent cases.

Reversed and remanded for proceedings consistent with this opinion.

LARSEN, J., joins this opinion and files a concurring opinion.

O'BRIEN, J., filed a dissenting opinion in which EAGEN, C.J., and POMEROY, J., joined.

POMEROY, J., filed a dissenting opinion in which EAGEN, C.J., and O'BRIEN, J., joined.

LARSEN, Justice, concurring.

I join in Mr. Justice Roberts' opinion and wish to add that I can think of no greater function or more honorable pursuit than for the sovereign (Commonwealth of Pennsylvania) to care for those whom it has injured or maimed. Over thirty other sovereigns share this philosophy.

O'BRIEN, Justice, dissenting.

I respectfully but emphatically dissent. The majority of this court has usurped the power of the Pennsylvania legislature

---

[23] *Ayala v. Philadelphia Board of Public Educ.*, 453 Pa. at 606, 305 A.2d 888. . . .
[24] . . . quoting collected Legal Papers of Oliver Wendell Holmes 187.

in abrogating the Pennsylvania Constitutional provision prohibiting suits against the Commonwealth unless the legislature directs that such suits may be filed.

Article I, §11, of the Pennsylvania Constitution provides:

> "All courts shall be open; and every man for an injury done him in his lands, goods, person or reputation shall have remedy by due course of law, and right and justice administered without sale, denial or delay. *Suits may be brought against the Commonwealth in such manner, in such courts and in such cases as the Legislature may by law direct.*" (Emphasis added.)

In *Biello v. Pa. Liquor Control Bd.,* 454 Pa. 179, 301 A.2d 849 (1973), this court stated:

> " . . . This language *consistently* has been interpreted to mean that no suit may be maintained against the state in tort until the legislature specifically has provided for such an action." [Cc.] (Emphasis added.)

Article I, § 11, is a Pennsylvania constitutional provision not a creature of the common law capable of judicial modification or abolition, without a judicial determination that another Pennsylvania constitutional provision supersedes it or that it is repugnant to the U.S. Constitution. This court has no power to abrogate Article I, § 11, of the Pennsylvania Constitution. While sovereign immunity may have arrived in Pennsylvania in *Respublica v. Sparhawk,* [C.] as a judicial creation that creation was elevated to constitutional stature in the Constitution of 1790 and retained in the Constitution of 1873, and has remained in all of the constitutions up to and including today's constitution.

This court, while having consistently upheld the Commonwealth's right not to be sued without its consent, has consistently told the legislature that they and they alone do possess the power to make the Commonwealth amendable to suit. See *Brown v. Commonwealth,* 453 Pa. 566, 305 A.2d 868 (1973).

The majority today usurps the legislative power granted to elected members of the General Assembly and Senate of Pennsylvania. I dissent and would affirm the order of the Commonwealth Court.

EAGEN, C.J., and POMEROY, J., join in this dissenting opinion.

POMEROY, Justice, dissenting.

Article I, Section 11 of the Pennsylvania Constitution provides in pertinent part:

> "Suits may be brought against the Commonwealth in such manner, in such courts and in such cases as the Legislature may by law direct."

The majority today holds that this constitutional provision does not mean what it says, and purports to abolish what it calls the "doctrine" of sovereign immunity. I respectfully dissent.

The majority's description of the lack of foundation in public policy for the continuance of the doctrine of sovereign immunity in the Commonwealth of Pennsylvania in the 20th Century is unexceptionable. Indeed, what the Court states in this regard is essentially a restatement of what has been quite clear to both courts and commentators for years. See generally, in addition to the authorities cited in the Court's opinion, *Laughner v. Allegheny County,* 436 Pa. 572, 576, 261 A.2d 607 (1970) (Pomeroy, J., dissenting). I would have no difficulty in joining the Court's abolition of sovereign immunity, and indeed would do so with enthusiasm, were I able to conclude that this Court is free to take such action. But I cannot so conclude. As I wrote in *Brown v. Commonwealth*, 453 Pa. 566, 574–75, 305 A.2d 868, 873 (1973) (concurring opinion):

> "When by their Constitution the people of Pennsylvania have expressly delegated to the legislative branch of government the task of determining in what manner and in what court and in what cases the Commonwealth may be subjected to suit (and, implicitly, to the liability that may result therefrom), I fail to see how this Court can properly hold that it has a right to preempt this legislative function. A proposition that had its ancient origin in the common law of England and colonial America was elevated to constitutional status in Pennsylvania as long ago as 1790. To ignore this development would be to warp the plain meaning of the Constitution to suit societal ends which now, one hundred and eighty-three years later, the entire membership of this Court thinks are much to be desired. We may lament the legislative failure to correct before the present date an inequitable situation, but impatience should not cause us to upset the balance of power in our tripartite system of government by making the correction ourselves."

I remain of this view, and I am not persuaded to the contrary by the majority's historical discussion. As the Court concedes, we do not have the benefit of any of the debates during the 1790 convention to guide us to determining the intent of the drafters. Thus I doubt that the majority's historical speculation is sufficient to change what has long been the accepted construction of the constitutional provision—a construction which has been relied upon by the other branches of Pennsylvania government. But I believe that discussion on this point is in any event irrelevant, for it is well settled that a court should undertake an examination of a constitutional provision's historical setting only if the wording of the provision itself is ambiguous. [Cc.] I cannot find such an ambiguity in the constitutional provision.

Today's decision contains a further irony. After numerous decisions in which this Court has called upon the Legislature to take the comprehensive action necessary to deal with the problem of the Commonwealth's immunity in tort, e.g. [C.], such action is now apparently forthcoming. After lengthy study, the General Assembly's Joint State Government Commission has issued a report recommending legislation that would permit negligence actions against the Commonwealth in eight specific areas but require that immunity be retained in all other areas. In addition, suits would be permitted only for causes of action arising on or after July 1, 1979.[25]

Having for a number of years invited the Legislature's attention to this subject and being now advised that a definitive response has been proposed after serious study, for this Court to inform the Legislature, as it does today, that the Commonwealth is liable to suit by any person on any cause of action (for the reach of today's decision cannot be limited to torts)

---

[25] The bill proposed by the Joint State Government Commission was introduced into the House of Representatives on April 19, 1978 with broad sponsorship as H.B. 2437 (Printer's No. 3435) and referred to the Committee on Judiciary. It has since been reported by the House Judiciary Committee to the floor for consideration by the full House. Pa.L.J., June 19, 1978, at 7.

comes with ill grace and without the justification of some compelling new reason.

For the reasons above stated, I dissent.

EAGEN, C.J., and O'BRIEN, J., join in
this dissenting opinion.

CASE QUESTIONS

1. Article I, §11, of the Pennsylvania Constitution reads as follows:

   > All courts shall be open; and every man for an injury done him in his lands, goods,
   > person or reputation shall have remedy by due course of law, and right and justice ad-
   > ministered without sale, denial or delay. Suits may be brought against the
   > Commonwealth in such manner, in such courts and in such cases as the Legislature
   > may by law direct.

   Does the second sentence carry out the purpose of the first sentence by providing suits against the commonwealth, or does it furnish an exception to the first
   sentence?
2. Which is more convincing, the majority opinion or the dissenting opinions?
3. Does the fact that the legislature was at the same time considering passage of a
   statute governing sovereign and governmental immunity shed any light on analysis
   of this case?
4. Why is the court not bound by *stare decisis*?
5. Is the force of the court's argument weakened by the fact that this is a 4–3 decision?
6. Is the court making law?

STATUTE B-1: The Pennsylvania Legislature Reinstates Sovereign Immunity: 1 Purdon's Pennsylvania Statutes Annotated §2310 (Supplementary Pamphlet, 1964 to 1978), 148

§2310. Sovereign Immunity Reaffirmed; Specific Waiver

Pursuant to section 11 of Article I of the Constitution of Pennsylvania, it is hereby declared to be the intent of the General Assembly that the Commonwealth, and its officials and employees acting within the scope of their duties, shall continue to enjoy sovereign and official immunity and remain immune from suit except as the General Assembly shall specifically waive the immunity. When the General Assembly specifically waives sovereign immunity, a claim against the Commonwealth and its officials and employees shall be brought only in such manner and in such courts and in such cases as directed by the provisions of Title 42 (relating to judiciary and judicial procedure) unless otherwise specifically authorized by statute.

1978, Sept. 28, P.L. 788, No. 152, §1, imd. effective.

QUESTIONS

1. Section 5, "Construction and Application," of the act states:

    This act is intended to specifically respond to and prescribe limitations on the decision of *Mayle v. Commonwealth*, decided by the Supreme Court on July 14, 1978.

    Does this mean that the legislature has the authority to cancel the effect of a ruling by the Supreme Court? Was the legislature angry with the Supreme Court?

2. The Legislature also enacted at the same time the Political Subdivisions Tort Claims Act, effectively repealing *Ayala*, but provided eight exceptions to immunity:
    a. Vehicle liability.
    b. Care, custody or control of personal property.
    c. Care, custody, or control of real property.
    d. Dangerous conditions of trees, traffic controls, and street lighting.
    e. Dangerous conditions of utility service facilities.
    f. Dangerous conditions of streets.
    g. Dangerous conditions of sidewalks.
    h. Care, custody, or control of animals.

    Does this list cover most items for which local governments might be liable?

CASE NO. B–2: The Court Upholds the Statute: Carroll v. County of York

At the same time the Legislature reinstated sovereign immunity for the commonwealth, it reinstated local governmental immunity, which had been abolished by the Supreme Court in 1973 in *Ayala v. Philadelphia Bd. of Public Educ.* In *Carroll v. County of York*, the Court was forced to decide who was to have the last word on the matter. Note that the decision was once again a 4–3 split, but some of the justices had been replaced. Justice Roberts wrote the majority opinion in both *Mayle* and *Carroll*.

CARROLL v. COUNTY OF YORK
496 Pa. 363, 437 A.2d 394 (1981)

Nancy D. CARROLL, Administratrix of the Estate of Craig S. Breeswine, Petitioner-Plaintiff,

v.

The COUNTY OF YORK,
Respondent-Defendant.

Supreme Court of Pennsylvania.
Argued March 2, 1981.
Reargued Sept. 17, 1981.
Decided Nov. 6, 1981.
Reargument Denied Dec. 14, 1981.

Before O'BRIEN, C.J., and
ROBERTS, NIX, LARSEN, FLAHERTY,
KAUFFMAN and WILKINSON, JJ.

OPINION OF THE COURT

ROBERTS, Justice.

At issue on this appeal is the constitutionality of the Political Subdivision Tort Claims Act enacted five years after this Court abrogated the judicially created doctrine of governmental immunity. See *Ayala v. Philadelphia Board of Public Education*, 453 Pa. 584, 305 A.2d 877 (1973). With the exception of eight areas of activity, not including the activity giving rise to the present action, the Act reinstates the immunity of political subdivisions from suit.

Plaintiff Nancy D. Carroll filed wrongful death and survival claims in the Court of Common Pleas of York County seeking to recover for the death of her son, Craig S. Breeswine. Decedent committed suicide on February 14, 1979 while in the custody of the York County Detention Home. Plaintiff alleges that Detention Home officials negligently contributed to the death of decedent by placing him in an isolated, inadequately supervised area, even though they knew of decedent's depressed emotional condition and his previous suicide attempt at the Detention Center. Defendant, County of York, filed preliminary objections to the complaint, asserting immunity from suit under the provisions of the Political Subdivision

Tort Claims Act. Plaintiff responded by challenging the constitutionality of the Act. Before the trial court entered a determination, plaintiff petitioned this Court for the assumption of plenary jurisdiction. We granted the petition. See 42 Pa.C.S. §726.

Because we conclude that plaintiff's challenges to the constitutionality of the Act are without merit, we sustain the defendant's preliminary objections and dismiss plaintiff's complaint.

The first sentence of Article I, Section 11 of the Pennsylvania Constitution provides:

> "All courts shall be open, and every man for an injury done him in his lands, goods, person or reputation shall have remedy by due course of law, and right and justice administered without sale, denial or delay."

Plaintiff relies on this first sentence to argue that, by prohibiting a tort victim from successfully suing the Commonwealth, the act unconstitutionally "closes" the courts to potential plaintiffs by denying them a "remedy by due course of law."

Plaintiff's argument, based solely on the first sentence of Article I, Section 11, completely ignores the concluding sentence of that section:

> "Suits may be brought against the Commonwealth in such manner and in such cases as the Legislature may by law direct."

This concluding sentence of Article I, Section 11 is an integral, unequivocal and controlling portion of the Constitutional provision upon which plaintiff would rely.

In 1978, this Court discussed the relationship between Article I, Section 11 and the doctrine of sovereign immunity:

"[W]e now believe that this constitutional provision does not forbid judicial abrogation of the doctrine. Rather, 'The Constitution is . . . neutral—it neither requires nor prohibits sovereign immunity.' It merely provides that the presence or absence of sovereign immunity shall be decided in a non-constitutional manner. . . . "

Mayle v. Pennsylvania Dep't of Highways, 479 Pa. 384, 400, 388 A.2d 709, 716 (1978). Thus, while the Framers of Article I, Section 11 did not intend to grant constitutional immunity to the Commonwealth, they

"intended to allow the Legislature if it desired, to choose cases in which the Commonwealth should be immune. . . . "

479 Pa. at 400, 388 A.2d at 717. Surely the Legislature's authority "to choose cases in which the Commonwealth should be immune" encompasses political subdivisions. It is axiomatic that

"'[m]unicipal corporations are agents of the state, invested with certain subordinate governmental functions for reasons of convenience and public policy. They are created, governed, and the extent of their powers determined by the Legislature and subject to change, repeal or total abolition at its will.'"

City of Pittsburgh v. Commonwealth of Pennsylvania, 468 Pa. 174, 179, 360 A.2d 607, 610 (1976), quoting *Commonwealth v. Moir,* 199 Pa. 534, 541, 49 A. 351, 352 (1901). Consistent with *Mayle,* the conferring of tort immunity upon political subdivisions is within the scope of the Legislature's authority pursuant to Article I, Section 11.

Nonetheless, plaintiff maintains that the Political Subdivision Tort Claims Act creates arbitrary and irrational classifications. Plaintiff seizes upon language in *Ayala,* supra, where this Court stated:

"We conclude that no reasons whatsoever exist for continuing to adhere to the doctrine of governmental immunity. Whatever may have been the basis for the inception of the doctrine, it is clear that no public policy considerations presently justify its retention."

453 Pa. at 592, 305 A.2d at 881.

Plaintiff's reliance on *Ayala* is misplaced. This Court has repeatedly emphasized the fundamental distinction between the abrogation of a judicially created doctrine, as in *Ayala,* and the review, as here of an act of the Legislature. As this Court stated in *Ayala,*

"the doctrine of governmental immunity—judicially imposed—may be judicially dismantled . . . : the controverted rule . . . is not the creature of the Legislature. *This Court fashioned it, and, what it put together, it can dismantle.*"

453 Pa. at 600, 305 A.2d at 885, quoting *Flagiello v. Pennsylvania Hospital,* 417 Pa. 486, 503, 208 A.2d 193, 202 (1965) (emphasis added in *Ayala*). So too, in *Hack v. Hack,* 495 Pa. 300, 433 A.2d (1981), where this Court recently abrogated interspousal immunity, the primary issue was whether the Legislature had intended to create the immunity. There was no serious question that, absent a controlling statute, this Court could and should abrogate the doctrine.

This Court has frequently recognized that the Legislature may permissibly limit liability on the basis of a defendant's status. For example, in *Sherwood v. Elgart,* 383 Pa. 110, 117 A.2d 899 (1955), this Court found no violation of Article I, Section 11, where a statute denied a remedy in tort to all victims of negligent trespass to personal property which occurred while the property was in the care of an innkeeper even though the same negligent trespass by an owner of an apartment house or an apartment building would have given rise to liability. So too, in *Freezer Storage, Inc. v. Armstrong Cork Co.*, 476 Pa. 270, 382 A.2d 715 (1978), our Court found no constitutional violation where the Legislature had provided that tort liability of architects and builders would terminate twelve years after completion of a structure despite the fact that others not engaged in the improvement of real estate, such as suppliers of property, were not made similarly immune.

> "This Court would encroach upon the Legislature's ability to guide the development of the law if we invalidated legislation simply because the rule enacted by the Legislature rejects some cause of action currently preferred by the courts. To do so would be to place certain rules of the 'common law' and certain non-constitutional decisions of courts above all change except by constitutional amendment. Such a result would offend our notion of the checks and balances between the various branches of government, and of the flexibility required for the healthy growth of the law."

476 Pa. at 281, 382 A.2d at 721. [Cc.]

It is not our function to displace a rationally based legislative judgment.

> "Evils in the same field may be of different dimensions and proportions, requiring different remedies. Or so the legislature may think. Or the reform may take one step at a time, addressing itself to the phase of the problem which seems most acute to the legislative mind. The legislature may select one phase of one field and apply a remedy there, neglecting the others."

Williamson v. Lee Optical Co., 348 U.S. 483, 489, 75 S.Ct. 461, 465, 99 L.Ed. 563, 573 (1955) (citations omitted). [Cc.]

The report of the Joint State Government Commission on Sovereign Immunity, which formed the basis for the Political Subdivision Tort Claims Act, explains that partial immunity will assure

> "that the Commonwealth will not be required to process and defend various litigation brought against it in areas where risk management is totally uncertain at this time. . . . "

May, 1978 Report at 10. Manifestly, it is within the province of the Legislature to determine that certain bars to suit are, in its judgment, needed for the operation of local government.[26]

Contrary to plaintiff's assertions, the Political Subdivision Tort Claims Act is a valid exercise of legislative authority specifically granted by our Constitution. Accordingly, defendant's preliminary objections are sustained and plaintiff's complaint dismissed.

LARSEN, J., files a dissenting opinion in which FLAHERTY and KAUFFMAN, JJ., join.

KAUFFMAN, J., filed a dissenting opinion in which LARSEN and FLAHERTY, JJ., join.

LARSEN, Justice, dissenting.

---

[26] Plaintiff also challenges the constitutionality of the Political Subdivision Tort Claims Act because it limits awards recoverable by claimants to $500,000 for each tort. However, because plaintiff is not among those who can recover under any one of the eight exceptions to governmental immunity enumerated in the Act, the issue is not properly before this Court.

I dissent. In 1973, this Court buried the "doctrine" of governmental immunity, as that "doctrine" had long since been deprived of any vitality which it might once have enjoyed. *Ayala v. Philadelphia Board of Public Education,* [C.]. There Justice Roberts described the decay of justice that had taken place in this area as stare decisis had advanced into rigor mortis. With the Political Subdivision Tort Claims Act of 1978, 32 P.S. §§5301.101–5301.803 (Supp. 1980–81) (the Act), the legislature now with the help of the majority, summons the corpse from its grave.

Petitioner's challenges are: 1) Section 201 of the Act, which grants immunity from tort liability to political subdivisions closes the courts to one who has suffered injury in violation of Article I, §11 of the Pennsylvania Constitution; 2) the classifications created by sections 201 and 202 of the Act are impermissible under the Equal Protection Clause of the Fourteenth Amendment to the United States Constitution; and 3) Sections 402, 403 and 405 of Chapter 4 of the Act, "Limitations on Damages", limit the amount of recovery for an injury in violation of Article III, §18 of the Pennsylvania Constitution.

As with all challenges to the constitutionality of lawfully enacted legislation, we must begin with the presumption in favor of constitutionality. The burden is on the challenger to rebut the presumption by demonstrating that the legislation "clearly, palpably and plainly" violates some constitutional directive. [Cc.] I would find that petitioner has met her burden.

Article I, §11 of the Pennsylvania Constitution declares, in *relevant* part:

> All courts shall be open; and every man for an injury done him in his lands, goods, person or reputation shall have remedy by due course of law, and right and justice administered without sale, denial or delay.

Petitioner contends that section 201 of the Act, 53 P.S. § 5311.201, violates this provision. Section 201 provides that, except for eight exceptions listed in section 202,[27] "no political subdivision shall be liable for any damages on account of any injury to a person or property caused by any act or omission of the political subdivision or an employee thereof or any other person." Petitioner's cause of action does not fall within the purview of section 202; therefore, the parties agree that, unless section 201 is declared unconstitutional, she will be barred from suit against respondent. Respondent and the friends of the court who intervene in the interests of political subdivisions deny that section 201 of the Act violates Article I, §11 because, in their view, the General Assembly has merely "abolished" a cause of action which this Court has stated is a permissible legislative exercise under that provision.

On several occasions, this Court has espoused the view that nothing in Article

---

[27] This section waives immunity in eight specific areas, to wit:
    (1) Vehicle l iability;
    (2) Care, custody or control of personal property;
    (3) Care, custody or control of real property;
    (4) Dangerous conditions of trees, traffic controls and street lighting;
    (5) Dangerous conditions of utility service facilities;
    (6) Dangerous conditions of streets;
    (7) Dangerous conditions of sidewalks;
    (8) Care, custody or control of animals.

I, § 11 prevents the legislature from extinguishing or modifying a cause of action. [Cc.] (Some of these cases have spoken of the authority of the legislature to "abolish" or "extinguish" a cause of action. None of these cases, however, dealt with legislation which extinguished a cause of action *in toto* leaving a plaintiff who had suffered a legal injury completely without any remedy. It is, therefore, doubtful whether the "abolition" language of these cases could support a total extinction of a cause of action without substituting some sort of remedy. For example, could the legislature abolish *all* causes of action for, say, the common law tort of trespass, leaving no viable, substitute remedy for injuries caused by *any* of the various types of trespass? I think not, despite the dicta to the contrary in the above cited cases. Or, could the legislature say "Because suits in assumpsit are a drain upon our judicial system, we hereby abolish all causes of action based upon breach of contract."? Again, such a sweeping "abolition" would probably not withstand the proscription of Article I, § 11.)

Article I, § 11 assures that every injured party will have redress for that injury so long as it retains its character as a "legal injury". [Cc.] This "legal injury" qualification of the broad language of Article I, § 11 recognizes that no one has a "vested right in the continued existence of an immutable body of negligence law . . ." *Singer v. Sheppard, supra* 464 Pa. at 399, 346 A.2d at 903. Changing societal conditions occasionally require modification of some of the substantive elements or the procedural prerequisites of a particular cause of action. [Cc.]

Hence, Article I, § 11 does not prohibit either the courts or the legislature from altering legal recognition of an injury. When societal interests and conditions have changed significantly, the cause of action based on such injury may be modified to keep pace. Thus, in *Sherwood v. Elgart*, 383 Pa. 110, 117 A.2d 899 (1955), this Court, with virtually no analysis of constitutional considerations, upheld a statute relieving from liability for lost or damaged personal property an innkeeper who provided a safe deposit facility for such personal property of his guests. The plaintiffs there had lost certain personal property in a hotel fire allegedly caused by the innkeeper's negligence and had contended that Article I, § 11 prohibited the legislature from "abolishing" the common law cause of action for recovery for the damage to their personal goods.

And in *Freezer Storage, Inc. v Armstrong Cork Co., supra,* this Court upheld a similar challenge against a twelve year statute of repose for negligent defects and designs that would bar suit against builders and designers who had undertaken improvements to real property beyond that time period, but not against others who might have been considered to be improvers of real property, namely landowners and suppliers. Justice Roberts, speaking for the Court, wrote:

"If in *Sherwood* the Legislature could redefine the long-established rights of hotel guests and operators, we should no less allow the Legislature to redefine the rights of builders, their customers and third parties, where those rights are not settled, but rather are in a period of growth and change.

This Court would encroach upon the Legislature's ability to guide the development of the law if we invalidated legislation simply because the rule enacted by the Legislature rejects some cause of action currently preferred by the courts. To do so would be to place certain rules of the "common law" and certain nonconstitutional decisions of courts above all change except by constitutional amendment. Such a result would offend our notion of the checks and balances between the various branches of government, and of the flexibility required for the healthy growth of the law." 476 Pa. at 280–81, 382 A.2d at 721. (emphasis added).

The legislature's ability to modify a cause of action consistent with Article I, § 11 is not, however, a *carte blanche*. There is a world of difference between the modification of a cause of action or the imposition of reasonable procedural prerequisites and the erection of insurmountable barriers to legal recognition of a cause of action. An immunity to liability is such a barrier.

We must pause a moment to reflect on the precedent of Article I, § 11. The rationale upholding constitutional challenges to statutes based on this section has been inconsistent, strained,[28] or sometimes non-existent.[29] This should not be surprising—it can be extremely difficult in a given case to decide whether an act works a change on a substantive element or procedural requirement of a cause of action or is merely effecting a change of result by some artificial expedient. The distinction can be, and often is, hazy. Reasonable men can differ.

Rather than straining to meticulously "distinguish" certain cases (which frequently leads to contortion of precedent),

the better tack would seem to be the isolation of the common thread which binds (perhaps too loosely) the cases. That "thread" was identified by Justice Roberts in *Singer v. Sheppard, supra*. Justice Roberts observed, albeit in the context of Article III, § 18 (a section frequently argued side-by-side with Article I, § 11), that the Constitution does not "limit the power of the legislature to create or abolish causes of action; to prescribe the essential elements of a cause of action; to specify what are recoverable items of damages or legally compensable losses; or to provide under what circumstances a person has a cause of action and what items of damage are recoverable by him in those circumstances." 464 Pa. at 415–16, 346 A.2d at 911–12.

This "thread" is the same one that runs, or should run, through the Article I, § 11 precedent. The cases represent attempts to reconcile the balance of powers between the judiciary and the legislature. Article I, § 11 represents a check on the legislature's powers to deny remedy for injuries done. Common sense—and precedent—indicate that the legislature *must* have *some* authority to modify existing causes of action, but that authority must be exercised *reasonably* and must not effectuate a complete denial of remedy for conduct which retains its character as "legal injury".

In the *Sherwood* (standard of care of negligence for damage to personal property modified for innkeepers who

---

[28] *Singer v. Sheppard, supra* is a good example of reasoning straining to fit within the constitutional parameters of Article I, § 11. (*See* lead opinion by Jones, C.J., 464 Pa. at 398–401, 346 A.2d at 899–907). Also note that no less than six separate opinions were written in *Singer*.

[29] *Sherwood v. Elgart, supra* is often cited for the proposition that a common law cause of action can be abolished by act of legislature. (*See, e.g., Freezer Storage Inc. v. Armstrong Cork Co., supra*, 476 Pa. at 279, 382 A.2d at 720–21). However, the *Sherwood* case was primarily a case of statutory construction; the only discussion of constitutional dimension was "the appellees may properly contend at this time that the Act of 1913 is unconstitutional [under Article I, § 11 and then applicable Article III, § 21]. However, after considering appellee's contention we find it to be without merit." 383 Pa. at 115, 117 A.2d 899.

provide safe deposit facilities—in effect, legislatively determined that duty *[of]* care was established when safe provided) and *Freezer Storage* (12 year statute of repose adopted—length of time between tortious conduct and commencement of action restricted for builders and designers) the Act of the General Assembly worked some change either on a substantive element of the cause of action or upon a procedural requirement which changes were reasonable exercises of legislative authority to modify a cause of action. These enactments were reasonable because they did not simply deny a remedy for an otherwise actionable injury. *See also Singer v. Sheppard, supra* (No-Fault Act abolished the common law tort of negligence for motor vehicle accident victims suffering personal injury damages under $750) and *Jackman v. Rosenbaum Co., supra* (common law tort for recovery for damages to party walls modified by statute—no recovery for consequential damages).

However, a barricade such as a grant of immunity stands in contrast to reasonable legislative modifications that have been sustained by this Court—the identity and status of the defendant are *in no way* elements or essential ingredients of the cause of action. An immunity does no more, *and no less,* than to close the door to suit for a particular cause of action against a favored defendant. "The immunity doctrine offends against fundamental justice and elementary logic in many ways . . . *it closes the doors to a person whose body has been injured. . . .* " *Flagiello v. Pennsylvania Hospital,* 417 Pa. 486, 506, 208 A.2d 193 (1965) (judicial abrogation of charitable immunity) (emphasis added).

In *Freezer Storage,* this Court approved the "rational distinction" between a statute of repose applicable to builders, engineers, architects and contractors but not to landowners or suppliers. The observations made in upholding the statute over an object that it was "special legislation" prohibited by Article III, §32 are equally cogent here. *Freezer Storage* held "[t]his Act . . . draws the sort of rational distinction, *based on real differences* in the business world, which our cases have consistently upheld." 476 Pa. at 177, 382 A.2d at 719. The Court then reviewed a case, *Goodman v. Kennedy,* 459 Pa. 313, 329 A.2d 224 (1974), which sustained a portion of a statute exempting food stores with fewer than ten employees from Sunday "Blue Laws." *Goodman,* however, struck down another exemption for stores where certain commodities were sold by the store's proprietor or immediate family. The first exemption we held was rationally related to a legitimate legislative purpose but the "family" exemption "gave business benefits to certain individuals *solely* on the basis of family *status.* We did not see that this distinction had any basis in the business situation to which the statute applied." *Freezer Storage, Inc. v. Armstrong Cork Co., supra* 476 Pa. at 277, 382 A.2d at 719. *Freezer Storage* continued:

> [I]n *Commonwealth v. Casey,* 231 Pa. 170, 80 A. 78 (1911), we struck down a law establishing a forty hour week for "mechanics, workingmen and laborers" employed by the state, municipalities or public works contractors, but not for laborers employed by private enterprise. This Court held that the distinction this statute drew between publicly and privately employed workers had *no relationship whatever to the type of work the employees performed* and therefore no relationship to the statutory aim of easing the burden of the workingman.

That is, *the statute did not draw upon real distinctions* in the relevant business environment, the conditions in which the worker labors, *but upon the artificial grounds of the identity of the employer.* *Id.*, 476 Pa. at 278, 382 A.2d at 719–20. (emphasis added).

Real distinctions versus artificial grounds . . . real modifications of causes of action versus artificial changes modifying nothing but result. The instructions of *Freezer Storage* regarding real and artificial distinctions are helpful to our determination. The legislature may not, under the guise of "modifying" a cause of action, simply carve two causes of action out of one on the basis of two classes of defendants, and then "abolish" the cause of actions as to one of those classes. Such a dichotomy does not *in fact* just alter the cause of action or procedural requirement of the "legal" character of the injury. If injury is a "legal injury" when committed by X, it retains its character as a "legal injury" when committed by Y. The following examples are illustrative:

A. (1) negligent supervision of patient/inmate *by* private institution;
(2) negligent supervision of patient inmate by political subdivision.
B. (1) negligent use of firearms *by* private security guards;
(2) negligent use of firearms *by* political subdivision.
C. (1) negligent dumping of garbage *by* private contractors;
(2) negligent dumping of garbage *by* political subdivision.

With each of these types of torts, an action based on the second theory would be barred by section 201 of the Act as none of these examples fall within the eight enumerated exceptions to general immunity enunciated in section 202. It cannot seriously be maintained that each of these examples illustrates two separate causes of action. The grant of immunity in section 201 does not, therefore, work any change in any heretofore recognized cause of action but, instead, plainly and simply denies access to the courts for the redress of a legal injury. The distinction between the asserted two causes of action is artificial.

Moreover, there is language in the Act which supports the conclusion that the Legislature did *not* purport, as amici suggest, to either abolish or modify causes of action. Sections 202 and 201 are, of course, in pari materia and must be construed together, if possible. The Statutory Construction Act of 1972, 1 Pa.C.S.A. § 1932 (supp. pamphlet 1980–81). Section 202(b) sets out the causes of action that the Act permits to be brought against the political subdivision. Section 202(a)(1) establishes a condition precedent to bringing an action for damages under 202(b), namely, that the "damage would be recoverable under common law or a statute creating a cause of action if the injury were caused by a person not having available a defense under section 201. . . ." Thus section 202(a)(1) "implicitly recognizes that the *quality* of an injury as "legal" or "non-legal" is unaffected by the status of the parties or the existence of an immunity. If an act did not give rise to a cause of action at common law, section 202(b) does not create a new cause of action. This section, coupled with the fact that section 201 uses no language evincing an intention to affect causes of action, demonstrates that the legislature worked no change upon existing causes of action.

For the foregoing reasons, I would hold that the general grant of immunity in section 201 of the Act, 53 P.S.

§ 5311.201, denies access to the courts for redress for legal injury and clearly, palpably and plainly violates Article I, § 11 of the Pennsylvania Constitution. Accordingly, respondent's preliminary objections asserting governmental immunity should, on remand, be dismissed.

The majority opinion glosses over the complex issues in this case by the simple expedient of equating "political subdivisions" with "the Commonwealth." The majority hones in on the second proviso of Article I, § 11 (suits may be brought "*against the Commonwealth* in such manner and in such cases as the legislature may b[y] law direct.") and, on *exceedingly* meager authority, concludes "surely the Legislature's authority 'to choose cases in which the Commonwealth should be immune' encompasses political subdivisions." At 396. By use of this legal sleight-of-hand, relying *only* on a case which states that municipal corporations are agents of the state, *City of Pittsburgh v. Commonwealth*, 468 Pa. 174 360 A.2d 607 (1976), the majority concludes that "the conferring of tort immunity upon political subdivisions is within the scope of the legislature's authority pursuant to Article I, Section 11." At p. 396.

The second sentence in Article I, § 11 provides: "Suits may be brought *against the Commonwealth* in such manner, in such courts and in such cases as the legislature may by law direct." (emphasis added); it does *not say* "suits may be brought against the Commonwealth *and its subdivisions*, etc." It is quite obvious that this proviso is *irrelevant* to the instant case. Whatever authority this proviso may grant to the General Assembly to enact legislation conferring immunity upon the Commonwealth (*See Mayle v. Pennsylvania dept. of Highways*, 479 Pa. 384, 388 A.2d 709 (1978)), it has no bearing on the authority of the General Assembly to confer immunity upon political subdivisions.

A political subdivision is most certainly not "the Commonwealth" and the parties do not seriously argue that the second proviso of Article I, § 11 supports the legislature's enactment of the Act. Such an argument is quickly answered with two same-day decisions of this Court. *Brown v. Commonwealth*, 453 Pa. 566, 305 A.2d 868 (1973) declined to overrule the "doctrine" of sovereign immunity in the absence of legislative action waiving the Commonwealth's immunity. *Ayala v. Philadelphia Board of Public Education, supra*, did not feel compelled, on the other hand, to await legislative action in order to abolish immunity's local government counterpart. The difference between these cases, as observed by Justice Pomeroy, was the second proviso, which provided a constitutional basis for sovereign immunity but not for governmental, thus freeing the courts to act in the latter case, while restricting them in the former. *Brown v. Commonwealth, supra*, 453 Pa. at 573–74, 305 A.2d at 872–74 (Pomeroy, J., concurring). Justice Roberts reiterated this theme in *Ayala* wherein he stated:

> The notion that the immunity of the school district is linked to the sovereign immunity of the Commonwealth and that, therefore, only the Legislature may act, is a notion without present vitality. Underlying this assumption is the theory that there is a distinction between municipal corporations and quasi-corporations, the latter being agents of the Commonwealth and, thus, entitled to the sovereign immunity enjoyed by the Commonwealth. . . .

We expressly rejected this theory in *Morris v. Mount Lebanon Township*

School District. [393 Pa.][633] at 636, 144 A.2d [737] at 738. . . .

Thus, municipal corporations and quasi-corporations are on an equal level with regard to immunity. The immunity of both these types of governmental units was judicially created and may be judicially abolished. *Whatever may be the need for legislative action in the area of sovereign immunity, it is clear that there is no requirement for legislative action to abolish—as we do here—the immunity of municipal corporations and quasi-corporations.* 453 Pa. at 601 n.8, 305 A.2d at 885 n.8, (emphasis added).

Because I would decide the grant of immunity of section 201 violates Article I, § 11, there is no need to resolve the equal protection issue. I would note, however, that *serious* equal protection problems are raised by legislative classification based *solely* on the identity and/or status of one of the parties. At [sic] this Court's recent decisions have uniformly and unequivocally stressed, there are "*no reasons whatsoever*" for immunities that are strictly status-based. *Ayala v. Philadelphia Board of Public Education, supra,* 453 Pa. at 592, 305 A.2d 877 (1973) (emphasis added). We further stated in *Ayala,* per Justice Roberts, "we must agree with Chief Justice Traynor of the California Supreme Court that 'the rule of governmental immunity is an anachronism, *without rational basis.* . . . ' " *Id.,* 453 Pa. at 592, 305 A.2d 877. *Cf. Dubree v. Commonwealth,* 481 Pa. 540, 393 A.2d 293 (1978) wherein the doctrine of official immunity was upheld but was restricted to cases where the public policy (of insuring that an official will exercise his judgment unhampered by the threat of personal liability) will be served. That is, automatic immunity was disapproved, while immunity on a case-by-case basis,

looking to the *function* performed by the official (the nature of the official's action or decision in question) and the need for immunity to ensure the continued diligent and unfettered performance of that function, was retained. *Also cf. Petition of Dwyer,* 486 Pa. ?85, 406 A.2d 1355 (1979) (quasi-judicial immunity from criminal prosecution for certain public officials adopted where performance of duties require unfettered discretion in rendering quasi-judicial decisions) *and* Restatement Second of Torts, Ch. 45 A, *especially* §§ 895C and 895D and comments thereto.

FLAHERTY and KAUFFMAN, JJ., join in this dissenting opinion.

KAUFFMAN, Justice, dissenting.

The majority not only has breathed new life into an antiquated doctrine, but also has erroneously given it constitutional underpinnings. This result is contrary to law, logic and fundamental justice.

In 1973, this Court abolished governmental immunity with respect to municipal corporations and political subdivisions. *Ayala v. Philadelphia Board of Public Education,* 453 Pa. 584, 305 A.2d 877 (1973). Mr. Justice Roberts persuasively wrote in that case:

[C]ities and states are active and virile creatures capable of inflicting great harm, and their civil liability should be co-extensive. Even though a governmental entity does not profit from its projects, the taxpaying public nevertheless does, and it is the taxpaying public which should pay for governmental maladministration. If the city operates or maintains injury-inducing activities or conditions, the harm thus caused should be viewed as a part of the normal and proper costs of administration. . . .

The city is a far better loss-distributing agency than the innocent and injured victim.

Id., 453 Pa. at 594–95, 305 A.2d at 882 (Emphasis supplied).

Just recently, we abrogated sovereign immunity with respect to the Commonwealth, concluding that the doctrine irrationally placed a victim's opportunity for justice "not upon the nature of his injury or of the act which caused it, but upon the identity or status of the wrongdoer." *Mayle v. Pennsylvania Department of Highways,* 479 Pa. 384, 386, 388 A.2d 709, 710 (1978). [Cc.]

These decisions clearly reflect one of the most basic and fundamental concepts of our common law: "one may seek redress for every substantial wrong." [Cc.]. Contrary to recent trends in Pennsylvania law, however, the majority concludes that Article 1, Section 11 of our Constitution, which expressly refers only to the *Commonwealth,* vests the Legislature with authority to immunize *political subdivisions* from suit.[30] Whatever authority this section might give the Legislature to insulate the *Commonwealth,* our decisions clearly establish that it does not extend to political subdivisions. On the very same day that this Court decided *Ayala,* we upheld the doctrine of sovereign immunity *as applied to the Commonwealth* upon the assumption that such immunity was *constitutionally mandated* by Article 1, Section 11 and could only be waived by the Legislature. *See Brown v. Commonwealth,* 453 Pa. 566, 571 A.2d 868, 879 (1973).[31] Nevertheless, in abrogating governmental immunity for political sub-divisions in *Ayala,* we found no such constitutional restraint:

> The notion that the immunity of the school district is linked to the sovereign immunity of the Commonwealth . . . is a notion without present vitality. . . .
>
> . . . Whatever may be the need for legislative action in the area of sovereign immunity, it is clear that there is no requirement for legislative action to abolish—as we do here—the immunity of municipal corporations and quasi-corporations.

Ayala v. Philadelphia Board of Public Education, supra 453 Pa. at 601 n.8, 305 A.2d at 885 n.8. Thus, when read together, *Ayala* and *Brown* squarely refute the majority's reasoning that the reference to the "Commonwealth" in Article 1, Section 11 also includes political subdivisions.

Moreover, Mr. Justice Roberts' dissent in *Laughner v. Allegheny County,* 436 Pa. 572, 261 A.2d 607 (1970) demonstrates the anomalous and inconsistent result which the majority reaches today. In *Laughner,* which we decided prior to *Ayala,* the majority *per curiam* affirmed the dismissal of a wrongful death action instituted against Allegheny County on facts strikingly similar to those now before us. In his dissent, Mr. Justice Roberts wrote that governmental immunity is distinguishable from sovereign immunity in that the latter applies solely to suits against the Commonwealth and is expressly created by our Constitution. Urging the Court to abolish governmental immunity, Mr. Justice Roberts concluded:

---

[30] The second sentence of Article 1, Section 11 provides: "Suits may be brought against the *Commonwealth* in such manner and in such cases as the Legislature may by law direct." Pa.Const. art. 1, § 11. (emphasis supplied).

[31] We later concluded in *Mayle* that Article 1, Section 11 was neutral in respect to sovereign immunity, and thus did not preclude us from abolishing the judicially imposed doctrine even as to the Commonwealth.

The county was under a duty to provide for Carol's care, yet we sanction the negligent way in which they provide that care. We refuse to use the historical tool at our disposal—tort law—to help prevent future abuses. Those who must accept the 'benefits' of governmental action will continue to be faced with what Carol faced. And governmental units will be secure in their knowledge that they may act with impunity. 436 Pa. at 575, 261 A.2d at 608-09 (Roberts, J., dissenting).

Thus, there is no constitutional or rational basis for permitting the Political Subdivision Tort Claims Act ("Tort Claims Act") to shield York County from potential liability for its alleged wrongs. We must not ignore the plain meaning of the first sentence of Article 1, Section 11:

All Courts shall be open, and every man for an injury done him in his lands, goods, person or reputation shall have remedy by due course of law, and right and justice administered without sale, denial or delay.

The immunity which the tort Claims Act affords, and which the majority upholds, is not only manifestly unjust and inconsistent with our most recent decisions, but unconstitutionally slams shut the doors of our courts solely on the basis of the county's status as an arm of the Commonwealth.

While we have recognized the Legislature's authority to define, within constitutional parameters, what constitutes a "legal injury," *Singer v. Sheppard*, 464 Pa. 387, 400, 346 A.2d 897, 903 (1975), the Tort Claims Act does not purport to modify or alter existing causes of action. Rather, it unconstitutionally denies victims not falling within any of its exceptions a "remedy by due course of law." The majority's resurrection of governmental immunity is a giant leap backwards denying substantial justice to countless innocent and injured victims of this Commonwealth.[32]

Accordingly, I would hold that plaintiff may proceed with her cause of action against the County of York.

LARSEN and FLAHERTY, JJ., join in this dissenting opinion.

CASE QUESTIONS

1. Is Justice Roberts' position in *Carroll* consistent with his opinion in *Mayle*?
2. Justice Larsen's dissent suggests that the issue before the court is considerably more complex than suggested by the majority opinion. Are his arguments convincing?
3. The cases and the statutes suggest a minor power struggle between the Pennsylvania General Assembly and the Pennsylvania Supreme Court. Who won? Was this a victory or a defeat for the doctrine of separation of powers?

---

[32] As Justice Musmanno has stated:

I would like to see this honored Court . . . take the lead and be in the vanguard rather than in the rear ranks of the forces battling to overcome outmoded reasoning, unrealistic precedents, mechanical adherence to illogical rules, and doctrines which have no place in the twentieth century of a greater appreciation of the sanctity of human life and all that life holds dear.

Knaub v. Gotwalt, 422 Pa. 267, 282, 220 A.2d 646, 653 (1966) (Musmanno, J., dissenting).

4. Has the meaning of Article I, §11 of the Pennsylvania Constitution changed over time? What does it mean after *Carroll?*

CASE NO. B–3: Loose Ends in Application of the Law: Marino v. Seneca Homes

Carroll did not resolve all the issues of sovereign immunity in Pennsylvania. Changing the law is even more complex than what is shown above. *Marino* raises issues not only of sovereign immunity but of when it was abolished and when reinstated and the effect of the times at which these occurred. Adjudication operates on past events, while legislation makes rules for the future. Does this explain the puzzles raised in the following case? Pay close attention to the chronology of events.

MARINO V. SENECA HOMES, INC.

439 A.2d 1287, 63 Pa.Cmwlth.
534 (1981) appeal dismissed
451 A.2d 444, 499 Pa. 61

[Daniel A. Marino, Jr. et ux. v. Seneca
Homes, Inc. et al.
Michael Bove t/a Bove Engineering
company, Appellant.]

Argued October 5, 1981, before Judges Mencer, MacPhail and Palladino, sitting as a panel of three.

Appeal, No. 845 C.D. 1980, from the Order of the Court of Common Pleas of Westmoreland County in case of Daniel A. Marino, Jr. and Marilyn L. Marino, his wife v. Seneca Homes, Inc. and The Hempfield Township Municipal authority and Duncan, Lagnese and Associates Inc. v. Michael Bove, t/a Bove Engineer-

ing Company v. Commonwealth of Pennsylvania, Department of Environmental Resources, No. 140 of 1979.

Complaint in equity in the Court of Common Pleas of Westmoreland County to enjoin water discharge. Additional parties joined. Department of Environmental Resources filed preliminary objections. Preliminary objections sustained. Complaint against Department dismissed. Hudock, J. Bove appealed to the Commonwealth Court of Pennsylvania. Held: Affirmed.

OPINION BY JUDGE MACPHAIL, December 31, 1981:

On January 5, 1979, Mr. and Mrs. Marino (Marinos) filed a complaint in equity against Seneca Homes, Inc. and Hempfield Township Municipal Authority seeking to enjoin those defendants from discharging upon their land water from a sewage treatment plant located on a site adjacent to their property. Several additional defendants have been added to the original suit, including Michael Bove, trading as Bove Engineering Company (Bove). Bove subsequently filed a complaint against the Department of Environmental Resources (DER) as an additional defendant, contending that DER negligently approved plans for the sewage plant. DER filed preliminary objections to the complaint including a demurrer alleging the defense of sovereign immunity[33] which was sustained by the Court of Common Pleas of Westmoreland County. This appeal followed.

Our Supreme Court in *Mayle v. Pennsylvania Department of Highways*, 479 Pa. 384, 388 A.2d 709 (1978) abrogated the doctrine of sovereign immunity in Pennsylvania. In response to *Mayle*, the General Assembly enacted the Act of September 28, 1978, P.L. 788 (Act 152), which reinstates the doctrine of sovereign immunity except for eight categories in which immunity was specifically waived. In determining that sovereign immunity barred the action against DER, the trial court in the instant case relied upon our decision in *Brungard v. Hartman*, 46 Pa. Commonwealth Ct. 10, 405 A.2d 1089 (1979). In *Brungard* we found that *Mayle* did not have retroactive effect and that Act 152 could be applied retroactively. The trial court held that since Bove asserted that its cause of action accrued prior to the decision in *Mayle*, the defense of sovereign immunity was available to DER under Act 152. The trial court also held that none of the allegations of Bove's complaint against DER would bring it within any of the eight categories wherein the Commonwealth had waived its defense of immunity. 42 Pa. C. S. §8522.

On June 2, 1980, after the trial court's order was filed, our Supreme Court, in *Gibson v. Commonwealth*, 490 Pa. 156, 415 A.2d 80 (1980), held that the provisions of Act 152 could *not* govern causes which became actionable prior to the effective date of that statute and that *Mayle* must be given retroactive effect. Finally,

on July 21, 1980 the Supreme Court vacated the decision of this Court in *Brungard. Brungard v. Mansfield State College*, 491 Pa. 114, 419 A.2d 1171 (1980). Thus sovereign immunity presently exists as a statutory defense within the limitations of Act 152 and governs causes of action which accrued on or after September 28, 1978, contrary to the opinion of the trial court which, as we have said, was rendered prior to the recent decisions of our Supreme Court.

It is now firmly established that as to causes of action which accrued prior to September 28, 1978, the defense of sovereign immunity will not lie and with respect to causes of action which accrued on or after September 28, 1978, sovereign immunity is a bar except as to those circumstances set forth in Act 152 where the Commonwealth has waived its immunity. 42 Pa. C. C. §8522.

Notwithstanding this change in the law with respect to the defense of sovereign immunity, DER contends, nevertheless, that the order of the trial court from which this appeal has been taken should be affirmed. Acknowledging that under the law as it now exists, the critical factor which determines whether the defense of sovereign immunity may be asserted successfully by DER is the date on which the cause of action accrued, DER contends that in this case, that date is November 10, 1978. That is the date Marinos allege in their complaint that a letter was sent to Seneca Homes, Inc., who had built the sewage treatment plant, informing that party that the anticipated discharge of effluent onto Marinos' property would

---

[33] Pa. R.C.P. No. 1030 requires that the affirmative defense of sovereign immunity shall be set forth in a responsive pleading under "New Matter." No objection to DER's demurrer was made, however, and therefore this procedural defect has been waived. As will appear in this opinion, much of the procedural morass in which the parties now find themselves could have been avoided had the defense been pleaded properly.

constitute a continuing trespass. If we conclude that Bove's cause of action against DER accrued on November 10, 1978, the defense of sovereign immunity may be asserted successfully by DER since such date is after the effective date of Act 152.

Bove, on the other hand, contends that his cause of action accrued when DER negligently approved the plans and specifications submitted by Bove. Unfortunately, Bove does not set forth in his complaint when that approval was issued.[34]

"The true test in determining when a cause of action arises or accrues is to establish the time when the plaintiff could have first maintained the action to a successful conclusion." 51 Am.Jur.2d *Limitation of Actions,* §107 (1970) (footnote omitted). As a general rule, in tort cases a cause of action accrues at the time of the act or failure to act upon which the claim is based. 22 P.L.E. *Limitation of Actions* §64 (1959). Bove's complaint, as we have noted alleges liability against DER in the alternative. First, Bove says that DER is liable solely or jointly to Marinos. Marinos' suit in equity is based upon a cause of action which alleges anticipatory injury to real property. The *earliest* date that that cause of action could have accrued is November 10, 1978, a date alleged by Marinos in their complaint. Since that date is beyond the effective date of Act 152 any recovery against DER based upon Marinos' cause of action would be barred by sovereign immunity.

In the alternative, Bove alleges that if he is found liable to Marinos, then DER is "liable over" to Bove. A determination of when that cause of action accrues is more difficult. It is true that DER's alleged negligence was its issuance of the approval letter, on a date which is not now known to us. Until there has been some damage to Marinos for which Bove has been held liable, however, there can be no liability over against DER. Thus, the cause of action based upon DER's liability over to Bove will not accrue until the date, if any, on which Marinos succeed in their original cause of action and Bove is among those found liable. *See* 8 Goodrich-Amram 2d §2252(a):9 (1977). Obviously, the accrual date of that right of action is sometime in the future and well after the effective date of Act 152.

Bove contends, however, that even though the provisions of Act 152 may bar his cause of action, the Act itself is unconstitutional. DER claims that argument is moot in view of our Supreme Court's decision in *Gibson.* Of course, DER is wrong. *Gibson* held that insofar as Act 152 would make its provisions applicable to causes of action which accrued prior to its effective date, the Act was unconstitutional. As we noted in *Picariello v. Commonwealth,* 54 Pa.Commonwealth Ct. 252, 421 A.2d 477 (1980), the Supreme Court in *Gibson* specifically avoided addressing the constitutional challenge to the act in its entirety.

Bove's constitutional challenge here is grounded upon the Federal and State constitutional due process clauses and Article I, Section 11 of the Pennsylvania Constitution. In *Picariello* we rejected a due process challenge to Act 152. The reasons for doing so there are equally applicable to the case now before us and

---

[34] In its opinion, the trial court refers to December 29, 1977 as the date when the approval was given but that date nowhere appears in Bove's complaint against DER. In ruling upon a demurrer, of course, the court is limited to the allegations set forth in the challenged pleading.

do not bear repeating. It was Article I, Section 11 that our Supreme Court relied upon in part in reaching its decision in *Gibson* that Act 152 could not have retrospective application to causes of action arising prior to its effective date. The issue which we must now resolve is whether Article I, Section 11 of the Pennsylvania Constitution renders the provisions of Act 152 unconstitutional as applied to causes of action which arise *after* its effective date.

Recently our Supreme Court addressed a constitutional challenge to the validity of Sections 8541–8564 of the Judicial Code, 42 Pa.C.S. §§8541–8564, *formerly* the Political Subdivision Tort Claims Act, which challenge was specifically grounded upon Article I, Section 11. *Carroll v. County of York,* _____ Pa. _____, _____ A.2d _____ (No. 152 W.D.Misc. Dkt. 1980, filed November 6, 1981). In that case the Court referred to its prior decision in *Mayle* where it said that while the framers of the Pennsylvania Constitution did not intend to grant constitutional immunity to the Commonwealth by the language in Section 11, that Section *did* give authority to the Legislature to choose cases in which the Commonwealth would be immune. The Supreme Court distinguished its action in dismantling a judicially imposed immunity, which the Courts

created and could therefore abolish, from an act of the Legislature granting immunity. The Court pointed to other situations where it had held in the past that the Legislature could permissibly limit liability on the basis of the defendant's status. Finally, the Court said that it would not displace "rationally based legislative judgment." It cited the report of the Joint State Government Commission of Sovereign Immunity with approval wherein it was said that the Commonwealth, by providing for limited immunity would not be required to process and defend litigation where risk management was totally uncertain. Our Court used this same financial consideration in *Picariello.*

We think the reasoning in *Carroll* disposes of the constitutional challenge here asserted.

Accordingly, having found that Act 152 is constitutional and that the provisions of that statute apply to the facts in the pleadings now before us, we will affirm the decision of the trial court which sustained the demurrer of DER raising the defense of sovereign immunity.

ORDER

AND NOW, this 31st day of December, 1981, the order of the Court of Common Pleas of Westmoreland County dated March 18, 1980 is affirmed.

CASE QUESTIONS

1. Are there any weak points in the reasoning of the court?
2. Is the court attempting to reconcile cases that are irreconcilable?
3. How does the retroactive effect of judicial decisions compare with the retroactive effect of statutes?
4. How does the result here compare with a similar problem posed in Chapter 4 regarding charitable immunity in Massachusetts?

APPENDIX C

NALA Code of Ethics and Professional Responsibility

It is the responsibility of every legal assistant to adhere strictly to the accepted standards of legal ethics and to live by general principles of proper conduct. The performance of the duties of the legal assistant shall be governed by specific canons as defined herein in order that justice will be served and the goals of the profession attained. The canons of ethics set forth hereafter are adopted by the National Association of Legal Assistants, Inc., as a general guide and the enumeration of these rules does not mean there are not others of equal importance although not specifically mentioned.

Canon 1. A legal assistant shall not perform any of the duties that lawyers only may perform nor do things that lawyers themselves may not do.

Canon 2. A legal assistant may perform any task delegated and supervised by a lawyer so long as the lawyer is responsible to the client, maintains a direct relationship with the client, and assumes full professional responsibility for the work product.

Canon 3. A legal assistant shall not engage in the practice of law by accepting cases, setting fees, giving legal advice or appearing in court (unless otherwise authorized by court or agency rules).

Canon 4. A legal assistant shall not act in matters involving professional legal judgment as the services of a lawyer are essential in the public interest whenever the exercise of such judgment is required.

Canon 5. A legal assistant must act prudently in determining the extent to which a client may be assisted without the presence of a lawyer.

Canon 6. A legal assistant shall not engage in the unauthorized practice of law.

Canon 7. A legal assistant must protect the confidences of a client, and it shall be unethical for a legal assistant to violate any statute now in effect or hereafter to be enacted controlling privileged communications.

413

Canon 8. It is the obligation of the legal assistant to avoid conduct which would cause the lawyer to be unethical or even appear to be unethical and loyalty to the employer is incumbent upon the legal assistant.

Canon 9. A legal assistant shall work continually to maintain integrity and a high degree of competency throughout the legal profession.

Canon 10. A legal assistant shall strive for perfection through education in order to better assist the legal profession in fulfilling its duty of making legal services available to clients and the public.

Canon 11. A legal assistant shall do all things incidental, necessary or expedient for the attainment of the ethics and responsibilities imposed by statute or rule of court.

Canon 12. A legal assistant is governed by the American Bar Association Model Code of Professional Responsibility and the American Bar Association Model Rules of Professional Conduct.

APPENDIX D

NFPA Affirmation of Professional Responsibility

NFPA MISSION STATEMENT

The National Federation of Paralegal Associations, Inc. ("Federation") is a non-profit, professional organization comprised of state and local paralegal associations throughout the United States. The Federation affirms the paralegal profession as an independent, self-directed profession which supports increased quality, efficiency and accessibility in the delivery of legal services. The Federation promotes the growth, development and recognition of the profession as an integral partner in the delivery of legal services.

NFPA has adopted an Affirmation of Professional responsibility, which is the code of ethics for its members. The Affirmation sets forth guidelines for paralegals in the delivery of legal services and affirms their responsibility to the public and their dedication to the development of the paralegal profession. NFPA has also taken steps to become a leader on the improvement of paralegal education programs throughout the country.

PREAMBLE

The National Federation of Paralegal Associations recognizes and accepts its commitment to the realization of the most basic right of a free society, equal justice under the law.

In examining contemporary legal institutions and systems, the members of the paralegal profession recognize that a redefinition of the traditional delivery of legal services is essential in order to meet the needs of the general public. The paralegal profession is committed to increasing the availability and quality of legal services.

The National Federation of Paralegal Associations has adopted this Affirmation of Professional Responsibility to delineate the principles of purpose and conduct toward which paralegals should aspire. Through this Affirmation, the National Federation of Paralegal Associations places upon each paralegal the responsibility to adhere to these standards and encourages dedication to the development of the profession.

I. PROFESSIONAL RESPONSIBILITY

A paralegal shall demonstrate initiative in performing and expanding the paralegal role in the delivery of legal services within the parameters of the unauthorized practice of law statutes.

Discussion: Recognizing the professional and legal responsibility to abide by the unauthorized practice of law statutes, the Federation supports and encourages new interpretations as to what constitutes the practice of law.

II. PROFESSIONAL CONDUCT

A paralegal shall maintain the highest standards of ethical conduct.

Discussion: It is the responsibility of a paralegal to avoid conduct which is unethical or appears to be unethical. Ethical principles are aspirational in character and embody the fundamental rules of conduct by which every paralegal should abide. Observance of these standards is essential to uphold respect for the legal system.

III. COMPETENCE AND INTEGRITY

A paralegal shall maintain a high level of competence and shall contribute to the integrity of the paralegal profession.

Discussion: The integrity of the paralegal profession is predicated upon individual competence. Professional competence is each paralegal's responsibility and is achieved through continuing education, awareness of developments in the field of law, and aspiring to the highest standards of personal performance.

IV. CLIENT CONFIDENCES

A paralegal shall preserve client confidences and privileged communications.

Discussion: Confidential information and privileged communications are a vital part of the attorney, paralegal and client relationship. The importance of preserving confidential and privileged information is understood to be an uncompromising obligation of every paralegal.

V. SUPPORT OF PUBLIC INTERESTS

A paralegal shall serve the public interests by contributing to the availability and delivery of quality legal services.

Discussion: It is the responsibility of each paralegal to promote the development and implementation of programs that address the legal needs of the public. A paralegal shall strive to maintain a sensitivity to public needs and educate the public as to the services that paralegals may render.

VI. PROFESSIONAL DEVELOPMENT

A paralegal shall promote the development of the paralegal profession.

Discussion: This Affirmation of Professional Responsibility promulgates a positive attitude through which a paralegal may recognize the importance, responsibility, and potential of the paralegal contribution to the delivery of legal services. Participation in professional associations enhances the ability of the individual paralegal to contribute to the quality and growth of the paralegal profession.

APPENDIX E

The Constitution of the United States of America

We the People of the United States, in Order to form a more perfect Union, establish Justice, insure domestic Tranquility, provide for the common defence, promote the general Welfare, and secure the Blessings of Liberty to ourselves and our Posterity, do ordain and establish this Constitution for the United States of America.

ARTICLE I

Section 1 All legislative Powers herein granted shall be vested in a Congress of the United States, which shall consist of a Senate and House of Representatives.

Section 2 (1) The House of Representatives shall be composed of Members chosen every second Year by the People of the several States, and the Electors in each State shall have the Qualifications requisite for Electors of the most numerous Branch of the State Legislature.

(2) No Person shall be a Representative who shall not have attained to the age of twenty-five Years, and been seven Years a Citizen of the United States, and who shall not, when elected, be an Inhabitant of that State in which he shall be chosen.

(3) Representatives and direct Taxes shall be apportioned among the several States which may be included within this Union, according to their respective Numbers, which shall be determined by adding to the whole Number of free Persons, including those bound to Service for a Term of Years, and excluding Indians not taxed, three fifths of all other Persons. The actual Enumeration shall be made within three Years after the first Meeting of the Congress of the United States, and within every subsequent Term of ten Years, in such Manner as they shall by Law direct. The Number of Representatives shall not exceed one for every thirty Thousand, but each State shall have at Least one Representative; and until such enumeration shall be made, the State of New Hampshire shall be entitled to chuse three, Massachusetts eight, Rhode Island and Providence Plantations one, Connecticut five, New York six, New Jersey four, Pennsylvania eight, Delaware one, Maryland six, Virginia ten, North Carolina five, South Carolina five, and Georgia three.

(4) When vacancies happen in the Representation from any State, the Executive Authority thereof shall issue Writs of Election to fill such Vacancies.

(5) The House of Representatives shall chuse their Speaker and other Officers; and shall have the sole Power of Impeachment.

Section 3 (1) The Senate of the United States shall be composed of two Senators from each State, chosen by the Legislature thereof, for six Years; and each Senator shall have one Vote.

(2) Immediately after they shall be assembled in Consequence of the first Election, they shall be divided as equally as may be into three Classes. The Seats of the Senators of the first Class shall be vacated at the Expiration of the second Year, of the second Class at the Expiration of the fourth Year, and of the third Class at the Expiration of the sixth Year, so that one third may be chosen every second Year; and if Vacancies happen by Resignation, or otherwise, during the Recess of the Legislature of any State, the Executive thereof may make temporary Appointments until the next Meeting of the Legislature, which shall then fill such Vacancies.

(3) No Person shall be a Senator who shall not have attained to the Age of thirty Years, and been nine Years a Citizen of the United States, and who

shall not, when elected, be an Inhabitant of that State for which he shall be chosen.

(4) The Vice President of the United States shall be President of the Senate, but shall have no Vote, unless they be equally divided.

(5) The Senate shall chuse their other Officers, and also a President pro tempore, in the Absence of the Vice President, or when he shall exercise the Office of the President of the United States.

(6) The Senate shall have the sole Power to try all Impeachments. When sitting for that Purpose, they shall be on Oath or Affirmation. When the President of the United States is tried, the Chief Justice shall preside: And no Person shall be convicted without the Concurrence of two thirds of the Members present.

(7) Judgment in Cases of Impeachment shall not extend further than to removal from Office, and disqualification to hold and enjoy any Office of honor, Trust or Profit under the United States: but the Party convicted shall nevertheless be liable and subject to Indictment, Trial, Judgment and Punishment, according to Law.

Section 4 (1) The Times, Places and Manner of holding Elections for Senators and Representatives, shall be prescribed in each State by the Legislature thereof; but the Congress may at any time by Law make or alter such Regulations, except as to the Places of chusing Senators.

(2) The Congress shall assemble at least once in every Year, and such Meeting shall be on the first Monday in December, unless they shall by Law appoint a different Day

Section 5 (1) Each House shall be the Judge of the Elections, Returns and Qualifications of its own Members, and a Majority of each shall constitute a Quorum to do Business; but a smaller Number may adjourn from day to day, and may be authorized to compel the Attendance of absent Members, in such Manner, and under such Penalties as each House may provide.

(2) Each House may determine the Rules of its Proceedings, punish its Members for disorderly Behaviour, and, with the Concurrence of two thirds, expel a Member.

(3) Each House shall keep a Journal of its Proceedings, and from time to time publish the same, excepting such Parts as may in their Judgment require Secrecy; and the Yeas and Nays of the Members of either House on any question shall, at the Desire of one fifth of those Present, be entered on the Journal.

(4) Neither House, during the Session of Congress, shall, without the Consent of the other, adjourn for more than three days, nor to any other Place than that in which the two Houses shall be sitting.

Section 6 (1) The Senators and Representatives shall receive a Compensation for their Services, to be ascertained by Law, and paid out of the Treasury of the United States. They shall in all Cases, except Treason, Felony and Breach of the Peace, be privileged from Arrest during their Attendance at the Session of their respective Houses, and in going to and returning from the same; and for any Speech or Debate in either House, they shall not be questioned in any other Place.

(2) No Senator or Representative shall, during the Time for which he was elected, be appointed to any civil Office under the Authority of the United States, which shall have been created, or the Emoluments whereof shall have been encreased during such time; and no Person holding any Office under the United States, shall be a Member of either House during his Continuance in Office.

Section 7 (1) All Bills for raising Revenue shall originate in the House of Representatives; but the Senate may propose or concur with Amendments as on other Bills.

(2) Every Bill which shall have passed the House of Representatives and the Senate, shall, before it become a Law, be presented to the President of the United States; If he approve he shall sign it, but if not he shall return it, with his Objections to that House in which it shall have originated, who shall enter the Objections at large on their Journal, and proceed to reconsider it. If after such Reconsideration two thirds of that House shall agree to pass the Bill, it shall be sent, together with the Objections, to the other House, by which it shall likewise be reconsidered, and if approved by two thirds of that House, it shall become a law. But in all such Cases the Votes of both Houses shall be determined by Yeas and Nays, and the Names of the Persons voting for and against the Bill shall be entered on the Journal of each House respectively. If any Bill shall not be returned by the President within ten Days (Sunday excepted) after it shall have been presented to him, the Same shall be a Law, in like Manner as if he had signed it, unless the Congress by their Adjournment prevent its Return, in which Case it shall not be a Law.

(3) Every Order, Resolution, or Vote to which the Concurrence of the Senate and House of Representatives may be necessary (except on a question of Adjournment) shall be presented to the President of the United States; and before the Same shall take Effect, shall be approved by him, or being disapproved by him, shall be repassed by two thirds of the Senate and House of

Representatives, according to the Rules and Limitations prescribed in the Case of a Bill.

Section 8 (1) The Congress shall have Power To lay and collect Taxes, Duties, Imposts and Excises, to pay the Debts and provide for the common Defence and general Welfare of the United States; but all Duties, Imposts and Excises shall be uniform throughout the United States;

(2) To borrow Money on the credit of the United States;

(3) To regulate Commerce with foreign Nations, and among the several States, and with the Indian Tribes;

(4) To establish an uniform Rule of Naturalization, and uniform Laws on the subject of Bankruptcies throughout the United States;

(5) To coin Money, regulate the Value thereof, and of foreign Coin, and to fix the Standard of Weights and Measures;

(6) To provide for the Punishment of counterfeiting the Securities and current Coin of the United States;

(7) To establish Post Offices and post Roads;

(8) To promote the Progress of Science and useful Arts, by securing for limited Times to Authors and Inventors the exclusive Right to their respective Writings and Discoveries;

(9) To constitute Tribunals inferior to the supreme Court;

(10) To define and punish Piracies and Felonies committed on the high Seas, and Offenses against the Law of Nations;

(11) To declare War, grant Letters of Marque and Reprisal, and make Rules concerning Captures on Land and Water;

(12) To raise and support Armies, but no Appropriation of Money to that Use shall be for a longer Term than two Years;

(13) To provide and maintain a Navy;

(14) To make Rules for the Government and Regulation of the land and naval Forces;

(15) To provide for calling forth the Militia to execute the Laws of the Union, suppress Insurrections and repel Invasions;

(16) To provide for organizing, arming, and disciplining, the Militia, and for governing such Part of them as may be employed in the Service of the United States, reserving to the States respectively, the Appointment of the Officers, and the Authority of training the Militia according to the discipline prescribed by Congress;

(17) To exercise exclusive Legislation in all Cases whatsoever, over such District (not exceeding ten Miles square) as may, by Cession of particular States, and the Acceptance of Congress, become the Seat of the Government of the United States, and to exercise like Authority over all Places purchased by the Consent of the Legislature of the State in which the Same shall be, for the Erection of Forts, Magazines, Arsenals, dock-Yards, and other needful Buildings;—And

(18) To make all Laws which shall be necessary and proper for carrying into Execution the foregoing Powers, and all other Powers vested by this Constitution in the Government of the United States, or in any Department or Officer thereof.

Section 9 (1) The Migration or Importation of such Persons as any of the States now existing shall think proper to admit, shall not be prohibited by the Congress prior to the Year one thousand eight hundred and eight, but a Tax or Duty may be imposed on such Importation, not exceeding ten dollars for each Person.

(2) The Privilege of the Writ of Habeas Corpus shall not be suspended unless when in Cases of Rebellion or Invasion the public Safety may require it.

(3) No Bill of Attainder or ex post facto Law shall be passed.

(4) No Capitation, or other direct, Tax shall be laid, unless in Proportion to the Census or Enumeration herein before directed to be taken.

(5) No Tax or Duty shall be laid on Articles exported from any State.

(6) No Preference shall be given by any Regulation of Commerce or Revenue to the Ports of one State over those of another; nor shall Vessels bound to, or from, one State, be obliged to enter, clear or pay Duties in another.

(7) No Money shall be drawn from the Treasury, but in Consequence of Appropriations made by Law; and a regular Statement and Account of the Receipts and Expenditures of all public Money shall be published from time to time.

(8) No Title of Nobility shall be granted by the United States: And no Person holding any Office of Profit or Trust under them, shall, without the Consent of the Congress, accept of any present, Emolument, Office, or Title, of any kind whatever, from any King, Prince or foreign State.

Section 10 (1) No State shall enter into any Treaty, Alliance, or Confederation; grant Letters of Marque and Reprisal; coin Money; emit Bills of Credit; make any Thing but gold and silver Coin a Tender in Payment of Debts; pass any Bill of Attainder, ex post facto Law, or Law impairing the Obligation of Contracts, or grant any Title of Nobility.

(2) No State shall, without the Consent of Congress, lay any Imposts or Duties on Imports or Exports, except what may be absolutely necessary

for executing its inspection Laws: and the net Produce of all Duties and Imposts, laid by any State on Imports or Exports, shall be for the Use of the Treasury of the United States; and all such Laws shall be subject to the Revision and Controul of the Congress.

(3) No State shall, without the Consent of Congress, lay any Duty of Tonnage, keep Troops, or Ships of War in time of Peace, enter into any Agreement or Compact with another State, or with a foreign Power, or engage in War, unless actually invaded, or in such imminent Danger as will not admit of Delay.

ARTICLE II

Section 1 (1) The executive Power shall be vested in a President of the United States of America. He shall hold his Office during the Term of four Years, and, together with the Vice President, chosen for the same Term, be elected, as follows:

(2) Each State shall appoint, in such Manner as the Legislature thereof may direct, a Number of Electors, equal to the whole Number of Senators and Representatives to which the State may be entitled in the Congress: but no Senator or Representative, or Person holding an Office of Trust or Profit under the United States, shall be appointed an Elector.

The Electors shall meet in their respective States, and vote by Ballot for two Persons, of whom one at least shall not be an Inhabitant of the same State with themselves. And they shall make a List of all the Persons voted for, and of the Number of Votes for each; which List they shall sign and certify, and transmit sealed to the Seat of the Government of the United States, directed to the President of the Senate. The President of the Senate shall, in the presence of the Senate and House of Representatives, open all the Certificates, and the Votes shall then be counted. The Person having the greatest Number of Votes shall be the President, if such Number be a Majority of the whole Number of Electors appointed; and if there be more than one who have such Majority, and have an equal Number of Votes, then the House of Representatives shall immediately chuse by Ballot one of them for President; and if no Person have a Majority, then from the five highest on the List the said House shall in like Manner chuse the President. But in chusing the President, the Votes shall be taken by States, the Representation from each State having one Vote; a quorum for this Purpose shall consist of a Member or Members from two thirds of the States, and a Majority of all the States shall be necessary to a Choice. In every Case, after the Choice of the President, the Person having the greatest Number of Votes of the Electors shall be the Vice President. But if there should remain two or more who have equal Votes, the Senate shall chuse from them by Ballot the Vice President.

(3) The Congress may determine the Time of chusing the Electors, and the Day on which they shall give their Votes; which Day shall be the same throughout the United States.

(4) No Person except a natural born Citizen, or a Citizen of the United States, at the time of the Adoption of this Constitution, shall be eligible to the Office of President; neither shall any Person be eligible to that Office who shall not have attained to the Age of thirty five Years, and been fourteen Years a Resident within the United States.

(5) In Case of the Removal of the President from Office, or of his Death, Resignation, or Inability to discharge the Powers and Duties of the said Office, the Same shall devolve on the Vice President, and the Congress may by Law provide for the Case of Removal, Death, Resignation or Inability, both of the President and Vice President, declaring what Officer shall then act as President, and such Officer shall act accordingly, until the Disability be removed, or a President shall be elected.

(6) The President shall, at stated Times, receive for his Services, a Compensation, which shall neither be increased nor diminished during the Period for which he shall have been elected, and he shall not receive within that Period any other Emolument from the United States, or any of them.

(7) Before he enter on the Execution of his Office, he shall take the following Oath or Affirmation:—"I do solemnly swear (or affirm) that I will faithfully execute the Office of President of the United States, and will to the best of my Ability, preserve, protect and defend the Constitution of the United States."

Section 2 (1) The President shall be Commander in Chief of the Army and Navy of the United States, and of the Militia of the several States, when called into the actual Service of the United States; he may require the Opinion, in writing, of the principal Officer in each of the executive Departments, upon any Subject relating to the Duties of their respective Offices, and he shall have Power to grant Reprieves and Pardons for Offenses against the United States, except in Cases of Impeachment.

(2) He shall have Power, by and with the Advice and Consent of the Senate, to make Treaties, provided two thirds of the Senators present concur; and he shall nominate, and by and with the Advice and Consent of the Senate, shall appoint Ambassadors, other public Ministers and Consuls, Judges of the supreme Court, and all

other Officers of the United States, whose Appointments are not herein otherwise provided for, and which shall be established by Law: but the Congress may by Law vest the Appointment of such inferior Officers, as they think proper, in the President alone, in the Courts of Law, or in the Heads of Departments.

(3) The President shall have Power to fill up all Vacancies that may happen during the Recess of the Senate, by granting Commissions which shall expire at the End of their next Session.

Section 3 He shall from time to time give to the Congress Information of the State of the Union, and recommend to their Consideration such Measures as he shall judge necessary and expedient; he may, on extraordinary Occasions, convene both Houses, or either of them, and in Case of Disagreement between them, with Respect to the Time of Adjournment, he may adjourn them to such Time as he shall think proper; he shall receive Ambassadors and other public Ministers; he shall take Care that the Laws be faithfully executed, and shall Commission all the Officers of the United States.

Section 4 The President, Vice President and all Civil Officers of the United States, shall be removed from Office on Impeachment for, and Conviction of, Treason, Bribery, or other high Crimes and Misdemeanors.

ARTICLE III

Section 1 The judicial Power of the United States, shall be vested in one supreme Court, and in such inferior Courts as the Congress may from time to time ordain and establish. The Judges, both of the supreme and inferior Courts, shall hold their Offices during good Behaviour, and shall, at stated Times, receive for their Services, a Compensation, which shall not be diminished during their Continuance in Office.

Section 2 (1) The judicial Power shall extend to all Cases, in Law and Equity, arising under this Constitution, the Laws of the United States, and Treaties made, or which shall be made, under their Authority;—to all Cases affecting Ambassadors, other public Ministers and Consuls;—to all Cases of admiralty and maritime Jurisdiction;—to Controversies to which the United States shall be a party;—to Controversies between two or more States;—between a State and Citizens of another State;—between Citizens of different States;—between Citizens of the same State claiming Lands under Grants of different States, and between a State, or the Citizens thereof, and foreign States, Citizens or Subjects.

(2) In all Cases affecting Ambassadors, other public Ministers and Consuls, and those in which a State shall be Party, the supreme Court shall have original Jurisdiction. In all the other Cases before mentioned, the supreme Court shall have appellate Jurisdiction, both as to Law and Fact, with such Exceptions, and under such Regulations as the Congress shall make.

(3) The Trial of all Crimes, except in Cases of Impeachment, shall be by Jury; and such Trial shall be held in the State where the said Crimes shall have been committed; but when not committed within any State, the Trial shall be at such Place or Places as the Congress may by Law have directed.

Section 3 (1) Treason against the United States, shall consist only in levying War against them, or in adhering to their Enemies, giving them Aid and Comfort. No Person shall be convicted of Treason unless on the Testimony of two Witnesses to the same overt Act, or on Confession in open Court.

(2) The Congress shall have Power to declare the Punishment of Treason, but no Attainder of Treason shall work Corruption of Blood, or Forfeiture except during the Life of the Person attainted.

ARTICLE IV

Section 1 Full Faith and Credit shall be given in each State to the public Acts, Records, and judicial Proceedings of every other State. And the Congress may by general Laws prescribe the Manner in which such Acts, Records and Proceedings shall be proved, and the Effect thereof.

Section 2 (1) The Citizens of each State shall be entitled to all privileges and Immunities of Citizens in the several States.

(2) A Person charged in any State with Treason, Felony, or other Crime, who shall flee from Justice, and be found in another State, shall on Demand of the executive Authority of the State from which he fled, be delivered up, to be removed to the State having Jurisdiction of the Crime.

(3) No Person held to Service of Labour in one State, under the Laws thereof, escaping into another, shall, in Consequence of any Law or Regulation therein, be discharged from such Service or Labour, but shall be delivered up on Claim of the Party to whom such Service or Labour may be due.

Section 3 (1) New States may be admitted by the Congress into this Union; but no new State shall be formed or erected within the Jurisdiction of any other State; nor any State be formed by the Junction of two or more States, or Parts of States, without the Consent of the Legislatures of the States concerned as well as of the Congress.

(2) The Congress shall have power to dispose of and make all needful Rules and Regulations respecting the Territory or other Property

belonging to the United States; and nothing in this Constitution shall be so construed as to Prejudice any Claims of the United States, or of any particular State.

Section 4 The United States shall guarantee to every State in this Union a Republican Form of Government, and shall protect each of them against Invasion; and on Application of the Legislature, or of the Executive (when the Legislature cannot be convened) against domestic Violence.

ARTICLE V

The Congress, whenever two thirds of both Houses shall deem it necessary, shall propose Amendments to this Constitution, or, on the Application of the Legislatures of two thirds of the several States, shall call a Convention for proposing Amendments, which, in either Case, shall be valid to all Intents and Purposes, as Part of this Constitution, when ratified by the Legislatures of three fourths of the several States, or by Conventions in three fourths thereof, as the one or the other Mode of Ratification may be proposed by the Congress; Provided that no Amendment which may be made prior to the Year One thousand eight hundred and eight shall in any Manner affect the first and fourth Clauses in the Ninth Section of the first Article; and that no State, without its Consent, shall be deprived of its equal Suffrage in the Senate.

ARTICLE VI

(1) All Debts contracted and Engagements entered into, before the Adoption of this Constitution, shall be as valid against the United States under this Constitution, as under the Confederation.

(2) This Constitution, and the Laws of the United States which shall be made in Pursuance thereof; and all Treaties made, or which shall be made, under the Authority of the United States, shall be the supreme Law of the Land; and the Judges in every State shall be bound thereby, any Thing in the Constitution or Laws of any State to the Contrary notwithstanding.

(3) The Senators and Representatives before mentioned, and the Members of the several State Legislatures, and all executive and judicial Officers, both of the United States and of the several States, shall be bound by Oath or Affirmation, to support this Constitution; but no religious Test shall ever be required as a Qualification to any Office or public Trust under the United States.

ARTICLE VII

The Ratification of the Conventions of nine States, shall be sufficient for the Establishment of this Constitution between the States so ratifying the Same.

ARTICLES IN ADDITION TO, AND AMENDMENT OF, THE CONSTITUTION OF THE UNITED STATES OF AMERICA, PROPOSED BY CONGRESS, AND RATIFIED BY THE SEVERAL STATES, PURSUANT TO THE FIFTH ARTICLE OF THE ORIGINAL CONSTITUTION

AMENDMENT I (1791)

Congress shall make no law respecting an establishment of religion, or prohibiting the free exercise thereof; or abridging the freedom of speech, or of the press; or the right of the people peaceably to assemble, and to petition the Government for a redress of grievances.

AMENDMENT II (1791)

A well regulated Militia, being necessary to the security of a free state, the right of the people to keep and bear Arms, shall not be infringed.

AMENDMENT III (1791)

No Soldier shall, in time of peace be quartered in any house, without the consent of the Owner, nor in time of war, but in a manner to be prescribed by law.

AMENDMENT IV (1791)

The right of the people to be secure in their persons, houses, papers, and effects, against unreasonable searches and seizures, shall not be violated, and no Warrants shall issue, but upon probable cause, supported by Oath or affirmation, and particularly describing the place to be searched, and the persons or things to be seized.

AMENDMENT V (1791)

No person shall be held to answer for a capital, or otherwise infamous crime, unless on a presentment or indictment of a Grand Jury, except in cases arising in the land or naval forces, or in the Militia, when in actual service in time of War or public danger; nor shall any person be subject for the same offence to be twice put in jeopardy of life or limb; nor shall be compelled in any criminal case to be a witness against himself, nor be deprived of life, liberty, or property, without due process of law; nor shall private property be taken for public use, without just compensation.

AMENDMENT VI (1791)

In all criminal prosecutions, the accused shall enjoy the right to a speedy and public trial, by an impartial jury of the State and district wherein the crime shall have been committed, which district shall have been previously ascertained by law, and to be informed of the nature and cause of the accusation; to be confronted with the witnesses against him; to have compulsory process for obtaining witnesses in his favor, and to have the Assistance of Counsel for his defence.

AMENDMENT VII (1791)

In Suits at common law, where the value in controversy shall exceed twenty dollars, the right of trial by jury shall be preserved, and no fact tried by a jury, shall be otherwise re-examined in any Court of the United States, than according to the rules of the common law.

AMENDMENT VIII (1791)

Excessive bail shall not be required, nor excessive fines imposed, nor cruel and unusual punishments inflicted.

AMENDMENT IX (1791)

The enumeration in the Constitution, of certain rights, shall not be construed to deny or disparage others retained by the people.

AMENDMENT X (1791)

The powers not delegated to the United States by the Constitution, nor prohibited by it to the States, are reserved to the States respectively, or to the people.

AMENDMENT XI (1798)

The Judicial power of the United States shall not be construed to extend to any suit in law or equity, commenced or prosecuted against one of the United States by Citizens of another State, or by Citizens or Subjects of any Foreign State.

AMENDMENT XII (1804)

The Electors shall meet in their respective states and vote by ballot for President and Vice-President, one of whom, at least, shall not be an inhabitant of the same state with themselves; they shall name in their ballots the person voted for as President, and in distinct ballots the person voted for as Vice-President, and they shall make distinct lists of all persons voted for as President, and of all persons voted for as Vice-President, and of the number of votes for each, which lists they shall sign and certify, and transmit sealed to the seat of the government of the United States, directed to the President of the Senate;—The President of the Senate shall, in the presence of the Senate and House of Representatives, open all the certificates and the votes shall then be counted;—The person

having the greatest number of votes for President, shall be the President, if such number be a majority of the whole number of Electors appointed; and if no person have such majority, then from the persons having the highest numbers not exceeding three on the list of those voted for as President, the House of Representatives shall choose immediately, by ballot, the President. But in choosing the President, the votes shall be taken by states, the representation from each state having one vote; a quorum for this purpose shall consist of a member or members from two-thirds of the states, and a majority of all the states shall be necessary to a choice. And if the House of Representatives shall not choose a President whenever the right of choice shall devolve upon them, before the fourth day of March next following, then the Vice-President shall act as President, as in the case of the death or other constitutional disability of the President—The person having the greatest number of votes as Vice-President, shall be the Vice-President, if such number be a majority of the whole number of Electors appointed, and if no person have a majority, then from the two highest numbers on the list, the Senate shall choose the Vice-President; A quorum for the purpose shall consist of two-thirds of the whole number of Senators, and a majority of the whole number shall be necessary to a choice. But no person constitutionally ineligible to the office of President shall be eligible to that of Vice-President of the United States.

AMENDMENT XIII (1865)

Section 1 Neither slavery nor involuntary servitude, except as a punishment for crime whereof the party shall have been duly convicted, shall exist within the United States, or any place subject to their jurisdiction.

Section 2 Congress shall have power to enforce this article by appropriate legislation.

AMENDMENT XIV (1868)

Section 1 All persons born or naturalized in the United States and subject to the jurisdiction thereof, are citizens of the United States and of the State wherein they reside. No State shall make or enforce any law which shall abridge the privileges or immunities of citizens of the United States; nor shall any State deprive any person of life, liberty, or property, without due process of law; nor deny to any person within its jurisdiction the equal protection of the laws.

Section 2 Representatives shall be apportioned among the several States according to their respective numbers, counting the whole number of persons in each State, excluding Indians not taxed.

But when the right to vote at any election for the choice of electors for President and Vice-President of the United States, Representatives in Congress, the Executive and Judicial officers of a State, or the members of the Legislature thereof, is denied to any of the male inhabitants of such State, being twenty-one years of age, and citizens of the United States, or in any way abridged, except for participation in rebellion, or other crime, the basis of representation therein shall be reduced in the proportion which the number of such male citizens shall bear to the whole number of male citizens twenty-one years of age in such State.

Section 3 No person shall be a Senator or Representative in Congress, or elector of President and Vice-President, or hold any office, civil or military, under the United States, or under any State, who, having previously taken an oath, as a member of Congress, or as an officer of the United States, or as a member of any State legislature, or as an executive or judicial officer of any State, to support the Constitution of the United States, shall have engaged in insurrection or rebellion against the same, or given aid or comfort to the enemies thereof. But Congress may by a vote of two-thirds of each House, remove such disability.

Section 4 The validity of the public debt of the United States, authorized by law, including debts incurred for payment of pensions and bounties for services in suppressing insurrection or rebellion, shall not be questioned. But neither the United States nor any State shall assume or pay any debt or obligation incurred in aid of insurrection or rebellion against the United States, or any claim for the loss or emancipation of any slave; but all such debts, obligations and claims shall be held illegal and void.

Section 5 The Congress shall have power to enforce, by appropriate legislation, the provisions of this article.

AMENDMENT XV (1870)

Section 1 The right of citizens of the United States to vote shall not be denied or abridged by the United States or by any State on account of race, color, or previous condition of servitude.

Section 2 The Congress shall have power to enforce this article by appropriate legislation.

AMENDMENT XVI (1913)

The Congress shall have power to lay and collect taxes on incomes, from whatever source derived, without apportionment among the several States, and without regard to any census or enumeration.

AMENDMENT XVII (1913)

The Senate of the United States shall be composed of two Senators from each State, elected by the people thereof, for six years; and each Senator shall have one vote. The electors in each State shall have the qualifications requisite for electors of the most numerous branch of the State legislatures.

When vacancies happen in the representation of any State in the Senate, the executive authority of such State shall issue writs of election to fill such vacancies: *Provided,* That the legislature of any State may empower the executive thereof to make temporary appointments until the people fill the vacancies by election as the legislature may direct.

This amendment shall not be so construed as to affect the election or term of any Senator chosen before it becomes valid as part of the Constitution.

AMENDMENT XVIII (1919)

Section 1 After one year from the ratification of this article the manufacture, sale, or transportation of intoxicating liquors within, the importation thereof into, or the exportation thereof from the United States and all territory subject to the jurisdiction thereof for beverage purposes is hereby prohibited.

Section 2 The Congress and the several States shall have concurrent power to enforce this article by appropriate legislation.

Section 3 This article shall be inoperative unless it shall have been ratified as an amendment to the Constitution by the legislatures of the several States, as provided in the Constitution, within seven years from the date of the submission hereof to the States by the Congress.

AMENDMENT XIX (1920)

The right of citizens of the United States to vote shall not be denied or abridged by the United States or by any State on account of sex.

Congress shall have power to enforce this article by appropriate legislation.

AMENDMENT XX (1933)

Section 1 The terms of the President and Vice President shall end at noon on the 20th day of January, and the terms of Senators and Representatives at noon on the 3d day of January, of the years in which such terms would have ended if this article had not been ratified; and the terms of their successors shall then begin.

Section 2 The Congress shall assemble at least once in every year, and such meeting shall begin at noon on the 3d day of January, unless they shall by law appoint a different day.

Section 3 If, at the time fixed for the beginning of the term of the President, the President elect shall have died, the Vice President elect shall become President. If a President shall not have been chosen before the time fixed for the beginning of his term, or if the President elect shall have failed to qualify, then the Vice President elect shall act as President until a President shall have qualified; and the Congress may by law provide for the case wherein neither a President elect nor a Vice President elect shall have qualified, declaring who shall then act as President, or the manner in which one who is to act shall be selected, and such person shall act accordingly until a President or Vice President shall have qualified.

Section 4 The Congress may by law provide for the case of the death of any of the persons from whom the House of Representatives may choose a President whenever the right of choice shall have devolved upon them, and for the case of the death of any of the persons from whom the Senate may choose a Vice President whenever the right of choice shall have devolved upon them.

Section 5 Sections 1 and 2 shall take effect on the 15th day of October following the ratification of this article.

Section 6 This article shall be inoperative unless it shall have been ratified as an amendment to the Constitution by the legislatures of three-fourths of the several States within seven years from the date of its submission.

AMENDMENT XXI (1933)

Section 1 The eighteenth article of amendment to the Constitution of the United States is hereby repealed.

Section 2 The transportation or importation into any State, Territory or possession of the United States for delivery or use therein of intoxicating liquors, in violation of the laws thereof, is hereby prohibited.

Section 3 This article shall be inoperative unless it shall have been ratified as an amendment to the Constitution by conventions in the several States, as provided in the Constitution, within seven years from the date of the submission hereof to the States by the Congress.

AMENDMENT XXII (1951)

Section 1 No person shall be elected to the office of the President more than twice, and no person who has held the office of President, or acted as President, for more than two years of a term to

which some other person was elected President shall be elected to the office of the President more than once. But this Article shall not apply to any person holding the office of President when this Article was proposed by the Congress, and shall not prevent any person who may be holding the office of President, or acting as President, during the term within which this Article becomes operative from holding the office of President or acting as President during the remainder of such term.

Section 2 This Article shall be inoperative unless it shall have been ratified as an amendment to the Constitution by the legislatures of three-fourths of the several States within seven years from the date of its submission to the States by the Congress.

AMENDMENT XXIII (1961)

Section 1 The District constituting the seat of Government of the United States shall appoint in such manner as the Congress may direct:

A number of electors of President and Vice President equal to the whole number of Senators and Representatives in Congress to which the District would be entitled if it were a State, but in no event more than the least populous State; they shall be in addition to those appointed by the States, but they shall be considered, for the purposes of the election of President and Vice President, to be electors appointed by a State; and they shall meet in the District and perform such duties as provided by the twelfth article of amendment.

Section 2 The Congress shall have power to enforce this article by appropriate legislation.

AMENDMENT XXIV (1964)

Section 1 The right of citizens of the United States to vote in any primary or other election for President or Vice President, for electors for President or Vice President, or for Senator or Representative in Congress, shall not be denied or abridged by the United States or any State by reason of failure to pay any poll tax or other tax.

Section 2 The Congress shall have power to enforce this article by appropriate legislation.

AMENDMENT XXV (1967)

Section 1 In case of the removal of the President from office or of his death or resignation, the Vice President shall become President.

Section 2 Whenever there is a vacancy in the office of the Vice President, the President shall nominate a Vice President who shall take office upon confirmation by a majority vote of both Houses of Congress.

Section 3 Whenever the President transmits to the President pro tempore of the Senate and the Speaker of the House of Representatives his written declaration that he is unable to discharge the powers and duties of his office, and until he transmits to them a written declaration to the contrary, such powers and duties shall be discharged by the Vice President as Acting President.

Section 4 Whenever the Vice President and a majority of either the principal officers of the executive departments or of such other body as Congress may by law provide, transmit to the President pro tempore of the Senate and the Speaker of the House of Representatives their written declaration that the President is unable to discharge the powers and duties of his office, the Vice President shall immediately assume the powers and duties of the office as Acting President.

Thereafter, when the President transmits to the President pro tempore of the Senate and the Speaker of the House of Representatives his written declaration that no inability exists, he shall resume the powers and duties of his office unless the Vice President and a majority of either the principal officers of the executive department or of such other body as Congress may by law provide, transmit within four days to the President pro tempore of the Senate and the Speaker of the House of Representatives their written declaration that the President is unable to discharge the powers and duties of his office. Thereupon Congress shall decide the issue, assembling within forty-eight hours for that purpose if not in session. If the Congress, within twenty-one days after receipt of the latter written declaration, or, if Congress is not in session, within twenty-one days after Congress is required to assemble, determines by two-thirds vote of both Houses that the President is unable to discharge the powers and duties of his office, the Vice President shall continue to discharge the same as Acting President; otherwise, the President shall resume the powers and duties of his office.

AMENDMENT XXVI (1971)

Section 1 The right of citizens of the United States, who are eighteen years of age or older, to vote shall not be denied or abridged by the United States or by any State on account of age.

Section 2 The Congress shall have power to enforce this article by appropriate legislation.

AMENDMENT XXVII (1992)

No law varying the compensation for the services of the senators and representatives shall take effect, until an election of representatives shall have intervened.

GLOSSARY

absolute liability   is liability without fault or negligence, often used interchangeably with *strict liability*, though many would contend there is a difference.

admiralty   is that branch of law pertaining to maritime commerce and navigation.

adversarial   In an adversarial legal system like ours, litigants, typically represented by attorneys, argue their respective sides in a dispute before an impartial judge and jury. Ideally, parties to a suit are at liberty to present their cases and challenge their opponents. The adversarial system is often contrasted with an inquisitorial one in which an accused is questioned by officials without rights of defense in a relentless search for the truth. An inquisitorial process provides no protection against abuse by the officials.

adverse possession   is a means of acquiring title by occupying and using land for a certain length of time even though the occupier does not have title. The period required by the common law was traditionally twenty years, which has been shortened in most states. Several other requirements must be met, which are spelled out in state statutes.

anticipatory breach   occurs when one party to a contract expresses an intention not to perform; the other party may then treat the contract as breached and sue for appropriate remedies rather than wait for the time performance is due under the contract.

appellant   is the party bringing the appeal; the **appellee** is the party against whom the appeal is brought.

appellate briefs   are written arguments submitted to an appellate (appeals) court. The party initiating the appeal (the appellant) files an appellant's brief, after which the other party (the appellee) is given a period to reply with appellee's brief.

assault   is putting someone in apprehension of a battery. The actor must have the ability to carry out the threatened battery.

associate   is the title usually given to a full-time member of a law firm who has not yet been elevated to partner. The associate is salaried, whereas the partners share in the profits of the firm.

attachment   is a procedure whereby property is seized and a lien placed on it to satisfy a debt or judgment or to secure property in anticipation of a judgment.

attorney–client privilege   Confidential statements made by a client to an attorney may not be disclosed to others by the attorney without the client's permission, including court proceedings. Staffs of law firms, including paralegals, enjoy this privilege and must scrupulously avoid breaking client confidentiality. The privilege is for the benefit and protection of the client.

bailiff   An officer of the court charged with keeping order in the courtroom, having custody over prisoners and the jury.

bailment   occurs when the owner of personal property delivers possession without intent to pass title, as when one leaves an automobile with an auto mechanic. The bailee in possession may or may not have authority to sell the property for the owner (bailor). The bailee may retain the property under certain circumstances, as when the owner does not pay the auto mechanic, who may keep the auto until the repair bill is paid (this is covered by the law governing **mechanic's liens**).

bankruptcy   While there are different forms of bankruptcy, the term generally refers to the situation in which a person, business, or government cannot or will not pay its debts, so its property is entrusted to a trustee in bankruptcy who distributes the property to creditors.

battery   is an unconsented offensive contact.

bicameral   legislature has two bodies, such as a House of Representatives and a Senate. Only Nebraska has a single, or *unicameral*, legislature.

black letter law   is lawyer's slang for the basic, well-established rules of law. It is a common custom in annotated statutes and legal treatises to bold-face (hence "black letter") the rules and statutes while leaving comments and annotations in normal type.

breached   commonly means breaking a law or obligation. In contract law, a breaching party is one who fails to perform part or all of his obligations under the contracts.

Canons of Ethics   Refers to a set of basic principles established by the ABA to govern professional conduct. Their meaning has been elaborated by additional rules and interpretations in the various states.

capitalist, socialist, and communist nations typically call themselves democratic. The major difference between them is the extent to which property is privately and publicly held. That differences in ownership of property have resulted in very different lifestyles for the people living under these regimes lends credence to the quotation from Reich about the relation between property rights and individuality. Our Founding Fathers were very much concerned about protecting private ownership of property.

certificates of deposit   are promises by banks to pay money deposited with the bank, ordinarily with interest.

chain of title   refers to the history of the transfer of title to real property. It is essential that a seller be shown to be the true owner by virtue of a documented chain of transfer of title up to the present owner.

civil procedure   courses address the complex rules governing the steps appropriate to noncriminal cases as they progress from the initial filing of a lawsuit through trial and even post-trial stages.

class action suits   are a modern form of suit in which a group of persons is represented by some members of the class in pursuing a lawsuit. It was designed to enable a class with numerous members to bring a suit in the name of all. In order to bring a class action, federal and state rules require that several criteria be met.

clearly erroneous and **substantial evidence** express the standard by which trial court fact-finding is measured by appellate courts. The appellate court will not reverse fact-finding unless it is clearly erroneous or there is no substantial evidence to support it. Clearly erroneous is more commonly applied; although technically speaking it applies to judicial fact-finding while substantial evidence applies to jury fact-finding, no one has ever been able to show the difference.

codification The term *codify* may refer to the simple process of turning a custom or common law rule into legislation, but usually it refers to making *codes*, i.e., comprehensive legislation covering a particular area, such as civil procedure. Codification movements have been inspired by efforts of lawyers, judges, and legislators to organize a body of law into a coherent and consistent statutory form.

collateral is property pledged to pay a debt; it is a security interest.

community property Eight states borrowing from French (Louisiana) or Spanish (Texas west to California) law incorporated the concept of community property into marital law. The most important feature of this concept is that earnings of husband and wife during the marriage are considered to be owned equally by both. Husband and wife form an inseparable *marital community.* Consequences of this law are important upon divorce or death of one of the spouses.

contingency fee contracts are agreements between an attorney and a client in which the attorney will receive compensation in the form of a percentage of money recovered in a lawsuit, whether the amount is negotiated without a trial or awarded at the end of trial. This is the usual form of compensation in personal injury cases but is unethical in most other sorts of cases. The contingency fee has come under attack through the years and is likely to be subject to statutory limitations in coming years.

contract implied in fact is a contract that can be inferred by the conduct of the parties in the absence of a verbal or express contract—enrolling in college and paying tuition creates a contractual relationship even though no words are exchanged. A contract implied in fact reflects the unspoken intentions of the parties to create a contract, whereas a contract implied in law arises when intent is lacking but the Court treats the relation as having contractual obligations in order to avoid unjust enrichment.

copyright A right in literary property giving an author the sole privilege to copy original literary or artistic works.

corporations are business entities registered with a state and conforming to state requirements. They are considered by the law as "persons" and can sue or be sued. A major feature of corporations is *limited liability*—ordinarily the owners may not be sued for their private assets when the corporation is sued.

Corpus Juris Corpus Juris Civilis, literally, "the body of the civil law," was the name later given to a compilation of Roman civil law ordered by the Emperor Justinian in the first half of the sixth century. In the late Renaissance under the desire to establish national codes of law, the Corpus Juris was revived and studied and served as a model for all European nations except England, which stubbornly kept the common law. A major American encyclopedia of the common law, the Corpus Juris Secundum ("the Second Body of the Laws"), borrowed from the name without borrowing from the early code.

counterclaim is a cause of action brought by a defendant against the plaintiff in a single case.

court reporters make verbatim recordings of court proceedings and, when necessary, reduce them to typewritten transcripts. They are also employed to make transcripts of out-of-court sworn statements such as depositions.

criminal procedure ordinarily is taught as a separate course from civil procedure because many of its rules are different, such as laws governing searches and seizure of evidence and the right not to testify against oneself (privilege against self-incrimination).

defamation is an injury to reputation (slander and libel are forms of defamation).

defenses In addition to defending by challenging the allegations and proof of the plaintiff, the defendant has available specific defenses in specific torts to prevent plaintiff from recovering anything. For example, while defamation represents an injury to reputation, truth is an absolute defense; i.e., even though plaintiff's reputation may have suffered, if the statement that caused the injury is true, the plaintiff does not recover damages.

disbarment is the most severe professional disciplinary sanction in which an attorney's license to practice law is canceled. In addition to professional discipline, an attorney may be subject to civil and criminal actions.

discovery refers to devices used to request information from the opposing side of a lawsuit prior to trial. The court is not ordinarily involved in this process unless one side refuses to comply with requests from the other.

docket as used here, refers to the court calendar with listings of court proceedings to be heard during a certain time period or term of court.

domestic relations is the traditional name for an area of law also referred to as family law, which is concerned with marriage, divorce, child custody, and guardianship.

dower and **curtesy** were interests in property held by wife (dower) and husband (curtesy), the primary purpose of which was to guarantee real property interests for the surviving spouse at death of the other. Since in early common law these interests favored the husband, they do not comport with the equal protection clause of the Fourteenth Amendment (they discriminate against wives). Most states have statutorily changed the marital estates to make them equal or have provided a modern substitute to protect surviving spouses.

draft is an order to pay money. A drawer orders a drawee to pay money to a payee. A **check** is a draft on a bank payable on demand.

due process The Fifth Amendment to the Constitution provides: "Nor shall any person . . . be deprived of life, liberty, or property, without due process of law . . ." Since this was construed only to apply to action by the federal government, in 1868 the Fourteenth Amendment was ratified, applying the same principle to action by the states. The very breadth of these provisions has allowed a great variety of lawsuits asserting property rights and challenging government restrictions on them.

easement is a right of use in another's property as, for example, when someone has a right of way to cross another's land. Cities and counties ordinarily have easements adjacent to streets and highways, allowing them control over drainage, road shoulders, etc.

ejectment is a common law cause of action designed to return rightful possession of real property. Its common name in modern landlord and tenant law is *eviction* to remove a tenant who no longer has a right to stay on the property, but ejectment has application to persons wrongfully occupying land without any prior relation to the owner.

emancipated minor is a person under the age of majority who is totally self-supporting or married, the definition varying from state to state.

equitable distribution Many of the states that are not community property states have by legislation or judicial decision established principles of equitable distribution for the purpose of dividing property at divorce. Among other features, this law incorporates the modern trend in family law that values homemaking on a par with earnings. The result often resembles what is achieved under community property principles.

estate Estate has several legal meanings but when used in reference to a decedent means the property rights distributed by someone appointed by the court (called the personal representative, administrator, or executor) to those entitled by law to receive the decedent's property.

estate planning An attorney and/or an accountant helps someone plan for the management of his or her property with particular concern for distribution at death. Much of estate planning is concerned with taxation, since large estates may be subject to heavy taxes at death.

estates and trusts deals principally with the distribution of the property of a deceased person, commonly referred to as *decedents' estates*. Trusts involve formal agreements that establish management of property by a trustee on behalf of someone else, called a *beneficiary*. Trusts are frequently associated with wills but may also be set up without reference to a will.

estoppel is a principle used by the courts to prevent someone from making an assertion inconsistent with prior words or conduct that led another to act, which action would be to his detriment if the later assertion were allowed. For example, if an imposter posing as a physician negligently treats a patient, the imposter should be estopped from later avoiding a malpractice suit on the grounds of never having had a license to practice medicine.

evidentiary facts the specific facts presented at trial as distinguished from **ultimate facts**.

executory contracts An executed contract is one that has been performed, completed by both sides; an executory contract is one that still has some obligation to be performed.

forcible rape is distinguished from *statutory rape*. Forcible rape has as one of its elements that force or threat of force be used. This goes further than mere lack of consent on the part of the victim. Statutory rape involves consensual sex when the victim is deemed not capable of consent because of age, mental condition, status, etc.

foreclosure is the process whereby real property is sold to satisfy a mortgage. Foreclosures are strictly governed by state law.

42 U.S.C. §1983 "Every person who, under color of any statute, ordinance, regulation, custom, or usage, of any State or Territory, subjects, or causes to be subjected, any citizen of the United States or other person within the jurisdiction thereof to the deprivation of any rights, privileges, or immunities secured by the Constitution and laws, shall be liable to the party injured in an action at law, suit in equity, or other proper proceeding for redress." (Civil Rights Act of 1871)

garnishment is an action by which one who is owed a debt may collect payments through a third party. For instance, creditors often garnish wages, i.e., have an employer subtract part of an employee's wages for payment to the creditor.

house counsel Many corporations and other businesses employ full-time attorneys, called house counsel, as part of their administrative staff. When attorneys from private firms are retained to represent corporate interests, they are usually called *outside counsel*.

implied warranty is a promise imposed by law, as distinguished from an *express warranty* stated in the contract. Of particular importance is the implied warranty of merchantability or fitness (for the use seller knows to be required) in the sale of a product.

Inns of Court For centuries, English lawyers were trained in the Inns of Court, where students learned the law in association with legal scholars, lawyers, and judges. (The reputation of these institutions has had its ups and downs, at times appearing more like young gentlemen's clubs than legal institutions.) English lawyers are divided into two groups: *barristers*, roughly equivalent to our trial lawyers, and the more numerous *solicitors*, who handle legal matters other than trial work. The Inns of Court provided the traditional training ground for barristers.

interrogatories are a discovery device in which one party sends written questions to the other party. These are particularly useful in obtaining factual information that cannot easily be denied, such as previous marriages, employment, addresses, etc. but would be troublesome to obtain through investigation.

invasion of privacy actually is composed of four different forms of misconduct that harm a person's reasonable expectations of privacy, including the wrongful use of another's name, likeness, or private history, as well as unreasonable intrusion into another's private life and affairs.

jurisprudence is commonly defined as the science or philosophy of law. It is generally concerned with the nature of law and legal systems and their rules rather than with ethics and morality, though these latter topics can rarely be excluded.

justice The judges on the United States Supreme Court and the highest state courts are called Justices, though the term may be used for other judges, depending on the custom of the jurisdiction.

law clerk Top law students often seek clerkships with judges after graduating from law school. It is a very great honor to serve as a clerk for a United States Supreme Court Justice. Law clerks frequently make major contributions to drafting written decisions. Law clerk also refers to law school students who work summers or part time for private attorneys. They do much the same work as paralegals.

law review Most accredited law schools publish a law review on a quarterly basis with scholarly articles and comments on legal issues. Law reviews are edited by outstanding students, who gain considerable prestige by serving on law review. Law reviews tend to reflect the prestige of their schools, the Harvard Law Review occupying center stage for most of this century.

lease is an agreement by an owner of property (**lessor**) with a renter (tenant or **lessee**) whereby the lessee pays for the right of possession and use but does not acquire title.

litigation Bringing a dispute to court; derived from the Latin *lis*, which means lawsuit. We Americans are said to be *litigious*, meaning that we are prone to resolve our disputes through lawsuits rather than by other means. In a curriculum, may serve as the title for a course called "Civil Procedure" at other schools.

long-arm statutes provide a state with jurisdiction over persons or entities ordinarily beyond its territory and usual jurisdiction.

malicious prosecution occurs when someone initiates or causes a groundless suit to be brought out of malice. It is essential that the original suit be terminated in favor of the person later suing for malicious prosecution.

marital settlement agreement refers to a contract drawn up for a divorcing couple to distribute marital property and set the terms for child custody, child support payments, and alimony.

mechanic's lien A lien arises when property is burdened by an obligation to pay money, as in a mortgage transaction. A mechanic's lien arises when someone (an auto mechanic, a carpenter working on a building) is not paid for work or improvements to property. Mechanic's liens are normally created by the operation of law (rather than agreement of the parties) under state statutes.

medical malpractice Malpractice generally refers to professional negligence. If a person is injured due to negligent performance of professional services, he or she may sue for malpractice. A major difference between professional malpractice and ordinary negligence is that the professional is held to a higher standard of care when providing professional services.

memorandum and **per curiam** opinions reflect unanimity of the appellate court without individual authorship. These are usually brief opinions dealing with a settled question of law not requiring lengthy explanation.

mortgage is a written instrument creating an interest in land as collateral for the payment of a debt. Originally a mortgage transferred legal title to the mortgagee (creditor) and returned to the mortgagor when the debt was paid, but most states now hold that the mortgagee has only a lien on the property rather than legal title. Similar security interests on personal property are called chattel mortgages but are usually now covered by the *UCC* provisions on secured transactions.

negligence is a cause of action based on a failure to meet a reasonable standard of conduct that results in an injury.

no-fault divorce refers to recent statutory changes in the grounds for divorce. Formerly, divorce in every state was an adversarial procedure in which one spouse sued the other for divorce on the basis of fault, asserting grounds like adultery or extreme cruelty. Under no-fault divorce, the basis for the action is "marriage irretrievably broken" or "irreconcilable differences" without alleging fault. No-fault divorce generally precludes defenses by the other spouse since no fault is alleged.

nuisance A private nuisance is basically a continuing trespass, as when one discharges polluting effluents that seep into a neighbor's pond.

obiter dictum *Dictum* is a Latin word meaning "said" or "stated." *Obiter* means "by the way" or "incidentally." *Obiter dictum*, then, means something stated incidentally and not necessary to the discussion.

partnerships are unincorporated business associations and as such do not have limited liability; suits that cannot be satisfied by partnership property may go after the personal assets of the partners. Most states have partnership statutes modeled on the Uniform Partnership Act.

patent A patent is an exclusive right granted by the government to use one's invention.

perjury A person who makes a false statement under oath in a judicial proceeding, knowing the statement to be false, has committed perjury. The false statement must concern a material issue or fact in the proceeding.

physical evidence consists of physical objects introduced as evidence, such as a gun, a lock, drugs, etc.

plea bargaining One accused of a crime can "bargain" through his or her attorney with the prosecutor. The trade usually involves an agreement by the accused to plead guilty rather than not guilty, in return for which the prosecutor agrees to charge the accused with a lesser crime, e.g., voluntary manslaughter in lieu of murder, or to recommend a lesser sentence. The court may enter a written agreement to this effect, though the rules vary by state.

pleadings   These are formal documents filed with the court that establish the nature of a lawsuit and its defenses. The initial pleading is usually called a *complaint* or a *petition.*

possession   includes more than physical possession. With land, occupancy and use constitute *actual possession* while the exercise of dominion and control may constitute *constructive possession* where direct physical control is absent. Conduct and intent are important evidence tending to prove possession.

prejudicial   error refers to mistakes made at trial that are sufficiently serious to prejudice the result against one of the parties; in other words, it is sufficiently serious that, if it had not occurred, the case might have reached a different result. It is also called *reversible* or *harmful* error. Error that does not reach this degree of seriousness is called *nonprejudicial* or *harmless* error.

privity of contract   The relationship between two parties to a contract. Originally this was a bar to a suit brought by a consumer against a manufacturer who did not have a direct contractual relationship, but this requirement has been abandoned in products liability cases.

products liability   is a branch of tort law that assigns liability to a manufacturer when injury occurs due to a "dangerously defective product." A major feature of products liability is that it dispenses with the traditional concept of fault that has been an essential element of intentional torts (e.g., battery, slander) and negligence.

promissory notes   are promises by the *maker* of the note to pay money to a payee, usually involved in loans or debts.

prosecutor   In criminal cases, suits are brought in behalf of a state or the United States. The attorney charged with prosecuting such cases is a public official, commonly called state attorney, district attorney, or United States attorney.

punishment   or retribution and **deterrence** of crime are traditional motivations behind the criminal law. In addition, criminal law aims at incapacitation, that is, removing the criminal from society through incarceration, and rehabilitation, helping the criminal toward a productive role in society. The relative importance of retribution, deterrence, incapacitation, and rehabilitation varies depending on one's view of the ultimate goals of the criminal law and is as much of a political and social issue as a legal one.

punitive damages   are sometimes awarded to punish the defendant, while **compensatory damages** are designed solely to repay the plaintiff for injuries sustained.

ratified   A contract is ratified when one suffering a disability approves the contract after the disability has terminated, as when a minor reaches the age of majority and subsequently agrees to the provisions of the contract.

real estate closing (settlement)   Real estate transactions are completed by a closing at which numerous documents are signed and exchanged, payment is made, and property deeds are transferred. Paralegals are frequently employed in the preparation and organization of documents, but states differ on the extent to which paralegals can actively participate in closings. Exceeding the limits set by the state may subject a paralegal to the charge of "unauthorized practice of law."

replevin   is a common law cause of action to recover personal property wrongfully possessed by another person.

rescind   To rescind a contract is to annul or cancel it, putting the parties back in the position they were in before, as if no contract had been made. This is the basis for the equitable remedy of rescission, which in some cases is an alternative to suing for damages for breach of contract.

Restatements The American Law Institute, which was founded in 1923, sponsored the compilation of major fields of common law and published a number of works, beginning with the *Restatement of Contracts* in 1932. These works state basic legal principles and provide comments on them. While courts are free to accept or reject these principles, they frequently quote them in cases.

restitution means the restoration of a party to the position enjoyed before a loss, applied in contract law to the equitable remedy of rescission.

restrictive covenants take many forms including minimum square footage, architectural approval before building, grass cutting, size of "for sale" signs, and even the length of time a garage door may be left open. In modern residential developments, restrictive covenants are commonly used to maintain upscale housing. Racially restrictive covenants and other discriminatory practices have long been held unconstitutional.

§402A The *Restatement of Torts* (Second) §402A covers products liability as follows: Special Liability of Seller of Product for Physical Harm to User or Consumer (1) One who sells any product in a defective condition unreasonably dangerous to the user or consumer or to his property is subject to liability for physical harm thereby caused to the ultimate user or consumer, or to his property, if (a) the seller is engaged in the business of selling such a product and (b) it is expected to and does reach the user or consumer without substantial change in the condition in which it is sold. (2) The rule stated in Subsection (1) applies although (a) the seller has exercised all possible care in the preparation and sale of his product, and (b) the user or consumer has not bought the product from or entered into any contractual relation with the seller.

slander is an injury to reputation ordinarily caused by the communication of lies to third parties that result in a loss of good reputation. Slander is the spoken form of defamation, while *libel* is the written form. Rules governing slander and libel are considerably more complex than this definition suggests.

sole proprietorships are unincorporated businesses owned by one person.

statute of limitations Nearly all civil and criminal actions have time limits within which suits must be filed. These are spelled out in state and federal statutes and vary from one action to another and from state to state. An attorney who neglects to file an action within the time period has committed a serious mistake that may be grounds for a malpractice suit.

substantial performance occurs when one party has attempted to complete performance in good faith, but a minor variance from the specific terms of the contract has occurred. This equitable principle can be applied by the Court to enforce the contract, though it is common to reduce the obligation to pay by the value of the variance. This applies particularly to construction contracts in which performance varies in a minor way from the specifications and the cost of remedying the variance would be extreme, e.g., moving a wall two inches.

substantive law and **procedural law** Our legal system makes a critical distinction between substance and procedure. Substantive law describes rights and duties, while procedural law outlines the procedures that are available or must be followed to enforce or remedy legal rights and duties. The property rights one enjoys are a matter of substantive law; the means by which a deed to property may become part of official records is a matter of procedural law.

substantive law of crimes includes not only specific crimes, such as burglary, embezzlement, and murder, but also the fundamental elements of criminal behavior, such as criminal act and criminal intent. Substantive law also covers issues of participation, such as conspiracy, accessories to crime, and attempted crimes. In general, substantive criminal law deals with culpability, while criminal procedure deals with the manner in which criminal cases are processed.

substitution of judgment refers to the standard for appellate reversal of trial court action on questions of law. The appellate court is free to substitute its judgment for that of the trial court. Compare this with the **clearly erroneous** test of judicial fact-finding. Since the appellate courts are a higher authority for statements of law, they need show no deference for rulings by the lower courts. In fact, their primary purpose is to correct improper statements of the law.

supremacy clause Article VI of the U.S. Constitution provides: "This Constitution and the laws of the United States which shall be made in pursuance thereof; and all treaties made, or which shall be made, under the authority of the United States, shall be supreme law of the land, and the Judges in every State shall be bound thereby, any thing in the Constitution or laws of any State to the contrary notwithstanding."

testimony consists of statements made by witnesses in the course of trial.

tortfeasor is a person who engages in tortious conduct.

torts is a major area of substantive law concerning causes of action to redress injuries that arise out of noncontractual incidents such as auto accidents and medical and other professional malpractice.

trademark A distinctive mark in symbols or words used to distinguish the products of manufacturers or merchants.

transcript refers to a written verbatim statement. In law, transcripts are used most frequently in reference to depositions and trials.

treatises in the legal context are scholarly books about the law, usually covering one of the basic fields of law, such as torts or contracts, or a significant subfield of the law, such as worker's compensation or products liability. The persuasiveness of the treatise rests largely on the prestige of the author.

trespass originally covered a wide variety of wrongs, one species of which, trespass *quare clausum fregit* constituted "trespass to land," which is a wrongful intrusion on land (real property). Also, an injury to a person's right of exclusive possession (e.g., where a neighbor builds a shed that encroaches on another's property).

trust A device whereby title to property is transferred to one person, the trustee, for the benefit of another, the beneficiary. An example might be the creation of a trust for a minor child, who might receive payments as directed by the trust until reaching a certain age, at which time the remainder of the trust would be transferred.

ultimate facts In pleading, a distinction is made between ultimate facts and **evidentiary** facts. Evidentiary facts are the specific facts presented at trial; ultimate facts are the general statements of fact that support a cause of action. The complaint should avoid a lengthy detailing of the events of the case and simply allege general facts that support a cause of action and notify the defendant of the basis for the suit. Nor is it sufficient to merely state *conclusions of law*, such as "The defendant was negligent." The boundaries between these three are not very clear.

Uniform Commercial Code The Uniform Commercial Code, commonly referred to simply as the UCC, is a set of comprehensive statutes governing most commercial transactions and has been adopted in every state except Louisiana.

will or **contract**   A document through which a person directs how his or her property will be distributed at death. The formal requisites of a valid will are established by state law. A person who dies without a valid will is called an *intestate*, and the decedent's property passes by state law governing *intestate succession*. Wills are sometimes challenged by those who would benefit if the will were declared invalid. If there is no challenge, the will is said to be **uncontested**.

workers' compensation   is a statutory scheme whereby fixed awards are made for employment-related injuries. Commonly this takes the form of state-regulated employers' insurance arrangements. A claimant does not need to show negligence, nor is contributory negligence a defense.

writ of mandamus   is an order requiring a public officer to perform a duty.

zoning variance   It is customary in the United States for local governments to create zones within city and county boundaries with restrictions primarily on the form of use, e.g., agricultural or residential zones. Permission by local government to depart from the restrictions is called a variance.

INDEX

References in italics appear as definitions in margins.